THE NEW YORKERS

A History of New York in 27 Buildings: The 400-Year Untold Story of an American Metropolis

Only in New York: An Exploration of the World's Most Fascinating, Frustrating and Irrepressible City

Grand Central: How a Train Station Transformed America

A History of New York in 101 Objects

America's Mayor: John V. Lindsay and the Reinvention of New York (editor)

A Kind of Genius: Herb Sturz and Society's Toughest Problems

The Brother: The Untold Story of the Rosenberg Case

Who We Are Now: The Changing Face of America in the 21st Century

Who We Are: A Portrait of America

The New York Times *Reader*

*"I Never Wanted to be Vice-President of Anything!":
An Investigative Biography of Nelson Rockefeller* (with Michael Kramer)

THE
NEW YORKERS

31 REMARKABLE PEOPLE,
400 YEARS, AND THE **UNTOLD BIOGRAPHY**
OF THE **WORLD'S GREATEST CITY**

SAM ROBERTS

BLOOMSBURY PUBLISHING
NEW YORK · LONDON · OXFORD · NEW DELHI · SYDNEY

BLOOMSBURY PUBLISHING
Bloomsbury Publishing Inc.
1385 Broadway, New York, NY 10018, USA

BLOOMSBURY, BLOOMSBURY PUBLISHING, and the Diana logo are trademarks
of Bloomsbury Publishing Plc

First published in the United States 2022

LIBRARY OF CONGRESS CATALOGING-IN-PUBLICATION DATA IS AVAILABLE

ISBN: HB: 978-1-62040-978-7; EBOOK: 978-1-62040-979-4

2 4 6 8 10 9 7 5 3 1

Typeset by Westchester Publishing Services
Printed and bound in the U.S.A.

To find out more about our authors and books visit www.bloomsbury.com and sign up
for our newsletters.

Bloomsbury books may be purchased for business or promotional use. For information on
bulk purchases please contact Macmillan Corporate and Premium Sales Department at
specialmarkets@macmillan.com.

For Shelby White

CONTENTS

PROLOGUE

On any person who desires such queer prizes, New York will bestow the gift of loneliness and the gift of privacy. It is this largess that accounts for the presence within the city's walls of a considerable section of the population; for the residents of Manhattan are to a large extent strangers who have pulled up stakes somewhere and come to town, seeking sanctuary or fulfillment or some greater or lesser grail. The capacity to make such dubious gifts is a mysterious quality of New York. It can destroy an individual, or it can fulfill him, depending a good deal on luck. No one should come to New York to live unless he is willing to be lucky.

—E. B. WHITE

I've written quirky accounts of New York through books titled *A History of New York in 101 Objects* and *A History of New York in 27 Buildings*. Those were told through material evidence. This book is a *living* history. It's told through people, which is what makes it a biography of the city. It's distinct in another way, too. The thirty-one people profiled in this book are among the most remarkable and noteworthy New Yorkers you've never heard of.

You'll meet the first woman to appear nude in a motion picture, who also became the face of Civic Fame in Manhattan. The couple whose affair ended the Gilded Age, and the husband and wife who invented celebrity talk shows. The victim of the city's first recorded murder in the seventeenth century, and the high school dropout who slashed crime rates in the twentieth. The woman who won her racial discrimination case against a bus company a century before Rosa Parks, and the mobster the mayor banished by fiat from the five boroughs. The man who refused to accept the familiar nostrum "You can't fight city hall," and the family who fought Trinity Church over four centuries in a dispute about property now worth billions of dollars. And you'll meet the father of Greater New York.

A few names might sound familiar. Several deserved monuments, but never got them. Others are included for reasons that have absolutely nothing to do with fame. Most, though, have not only been lost to history. They never made it into narratives of New York in the first place. Yet in some way, each was transformative. Some also personified an epoch in the city's perpetual transmutation. Some overlapped. Several even knew each other. What bound virtually all of them was oblivion, obscurity rather than celebrity. Hardly any could be found in history books or have portraits now hanging in museums and public buildings. (And, to be honest, a few are here because I considered their lost personal stories so irresistibly bizarre that they demanded to be shared.)

A deliberate search for diversity was not a factor in choosing whom to include. It didn't need to be. There were plenty of people of color and women who, though they played formative roles, were largely overlooked both in their own lifetimes and since then. Winston Churchill once said that history would be kind to him because he intended to write it. For the most part, the legacies of the New Yorkers about whom you'll read in this book are presented unvarnished, without benefit of autobiography.

Who qualifies as a New Yorker? NYC & Company, the city's official tourism agency, offers one abiding definition: "Some are born. Some are made. All are welcome." Having been born in the five boroughs and being proud of it is a surefire credential. So is moving to the city and staying long enough to be lucky, or at least, as the star of the musical *Hamilton* declares, to give it their best shot. Almost all of the New Yorkers in this book did just that: for one reason or another, they came from someplace else, and were seduced by what they discovered.

The idea behind *The New Yorkers* was to create, as Graham Robb put it at the beginning of his book *Parisians: An Adventure History of Paris* (2010), an impressionistic tone poem, a potent antidote to the way one of the jaded students in Alan Bennett's play *The History Boys* indolently mocked history as "one damn thing after another." *Parisians* was intended as a kind of mini version of Balzac's *Comédie humaine* "in which the history of the city would be illuminated by the real experience of its inhabitants," Robb wrote.

Paris was ancient by the time Europeans settled what was then New Amsterdam in the 1620s. The thirty-one people profiled in this book all lived during the last four centuries. Each appeared in a written record. That means most stories of the indigenous natives who arrived from Asia thousands of years earlier have been tragically lost. While *The New Yorkers* is not an omnibus of obituaries, being dead was one criterion for those people who are included. (In fact, the first person profiled qualified only *because* he died in New York.) In an era of pop-up accomplishments and fifteen-second fame, predicting the indelible impact of someone who's still alive seemed like a dubious undertaking.

Even so, the potential universe of New Yorkers left to profile was galactic. How many people had ever lived in what became the five boroughs? I asked Neil G. Bennett, director of the City University of New York's Institute for Demographic Research, to guesstimate. He prudently began as late as 1790, when New York was the nation's first capital and the first U.S. Congress authorized the first census. Then he factored in variables like changing longevity, and compensated for double counting from one year to the next. The iffiest component of the hypothetical equation is residential life span—how much time people spent in the city between their arrival, by birth or migration from abroad or from out of town, and their departure, by moving away or by death. If their average residential life span was only one year, the rapid turnover in newly minted New Yorkers would result in the highest number of people who had ever lived in the city: 923,380,602, or nearly one billion.

It's that churning, that tidal ebb and flow in the maritime city, that for more than four hundred years has sustained the *New* in New York. What, from the earliest days of the Dutch, distinguished the city from other European colonies in the New World was that New Amsterdam was largely a magnet for gutsy pioneers who discerned the potential manna in Mannahatta. No wonder the city never sleeps. It's in constant motion. A snapshot of even a single day in New York would be a blur. Joseph Salvo, who recently retired after thirty years as the city's chief demographer, crunched the numbers for me to simulate a population clock. The pace is staggering. Every twenty-four hours, on average, 389 people move to the city from other states; 655 decamp from New York to elsewhere in the nation; 239 immigrants arrive from abroad; 92 New Yorkers leave for other countries; 317 babies are born to New York City residents; and 149 New Yorkers die. Now you know what they mean by a New York minute.

"The history of the world," Thomas Carlyle said, "is but the biography of great men." That leaves a lot of discretion in choosing which people belong in a biography of a great, organic city (and what makes them great). "New York is a city of things unnoticed," Gay Talese observed in his 1970 book *Fame and Obscurity*. Also, he wrote, it's a city of the anonymous, of characters, of the forgotten. Not all the characters from the past whom you'll meet in *The New Yorkers* may be deserving of fame. I've tried to rescue some of those forgotten, though, from undeserved obscurity.

People, after all, are at the nexus of ideas and events. Sometimes people who seem small at the time leave a larger-than-life legacy. They would be surprised to discover their names—which are never even in the indexes of so many histories—as the chapter titles in this biography of New York. Yet each shaped the city, which is celebrating its four hundredth anniversary, in some extraordinary way.

John Colman

Whodunit? The First Recorded Homicide

On the night of Sunday, September 6, 1609, John Colman, second mate on Henry Hudson's three-masted Dutch carrack, the *Halve Maen* (in English, the *Half Moon*), bled to death in a rainswept rowboat in New York Bay. The next morning, after he was hastily buried on the beach, nobody second-guessed the witness accounts of how Colman was killed. They were identical; in retrospect, perhaps, they all corresponded too precisely. No autopsy was conducted. His grave site has never been identified (was it in Brooklyn, Staten Island, or Sandy Hook?). A weapon—an arrow tipped with a stone—was recovered as evidence, but it could have been faked to conceal another source of blunt force trauma. Anyway, it, too, vanished. The suspects were never apprehended, much less questioned. Accounts of the cause were corroborated solely by narratives from colleagues, some of whom might have harbored a grudge against the victim: a white man who, mates concurred, had been killed in cold blood by hostile Native Americans. And the singular written record of the crime remains a secondhand account from Robert Juet, the *Halve Maen*'s mean-tempered first mate—Henry Hudson's "evil genius," as one historian put it—who would later launch a mutiny against him.

Even the victim's name (Colman, or was it Coleman?) has been forgotten. Accounts of his death would largely vanish from schoolbooks and other narratives, deemed inconsequential in a city where four hundred years later the homicide toll would briefly top two thousand annually and where it might be considered impolitic to mention the presumed perpetrators' ethnicity. But history has a funny way of reverberating in current events, carrying the benefit and baggage of centuries of hindsight into the context of today's perspective and prejudices.

The ship's log that Juet kept mentions John Colman's death only in passing. But through the prism of contemporary events, his homicide takes on a riveting significance: it can be considered the coldest case in the city's history of crime, a bloody trail now four hundred years long. Not only is it the first recorded murder in New York (of a European, at least), but also its investigation could be considered the first example of racial profiling, given the reflexive and undisputed presumption of the Native American suspects' guilt.

Two years before Hudson sailed into what became known as New York Bay, he had been contracted by the Muscovy Company, an English trading monopoly that controlled commerce between Britain and Moscow, to find an arctic northeast route to the Pacific coast of Asia. In May 1607, he set sail on the discordantly christened ship *Hopewell* from Gravesend, England, with a crew of eleven, including his

A probable depiction of the first murder in the City of New York, occurring September 6, 1609. The victim was recorded as Englishman John Colman (or Coleman), who was killed by an arrow shot from a bow. Depiction from the fourth-floor rotunda of the Justice Brennan Court House at 583 Newark Avenue in Jersey City, New Jersey. (Photo by Ozier Muhammad via the *New York Times*)

fourteen-year-old son John. It was a portentous voyage that would bode ill not only for Hudson's two subsequent transatlantic passages but also for their own fates and John Colman's alike. Before the ship even reached the Arctic Circle, Hudson headed west and wound up off Greenland, squabbled with the crew, sacked his experienced first mate, William Collins, and replaced him with Colman, a young boatswain. Impregnable ice floes barred his way farther east toward Asia.

In 1608 Hudson tried again, sailing past the Russian Novaya Zemlya archipelago in northeasternmost Europe, where he was supposed to turn south, presumably into the Pacific Ocean. Once again, he was thwarted by glacial masses. According to his journal, he encountered a mermaid and plenty of whales for the Muscovy Company to harvest, but he was fired nonetheless because he had failed to fulfill the terms of his contract, which was to find a faster route to Asia.

In January 1609 Hudson was hired to take a third stab at the elusive alternative nautical route to the East, this time by the entrepreneurial Dutch East India Company. He sailed from Holland on the *Halve Maen* on April 6, 1609. Encountering heavy ice floes yet again, the tenacious captain defied his orders from the start. Imperiously—and courageously—he changed course and ventured into largely unchartered waters. His sailors, cantankerous to begin with, were none too pleased with the surprise shift, which added to the customary early seventeenth-century uncertainty of what they might confront on the voyage and when, or if, they would return home.

Few of Hudson's written records survive. But among them is an acidulous reflection on his crew, written to the Dutch East India Company directors within twenty-four hours of returning to Amsterdam on the *Halve Maen*, months later. In it he made two recommendations. He proposed that the following spring the company commission him to embark on an officially sanctioned search for a north*west* passage to Asia, so that he wouldn't have to surreptitiously conduct the quest on his own initiative. And, without elaborating much on his motivation or the events of the *Halve Maen*'s voyage, he demanded to be allowed to replace six or seven sailors— fully a third of his crew—to make this fourth voyage more harmonious than the ones before it.

Navigating the river that would be named after him and reporting his findings to his patrons, the enterprising merchants of Amsterdam, would prove to be Hudson's greatest accomplishment. The impact of his findings was twofold. The Hudson River, it turned out, was not after all Europe's long-sought Northwest Passage to Asia, as Hudson thought it might be when he sailed into the broad Tappan Zee. But it would become a priceless nautical corridor to the inner continent, with a great harbor at its mouth. It would also cement Holland's global maritime preeminence and foothold in New Netherland. (Water, naturally, figured prominently in a country that lies largely below sea level and a city that grew as a port: the orange in both the Dutch and New York City flags is derived not from the color or the fruit but from the Roman city of Arausio, named for the local Celtic water god.)

No less a Dutch chauvinist than Adriaen van der Donck, who arrived in New Amsterdam in 1641 and rapidly ascended in the colony's political hierarchy, would question the novelty of Hudson's discoveries. Conceding that the so-called Indians were the original inhabitants of America, van der Donck assumed the continent had been populated by means of a diaspora over some ancient land bridge, perhaps reached via the Cape Verde archipelago, the westernmost point on the African land mass. By the time Hudson arrived, an estimated fifteen thousand people, predominantly the Munsee nation of the Lenape branch of the Algonquins, were living in what is now New York City. "For the peopling of America must necessarily have happened by migration and not by creation," van der Donck wrote, "or the very foundation of Scripture would be destroyed." The migration theory challenged universal historical convention, prompting van der Donck to pose this question: "If at any time America could actually be seen from Cape de Verde or thereabouts, did Christopher Columbus and Americus Vespucci"—or Hudson, for that matter—"discover what had never been lost?"

Still, what Hudson found was new to the Old World. White explorers pronounced the New York region to be a pristine, untamed wilderness, even if some of what they took to be virginal land had been cultivated for generations by Native Americans who used fire to clear their forests and rotated their crops. What Hudson immediately understood, though, was the majesty of the river, which at that time went by several names—the Manhattes River or the Mauritius River, after Maurice of Nassau. Hudson dubbed it the Great River of the Mountains, and the company called it the Great North River of New Netherland, to distinguish it from the Delaware to the south. "The navigability of the Hudson River and its access to the hinterland were great assets," Jaap Jacobs wrote in the *Hudson River Valley Review* in 2014, "arguably the single largest factor why New York eventually became the gateway to America, thus shaping the metropolis we know today."

Also, because the East India Company was the first to capitalize on Hudson's explorations, New Amsterdam would differ from other seventeenth-century North American settlements founded by Europeans. Unlike the English, Spanish, and

French, the Dutch pioneers were primarily capitalists; they came to make money. And if immigrants of other nationalities enriched the company, or at least didn't get in the way of its pecuniary goals, they were more or less accepted. Call it tolerance or, more likely, indifference; either way, that pragmatic pursuit of material success would largely define New York to the rest of the nation and America to the rest of the world.

The *Halve Maen*'s crew, however, showed none of that tolerance. Given the nationalist rivalry onboard, it could be considered a great accomplishment that Hudson, Juet, and Colman even got the ship across the Atlantic. The crew's ethnic conflicts reflected a global economic struggle that more than once escalated into combat. The Dutch and the English were historically maritime and imperialist competitors, which was one reason that Henry—not Hendrik—Hudson never fully enjoyed the confidence of either country's mercantile class. In this way the *Halve Maen*—whose name was inspired by a crescent-shaped silver medal worn by the so-called Sea Beggars, supporters of the Dutch revolt against Spanish rule—was a microcosm of the political and economic rivalry between the two nations, and arguably presaged four seventeenth-century Anglo-Dutch wars.

The English crew members included Juet, the thirty-one-year-old mate and captain's clerk, whose journal is the primary first-person account of the seven-and-a-half-month voyage that ended when the ship docked at Devonshire the following November. John Colman (who, unlike Hudson, spoke Dutch), was second mate. Hudson's son John was listed on the manifest as a passenger.

Born in Ireland, Colman himself had voiced concern and contempt for the Hollanders among the *Halve Maen*'s crew—who were less familiar with the North Atlantic than with the more temperate climates of the Southern Hemisphere frequented by ships flying the flag of the East India Company—even before the voyage began. Juet's log doesn't reveal whether Colman ever expressed his repugnance to the crew directly, but Colman wrote his wife warily, "I hope that these square-faced men know the sea. Looking at their fat bellies, I fear they think more highly of eating than of sailing." Just to leave no room for doubt, he added gratuitously: "They are an ugly lot."

By mid-May, barely a month after the *Halve Maen* had sailed, tempers were already flaring. With the ship still languishing in fog, hail, snow, and ice near Norway, ugly quarrels had broken out between the English and Dutch on board. By one account, while the crew was eating in the galley, Colman slunk into their sleeping quarters and confiscated knives and other weapons.

What united the crew, perhaps, was their apprehension about the natives they encountered as they approached the East Coast. By the beginning of July, three months into the voyage, the ship finally skirted the Grand Banks off Newfoundland, then sailed south to what is now Penobscot Bay in Maine, where the mariners went ashore, traded peacefully with the indigenous peoples, and feasted on lobsters. Then, apparently without any provocation, after returning to the ship and arming themselves with muskets, they rowed back to the coast and "drove the savages from their houses, and took the spoil of them, as they would have done of us."

In his log, Juet described the natives verbatim as "suages," an archaic term that peppers late sixteenth- and early seventeenth-century British travelogues of the Western Hemisphere, and even descriptions by some Englishmen of untamed segments of rebellious Northumberland and Wales. Derived from the French word for living in a natural, uncivilized state, the term can imply both a degree of purity and a wild, uncultivated unwillingness to acknowledge a social contract of acceptable group behavior, much less abide by it.

Giving Robert Juet every linguistic benefit of the doubt, the crew of the *Halve Maen*—English and Dutch alike—were wary of the natives they encountered, suspicious of their motives, and governed, as Juet suggested, largely by the maxim "Do

"Indian Village of the Manhattans," from Annals of Old Manhattan, 1609–1664 *by Julia M. Colton (New York: Brentano's, 1901), xii.*

unto others before they do unto you." That maxim may also have prevailed among some of the indigenous tribes suddenly exposed to white men who, dressed in strange costumes, arrived in giant vessels riding high above the waterline and propelled by billowing white wings.

The sailors might have considered the natives heathens, but they themselves, superstitious by nature, were unstrung by every omen. On July 21 the ship's mascot, a cat, inscrutably went berserk and ran "crying from one side of the ship to the other, looking overboard." The *Halve Maen*'s log recorded dryly: "This made us wonder, but we saw nothing." Ten days later a small boat, stolen from the natives, that was being towed behind the *Halve Maen* inexplicably self-destructed, further unnerving the crew. The ship continued south, hugging the coast to roughly the Jamestown settlement in Virginia (which would shrink from three hundred to sixty during the "starving time" the following winter), then reversed course. Hudson sailed about nine miles into Delaware Bay and back, then proceeded north again. On September 2, after the lookout observed a fire ablaze atop the ironstone Navasink Highlands flanking Raritan Bay in New Jersey. Hudson anchored off the spit that would become known as Sandy Hook.

The ancestors of the Lenape people Hudson encountered in New York Bay had settled on the continent thousands of years earlier, probably having traveled from Asia across what, when the oceans rose, would become the Bering Strait. They lived in bark-covered, dome-shaped shelters along the Shatemuc (the present-day Hudson), whose name meant "the river that flows both ways," which it does, technically as a brackish tidal basin or estuary, for some 150 miles. Originally hunters and gatherers, the Lenape supplemented their diet by altering the landscape for the first time, burning patches of forest to cultivate beans, maize, pumpkin, squash, and tobacco. Their deep reverence for the environment that sustained them would shortly provoke bloody vendettas over the definition of private property.

As late as 1655, Adriaen van der Donck in his *Description of New Netherland* still expressed trust in the natives, if somewhat condescendingly: "It is true that they appear singular and strange to our nation, because their complexion, speech and dress are so different, but this, on acquaintance, is disregarded . . . And as unlearned persons never reflect much but speak their first thoughts, in this manner it has probably happened that this people received their national name, because they seemed to be wild and strangers to the Christian religion." Van der Donck added that "no lunatics or fools are found amongst them, nor any mad or raving persons of either sex," and that "they are naturally civil and well disposed, and quick enough to distinguish between good and evil, but after they have associated amongst us, they become cunning and deceitful."

Hudson's own first impression of the indigenous people was mixed: friendly, not necessarily violent, but with "a great propensity to steal." After being invited to one of their feasts, he reported that "the natives are a very good people, for when they saw that I would not remain, they supposed that I was afraid of their bows, and taking the arrows, they broke them in pieces, and threw them into the fire." Hudson's other observation could, in fairness, be applied to many people: "The natives are very well disposed, if they are only well treated; although they are very changeable, and of the same general character as all the savages in the earth."

A few days later, Juet wrote, "the people of the country" approached the ship and "seeming very glad of our coming" and "are very civil" and "go in deer skins loose, well dressed" and brought with them green tobacco, which they traded for knives and beads. Perhaps foreshadowing New York's fashionista fixation, Juet was struck that the natives expressed few demands, but repeatedly alluded to one: "They desire clothes," he wrote. On September 5, more natives visited the ship, bringing hemp and red copper tobacco pipes. "At night they went on land again," Juet recorded, "so we rode very quiet, but durst not trust them." According to one later account, the welcoming Canarsie tribe allowed onto the *Halve Maen* that night was horrified to see the cook cutting up a giant manta or devil ray, a prize catch to the crew, but a sacred fish to the natives.

Juet recorded the events of the next day, September 6, 1609, dispassionately, almost parenthetically. Yet what occurred was unprecedented, heralded hundreds of years of conflict, and would resonate into the twenty-first century in questions that remain unanswered and challenges still unresolved. "The sixth, in the morning was faire weather, and our Master sent *John Colman*, with foure other men in our Boate over to the North-side, to sound the other River," Juet wrote. They left immediately after morning prayers and proceeded in their sixteen-foot-long shallop, a wooden gig equipped with a sail, on a reconnaissance mission to take depth soundings, navigating some dozen miles from the Raritan past the mouth of what would become the majestic Hudson.

Historians and geographers disagree on the shallop's exploratory route, which they have periodically tried to reconstruct from the tides, currents, depths, and landscape believed to have existed at the time or as described in Juet's log. According to the most detailed account, the expeditionary force rowed up the East River, breached the Harlem River, then headed east toward Long Island Sound. As the weather worsened, they stumbled into the mouth of the Bronx River near Hunts Point and, Evan T. Pritchard of the Center for Algonquin Culture speculates, inadvertently into a wampum manufactory, out of which they were driven by warriors who launched a preemptive strike. "The Lands they told us were as pleasant with Grasse and Flowers, and goodly Trees, as ever they had seene, and very sweet smells came from them," Juet wrote. "So they went in two leagues and saw an open Sea, and returned; and as they came backe, they were set upon by two Canoes, the one having twelve, the other fourteene men."

Juet did not identify the occupants of the canoes. (They may have been Raritans or Navasinks, harbingers of the mid-twentieth-century weekend bridge-and-tunnel influx from what would become New Jersey.) Armed with bows and arrows tipped with flint, the assailants were outgunned by Colman and the four crew members, who were armed with muskets and whose boat was also equipped with a small cannon. But a late summer squall suddenly developed, and the steady downpour extinguished the smoldering, cigar-shaped portable lighter Colman's men needed to fire the cannon. "The night came on, and it began to rayne, so that their Match went out; and they had one man slaine in the fight, which was an *English*-man, named *Iohn Colman*, with an Arrow shot into his throat, and two more hurt," Juet wrote. "It grew so darke that they could not find the ship that night, but labored too and fro on their Oares." The current was so swift that their anchor would not hold. By dawn, the sky had cleared. The shallop continued south, presumably toward the Narrows, "and by ten of the clocke they returned aboord the ship, and brought our dead man with them, whom we carryed on Land and buryed, and named the point after his name, *Colmans* Point."

What Juet related matter-of-factly in his log was the first homicide logged in what would become metropolitan New York. Whoever the perpetrator, as E. B. O'Callaghan wrote in his 1845 *History of New Netherland*, "This was the first Euro-pean blood that was shed in these waters." Given the agitation among the crew, the hostility toward Hudson and his officers, and the conflict between the English and the Dutch, how natural, how simple—and in the end, probably, how accurate—to dispose of the case by blaming the Native Americans. Colman's body was never found. The protrusion of beach where Hudson's crew said he was buried after being rowed to shore from the ship, anchored near Ambrose Channel, and which they memorialized as Colman's Point, has never been precisely identified, although geog-raphers guess it is somewhere in either Coney Island, Sandy Hook, Staten Island, or Keansburg, New Jersey, where a Colman's Point still exists at the tip of Carr Avenue.

One account has it that the *Halve Maen*'s sailors dubbed the river that flowed into Raritan Bay at Colman's Point "der Rivierten achter Kol" ("the River Named after Kolman," which was lager mangled into Arthur Kill). In his *History of Flatbush*, the Reverend Dr. Thomas M. Strong considers "Coney" a corruption of Colman. CONYNE EYLANDT appears on a Hollander's map dated 1639, although the consensus among historians is that the name was derived from abundance of *konijn*, Dutch for the island's ubiquitous wild rabbits. (Douglas Hunter writes that if the mate's surname was mangled into Coney, then according to Dr. Strong, John Colman's unlikely legacy would be the name of the world's first amusement park.) The *Proceedings of the New Jersey Historical Society* of 1847 suggests that the site is seven miles west of Sandy Hook at what the Native Americans called Mones'-conk and what was later known as Port Comfort; the *History of Union and Middlesex Counties, New Jersey* (1882) by W. Woodford Clayton says "his body was buried on Sandy Hook, at a place which still bears the name of Coleman's Point." (Clayton blamed the murder on "hostile savages of a different tribe from those who met Hudson in so pleasant a manner at his first landing.") His death is commemorated by a chimerical mural at the Hudson County Courthouse in Jersey City.

The only surviving account of the murder is secondhand, from Juet, which was presumably related to him by one of the four crewmen, probably all Dutchmen, who accompanied Colman, an Englishman. While no motive was established, according to a nineteenth-century manuscript by Gabriel Furman, a Brooklyn state legislator, judge, and meticulous amateur historian, the grounds might well have been self-defense. "Although nothing is said in Hudson's journal about any provocation to the Indians," Furman wrote in 1874, "yet it is certain some must have been given, and most probably not of a trivial character, or the people who had welcomed their arrival in such a friendly manner would not have become so immediately changed as to attack this party of the crew on this occasion. The result of this contest was that John Colman was killed by an arrow shot into his throat, he probably being the principal offender in this instance, as the Indians shoot no chance shot, but invariably aim at a particular object." In 1910, the American Scenic and Historic Preservation Society, founded by Andrew H. Green, who, for consolidating all five boroughs into one city, would become known as the father of Greater New York, agreed. "In some way," the society reported to the state legislature, "Colman's party incurred the hostility of the natives and was attacked." Hudson made no attempt to retaliate against the Lenape or any other natives.

The most complete hypothetical account was provided by E. M. Ruttenber in his *History of the Indian Tribes of Hudson's River* (1872). Ruttenber described Colman as "the first European victim of an Indian weapon on the Mahicanituck"—what the Mohicans, an Eastern Algonquin tribe, called the river. He, too, was more inclined to believe the Native Americans, suggesting that the Europeans instigated the confrontation: "The offense which had been committed by himself and his companions is not stated, but may be inferred. They were far from the ship, the night came on and a thick cloud of rain and fog settled over them; seeing their condition, the Indians sprang to their boards to rescue them, fear seized them, the savage was more dreaded then the tempest, a falcon shot was hurled at the approaching canoes, the swift arrow replied, and 'in the fight one man was slain and two more hurt.'"

In their 1877 *History of the City of New York*, Martha Joanna Lamb and Constance Cary Harrison—whose husband, Burton Harrison, was secretary to Confederate president Jefferson Davis and who, with her two cousins, sewed the first version of the Confederate battle flag—also suggested that the encounter was inadvertent and isolated or was precipitated by some rogue faction. "The Indians doubtless fired at random as there is no evidence that hostilities were continued, or any attempt made to capture the boat, which in the confusion might have been done with the greatest ease," they wrote. "For some days afterward Hudson spent his time in examining the shores, sounding the waters, and bartering with the Indians. The latter were closely watched, but manifested no knowledge of the fatal affray by which John Coleman had lost his life."

Juet's narrative reads in sharp relief to the overwhelmingly positive account of the *Halve Maen*'s voyage that Hudson himself provided to the Flemish historian Emanuel van Meteren, or at least to the way that van Meteren later related it. As Kelly K. Chaves and Oliver C. Walton wrote in *Explorers of the American East* (2019), "This positivity is taken to extremes by omitting any reference to the death of John Colman, which Juet included, describing the Natives near the lower Hudson as merely 'sensible and warlike.' . . . Van Meteren's version also exonerates Hudson from responsibility for any of the difficulties that the voyage faced, consistently blaming the crew and in particular its international composition. Indeed, it is with some subtlety that the Dutch are framed as the 'troublemakers.'" In 1866 John Meredith Read Jr. would write that Hudson was "afraid of his mutinous crew, who had sometimes savagely threatened him."

After a few more chary encounters, the *Halve Maen* sailed through the Narrows in September, then up the river and back. The ship was greeted graciously by the local people, who bartered for three weeks, until October 1, when a native, one of several on board to trade, stole Juet's pillow and two shirts and was summarily shot dead. The crew chased the others and, when they tried to capsize the ship's boat, shot one in the chest and with a sword amputated the hand of another. The next day the crew skirmished with two canoes full of men armed with bows and arrows, and about a hundred more from the shore. The crew fired muskets, killing six or seven.

Hudson had sailed some 140 miles up the mighty river that would bear his name. Two years later, commissioned this time by the English, he embarked on another futile voyage to find a northwest passage to China and Japan. Having survived a harsh winter frozen in place in what would become known as Hudson's Bay, he was determined in June 1611 to continue his quest, but his weary and hungry crew just wanted to go home. Led by Robert Juet, among others, they mutinied. Hudson, his teenage son, and seven loyal and infirm crewmen were set adrift in a shallop. They were never seen or heard from again.

Hudson's greatest legacy was already beginning to take hold, though, two thousand miles southeast of where he was marooned. By 1611 the thirty-one-year-old Amsterdam fur trader Arnout Vogels, who had sailed the summer before with Captain Adriaen Block around Long Island, chartered a ship to duplicate Hudson's route, find his river, and begin regular fur trading with the natives. In late 1613 another trader representing the Dutch, Juan Rodriquez, born in Santo Domingo of Portuguese and African heritage, became the first known non-native inhabitant of New York.

All things considered, the chances are pretty good that Colman was in fact killed by an arrow shot by a native. "I'm sure they were Indians," James Ring Adams, a senior historian at the National Museum of the American Indian, said of the perpetrators. "That leaves a question: Was this a renegade band or another tribe?" But on September 7, 1609, when Colman's body was returned to the *Halve Maen*, apparently nobody questioned the unequivocal group finger-pointing, despite the possibility that the sailors had been covering up their own complicity in or instigation of the murder. "The many complaints Hudson and Juet made suggest that the *Halve Maen* crew was a typical blend of sociopaths and working men," said Kathleen Hulser, public historian at the New-York Historical Society.

While the encounter has been largely overlooked in sanitized histories of seventeenth-century exploration, an unidentified sailor (unarmed) and a Native American man (gripping a bow, apparently bereft of arrows) are immortalized on the official New York city seal. Colman may not be remembered by name, but he survives in myth as the Dwerg, Heer of Dunderberg, a goblin empowered to summon up violent storms and roil the river north of West Point, where, plunging in depth from thirty feet to about two hundred, it becomes a watery grave for doomed ships, according to superstition perpetuated in the early nineteenth century by Washington Irving. (Superstitious sailors still tip their caps to the Dwerg in respect as they pass the forbidding mountain.) The murder was also immortalized in a poem by Thomas Frost, which hints at recurring tension between Colman and the crewmen whose eyewitness accounts of his death provide the basis for history's enduring verdict:

> *"What! are ye cravens?" Colman said;*
> *For each had shipped his oar.*
> *He waved the flag: "For Netherland.*
> *Pull for yon jutting shore!"*
> *Then prone he fell within the boat,*
> *A flinthead arrow through his throat!*
>
> *And now full many a stealthy skiff*
> *Shot out into the bay;*
> *And swiftly, sadly, pulled we back*
> *To where the Half Moon lay;*
> *But he was dead—our master wept—*
> *He smiled, brave heart, as though he slept.*

Legend has it, though, that Colman's dwarfed doppelgänger, the Dwerg, and his gnome crew still haunt Dunderberg (Dutch for "thunder") Mountain, on the west bank of the Hudson in Stony Point, New York. That was where, in Irving's version, Rip Van Winkle encountered them on the eve of his multiyear hibernation and where they return to play ninepins every two decades, which would mean they're probably already practicing for their next tournament, scheduled for September 2029.

2

Anneke Jans Bogardus

This Land Is Our Land

Envision fog everywhere, rising literally and metaphorically from a pristine river as it flows downstream past green meadows, only to be despoiled by the maritime commerce and collateral pollution of the great city emerging on its banks. Charles Dickens was describing the Thames, but in 1852—when Dickens began serializing *Bleak House*, his burlesque of the British legal system told through a contested bequest that had already dragged on for nearly two decades and, with a twist, more than justified the adage familiar to estate lawyers that where there's a will, there's a way—his vivid depiction could just as well have been of the Hudson.

Dickens wrote *Bleak House* after an 1842 visit to New York, where he might well have been further inspired by a still-pending court challenge involving a 1636 grant of farmland along the Hudson River. It would take fully three centuries to resolve, and even now, not all the potential heirs are persuaded that they weren't swindled somewhere along the way. The legal wrangling over the Lower Manhattan farm by the descendants of Anneke Jans Bogardus would, by comparison, shrink the interminable motions, rulings, appeals, and further judgments of Dickens's fictional lawsuit *Jarndyce v. Jarndyce* into a piddling dispute barely worthy of a small claims court. The historian John Fiske has described the legal fight over Anneke Jans Bogardus's farm as "one of the most pertinacious cases of litigation known to modern history."

Few historians of the city, much less untutored New Yorkers, have ever heard Anneke Jans Bogardus's name, much less remember it. But her biography and her descendants' legal claims are worth recounting for several reasons. Her legacy is about real estate, the foundational myth on which Manhattan was built. It originated with Peter Minuit's legendary purchase of the island for gewgaws and other goods supposedly worth around twenty-four dollars from Native Americans who (a) were probably out-of-towners from Brooklyn and didn't own the island but hoodwinked the Hollanders; and (b) as indigenous people, believed that the land belonged to everyone anyway and wasn't theirs to permanently grant, no matter how great the compensation. For all that the bedrock bargain would become mythologized, Peter Schaghen only mentioned the purchase in passing when he delivered the latest news from North America to the High and Mighty Lords of the States General of the United Provinces of the Dutch Republic. Schaghen reported matter-of-factly in November 1626 that a ship had just arrived from New Amsterdam laden with thousands of pelts and oak timbers destined for the West India Company, that grain had been harvested over the summer and some children had been born, and that, by the way, some twenty-two thousand acres of Manhattan Island had been purchased from the Native Americans for the equivalent of sixty guilders, which was later recalculated as the fabled twenty-four dollars.

In 1629, as the decade ended, with the Dutch still ambivalent about whether their new beachhead was destined to be a prosperous trading post or a fledgling colony, its "high and mighty"—as they were accustomed to being addressed—directors in Amsterdam voted to grant patroonships, or massive land grants. Their purpose: to attract more pioneers to New Netherland before it was subsumed by Swedes migrating from the south and English immigrants encroaching from the north. Among the first beneficiaries of the mammoth patroonships was Kiliaen van Rensselaer, an Amsterdam diamond and pearl dealer and West India Company founder. His estate, which measured twenty-four by forty-eight miles and was ostensibly purchased from local Native Americans, surrounded Fort Orange, which would become the city of Albany and eventually the state capital. His Rensselaerswyck would prove to be the sole successful patroonship, remaining in his family for two centuries. Among the first estate managers whom Van Rensselaer recruited was Roelof Jansen, a seaman who immigrated to New Netherland from Amsterdam on May 24, 1630, on the ship *Eendracht* with his twenty-five-year-old wife, Anneke Jans, and their daughters Sarah and Fytje. The couple had been born in what was then Norway but may have had Dutch roots.

Four years later, after Jansen was dismissed or his contracted service as a farmer expired (Van Rensselaer accused him of "bad management" for failing to procure sufficient seed, and his wife of frittering away provisions), he became foreman of a

Anneke Jans Bogardus, Everardus Bogardus, and genealogy chart. (Illustration via the New York Public Library)

sixty-two-acre West India Company farm in Manhattan. In 1636 Wouter van Twiller, the director of New Netherland (and Kiliaen van Rensselaer's nephew), granted the plot jointly to Jansen and his wife. One acre is relatively small, roughly two hundred feet by two hundred feet. Even sixty-two acres is merely one seventh the size of Central Park. Still, these sixty-two acres were no ordinary piece of property. What would be hallowed in turn as Trinity Church Farm, the King's Farm, the Queen's Farm, the Jans Farm, and the Bogardus Farm developed into Greenwich Village early in the eighteenth century and, much later, was rebranded by savvy real estate speculators, who dubbed the neighborhoods farther downtown as SoHo (south of Houston) and Tribeca (the triangle below Canal Street).

William Wolfman, chief counsel of the Title Guarantee & Trust Co., calculated around 1950 that to circumnavigate the farm, you would start at Broadway and Fulton Street, in front of St. Paul's Chapel, and walk west to the Hudson River. Turn right and continue north for about a mile and a half to Christopher Street, then east on Christopher to Hudson Street. From there, proceed south, then east to Broadway near today's Duane Street and then downtown about a half mile, past what became known as Lispenard's Meadows and New York City Hall on your left, to the departure point at Fulton Street. Each year, as New Amsterdam and then New York spread farther and farther from the downtown tip of the Battery, the value of those sixty-two acres soared as rapidly as Manhattan's skyscrapers would, but unbounded by the laws of physics.

One year after the Jansens were jointly granted their sixty-two-acre tract, Roelof died when he was thirty-five, leaving what then became known as the Anneke Jans Farm to his wife and the couple's four children. Jansen was memorialized locally in the name of a tributary (Roeliff Jansen Kill) that empties into the Hudson River in Columbia County. Jans would be immortalized around the world as a founding matriarch of New Amsterdam (her mother was the first official midwife). Her name would become a legal benchmark: "Although she may not have seemed rich in the days when great landed estates were to be bought for a few strings of beads," the historian Mary Lamb wrote, "yet she is reverenced by her numerous descendants as among the very goddesses of wealth." As John Oluf Evjen concluded in his profile of Scandinavian immigrants in New York, "Anneke Jans's fame rests on property and progeny."

Two years after she was widowed, Anneke married the Reverend Everardus Bogardus. He had arrived in New Amsterdam in 1633, a newly ordained clergyman and, barely twenty-six, the second dominie, a Dutch Reformed Church minister commissioned by the West India Company. Bogardus was enlisted to infuse a spiritual dimension into the pecuniary colony, which still numbered only several hundred inhabitants, lured from the Netherlands with the promise that the streets were lined with fur. Orphaned before he was ten when his father died, he was destined to become a tailor, but vowed in his teens that if he fully recuperated from an unidentified illness that had rendered him blind, deaf, and speechless, he would devote his life to God. He was so stoked by his miraculous recovery that from then on, he insisted on holding others, regardless of their station, to the same high standards of piety he had set but did not always pursue (much less meet) for himself.

Characterized as a character "of choleric temper and given to plain speech," the guardian of New Amsterdam's ethical and devotional values was described as "a large, dignified, portly man, with a determined, grave expression on his square Dutch face, relieved by a kindly eye and a benignant smile." Bogardus took on all comers with gusto. He challenged Wouter Van Twiller, the director who had granted his wife and her first husband the farm, with being "a child of the devil" and infused with alcoholic spirits too frequently.

In subsequent historical accounts, written by both men and women, Anneke was often described none too favorably as "buxom" and "coquettish." Once a notorious scandalmonger, Grietje Reiners, accused her of immodestly exposing her ankles when she lifted her petticoat to protect it from the muddy street. Jans successfully sued her accuser for slander. (Reiners and her husband, Anthony Janszoon Van Salee, the wealthy son of a Dutch pirate and Moorish mother, were branded as "troublesome" by the church and in effect banished to Brooklyn, where they pioneered the settlements of New Utrecht and Gravesend.) Bogardus himself was upbraided more than once for defaming members of his flock whom he considered wayward.

Bogardus and his wife rented out their farm and lived not far from Willem Kieft, the dictatorial director of New Netherland, but to whatever degree their proximity bred familiarity, it exponentially engendered contempt. One source of conflict was Kieft's incitement of Native Americans—taxing their crops, coercing them to sell property, and additional provocations to violence. Engaging in an infantile form of cancel culture, Kieft would rudely interrupt the minister's sermons with cannon fire. He also summoned Bogardus before the Council of New Amsterdam in 1646 to answer charges that he had berated Kieft as "an incarnate villain, whose buck goats are better than he." They split so irreparably that both he and the director, the West India Company's leading surrogates in the colony, were recalled to Amsterdam to defend themselves.

A stroke of divine justice spared the company's high and mighty lords from having to choose between the two. In 1647 Bogardus and Kieft both sailed to the Netherlands on the *Princess Amelia*. Instead of steering for the English Channel, the ship mistakenly strayed into the Bristol Channel off the Welsh coast and sank, drowning them both. Bogardus's death left Anneke, then forty-two, a widow again, now with four surviving children from Roelof and four more sons—Jonas, Pieter, William, and Cornelis—from the dominie. In 1653, when New Amsterdam was incorporated as a city (a legal benchmark that Philadelphia would not achieve until 1701 and Boston only in 1822) and was no longer technically a company town, Anneke's family reaffirmed her title to the farm under director general Peter Stuyvesant.

By then, Anneke herself had already decamped from 23 Whitehall Street for Beaverwyck, later Albany, to live with her daughter Fytie. She died there at fifty-eight on March 19, 1663. Anneke bequeathed "all her real estate" and "all property whatsoever, without reserve or restriction of any kind, to be disposed of after her decease and divided by them in equal shares, to do with the same at their own will and pleasure without any hindrance whatsoever" to her children. Being illiterate, she witnessed the will with an *X*.

In 1667, after the English seized New Amsterdam, Anneke's heirs' ownership of the farm was ratified by Richard Nichols, the new royal provincial governor of what was renamed New York. On March 9, 1670, five of Anneke's six living heirs or their descendants sold their interest in the farm to Nichols's successor as provincial governor, Francis Lovelace. One of her second set of sons, Cornelis Bogardus, a gunsmith, had died in 1666, but for some reason—unknown but potentially pivotal—his widow and his three-year-old son were not signatories to the 1670 deed.

Under the Treaty of Breda, after seizing New York briefly during another kerfuffle with the British, the States General of the Netherlands concluded in 1667 that it was outbargaining even Peter Minuit by surrendering its North American territory, where fur trading was lagging, in return for the volcanic Banda Islands east of Java, where the East India Company could monopolize the global supply of nutmeg, a spice valued as a seasoning, aphrodisiac, and curative. The British governor Benjamin Fletcher leased the sixty-two acres in Manhattan, which was by then known as the Duke's Farm (and, when the duke became king, as the King's Farm), for sixty bushels of wheat annually for seven years to Trinity Church, which had been incorporated by the crown that same year.

In 1699, though, the colonial legislature deemed the conveyance excessively long and limited leases to the length of a governor's term. In 1702 that act was repealed, but the repeal was overruled in 1708 by Queen Anne, in whose name the farm had been leased to Trinity by Governor Edward Hyde (Lord Cornbury) in 1700 and granted outright by the governor, Anne's cousin, as a subsidy to the struggling Anglican Church. In the interim, Trinity had leased the plot, now known as the Queen's Farm, in 1704 to George Ryerse in a deal that described the property as bounded by Broadway and the Hudson River, but left its northern and southern borders unspecified. That ambiguity would provide Anneke Jans's descendants an avenue to challenge the church's title. So would the colonial act of 1699 annulling the lease, which left judges yet unborn to decide whether that act barring governors from leasing property beyond their terms of office prevailed, or whether the act had been superseded by royal decree.

Originally the farm wasn't worth much, except to grow tobacco and pasture cattle. Swampy, rocky, uncleared, and unfenced, it was far from the fort at the southern tip of Manhattan, well north of the city walls, and, as William J. Parry wrote in the *New York Genealogical and Biographical Review*, "unprotected and subject to the depredations of native peoples and wild animals." But while the farmland wouldn't be fully settled until after the American Revolution, even by 1738, Parry wrote, "the city had expanded to the point where the farm had become desirable residential property, and was now sufficiently valuable to be worth fighting over." That year, the vestry minutes of Trinity Church record the first mention that some of Anneke Jans's descendants believed that the farm, or part of it, still belonged to their family. "Their extraordinary efforts, displaying a remarkable mixture of faith, righteousness, stubbornness, naiveness, and delusion," Parry wrote, would persist for two centuries. "It pitted English against Dutch, Anglican against Reformed, Establishment against Anti-Establishment, and Tory against Whig."

Around 1738, in what appears to have been the first formal challenge to Trinity's ownership, the family of Jacob Brouwer and his wife, Annetje Bogardus, Anneke's granddaughter, seized a portion of the farm and ejected the church's tenant, Adam Vandenburgh. Trinity pressed charges. In 1746 family members of Anneke Jans were convicted of forcible entry and trespass. The descendants eventually sued Trinity, but in 1760, after a two-day trial, a jury took twenty minutes to return a verdict in favor of the vestry. In 1773 the great-grandson of Anneke's son Cornelis, who insinuated himself onto the property as a farmer, was threatened with eviction by force as a squatter by Trinity's "representatives" (or goons), four of whom were convicted of stealing and destroying his crops. He would sue, claiming one sixth of the farm on the grounds that the family of his great-grandfather, who died in 1707, had neither agreed to the original sale nor signed the conveyance to Governor Lovelace.

By then, though, it was a wonder that Trinity wanted to be associated at all with the property. The contested site north of the church had been transformed into a bawdy nest of brothels and bars. Facetiously dubbed "the Holy Ground," it was plied by prostitutes and pimps who, for the time being, posed a greater danger to George Washington's fledgling army than the British armada that would soon be assembling to invade Brooklyn and bombard Manhattan. When the British overran and occupied New York after 1776, most of the Bogardus descendants fled for colonialist enclaves. The Anglican Church evicted all the Bogardus family members who remained. The farm itself was largely deserted and lay fallow. Old Trinity Church, built in 1698, fared even worse: the Dutch gambrel-roofed building on Broadway was destroyed with hundreds of other Lower Manhattan structures in a cataclysmic conflagration often blamed on pro-independence New Yorkers who followed General George Washington's fleeing Continental Army north.

Then, when the war ended and the British finally evacuated New York in November 1783, the already legally tendentious debate over the Bogardus tract became even more ambiguous. The church claimed that Bogardus descendants who fled the city to enlist in the Continental Army had abandoned whatever claim they had to the farm. Returning from the army, Cornelius B. Bogardus, another heir of Anneke's son Cornelis, published a notice in the *New York Packet* inviting other descendants of Anneke Jans Bogardus to meet at Cape's Tavern "on business of high importance relative to the lands called Dominie's Hook, which formerly belonged to her." In 1784 the church enlisted Aaron Burr—who had represented the heirs but switched sides after Trinity granted him the lease to Richmond Hill, a twenty-six-acre estate in the village of Greenwich—to fend off the family.

Violent confrontations ensued between tenants with competing claims. The family installed relatives or surrogates on the property. Trinity mustered a small army under

George Trenis, a Hessian, to burn the descendants' newly installed fences. The family retaliated by destroying barriers implanted by the
church's tenants. Shots were fired, and an
elderly diehard descendant literally dug in her
heels and drove away intruders by pouring
boiling water on them. The physical skirmishes were followed by several legal setbacks
for the family, including the discovery by
Balthazar De Hart, an associate of Alexander
Hamilton, of Anneke's five sons' actual 1670
deed to Governor Lovelace. (Grateful Trinity
elders rewarded De Hart with a silver
tankard.) About the same time, another
group of Bogardus descendants began
meeting to pursue their own claims. Their
collaboration encouraged another lawsuit,
this one filed in 1830 by John Bogardus on
behalf of all the heirs of Cornelis, the son who
had not signed the conveyance to Governor
Lovelace.

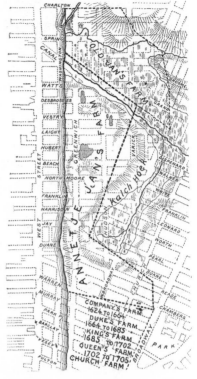

*"Map of Jans or Bogardus Farm with
position of streets indicated," from
Historic New York During Two
Centuries, edited by Maud Wilder
Goodwin et al (New York: G. P.
Putnam's Sons, 1897), 120.*

In an account written for Trinity in 1896,
Stephen Payne Nash, a senior warden of the
Episcopal Church and former president of
the Association of the Bar of the City of
New York, pointed out that the deed to Lovelace was "for the first time produced
as the basis of any claim upon the part of any of the descendants of Anneke Jans, and
it was brought forward by Bogardus to show that his ancestor Cornelis had not
joined in it." As a result, the heirs asserted that the lapsed statute of limitations on
challenging the title was immaterial, since Cornelis had never relinquished it. They
professed that since Trinity acquired the title under the deed to Lovelace, the
church held possession of the farm not adversely to Cornelis Bogardus and his
descendants, but as a tenant in common with him.

Among the witnesses testifying for Trinity in the crucial mid-nineteenth-century
case were the tobacconist Peter Lorillard, the master builder Ezra Weeks, and Morgan
Lewis, whose father, Francis, had been a member of the Trinity Church vestry and

had signed the Declaration of Independence. In 1847, the plaintiffs must have been buoyed as they began reading what Vice Chancellor Lewis Halsey Sanford of New York assumed would be the definitive opinion, indelibly precluding further litigation. Sanford acknowledged that, had he approached the case with any predisposition, it was "a hearty dislike to clothing an eleemosynary institution with either great power or extensive patronage." He also admitted to "a settled conviction that the possession by a single religious corporation, of such overgrown estates as the one in controversy" is, he said, "pernicious to the cause of Christianity." Those reservations, he wrote, "have disposed me to give an earnest scrutiny to the defense in this case; as, in the instance of the Dutch Church, they prompted me, in my capacity of counsel, to more zealous efforts to overthrow their title to the lands."

Yes, Sanford wrote, the deed to Lovelace "does not appear to have been executed by or for Cornelis Bogardus." Moreover, determining whether Queen Anne actually possessed the farm 150 years earlier required the court to rely on inconsistent testimony and evidence. Sanford's reasoning would be cited again and again: that the family's deed to Governor Lovelace was valid "unless he knew, (and of this there is neither proof nor probability,) that there was one heir of Anneke Jans who was not named in the instrument"; that statutes enacted by the assembly and approved by the governor were valid unless and until they were disapproved by the Crown; and that rights acquired by colonial statute before being disapproved by the Crown were not impaired by subsequent disapproval (which seemed contradictory), but regardless, "the Church had acquired a perfectly valid title by undisputed possession longer than the limitation at which title might be gained by possession in 1705, when the land came to the Church."

"A plainer case has never been presented to me as a judge," Sanford declared in deciding against the heirs and their lawyer, who had pursued the case for twenty-two years. "Were it not for the uncommon magnitude of the claim, the apparent sincerity and zeal of the counsel who supported it, and the fact (of which I have been often admonished by personal application in their behalf,) that the descendants of Anneke Jans at this day are hundreds, if not thousands, in number, I should not have deemed it necessary to deliver a written judgment on deciding the cause." By the mid-nineteenth century, Sandford warned, perhaps hyperbolically, that if the descendants won the case on the basis of a claim that had been suspended for five generations, the ruling in their favor "would lead to scenes of fraud, corruption, foul injustice, and legal rapine, far worse in their consequences upon the peace, good order and happiness of society than external war or domestic insurrection."

In layman's terms, the Bogardus family lost their claim on the grounds of adverse possession—because Trinity or its tenants had occupied the property for more than twenty years without challenge, and the statute of limitations had lapsed. "There were some prior grants made by the Dutch governors prior to Queen Anne's grant," William Wolfman wrote in *Title News*. "The description in these grants are even more vague and more difficult to follow than the description in the Trinity grant." But, he added, "The full and complete answer to these claims is, of course, adverse possession, and adverse possession, continued long enough, gives just as good a title as title by grant."

Sandford's dire and unequivocal warning did nothing to discourage future claimants or the lawyers who sincerely believed that their clients had a legitimate case for the compensation they had been defrauded of two centuries before, or had fortuitously stumbled upon another generation of easy marks. He underestimated the corresponding geometric explosion in property value of the sixty-two disputed acres and the unquenchable thirst of vulnerable people who are persuaded that powerful fixers have denied them some entitlement. Each accusation of professional misconduct seemed to embolden the claimants' advocates and legal surrogates, to the point that parties willing to underwrite the court challenge and, therefore, collect a share of the anticipated settlement were no longer required to have any ancestral connection to Anneke Jans Bogardus at all to join in the class-action lawsuit by anyone who felt aggrieved.

By the late 1800s Trinity's reputation as a steward for what was originally the Anneke Jans farm had not improved much from what it had been a century before. The church was even sued by the city's health department for violating the minimal municipal standards imposed in 1887, which required it to provide running water to residents of the nearly 150 immigrant-packed tenements on its properties. Trinity objected to the cost, cited the danger posed by freezing pipes, and professed furthermore that "no complaints in reference to the want of water had been made to defendant by the occupants of the buildings." Trinity's argument that the law, by depriving it of its property, was unconstitutional was rejected by the court of appeals (which admitted that the legislature might someday go too far—by requiring a toilet in each apartment—but that running water would mitigate "the tendencies to immorality and crime where there is very close packing of human beings of the lower order in intelligence and morals"). Nothing stanched the periodic claims that the church had illegally usurped the private property of the Bogardus family.

As late as 1891, Trinity published a public notice advising "all persons who suppose themselves to be descendants of Anneke Jans, or otherwise interested in claims hostile to this corporation, are cautioned against paying out money to any person alleging the pendency of such suits or negotiations." Trinity not only warned away potential patsies but also, in a pamphlet written for the church by Stephen Payne Nash in 1896, offered several hypothetical answers to a pivotal question: Why was there no reference in the Lovelace deed to the widow of Cornelis or to his son? One answer Nash suggested and then discounted was that "if they were defrauded, they were defrauded by other members of the family, by the aunts and uncles of the young Cornelius, and not by anyone else"—certainly not by the corporation of Trinity Church.

Subsequent cases were filed in 1892 on behalf of another group of claimants with bogus belletristic pretentions: the Anneke Jans Bogardus Literary Association, whose more than six hundred members subsidized the suit with fifty-dollar contributions. In 1901 still another suit was dismissed because the plaintiffs' lawyer was unlicensed; he was later convicted for collecting money from the heirs under false pretenses. John H. Fonda, a licensed lawyer who in 1896 had organized an association of heirs of Anneke Jans Bogardus, was charged in 1913 with mail fraud in connection with soliciting funds from family claimants. Fonda's case was dismissed by U.S. district court judge Learned Hand, who attributed his perseverance to "an obsession from childhood" rather than criminal motives and spared him a prison sentence because he was by then eighty-eight. After Fonda died in 1915, his lawyer, Willis T. Gridley, became head of the association of heirs and with his secretary, Gladys Wright, began soliciting descendants again to subsidize legal challenges against Trinity.

Gridley was convicted of fraud and disbarred in 1917 because "he knew that there was no chance of success, and had no new information and was unable to advance any theory upon which probably success could be based." Undeterred, in 1923, he relinquished his full-time job manufacturing fire extinguishers to establish the Order of the Advocates of Justice for the Descendants of Anneke Jans Bogardus, soliciting donations of $50 (about $800 in current dollars)—for a total at the time of at least $100,000 and possibly as much as $1 million from as many as seventy-five thousand self-described advocates—for research, publication costs, and copies of his book titled *Trinity! Break Ye My Commandments?* The book was eventually published after Gridley was convicted in Detroit for mail fraud in 1928 and sentenced to five years in Leavenworth Prison. His conviction was upheld, and in 1931 the Supreme Court declined to review it.

Gridley remained a hero to the claimants he represented, including one who had donated seventy dollars to qualify for his share of a settlement and later said of his lawyer: "I cannot do much, but God hates a quitter, and so do I." After Gridley was released from prison, he settled in Emporia, Kansas, where he died in 1943. His obituary, which made no mention of his most famous case or its aftermath, reported only that "Mr. Gridley, who formerly was a lawyer, had been retired for the past 12 years." Even Gridley's detention and death didn't put an end to the claims. William Wolfman, chief counsel for the Title Guarantee & Trust Company of New York, said that in 1947 he received a letter from Springfield, Ohio, signed by 2,458 Bogardus heirs still seeking to prosecute their claim.

Dickens began serializing *Bleak House* in 1852, a decade after his visit to America, where the descendants of Cornelis Bogardus harbored a spark of hope that they would inherit his share of the sixty-two-acre farm that had been deeded to his great-grandmother and her husband in 1636. Their on-again, off-again legal skirmishes would endure for another century, but as of the date of writing, they have lost every battle and their war. "Injustice breeds injustice," Dickens wrote. "The fighting with shadows and being defeated by them necessitates the setting up of substances to combat." After three centuries, the shadows of skyscrapers and apartment high-rises have obscured evocations of any uncultivated fields west of Broadway in Lower Manhattan, and the name Bogardus largely evokes the pioneering mid-nineteenth century cast-iron architecture of another descendant, James Bogardus, in Tribeca.

Trinity Realty remains the predominant landlord in an area dominated by the gaping mouth of the Holland Tunnel and the high-ceilinged loft buildings that once housed the city's printing industry. Trinity still owns about fourteen square blocks in what has been rebranded as Hudson Square, which since 2010 has added some fifteen million square feet of office space for high-tech tenants, including a $1 billion Google campus and a $650 million Walt Disney Company headquarters.

A triangular one tenth of an acre plot purchased for five dollars from Trinity Church in 1797 at what is now Hudson and Duane Streets was the first property bought by the City of New York specifically as a public park. Municipal signage describes it as "the last remnant of the greensward of the Annetje Jans farm." But to add insult to injury, the park is named for James Duane, New York's first post–Revolutionary War mayor, who was not only a Trinity vestryman but also, as a lawyer, represented the church against Anneke Jans's heirs' claims.

3

John Bowne

Practicing What They Preached

At the northern boundary of New Amsterdam, south of what would later be De Waal Straat, a wooden palisade stood as early as 1644, presumably to guard colonists against Native American attacks. The motivation behind the more formidable fortified "high stockade and small breastwork" ordered by the city's director general Peter Stuyvesant in 1653 was unambiguous: England and the Netherlands had just embarked on the first of four Anglo-Dutch wars. That the British, perhaps in league with Native Americans, might swoop down from New England and overtake Manhattan was no idle threat.

Despite the walls and Stuyvesant's provincialism, New Amsterdam had already distinguished itself from many North American settlements populated by refugees who, denied freedom of worship in Europe, managed to find one religious group or another to bedevil once they got to the New World. Puritans escaping the heavy hand of the Church of England banished Roger Williams from Massachusetts for his "dangerous ideas" of religious diversity. He transplanted himself to Providence Plantations in Rhode Island, where his First Baptist Church in America challenged what his flock feared was the dangerous theological foundation of Quakerism.

Few settlers would come to New Netherland and later to New York solely to freely express and practice their religious beliefs. Even fewer came to proselytize. New Amsterdam began as a company town—a wholly owned subsidiary, in effect, of the Dutch West India Company. Most immigrants were lured there with one goal in mind: to make money. Don't interfere with that objective, the message was, and generally, you'll be indulged. Idealists, with benefit of hindsight, have attributed this distinguishing forbearance to a tradition of tolerance grounded in the religious liberties guaranteed by the landmark 1579 Union of Utrecht, which united the northern provinces of the Netherlands.

Yet like everyone else, the Dutch did not always practice what they preached, particularly under the capricious and imperious director general of New Amsterdam, Peter Stuyvesant, and the Reverend Everardus Bogardus, minister of the Dutch Reformed Church (and the husband of Anneke Jans). All public officeholders were required to be communicants of the church, but most ordinary citizens could pray privately—or not at all—according to their own beliefs, while the town's busybodies and magistrates looked the other way. Bogardus wielded religion as a vehicle to futilely impose social control on a froward, independent congregation, while Stuyvesant used his church as a cudgel against the Quakers, whom he considered beards for the dreaded English.

Quakerism had begun in the 1640s as a reaction against the elaborate rituals of the Church of England. It spread to America, where its adherents became known to the Dutch as "strolling people," because they were missionaries seeking converts. The early Quakers (who figuratively and literally "trembled at the Word of the Lord") defied the benign modern, salubrious cereal-box stereotype. Among them was John Bowne (pronounced as in *town*), who was born in 1627 and emigrated with his father and sister from Matlock, Derbyshire, in the East Midlands. After a brief stay in Boston, he settled in Vlissingen—named for the home port in Holland of the West India Company and later anglicized as Flushing, Queens—where in 1656 he married Hannah Feake, a great-niece of Massachusetts governor John Winthrop. While Flushing was politically part of New Netherland and chartered by the West India Company, it had attracted a cluster of English settlers. It bestowed upon its residents the right "to have and enjoy the liberty of conscience, according to the custom and the manner of Holland, without molestation or disturbance."

Flushing also attracted a congregation of Quakers. Most residents—unless they were devout members of the Dutch Reformed Church or professional buttinskies—couldn't care less what the Quakers were doing in private, but Stuyvesant relentlessly badgered them. The same year that John Bowne married, thirty of his English neighbors, none of whom were Quakers themselves, signed a petition to Stuyvesant protesting the director general's cavalier treatment of their Quaker neighbors. In what became known as the Flushing Remonstrance, the petition objected to the

"The Surrender of Petrus Stuyvesant" by Henry
Alexander Ogden, from New York New
Amsterdam: The Dutch Origins of
Manhattan *by Martine Gosselink*
(Amsterdam: National Archives of
Netherlands, 2009), 146. (Illustration
via the New York Public Library)

director general's ban on public *and* private religious gatherings not conducted in
accordance with the customs of the Reformed Church. His edict even barred New
Netherlanders from harboring Quakers.

What was so striking about this formal reproach was that it daringly reached far
beyond any concept of religious freedom expressed up to that point, much less
demanded, in the colonies—or in Europe—in the mid-seventeenth century. The
Remonstrance was revolutionary on two counts: it set a bold precedent for the people's
right to petition to redress their grievances; even its wording had profound political
and theological implications, too.

The signers said they desired "not to judge lest we be judged, neither to condemn lest we be condemned, but rather let every man stand or fall to his own master." If the Quakers or anyone else "come in love unto us, we cannot in conscience lay violent hands upon them, but give them free egress and regress unto our Town, and houses" under God's law, the signers wrote. They then specified "Jews, Turks, and Egyptians" as among the "sons of Adam" and went so far as to add tolerantly that they would "be glad to see anything of God," too, in Presbyterians, Independents, Baptists, and Quakers (although Catholics, by the signers' standard, apparently did not qualify). The Remonstrance expressed a broad (if not universal) degree of tolerance. But it went well beyond previous expressions of forbearance in a fundamental way: it described religious persecution as a sacrilege—reversing the conventional orthodoxy that any heresy should be aggressively resisted. Therefore, it laid a legal foundation for the separation between church and state while also setting a bold precedent for the people's right to petition to redress their grievances.

Not only did Stuyvesant reject the Remonstrance, but he also ordered the arrest of the sheriff and town clerk who delivered it, imprisoned the two magistrates who signed it, and fined all the others whose names were affixed to the document. Nonetheless, Hannah Bowne, and then John, graduated from their initial curiosity about the idiosyncratic Quakers to further expressions of support. In 1661 Bowne invited them to meet in the one-room house he had just built and, persuaded by his wife and impressed with the "primitive Christianity" of the worshippers, converted to Quakerism himself.

By midsummer 1662 the magistrate of Flushing was complaining to Stuyvesant that every Sunday a large group "of that heretick and abominable sect" was assembling thanks to John Bowne, who "moreover has condescended unto them at several times to hold their conventicles and meetings in his house." Bowne ambiguously denied only hosting meetings of "heretics and deceivers." He was fined and, refusing to pay, confined to prison. (His sentence was written in Dutch; Bowne obstinately declined even to pay the three guilders to have it translated into English.) That December, he was ordered to leave the colony. After rejecting an offer to depart voluntarily, Bowne was banished from New Amsterdam in perpetuity and placed aboard a ship bound for Europe.

But instead of vanishing into ignominious exile, Bowne was bent on pursuing his defiance of Stuyvesant in person before the directors of the West India Company. In a preemptive strike, members of the New Amsterdam council had already written to the company to tell them that Bowne had been ostracized and why. Figuring on further ingratiating themselves to the West India directors, the burghers of New Amsterdam dauntlessly proclaimed that if the Quakers violated the law again, the council would "against our inclinations, be compelled to prosecute such persons in a more severe manner."

Resorting to Dutch doublespeak, the "wise and foreseeing" company directors declared in April 1663: "Although it is our cordial desire that similar and other sectarians might not be found there, yet as the contrary seems to be the fact, we doubt very much if vigorous proceedings ought not to be discontinued, except you intend to check and destroy your population, which however, in the youth of your existence, ought rather to be encouraged by all means." To burnish New Amsterdam as a paradigm of unbounded entrepreneurship, the company added a cynical coda: "It is our opinion that connivance would be useful, that the conscience of men, at least, ought to remain free and unshackled. Let everyone be unmolested as long as he is modest, as long as he does not disturb others or oppose the Governments." While the directors understood and perhaps even shared the concerns of the New Amsterdam councillors who sought to halt the further influx of "vagabonds, Quakers, and other Fugitives," the company plainly recapitulated the principle that "moderation has always been the guide of the magistrates of this city, and the consequence has been that, from every land, people have flocked to this asylum."

Bowne, who had further alienated his inquisitors by declining for religious reasons to remove his hat during the inquiries, stubbornly refused to take yes (which, as ambiguous as it was, may have been lost in translation from the Dutch) for an answer. After a fair amount of unproductive give-and-take, he grudgingly agreed to obey future laws in New Netherland. The directors skirted the substance of the conflict but left no doubt that, however good their intentions on behalf of the West India Company and the colony, Stuyvesant and his council had overreached. Their decision again dramatized the distinction between New Amsterdam and the other American colonies and, arguably, set the stage for the passage of the First Amendment when the first Federal Congress convened in New York in 1789 and for President George Washington's historic pledge, written from New York to the Hebrew Congregation in Newport, Rhode Island, in 1790, that the U.S. government would "give to bigotry no sanction, to persecution no assistance."

John Bowne sailed back to America, arriving on the winds of change in New Amsterdam in January 1664. His courage and audacity in defying—and one-upping—Stuyvesant further drained the director general of whatever reservoir of

JOHN BOWNE BEFORE GOVERNOR STUYVESANT.

"John Bowne before Governor Stuyvesant." (Courtesy of the Bowne House Historical Society)

goodwill he had to draw upon when his leadership was again challenged later that year, this time from without. Seeking a popular and profitable war with the Dutch, King Charles II of England had unilaterally awarded New Amsterdam to his brother, the Duke of York. After four British warships cruised unmolested into the harbor and demanded that the Dutch surrender, Stuyvesant desperately summoned New Amsterdammers to defend the city.

The British gave residents a choice: loyally stand with Stuyvesant on what remained of the city's decrepit ramparts as they endured a naval siege, or accede to the magnanimous, if undiplomatically dubbed, Articles of Capitulation. If they abandoned the crotchety director-general and the Dutch West India Company, they could keep their taverns, their guns, their language, their legal system, their customs, and "the liberty of their consciences in Divine Worship." They convincingly voted with their feet. On September 8, 1664, the British seized the city without firing a shot.

After Bowne returned home (where under English law he could now practice religion unmolested), he farmed, sold books, and invested in real estate in Queens and Pennsylvania. Hannah Bowne became a Society of Friends minister and joined several religious missions to Europe. In 1676 her husband joined her in London, where she died the following year. When John Bowne died in 1695 at the age of sixty-eight, his fellow Quakers recalled that he had not only hosted his neighbors in his home for forty years but also even accommodated George Fox, the movement's founder. As the Quaker minutes said of Bowne, he "suffered very much for ye truth's sake."

John Bowne left a durable family legacy, fathering sixteen children in all, eight of whom survived, with Hannah and two more women whom he married after he returned to New York. One of his sons, Walter Bowne, became a mayor of New York; another, Samuel Bowne, a congressman. In 1775 his great-grandson Robert founded Bowne & Co., a financial printing firm that was the first publicly traded company in the United States. He also joined with George Clinton (who was married to his cousin), Alexander Hamilton, and John Jay in forming the Manumission Society of New York. In 1806 Mary Bowne, the daughter of John Bowne IV, married Samuel Parsons. The original John Bowne's ninth-generation descendants, two sisters, Anna Hinckley Parsons and Bertha Parsons, lived in the home he built, now the oldest house in Queens, until 1945, when it was dedicated as a national shrine to religious freedom.

4

Isaac Sears

America Began in New York

I no longer even hated Rivington Street but the idea of Rivington Street,
all Rivington Streets of all nationalities allowed to pile up in cities like
gigantic dung heaps smelling up the world, ambitions growing out of
filth and crawling away like worms.

—AL MANHEIM, IN BUDD SCHULBERG, *WHAT MAKES SAMMY RUN?*

Rivington Street on the Lower East Side has been immortalized as a feverish
melting pot in novels, ballads, poems, lyrics, films, and even album covers
by everyone from the Beastie Boys to Lady Gaga. But in the late 1700s, when it
was originally mapped, the street was an anodyne, pastoral expanse sandwiched
between Delancey Street and North Street. Later renamed Houston Street, North
Street originally defined New York's urban outer boundary at the time when,
since livestock still outnumbered people, the landscape was indeed punctuated by
dung heaps, though they were not uncommonly gigantic by eighteenth-century
standards.

Rivington and Delancey Streets run parallel (unlike their namesakes). That the
street names have endured is further proof that New Yorkers don't know—or care—
much about their history. Given the Anglophobia of the nineteenth century, at
least one of them would have been renamed for, among others, Isaac Sears. (There *is*

a two-block-long Sears Street in the borough of Manhattan, on Randalls Island, but it's named for a firefighter trainee who died in 2008.) Neither Rivington Street's undistinguished geography nor its demography reflects the gratitude that James De Lancey Jr. intended to convey by naming the thoroughfare for James Rivington. The beleaguered fellow Loyalist and blisteringly pro-British publisher had helped De Lancey dispose of his property once it became apparent that the insufferable British subjugation of New York, which had begun in 1776 and would continue for seven years, could not be sustained indefinitely. All other considerations aside, it's no surprise that the screenwriter and novelist Budd Schulberg was professionally predisposed to harbor ill will against a street named for a publisher.

Born in London, Rivington emigrated to America in 1760. Thirteen years later, he started publishing the *New York Gazetteer*. The newspaper began as a relatively objective journal, although Rivington's personal loyalties were unconcealed. A favorite target of his vilification was the merchant patriot provocateur Isaac Sears, whom he maligned as "a *tool* of the lowest order; a *political cracker*, sent abroad to *alarm and terrify*." Sears gave as good as he got, denouncing Rivington as "a servile tool, ready to do the dirty work of any knave who purchases."

James De Lancey Jr. was a native New Yorker, his Huguenot grandfather, Stephen, having fled France and arrived in America in 1686. James Jr. inherited the family's mercantile business and, like many fellow merchants, opposed Parliament's heavy-handed taxation. James Jr. opposed the Stamp Act and other barriers to the colony's commerce, a self-serving mindset that temporarily endeared him to the radicals. But he sacrificed his credibility with patriotic Americans by belatedly agreeing to subsidize the care and feeding of British troops under the Quartering Act. Presciently, he packed his belongings and left New York in April 1775 for England, never to return.

Historians still debate whether the ensuing conflict was a revolution, a war for independence, or a civil war, and what proportion of Americans—some say more than half—were neither zealous Loyalists nor passionate patriots. The radicals revolting against an unrepresentative government some 3,500 miles away were the most identifiable by their words and deeds. They were dominated in the city by the triumvirate of Isaac Sears, John Lamb, and Alexander McDougall, men who, Pauline Maier wrote in *The Old Revolutionaries* (1980), were ambitious when "the obscure might rise to positions of power and prominence" through politics and "played the role of brokers, mediating between the various social and economic groups that made up the community." Lamb, a writer, was the son of a convicted robber exiled from England. McDougall, a Scottish-born merchant, had been a privateer.

Sears, a fifth-generation New Englander, was born in Massachusetts in 1730. When Isaac was four, his family moved to Norwalk, Connecticut. At sixteen he was apprenticed to a captain; at twenty-two, he was already commanding a sloop that shuttled cargo between New York and Canada. He captained a trading vessel until, in the Seven Years' War, he was commissioned as a privateer. As the *Magazine of American History* recounts, his exploits "gave him a great moral ascendancy over his fellow-citizens, and he seems to have fairly won over the title of 'King.'" By the early 1760s Sears had profited so handsomely as a privateer that he removed to New York, where he invested in trade with the West Indies. He married Sarah Drake, whose father owned the Water Street Tavern, at Trinity Church. Like so many other reluctant revolutionaries in New York, he seemed the antithesis of the rabble in arms that the British identified with the mobocracy.

Boston and Philadelphia would always maintain a friendly rivalry for the status of America's cradle of liberty; arguably, New York's role as the amalgamator of competitive colonies into symbiotic states and the site where the nation's government was invented has often been overlooked. New York was the only one of the thirteen colonies that the British had seized by force rather than settled in the seventeenth century. The nineteenth-century historian Henry B. Dawson dated the first revolt against the crown to as early as 1681, when New York merchants refused to pay custom duties. On October 18, 1764, the Provincial Assembly of New York was first among the colonies—before Massachusetts in 1770, and Virginia in 1773—to appoint a Committee of Correspondence, to collaborate with its legislative counterparts on the East Coast "on the Subject of the impending Dangers which threaten the Colonies of being taxed by Laws to be passed by Great Britain."

Britain, under a newly crowned king and an equally stubborn prime minister, ham-handedly forced the colonies to foot the lion's share of their own defense during and after the Seven Years' War—without giving the English expatriates and their progeny any say in the matter. Worse still, a 1763 proclamation barring American settlement west of the Appalachians, while its bestowal of title on Native Americans made it a legal benchmark of sorts, infuriated land-grabbing colonists, including George Washington, who would own some thirty-two thousand acres within the circumscribed territory. After the war, Parliament asserted its dominion by vigorously enforcing the Navigation Acts, all but granting Britain a monopoly on trade

"Sons of Liberty raising the flag, June 4th, 1766," from A Brief History of the City of New York *by Charles B. Todd (New York: American Book Co., 1899), 145.*

with America. The following spring, Parliament passed the odious Stamp Act. Effective November 1, 1765, the act required that officially stamped paper be purchased for all legal documents and that tax stamps be affixed to everything from pamphlets to playing cards.

On October 7, 1765, barely three weeks before the Stamp Act was to take effect, nine of the thirteen colonies, prodded by Massachusetts and Virginia, dispatched representatives to a Stamp Act Congress, which convened at New York's city hall. Even as the Congress was still meeting in New York, the first tax stamps were delivered from England on October 23. Sears, McDougall, and Lamb threatened a licking to anyone who used them. On October 25, delegates to the congress signed a fourteen-point Declaration of Rights and Grievances, which affirmed the supremacy of Parliament but argued that the rights of Englishmen precluded the august body from levying taxes because they could only be imposed by representatives of the people. John William Leonard, writing in his *History of the City of New York, 1609–1909* (1910), proclaimed the congress "the beginning of the American union."

On October 31, one day before the Stamp Act was to take effect, the city's merchants struck an even greater strategic blow against the crown. Two hundred voted unanimously to boycott British goods altogether until the act was repealed. "New York thus led in the great and effective movement which proved to be America's greatest commercial attack upon Great Britain," Leonard wrote. Philadelphia merchants followed suit on November 7; Boston's on December 3. When the underground Sons of Liberty emerged publicly to export its strategy of defiance to other colonies, the first name on its membership roster was Isaac Sears.

It's debatable whether Sears and many of his compatriots would have been much more amenable to subsidizing British troops had the Stamp Act and similar levies been imposed by legislators duly elected in the colonies instead of by distant, unrepresentative members of Parliament. He and other self-proclaimed patriots insisted, though, that "taxation without representation" was more than a bumper sticker. It was a matter of principle—although, in truth, because of gender, race, and property qualifications, fewer than one third of the colonists were eligible to vote for their own representatives, which meant that some two thirds of the population would have been taxed without direct representation anyway.

On June 4, 1766, the Sons of Liberty convened on the Commons, ostensibly to mark the king's birthday and celebrate Parliament's repeal of the Stamp Act by brazenly erecting a flagstaff called a Liberty Pole directly facing the British barracks—a defiant invitation for the Red Coats to topple it, which they did, three times, only to have the colonists immediately replace it. (After the Common Council refused to give the Sons of Liberty permission for another provocation, Sears bought a plot of land nearby and erected a twenty-two-foot totem on his own property.) On January 18, 1770, an altercation between Sears and several British soldiers posting broadsides belittling the Sons of Liberty as "great heroes who thought their freedom depended on a piece of wood" escalated into what became known (but not famous) as the Battle of Golden Hill—for the "golden grain" grown there in Dutch times—in Lower Manhattan. The British, whose broadsides presumably constituted an exercise of their free speech rights, derided the Sons of Liberty as drunken rabble while the soldiers stoically defended the populace. Accounts of casualties during the ensuing clashes varied widely (including possibly one death and several serious injuries). The better-known Boston Massacre occurred six weeks later.

New Yorkers almost beat Boston to a tea party, too. The first shipload of taxed tea was due in New York on November 25, 1773, and the Sons of Liberty were fully prepped to dump the tea chests overboard as soon as they arrived. But the tea-laden vessel was delayed, blown off course in a storm. By the time the ship was finally sighted off Sandy Hook the following April, Boston had stolen New York's thunder.

Undeterred, Isaac Sears prevented the tea from being marketed in Manhattan. A ditty at the time by the patriot poet Philip Freneau immortalized his exploits in rhyme:

> At this time there arose, a certain "King Sears,"
> Who made it his duty, to banish our fears,
> He was, without doubt, a person of merit,
> Great knowledge, some wit, and abundance of spirit,
> Could talk like a lawyer, and that without fee,
> And threaten'd perdition, to all that drank Tea.

A year later, in April 1775, Sears was publicly advocating revolution, a defiant act of sedition that inevitably resulted in his arrest. Freed from prison by fellow patriots who paraded him triumphantly through the city's streets, Sears and his allies commandeered city hall, where they seized five hundred muskets that had recently arrived from England for shipment to British troops in Boston. Less than a week later, Sears and a small army of 350 men raided the custom house, where duties were collected on imports, seized control, and proclaimed that the Port of New York was closed.

The following November, for the second time, Sears violently suppressed free speech—a right that had been won by the printer Peter Zenger when he was acquitted of libeling the royal governor in 1735. (He was tried at New York's city hall, where in 1789 the First Amendment, which would be enshrined in the Bill of Rights, was approved by Congress and sent to the states for ratification.) After Sears learned that the British governor of Virginia had seized a printing press operated by the nephew of John Holt, the patriot New York publisher, he mobilized a vigilante posse that raided the offices of Rivington's *Gazetteer*. The mob confiscated the newspaper's lead type, recasting it as bullets. (So much for the pen being mightier than the sword.) "Though I am fully sensible how dangerous and pernicious Rivington's press has been," Alexander Hamilton complained to John Jay, "I cannot help disapproving and condemning this step."

Sears repaired to New Haven, then forayed episodically into New York, where he forced Loyalists, including the Reverend Samuel Seabury (the future first American Episcopal bishop), to swear allegiance to the "United States of America." If, by the spring of 1776, the mission could be judged a success, a Connecticut delegate to the Continental Congress wrote to Samuel Adams, it was "much owing to that Crazy

Capt. Sears." Sears appropriated a British cannon from the Battery and sabotaged efforts to resupply British warships. Infuriated, Vice Admiral Samuel Graves ordered the sixty-four-gun HMS *Asia* to "fire upon the House of that Traitor, Sears."

That July 9, after Washington read the newly printed Declaration of Independence to his troops in New York, Sears mustered a mob of patriots to march the mile and a half downtown to Bowling Green, where they lassoed the two-ton statue of King George III, toppled it, cleaved it into portable segments, and carted off most of the gilded lead remnants to Litchfield, Connecticut, to be melted and delivered back to the British in the form of 42,088 musket balls. Toppling an effigy was one thing, but another of Sears's extremist provocations that same month proved too much: Washington himself thwarted the arrest of William Tryon, New York's royal governor. (Ironically, Tryon would conspire in a bollixed scheme to kidnap Washington the following spring.)

Once independence was declared, though, Washington became considerably less circumspect. There are suggestions that he was complicit in the Great Fire of September 1776, which broke out less than a week after the redcoats occupied Manhattan. The cause was never conclusively determined: radical patriots favored a scorched-earth campaign against the British, while Washington was ambivalent. The same was said about a plot to kidnap Prince William Henry, who was serving as a Royal Navy midshipman in New York. Washington gave the go-ahead in 1782, but the operation failed. (After the prince was crowned William IV in 1830, he was informed of the scheme by the American ambassador, who also assured him of Washington's edict that had the mission succeeded, the young prince should suffer no "insult or indignity." To that, the new king replied: "I am obliged to General Washington for his humanity, but I'm damned glad I did not give him an opportunity of exercising it towards me.")

The radical triumvirate fractured amid transactional alliances with one faction or another and as moderates embraced independence as the only realistic alternative. Once fighting broke out full-time and the British occupied the city, Sears transplanted himself to Boston. There, he profited handsomely as a merchant, outfitting the Continental Army and supplying a fleet of privateers. After the war he returned to New York, where he was elected to the assembly and tormented former Tories with confiscatory legislation.

Finally, after seven years of mercilous occupation, on Evacuation Day, November 26, 1783—a day that would be celebrated regularly and raucously in the city until the British came back into favor during World War I—the redcoats skulked away from New York. Loyalist refugees left in droves for England and Canada as well. Conspicuously, one unabashed Tory remained behind.

James Rivington had been driven from New York after his war of words with Isaac Sears descended into violence and vandalism, but he returned during the British occupation in mid-1777 with a lucrative royal appointment as "Printer to the King." He relaunched his journal as the *Royal Gazette*, the name it retained until November 19, 1783, a week before Evacuation Day. Although he hoped to attract new readers among returning American troops and patriots, he ceased publication on New Year's Eve, 1783, after pressure from Sears and other avenging alumni of the Sons of Liberty. This time, Rivington gave up without a fight—giving Sears the last word—and became a bookseller, having presciently imported British classics before the war ended.

As time passed, though, Rivington became an enigma. In December 1783 the *Massachusetts Gazette* in Springfield, without elaboration, cryptically printed the following item: "It is reported as an undoubted fact, that Mr. James Rivington, Printer at New-York, was, as soon as our troops entered the city, protected in person and property, by a guard, and that he will be allowed to reside in the country, for reasons best known to the great men at helm."

Rivington operated a private coffeehouse next door to his print shop, where he intimately insinuated himself into Loyalist and British military circles. His silent partner was Robert Townsend, the pseudonymous Samuel Culper Jr. of George Washington's spy ring organized under the nation's first chief of counterintelligence, John Jay. (It was in Rivington's print shop that Jay's brother invented the invisible ink with which secret messages were written.) Rivington also was said to have procured the Royal Navy's signal book, which helped the Americans and French win the decisive battle of Yorktown.

Rivington's coffeehouse, "a favorite gathering place for the British, was a principal source of information for Culper, Jr.," a Central Intelligence Agency history of spycraft concluded. George Washington Parke Custis, Martha Washington's grandson and the editor of the first president's memoirs, wrote that Rivington's motive was monetary, but that he "proved faithful to his bargain."

While the winners, apart from Sears and the Liberty Boys, left Rivington unmolested, the losers, in the person of Sir Guy Carleton, the British commander during the peace negotiations, presented Rivington's nine- and ten-year-old sons in 1782 with commissions into the British army, guaranteeing them half pay for life. Rivington may never have revealed his role as an American spy for fear of jeopardizing their pensions. His fear was well founded. While his great-nephew Percy Rivington Pyne

"Isaac Sears addressing the mob," from Harper's
Magazine, *1882*. (Illustration via the New York
Public Library)

would emigrate from England in 1835 and become president of City National Bank
of New York, the predecessor to Citigroup, Rivington's own sons, even with their
pensions, invested improvidently. Assuming their liabilities, Rivington wound up
spending four years in debtors' prison. Released in 1801, he died in New York the
following year, evocatively on July 4.

Isaac Sears was himself accused of buying Continental Army veterans' overdue
pay certificates at a discount and using the proceeds to speculate in Loyalist properties at distressed prices. Only by claiming immunity as a legislator did he manage to
avoid formal charges. He conveniently left town after he partnered with Samuel Shaw,
who was designated as the nation's first consul to China, and other investors, on the
ship *Hope*, which sailed from New York in February 1786. The *Hope* followed the
six-month, eighteen-thousand-mile course pioneered two years earlier by the *Empress
of China*, the first American merchant ship to enter Chinese waters. When the ship

arrived late in Canton (modern Guangzhou) in 1783, laden with thirty tons of medicinal ginseng root, it was the first American merchant vessel to enter Chinese waters. Disembarking en route in 1786 in Batavia—the capital of the Dutch East Indies, administered by the company that had hired Henry Hudson, and today's Jakarta—Sears contracted dysentery that July. He died in Canton on October 28 later that year, at the age of fifty-six.

Sears still insisted on having the last word. New Yorkers would later become familiar with political bosses ordering ballots cast on behalf of long-deceased voters, but he did them one better. News of his demise having been delayed for months, he was reelected to the state assembly effective January 1787—despite his death.

5

John Jay

The Capital of Capital

After seven years of pitiless occupation and a desolating fire blamed on fleeing patriots, much of Manhattan was in ruins when the American Revolution ended. It was as if New York, which more than any other colony had borne the brunt of the conflict and contributed more to the cause, had won a battle but lost the war. The population, which had peaked at about twenty-five thousand before 1776, had plummeted by about half once British troops finally evacuated the city in 1783, a combined exodus of patriots departing before the war and diehard Loyalists fleeing with the redcoats.

John Jay, a native New Yorker, had been among the founders and patriots who in 1776 urged General George Washington to level the city as he retreated from the advancing British troops. "If I ever see New York again I expect to meet with the shade of many a departed joy," Jay wrote a friend. "My heart bleeds to think of it." By the first official U.S. census in 1790, though, New York's population had burgeoned to 33,131 residents a mere seven years later. The city has remained the largest in the nation ever since.

John Jay is an anomaly in this book, known widely as an American diplomat, secretary of state, chief justice of the Supreme Court, and governor. But lost to history is his pivotal role in reviving New York City after the revolution. The artist Charles Willson Peale immortalized George Washington's triumphant return to New York on his white horse on Evacuation Day in 1783, but Washington went

home to Mount Vernon a month later. It was John Jay who would rescue the smoldering city, with "the deplorable 'Canvastown' and blackened ruins right in its
center," so vividly described by Daniel Van Pelt in *Leslie's History of the Greater New
York* (1898), reverberating in a late twentieth century urban vista that would be
ravaged not by a foreign occupying army but from within, by neglect, greed, and
the myopic cost of good intentions. No artist captured John Jay faithfully rejoining
his family in New York. But the city's revival never would have occurred so
quickly—or, perhaps, at all—had it not been triggered by the motion to relocate
the seat of government after hopscotching from Philadelphia to Princeton to
Annapolis to Trenton over four years. The consequential motion was introduced by
Charles Pinckney of South Carolina and seconded by Jay, just a few weeks before
the Fifth Congress of the Confederation was to convene in January of 1785. Little
more than a year after its British occupiers had been ousted, New York became the
capital of the young nation. That designation profoundly accelerated the city's
ascendancy.

John Jay was born in New York City in 1745, the grandson of Augustus Jay, a French
Huguenot refugee from religious persecution. Augustus settled in New York after
rejecting South Carolina (where he said the climate was "intolerable") and Philadelphia (which he ranked an "infant state"). Jay's maternal grandfather, Jacobus Van
Cortlandt, was a New Amsterdam–born former mayor of New York. John was the
seventh child of Augustus's son Peter Jay, a wealthy merchant (and slaveowner) and
Trinity vestryman, and Mary Van Cortlandt. In 1760 John enrolled in King's College,
then a six-year-old institution that would become Columbia University.

After graduating, Jay was clerking with a lawyer in 1765 when delegates from
the colonies gathered in New York for the Stamp Act Congress. The conclave
concluded with a riot by about two thousand New Yorkers—"a most surprising
ferment," as Jay described it. He withdrew with his parents "to our more peaceable
habitation in the country" in Westchester, foreshadowing his predisposition a
decade later to avoid a violent confrontation with the mother country. Relations
with Parliament deteriorated, though, and war became inevitable. As Walter
Stahr wrote in *John Jay: Founding Father* (2012), Jay chose to fight for his
commitment to the traditional rights enjoyed by Englishmen rather than maintain his sworn loyalty to the British king.

In the spring of 1776, Jay was elected to the New York Provincial Congress,
where he remained even as the Continental Congress was declaring the nation's
independence (which he might well have voted against had he been a delegate in

Portrait of John Jay, from The Memorial History of the City of
New-York: From Its First Settlement to the Year 1892, *vol. 2,
edited by James Grant Wilson (New York: New-York History Co.,
1892), 175.*

Philadelphia at the time). Once war came, though, he became fully committed. That
summer of 1776, with British ships and troops descending on New York City, Jay
secretly conspired to sabotage an expected Royal Navy foray up the Hudson and to
organize the New York legislature's Committee for Detecting and Defeating
Conspiracies, which in effect made him the fledgling nation's first chief of counterintelligence. During the revolution, he helped draft New York's constitution
and served as the state's chief justice and then president of the Continental
Congress until September 1779. At that time, he was dispatched as ambassador to
persuade Spain to recognize American independence (it declined to do so, fearing
its own colonies would catch the spirit, but agreed to support the new nation with a
loan). In June 1782 he arrived in Paris, where he joined John Adams and Benjamin
Franklin to negotiate a peace treaty with Britain.

The Articles of Confederation ("and Perpetual Union," as they were euphorically known), written in 1777, weren't ratified until four years later, which meant that the Congress of the Confederation (which was still calling itself the Continental Congress) didn't convene until 1781. Northern and southern members of the new congress first compromised by proposing *two* federal towns—one on the Delaware River near Trenton, and another on the Potomac near Georgetown, Maryland—and vacillate between them every six months. The engineer of this plan, Elbridge Gerry of Connecticut, would prove so adept at geographic jujitsu that his name would be combined with *mandering* ("aimless wandering") as a synonym for imaginative legislative mapmaking. But over nearly nine years the proposed two-capital scheme would self-destruct.

The Continental Congress fled Philadelphia in the summer of 1783, after its members were menaced by fever and by Continental Army veterans who demanded back pay. In deciding on a place to roost, the nation's governing body sought to address delegates' arduous travel demands and accommodate competing political agendas on vital issues like war debts, tariffs, slavery, and the supremacy of the national government, which the location of the capital would symbolize. By January 1784 the congress had ratified the peace treaty with Britain negotiated by Jay, Adams, and Franklin. But handcuffed under the feckless Articles of Confederation, its members struggled even to muster a quorum. After meeting at Princeton and in Annapolis, the Fourth Congress of the Confederation adjourned for Trenton on November 1, 1784.

Flush with wringing more concessions from the British than expected in the Treaty of Paris (the crown relinquished its claim to all land east of the Mississippi), Jay visited England for several months to recuperate. He sailed home from France in May 1784, arriving in New York on July 24 to learn that he had not only been elected as a delegate to the Continental Congress, but also that two months earlier, the congress had named him in his absence to the cabinet as secretary for foreign affairs. "I do not know how you will be pleased with this appointment, but I am sure your country stands in need of your abilities in that office," Charles Thomson, the secretary of Congress, wrote him.

"For this office he had not been an applicant and he was not anxious to accept it," Samuel Flagg Bemis wrote in *The American Secretaries of State and Their Diplomacy* (1928). Jay had already rejected offers to be ambassador to France or Britain so he could return to his private law practice, already neglected too long due to his government service.

Before accepting the job, Jay imposed several bureaucratic provisos. First, he insisted that he be allowed to choose his own staff. Second, third, and fourth: location, location, location—a stipulation that would prove instrumental in resuscitating the city that Jay himself had urged General Washington to vaporize before it fell into British hands just eight years earlier. Jay would consent to join the cabinet only if Congress agreed to relocate from the French Arms Tavern in Trenton when it reconvened in January 1785. "Not until he was assured that Congress would sit thenceforth in New York City instead of the less accessible town of Trenton, New Jersey," Bemis wrote, "would Jay take the office of secretary."

On December 21, Jay seconded the two-part motion by Charles Pinckney of South Carolina. It stated that Congress should expediently "determine on a place at which they will continue to sit until proper accommodations in a federal town shall be erected" and then specified "that the subsisting resolutions respecting the alternate temporary residence of Congress at Trenton and Annapolis, be repealed." That same day, Jay was sworn in as foreign affairs secretary. Two days later the delegates agreed to begin planning for a federal town on the banks of the Delaware, but meanwhile to adjourn and "to meet at the city of New York, on the eleventh Day of January following, for the dispatch of public business, and that the sessions of Congress be held at the place last mentioned, until the buildings aforesaid shall be ready for their reception." As Walter Stahr wrote, "Jay's desire to be in New York City, and Congress's desire to have Jay as its Secretary for Foreign Affairs, no doubt influenced this decision." Jay regarded the government's migration as so enduring that he began to build a new house in Manhattan.

New Yorkers might have harbored few hopes of keeping the capital permanently, but municipal boosters placed their faith in the mighty bureaucratic power of inertia and politics of entropy to keep Congress in the city longer than it originally expected to stay. They were right. Thanks first and foremost to John Jay, the Congress of the Confederation would remain in New York for more than four years, without ever fulfilling its commitment to proceed with the proposed federal towns on the Delaware and Potomac. New York would also become the first federal capital city under the Constitution in March 1789. "Remarkably," Stanley Y. Klos wrote in *America's Four Republics: The More or Less United States* (2012), "the capital of the United States of America, for the first and last time, had been moved to persuade a member of Congress to accept an executive position in the federal government."

Moreover, Jay's title as foreign secretary belied his singular muscularity under the Articles of Confederation. Without an appointed or elected president, the center of gravity in the national government belonged to Congress, which was why another one of Jay's conditions in accepting the job was that his office be the fulcrum for all legislative branch international communications. By dint of his political and social position, his wife, Sarah Jay, emerged as a savvy and gracious hostess and First Lady. And Jay himself "was really the only concrete expression of the government by, of, and for the people, which had just been wrested from Great Britain, to which other nations could at all clearly address themselves," the historian James Grant Wilson wrote. "He, too, was the person to whom the several states must look as the link for communication between themselves and that delusive thing—the general government. Hence, John Jay's position made him in effect the chief of state"—that is, the nation's first president, though no one said so at the time.

Jay fulfilled still another role in the mid-1780s: he was instrumental in persuading New York State to ratify the proposed constitution. In a compromise engineered in large part to keep the new federal government in New York City, the convention finally endorsed the Constitution on July 26, 1788, but barely. The delegates voted 30–27 for ratification, though they formally expressed their reservations about the document as written. They also appended thirty-one proposed amendments, a Bill of Rights that included twenty-five guarantees, and a ratification message, the longest of any state. It was drafted, of course, by John Jay.

Once the Constitution was ratified, all that was left to decide was when and where the incoming federal Congress would meet. The "when" was easy: under the Articles of Confederation, the new constitutional government would open for business on March 4, 1789. "Where" was an open question. The perennial rivalry between New York and Philadelphia resurfaced, and on September 12, 1788, delegates from New Hampshire and Virginia proposed that plans to reconvene, even temporarily, at "the present seat of Congress"—meaning New York—be stricken "to prevent jealousies in one part of the Union, of undue bias in the public councils or measures toward another part" and to identify a more central location "more likely to obviate disagreeable and injurious dissensions concerning the place most fit for the seat of federal business." A blank space was left to be filled in by some location between the Hudson and the Potomac. The resolution was defeated. "This being rejected," James Madison recalled, "the alternative remaining was to agree to New York or to strangle the government in its birth."

After weeks of rancorous debate, the Congress of the Confederation agreed— amid claims that New York had been guaranteed the seat of government in return

"Federal Hall, the Seat of Congress, the only surviving eyewitness rendering of Washington's inauguration," engraving by Amos Doolittle, circa 1790, after a drawing by Peter Lacour. (Illustration via the National Park Service)

for ratifying the Constitution (to say nothing of quid pro quo for Jay's agreement to become foreign affairs secretary)—that the First Federal Congress would convene there the following March. The lame-duck lawmakers were so embittered, though, that the city was initially enshrined as the government headquarters that dare not speak its name: the vote on September 13, 1788, didn't specify the location, except to say that the spring session would be held at "*the present seat* of Congress."

Once it was decided, Jay was instrumental in advancing funds for the redesign of New York's city hall by the Paris-born military engineer Pierre Charles L'Enfant, who called himself Peter in America. L'Enfant's new design tripled the Wall Street building's size and transformed it into the first example of Federal architecture in the United States. Finishing touches were still being put on the building—now renamed Federal Hall—by the March 4 deadline, as the sixty-five congressmen and twenty-six senators began to straggle in. So torturous was their journey by boat and over roads muddied by late-winter thaws that a quorum was not declared by the House until April 1 and the Senate on April 6. Still protesting that he neither wanted nor deserved the presidency—although even before he was elected he had begun drafting a surprisingly solipsistic seventy-three-page inaugural address, which he was persuaded not to deliver—George Washington was finally inaugurated on Federal Hall's banner-festooned second-floor balcony on April 30.

In early 1790 pressure was already building on Congress, which had deferred the decision again, to choose a permanent seat of government. Whether New York was ever a serious contender is arguable, given that the federal district envisioned was to be ten miles square, and all of Manhattan measures roughly thirteen miles by two. Lewis Morris, a former member of the Continental Congress, signer of the Declaration of Independence, and New York legislator, proposed his two-thousand-acre estate in the Bronx, but the offer—long before the borough would be stereotyped by the Bronx cheer and by Ogden Nash's "No thonx" ditty—was never seriously contemplated.

For all its assets, even then New York was an outlier in the eyes of other citizens of the newly constituted United States. Thomas Jefferson, the farmer-philosopher who inherited the duties of secretary of state from Jay in March 1790, invoked the Roman goddess of the sewers to pronounce New York a "cloacina of all the depravities of human nature." Jefferson also dubbed the city "Hamiltonopolis" in mock deference to the treasury secretary, who was initially among the city's biggest champions. That changed with a legendary dinner-table compromise forged in June 1790 between Hamilton, Jefferson, and Representative James Madison, a fellow Virginian, at Jefferson's New York home at 57 Maiden Lane.

Hamilton's single-minded goal during the first Congress was for the national government to assume the states' war debts—a goal that, New York senator Rufus King later wrote, "was the primary object, all subordinate points which oppose it must be sacrificed." Hamilton was willing to swap power for money, transplanting the seat of government to Philadelphia temporarily and then relocating it permanently even farther south to the Potomac site that Washington favored. By 1790 Hamilton was importuning Jay, who the previous fall had accepted Washington's offer to become chief justice of the Supreme Court, to formally grant his imprimatur to the plan. Jay balked, in an informal reply that nonetheless set a precedent: he would only officially rule on the debt legislation's constitutionality if and when a legal challenge came before the High Court.

Historians would deconstruct the separate votes on residence and assumption in every conceivable permutation, but the arithmetic was simple: states (and speculators) in the North owed more than those in the South. Hamilton sold his city down the river to buy southern votes for the debt deal, agreeing, in turn, to place the capital on the Potomac. The Residence Act, as it was officially called, transplanted the seat of government to Philadelphia for ten years while a permanent capital was being constructed in a swamp just north of George Washington's mansion in Mount Vernon, Virginia. In this way, Jefferson concluded, there would be "something to displease and something to soothe every part of the Union, but New York, which must be contented with what she has had." She was not.

On August 12, 1790, Congress convened for its final session at Federal Hall. On August 28, President Washington hosted his last state dinner in New York. Two days later, he and his family proceeded to McComb's Wharf on the Hudson River, boarded the same barge that had brought them to Manhattan sixteen months before, waved his hat, said "Farewell," and never returned to New York. If Congress guessed wrong about New York's graciousness, Philadelphians overestimated the degree to which federal officials would become besotted by their city. "You will see by the public papers that we are destined for Philadelphia," the forthright Abigail Adams wrote to John Quincy, "a Grievous affair to me I assure you, but so it is ordained." She informed her daughter that the Bush Hill mansion that her husband, the vice president, had secured for her in Philadelphia was beautiful and was indeed on a hill, but "there remains neither bush nor shrub upon it." Still, she acknowledged, she was better off than Martha Washington. The First Lady's new home in Philadelphia wouldn't even be finished in time for her arrival. Worse still, Adams wrote tartly, "when all is done, it will not be Broadway!"

Yet not every New Yorker was apoplectic that a city founded on the accumulation of capital would now be freed to return to its original mission. The loss cost some self-confidence, but Thomas Bender wrote in *New York Intellect* (1987), "the result was the strengthening of an elite civic consciousness, a sense of the city fundamentally localistic and based on the complementarity of commerce and culture. It was as if, having been shunned as being unsuitable for the nation's capital, New York decided to go it alone. New York would not be America." Ric Burns and James Sanders wrote in *New York: An Illustrated History* (1999) that no longer "weighted down with the symbolic obligations and ceremonial trappings a national capital entailed," the city would "dedicate itself unswervingly to what since the days of the Dutch had come most naturally: making money."

After 1790 New York City still remained the state capital, at least. Chief Justice Jay ran as the Federalist candidate for governor against Democratic-Republican incumbent George Clinton in 1792. He won more votes but, heralding two centuries of political machinations in New York, lost due to election law technicalities.

In 1794 Jay was dispatched to London to negotiate loose ends that lingered from the 1783 Treaty of Paris, threatening renewed hostilities with the British. Jay achieved an accord that eked out few givebacks but would at least avert a full-fledged declaration of war for nearly three decades. After details were leaked, the treaty proved enormously unpopular among Americans back home. But by then Jay had not only returned to the States but also been greeted, as in 1784, with word that he had gotten another unsolicited job: he had just been nominated *and elected* governor of New York after Clinton retired. Jay moved into the governor's mansion downtown, where he and Sarah joyfully returned to the center of New York social life.

Jay would serve as governor until 1801. As a committed abolitionist, he would finally get to approve legislation that abolished slavery in the state. Jay owned slaves himself, but had glossed over the inconsistency when, in 1785, he became a founding member of the New-York Society for Promoting the Manumission of Slaves, promoted subsidized education for free Black people, and, in 1799, signed the Act for the Gradual Abolition of Slavery. "I purchase slaves and manumit them at proper ages and when their faithful services shall have afforded a reasonable retribution," he explained. Similarly, as its title clearly stated, the state law was *gradual*: as of July 4, 1799, all children born to slave parents would be free—but they would be required to serve the mother's owner as, in effect, indentured servants, until age twenty-eight for males and age twenty-five for females.

Jay would retire to his farm in Bedford, where he died in 1829. His legacy would include freeing the slaves but also forever subjugating New York City to Albany. Legislators assembled in Albany in 1789, moved to New York from 1791 to 1793, returned to Albany in 1794, convened in Poughkeepsie in 1795, and came back to New York in 1796 to be close to Governor Clinton, who was ailing. Tired of convening in makeshift spaces and moving intermittently, New York's nomadic legislature had decided that it was time to take root.

On November 9, 1796, senators split evenly on a resolution to reconvene on the first Tuesday in January 1797—leaving the space after "at" unspecified. But lieutenant governor Stephen Van Rensselaer III (a descendant of Kiliaen van Rensselaer, the patroon whose estate Roeloff Jansen helped manage before he and his wife, Anneke, settled in Manhattan) cast the deciding vote. New York City and

Poughkeepsie vied for the blank space after the word *at*, but apparently, with some Manhattan boosters missing, Albany was inserted instead. When the complete resolution with time and place was put to a vote, the senate deadlocked. Once again, the lieutenant governor broke the tie. The next day, on November 10, the assembly adopted the senate version by a slim 53–50 margin.

Diarist and doctor Elihu Hubbard Smith of Manhattan predicted that the shift to Albany would have the same unifying effect on the state as transplanting the federal capital to Washington would on the nation. Smith injected a modicum of caution, however: "The only danger arises from the ardent temper of the many young men who represent the western & northern Counties," he wrote. "They feel their power; and are almost too fond of exercising it; they perceive their own superiority & are too prodigal of contempt for the imbecility of others."

Even some assemblymen from the western part of the state had cautioned against a precipitous move, though, arguing that Albany was ill prepared to house the state government immediately, and that a disruptive departure from New York City would so alienate downstaters that they would never agree to remain upstate permanently. Evading the question of a permanent capital altogether, legislators changed the title of the bill they were considering to an "act for erecting and establishing certain public offices in the city of Albany and for other purposes therein mentioned." The bill passed on March 11, 1797.

The legislature's Romanesque and Renaissance hilltop home, the one that still stands, was begun in 1867. It took thirty-two years to complete. It is dominated now by a 166-foot-long exterior staircase rather than the originally envisioned massive dome, its builders having calculated that the dome's weight would have thrust the 220-foot-tall granite building down the incline of State Street toward the Hudson River. In 1878, still incomplete, the building was officially designated the New York State Capitol.

As for the city itself, the lawmakers may have felt the need to leave the door open to fleeing the jurisdiction in the dead of night. Not until nearly a century later, in 1971, did the legislature correct its 1797 subterfuge and officially declare the City of Albany to be the state capital.

Jay's role in 1796 in moving the state capital is uncertain, but his reaction, as recorded secondhand, was unambiguous. "Our friend the Governor is well but rather out of temper with the abrupt adjournment of our Legislature to meet in January next, and at Albany," his former law clerk, Robert Troup, wrote to former senator Rufus King on November 16, 1796. Following a sleigh ride to Albany from New

York—the stagecoach took three days—Jay arrived on New Year's Eve for the first session of the newly relocated legislature and wrote his family, "I shall not, and cannot forget that I am not at home."

This may help explain why Jay was snubbed when Albany's monumental Empire State Plaza was built to replace the slums that had embarrassed Governor Nelson A. Rockefeller in 1959, when Princess Beatrix of the Netherlands visited to celebrate the region's Dutch heritage. Construction of the plaza, meant to supplement office space in the anachronistic and dwarfed Capitol, would obliterate most of Jay Street, the former governor's most visible public legacy in the capital city.

6

Levi Weeks

The Manhattan Well Mystery

On Monday, December 23, 1799, the morning after Elma Sands disappeared, the death of George Washington dominated New York newspapers. Muffled church bells tolled continuously for an hour beginning at noon, as they would each day up to the former president's ceremonial funeral in Manhattan a week later. To memorialize the general who liberated New York from the British on Evacuation Day in 1783 and was inaugurated in the city as the nascent nation's first president six years later, marchers accompanied a symbolic three-foot-tall urn to a service at St. Paul's Chapel on Broadway, where Washington had worshipped after he was sworn in. "Every kind of business ceased, and every thought was employed in preparation for the melancholy solemnity," according to one account. But by the following Monday, after it was reported that Washington had been buried at Mount Vernon, New Yorkers were already turning their thoughts to somebody else. Elma Sands was still missing.

Born as Gulielma Elmore Sands, she apparently came to New York City from the Connecticut Valley. Everyone knew her as Elma. The vivacious twenty-two-year-old had boarded since the previous July in a house on Greenwich Street owned by her married cousin, Catherine Ring, and her cousin's husband, Elias. On Sunday night, December 22, Elma mysteriously vanished. Witnesses heard her in her room upstairs. Supposedly she was preparing to elope. Her presumptive fiancé, fellow boarder Levi Weeks, was waiting in the sitting room, possibly with his brother, then stepped into the entryway. A whispered conversation was overheard. The front door opened and closed. A moment later a friend encountered Sands by chance on Greenwich Street, but her companion, whom the friend could not identify, pulled her away. As far as anyone knows, Elma Sands was never seen alive again.

Winter had only officially arrived the day before, but the season already had been lustily heralded: snow coated the narrow streets and blanketed the spacious and sparsely populated Lispenard's Meadows, part of the old Anneke Jans farm between New York City and the village of Greenwich, where Elma Sands and her companion appeared to have been heading. The night was frigid, so bone-chilling that she had borrowed a fur muff from a neighbor before she left the house on Greenwich Street. Searchers dragged the Hudson River for her body but came up empty-handed. Two days later her muff was found about half a mile inland, near the fresh tracks of a one-horse sleigh and not far from a well recently commissioned by the Manhattan Company and built with lumber and other building supplies purchased from Levi Weeks's brother, Ezra.

Given New York's exponential growth in population once it became the nation's capital after the Revolutionary War, guaranteeing a permanent supply of water would have challenged any engineering genius. Assemblyman Aaron Burr was undeterred, though; the obstacles would only marginally affect his primary objective, which was to slake his personal thirst for power and money by priming a metaphoric pump.

The previous spring, Burr had bamboozled (and probably bribed) the state legislature—even enlisting his on-again, off-again nemesis Alexander Hamilton— into chartering the ambiguously titled Manhattan Company to provide the parched city, dependent largely on the befouled Collect Pond just north of the Commons (now City Hall Park), with a sufficient supply of fresh water. Burr had already persuaded city officials that by providing water through a private company, he would save New Yorkers money and spare politicians from being blamed for higher taxes to pay for the pumps, pipes, and other paraphernalia that a municipal water works would require.

What Burr did not reveal, however, was that water was not the liquid asset that ranked highest on his business development agenda. A provision buried in the Manhattan Company's charter allowed it to invest whatever surplus it accumulated in any potentially profitable venture it pleased, which was Burr's way of circumventing the Federalists' monopoly on finance through the Bank of New York. Faster than he could open a spigot, Burr created the Bank of the Manhattan

Company, the antecedent (by several incarnations) of Chase Manhattan and what today is JPMorgan Chase.

On November 13, 1799, the *Mercantile Advertiser* printed a public notice announcing duplicitously that the legislature had incorporated the Manhattan Company "for the purpose, among others, of supplying pure and wholesome water." The company spared no words when it came to self-promotion. "The directors, impressed with the importance of this trust, determined to lose no time and to spare no expense in carrying into full effect the benevolent design of their incorporation," the newspaper announcement continued.

But by the late eighteenth century, many downtown wells were already adulterated by uncollected offal, the excrement of horses and free-ranging pigs, and other unregulated industrial pollutants that had seeped downtown from the Collect Pond. Like many early New York names, Collect was a corruption of the Dutch *kolck*, which meant a small lagoon. By the late eighteenth century, the Collect had become so contaminated by animal carcasses and runoff from tanneries and other chemicals that its other name, the Fresh Water Pond, had long ago been rendered an anachronism. Its western outlet to the Hudson River was south of the village of Greenwich, bordering the marshy Lispenard's Meadows, where the Manhattan Company, rejecting less polluted but more distant sites, had sunk its new well on a blip called the Sand Hills.

New York City has always had two water priorities: a distribution system vital to firefighting, and a pure and ample supply for human consumption. In 1796, responding to a public request for proposals, Joseph Browne, a medical doctor and engineer, ambitiously urged the Common Council to create a private company that would deliver water to Lower Manhattan from the Bronx River. The council embraced the end, but not the means. Early in 1799, the request was referred to a committee composed of the thirteen state assemblymen representing the city. The panel was chaired by Joseph Browne's brother-in-law, Aaron Burr. Assemblyman Burr first enlisted Hamilton and the city's leading merchants to persuade the Common Council to admit the possibility of private ownership, since it would spare the taxpayers and accelerate a solution to a crisis that had been worsening since a yellow fever outbreak the year before. Then he maneuvered the legislature into rejecting the city's request to finance a publicly owned water supply. In twenty-four hours and without a hearing, he engineered the assembly's approval of a bill that could not have been described more salubriously: "An act for supplying the city of New-York with pure and wholesome water."

Going well beyond the public-private partnership that Hamilton had envisioned, the legislated charter empowered the new entity "to employ all such surplus capital as may belong or accrue to the said company in the purchase of public or other stock, or in any monied transactions or operations not inconsistent with the constitution and laws of this state or of the United States, for the sole benefit of the said company." Hamilton saw through the subterfuge, but too late. Explaining his opposition to Burr's presidential candidacy in 1800, Hamilton would write James A. Bayard, a Federalist congressman from Delaware: "He has lately by a trick established a *Bank*, a perfect monster in its principle; but a very convenient instrument of *profit &* *influence.*"

To produce a surplus, the company had to spend less money on what was supposedly its principal mission. A panel of three Manhattan Company directors immediately concluded that the Bronx River proposal was, after all, impractical because of insufficient gravity to drive the flow downtown and the likelihood that open canals would freeze in winter. Shortly after its authorizing legislation was approved early in 1799, the directors advertised for suggestions on what any sanitarian would have considered a virtual impossibility: where in Lower Manhattan to sink a well that would yield the city's households and commercial establishments some three hundred thousand gallons a day of potable water from the Collect Pond.

"Reservoir of Manhattan Water Works in Chambers Street, 1825," from Valentine's Manual of Old New York, *edited by Henry Collins Brown (New York: Valentine's Manual, 1923), 199.*

Among those who responded were none other than Dr. Joseph Browne. Reversing himself, Browne now argued that "it is not impossible that the water taken from the vicinity of the Collect, after it has been renewed by a constant pumping, for a few months, might be thought sufficiently pure for culinary purposes." Browne was hired by the Manhattan Company as water superintendent and elected to the board of directors. The first bid received in response to the company's advertisement came from Elias Ring, the Greenwich Street boardinghouse owner and dry goods merchant, who had shown no previous passion for hydrology other than having once patented a waterwheel. Elias Ring's bid was rejected, but before the end of the year, he would be indelibly linked to the Manhattan Company's well for another reason altogether.

Ring's dry goods store shared the ground floor of 208 Greenwich Street with a booming millinery shop run by his wife, Catherine, the daughter of David Sands, a prominent minister from Cornwall in the Hudson Valley's Orange County. (Sands Point, Long Island, was named for the same Sands family; George Washington would have slept in the Sands home in Cornwall on his way to his Newburgh headquarters, had he not left early after his officers suspected a kidnap plot.) Above the shops on Greenwich Street was the boardinghouse where Catherine's cousin Elma lived. The Rings were practicing Quakers; Elma was not.

Elma Sands had been missing for ten days when, on January 2, 1800, her body was discovered at the bottom of the Manhattan Company's well, half a mile from the Rings's boardinghouse. She was bruised; her dress was torn. But the evidence was inconclusive: Had she jumped, fallen, or been pushed? While the January 4, 1800, *New York Daily Advertiser* was still crammed with dispatches about the nation's official and informal displays of mourning for George Washington, the editors found space to report on the "somewhat singular" circumstances of what was still being described as a missing persons case involving a young woman who left with her lover "with an intention of going to be married" and had not been seen since.

On January 6, a grand jury concluded that Sands had been deliberately killed. She was laid out in the parlor of the boardinghouse at 208 Greenwich, a common Quaker ritual, above the millinery shop where she had worked. Very little else was reported about Elma except that she might have been the daughter of an unwed mother, Mary Sands, whose father was from Charleston, South Carolina. To accommodate the crowds that came to pay their respects, Elma's coffin was carried from the house and displayed outside.

Four days after the grand jury decided on a cause of death, Elma's lover and rumored fiancé Levi Weeks, a twenty-three-year-old carpenter (described as a laborer in the indictment) of previously unblemished morals, was charged with her murder. He was apparently released on bail, as the record shows that he was rearrested on the eve of his March 31, 1800, court appearance. The charge set off what would become the nation's first media circus over a murder case, as well as its first transcribed murder trial. By then, though, Levi Weeks had already been convicted in the court of public opinion.

"Elma's body and the well in which it had been found served as twin omens for the rapidly expanding city," Angele Serratore wrote in the *Paris Review* in 2014. "If beauty like hers—vibrant, hopeful, alive—could be mangled by the brute ugliness of murder, what beauty was safe?" New Yorkers must have been relieved when Weeks was arrested. If he were found guilty, they wouldn't have to imagine that Elma Sands was murdered indiscriminately, the random victim of highwaymen on a frigid winter night, beneath a waning moon too slim to illuminate the snow-covered Lispenard's Meadows for any eyewitnesses.

Elma and the Rings shared the boardinghouse with Hope Sands, Catherine Ring's sister; two unrelated boarders, Margaret Clark and Richard Croucher; a recent immigrant from England who sold fabric; William Anderson, Levi Weeks's bedmate and apprentice; and Weeks himself, who had moved in the previous July. "He is a young man of reputable connections," prosecutor Cadwallader Colden, the grandson of a former lieutenant governor, would say in court, "and for ought we know, till he was charged with this crime of irreproachable character, nay of amiable and engaging manners, insomuch that he had gained the affections of those who are now to appear against him as witnesses on this trial for his life."

The affections of Weeks's fellow boarders, however deeply they might have developed over six months or so, were obviously fleeting. Virtually no one rushed to his defense besides his brother, Ezra. Four years older than Levi and married with children, Ezra had moved from western Massachusetts to New York, where Levi joined him in 1798. In a city still rebuilding after the Great Fire and the ruthless British occupation, Ezra was a prominent, prosperous architect erecting handsome public works and constructing country homes for the wealthy. If Levi, as an accused murderer, was universally considered to have had an "irreproachable character" only a few months before, then Ezra was indefectible. His motto, adopted from the early eighteenth-century English essayist Joseph Addison, defined his persona: "A well-bred man will not offend me, and no other can."

Ezra and Levi had been working together to build the Grange, Alexander Hamilton's Harlem Heights manse, designed and built by John McComb to rival Aaron

Burr's Richmond Hill near Charlton and Franklin Streets in the village of Green-wich. They would also help build a mansion for Archibald Gracie overlooking the East River, which in 1942 would become the official residence of New York City's mayors. McComb, who would also win the commission to design the new city hall, would join Ezra as the most reputable witnesses for Levi, who had few other friends in court and a contestable alibi. He had something else going for him, though, thanks to Ezra Weeks: the first publicity-savvy dream team of lawyers—Aaron Burr and Alexander Hamilton—to mount his defense.

The legal duo were fierce political rivals but, as virtuoso litigators, thoroughly respected each other's courtroom skills. They shared another common denomi-nator: as clients of Ezra Weeks (Hamilton for the Grange, Burr for three-miles of hollowed-out pine logs to pipe the water from the Manhattan Company's wells), both owed him substantial amounts of money. (Neither submitted a bill for defending Levi.) Moreover, given their penchant for one-upmanship, Bill James wrote in *Popular Crime: Reflections on the Celebration of Violence* (2011), "once one of them accepted, the other could not refuse." Enlisting both Burr and Hamilton not only guaranteed Levi Weeks a superlative defense at a time when even murder cases were often tried without a lawyer, but also provided bipartisan spin control when most publications were unabashedly political party organs. "Newspapers which days earlier had flatly stated that Weeks was guilty," James wrote, "now began to emphasize the need to reserve judgment." The third member of Weeks's defense dream team was Brockholst Livingston, John Jay's brother-in-law, who had been his private secretary when Jay was ambassador to Spain.

The Court of Oyer and Terminer (from the Anglo-French *oyer et terminer*, "to hear and to determine") convened at ten A.M. on March 31, 1800, in the building on Wall Street where Washington had been inaugurated and which had reverted to city hall when the federal government vamoosed. Presiding over the jury trial was John Lansing, a former legislator and congressman, and now the chancellor, or ranking judicial officer in the state. Also forming the special court panel were New York mayor Richard Varick, the city recorder, and an alderman. Breathtakingly speedy trials were the norm in those days. They proceeded without pause, typically with barely a bathroom break, until a verdict was rendered. After acknowledging that Levi Weeks defied the profile of a common murderer, Cadwallader Colden wasted no time homing in on the heart of his case.

"The deceased was a young girl, who till her acquaintance with the prisoner, was virtuous and modest," Colden said, "of a cheerful disposition, and lively manners, though of a delicate constitution. We expect to prove to you that the prisoner won her affections, and that her virtue fell a sacrifice to his assiduity that after a long period of criminal intercourse between them, he deluded her from the house of her protector under a pretense of marrying her, and carried her away to a well in the suburbs of this city, and there murdered her."

"Most barbarously murdered," Colden added for good measure.

The prosecution's case was simple but largely circumstantial. The previous September, when Catherine Ring fled the city during a fierce yellow fever outbreak, Levi Weeks and Elma Sands "lived together in the most intimate manner." That December, Elma cheerfully confided to Hope Sands, Catherine's sister, that she and Levi would elope on the following Sunday, and that for unstated reasons, he wanted to keep their marriage a secret. On Saturday, December 21, Hope blurted out the wedding plans to Catherine Ring, who confronted Elma the next evening. She admitted as much, and said that Levi, who had left the boarding-house around five P.M. that afternoon, was coming to fetch her at eight. He apparently arrived with his brother, Ezra. As Levi opened the sitting room door to leave, Catherine heard someone walk downstairs and whisper near the front door, which was opened and immediately shut. "If you believe that the prisoner, at this time, went out of the house with the deceased, I do not see how he can be acquitted," Colden declared. "From this time the deceased was never after seen till her corpse was found in the Manhattan well."

Elma suffered from stomach cramps (presumably the "delicate constitution" that Colden referred to). She had been prescribed small doses of laudanum, a painkiller typically sold without prescription. Levi, planting a seed that Elma was suicidal, testi-fied that she once threatened to swallow a whole vial of the opium derivative. The defense also sought to portray Levi as no more affectionate toward Elma than he was to any of the other female boarders and to divert suspicion to Elias Ring and to another boarder, Richard Croucher, who had been vigorously inflaming public passions against Levi since his arrest—but also had his own alibi for his whereabouts on the night that Elma vanished.

The prosecution produced a witness who placed Elma Sands walking toward the well with two men. Another witness recalled seeing a one-horse sleigh—like the one owned by Ezra Weeks—on Broadway carrying two men and a woman heading toward the Meadows. (Ezra's apprentice, however, swore the sleigh never left his lumberyard that night.) Witness accounts of the evening were riveting but also prob-lematic, given the anemic moonlight and the distance between their vantage points.

"From behind the hill at Lispenard's," Catherine Lyon recalled hearing a woman cry "Murder, Oh! Save me," adding inconclusively: "I did not see Elma's face, but I saw her form and shape." From a hundred yards away, Lawrence van Norden claimed to have heard a woman scream, "Lord have mercy on me, Lord help me." Foreshadowing the twentieth-century New York murder of Kitty Genovese, during which some Queens neighbors overlooked the victim's pleas for help, van Norden added: "In a little time the cries stopped, and I went to bed again." Still another witness said a man who identified himself as a carpenter was seen a week earlier sounding out the depth of the water in the well (about six feet at the time), but the prosecution abandoned that line of questioning when the man's clothes didn't match Levi's.

By one thirty A.M., some jurors were nodding off. When testimony finally ended an hour later, some seventy-five witnesses had appeared. Even with all that testimony, the trial transcript leaves a number of questions unanswered—and unasked. Levi said he would never have married without his brother's approval. Did a last-minute refusal by Ezra trigger the murder or, perhaps, Elma's suicide? If Elma was in a sleigh with two men heading toward the well, who were they? If one was Levi, was the other Ezra? Where were they going?

After hearing all the testimony, or perhaps earlier (and undeniably before the jury retired), Judge Lansing seemed convinced of the verdict. The jury was superfluous. Exhausted, Colden sought an adjournment until the next morning. But when both sides agreed to waive closing arguments, the judge jumped at the opening. He charged the jury with a point-by-point rebuttal of the prosecution's case that doubled as a brief for the defense. When Hamilton said he would "rest the case on the recital of the facts," Catherine Ring supposedly thrust her fist in his direction and shouted prophetically: "If thee dies a natural death, I shall think there is no justice in heaven."

Judge Lansing handed the jury a two-headed coin. He expressed doubt that Elma had left the Rings' boardinghouse with Levi the night of December 22, 1799, and that Ezra's one-horse sleigh left his lumberyard. He also suggested that Levi lacked a motive for the murder and that, "excepting a few minutes" between visits to Ezra's house that night, Levi could account for his whereabouts. Moreover, Lansing concluded, without any forensic confirmation from an autopsy of Elma, it was "very doubtful whether she had been exposed to any other violence than that occasioned by the drowning." (She apparently was not pregnant.) Without equivocation, he pronounced his own belief in Levi's innocence: "The court is unanimously of the opinion that the proof is insufficient to warrant a verdict against him." The jurors had barely left the courtroom when they returned, less than five minutes later: Not guilty!

"The popular version of the result of the trial was that Weeks was acquitted by the jury," Edward S. Gould wrote in *Harper's New Monthly Magazine* years later; "the true version is that he was acquitted by the Court." The *Commercial Advertiser* opined on April 2, 1800, "It must be a pleasing circumstance to this young man, whose character on the trial appeared irreproachable and uncommonly amiable, and to his respectable connections that he does not owe his acquittal to the eloquence of his counsel, but solely and entirely to the clear and unequivocal proof he produced of his innocence."

Yet the jury's hasty verdict hardly reversed the public's conviction that Levi Weeks was guilty and that some people were inevitably more equal than others in the eyes of justice, peeking from behind its blindfold. Ezra Weeks was reportedly so concerned that the testimony was damaging, if not flatly incriminating, that he considered bribing William Coleman, the court clerk, to expurgate the most inculpating passages. In the interests of justice, or having gotten a better offer, Coleman produced the first verbatim murder trial transcript—and of the longest criminal trial to date—for publication. Assuming, then, that Elma Sands's death was not a suicide, someone got away with murder. One subsequent suspect was her fellow boarder Richard Croucher. Two months after the Weeks trial, he was convicted of raping his thirteen-year-old stepdaughter when he took her to visit the scene of Elma's disappearance, the Rings' house on Greenwich Street.

Elias Ring apparently never patented his innovative waterwheel. He went bankrupt, lost the boardinghouse, and moved his family to Alabama, where he died of yellow fever. Meanwhile, the Bank of the Manhattan Company thrived. According even to its own authorized history, however, "while the water was said to be 'wholesome,' its quality did not give entire satisfaction." Thanks to Burr, the company had been granted a perpetual monopoly, but in 1830 the alderman Samuel Stevens ingeniously challenged its charter by claiming that the poor quality of the water was driving New Yorkers to drink alcoholic beverages instead.

Spurred by more epidemics and two more major fires in 1828 and 1835, the city fathers finally ended their dawdling. In 1836, the year that Burr died, New Yorkers voted overwhelmingly for a municipal water system. By 1837 they envisioned an ambitious five-year project, overseen by chief engineer John B. Jervis, that would deliver water from the dammed Croton River, more than forty miles north of the city in suburban Westchester County. From there, it would flow by gravity across the Harlem

"The home of Juliana Elmore Sands, Southwest corner of Greenwich and Franklin Streets," from As You Pass By *by Kenneth Holcomb Dunshee (New York: Hastings House, 1952), 206.*

River and downtown to a receiving reservoir in what is now Central Park, and to a distributing reservoir on the site of what today is the home of the New York Public Library on Fifth Avenue and Forty-Second Street, three miles north of New York City Hall. By 1840 the Manhattan Company was largely defunct as a waterworks, although it kept its pump on Reade Street going for nearly a century, fearing that its corporate charter—and thus its banking business—might be jeopardized if the company's original mission was abandoned altogether. Its revenue that year from sales of water was $1,910. During the same period, its bank reported a profit of $7,082,530.

After the trial, Burr and Hamilton resumed the rivalry that would culminate in their fatal duel four years later. Before then, though, Burr mustered the political clout of the Manhattan Company and Tammany Hall (the party machine that had been founded in 1786 as the fraternal Society of Saint Tammany, or the Columbian Order) to defeat Hamilton's Federalists and send Thomas Jefferson to the White House, with himself as vice president. Burr later survived treason charges, returned to New York, and was briefly married to Eliza Jumel, a wealthy widow on whose land in Upper Manhattan the Croton conduit passed. She divorced him after four months, employing Alexander Hamilton Jr. as her lawyer. William Coleman, the court clerk who employed an innovative form of shorthand to produce his verbatim transcript of the trial, was hired on Hamilton's recommendation by Governor Jay as clerk of the circuit court and later became the first editor of Hamilton's *New York Evening Post*. On December 12, 1829, eight months short of a century before Judge Joseph Force Crater famously stepped from a Times Square restaurant into the annals of missing persons mysteries, Judge Lansing left Ezra Weeks's City Hotel on Broadway to mail a letter on the Albany boat leaving from the Cortlandt Street pier. Lansing was never seen again.

Since Levi Weeks was acquitted and no one else had been formally accused, the Manhattan Well murder remained a cold case, resuscitated episodically by reports of spectral visions of Elma Sands haunting the vanished meadow in perpetual pursuit of her departed lover. The spellbinding saga lingered for decades, sustained by a body of literature that was inspired by William Coleman's verbatim courtroom narrative, complete with stage directions, which provided a template for novelistic storytelling.

While the murder persisted in the public mind, uncertainty surrounded the precise location of the notorious well itself. The brick-lined cylinder that was excavated in Lispenard's Meadows in 1799 had been buried when the marsh was dewatered and built over as the first full-scale influx of immigrants and the profusion of commerce pushed the city's population and peopled boundaries uptown. In 1806 Brannon Street, the route that ran east toward Lispenard's Meadows from Hudson Street, was renamed Spring Street, a reference to the surface and subterranean streams that fed the Collect Pond and supplied the Manhattan Well. Within decades, a matrix of other streets had been superimposed. The sparsely populated neighborhood that would much later be branded as SoHo was bordered by a nearly unbroken facade of residential and commercial buildings.

No. 129 Spring Street, near Greene Street, was variously occupied by a pawnbroker and the mail-order headquarters for O. Spotswood, which promised in *Scientific American* to prevent a craving for tobacco to anyone who replied with thirty-four one-cent stamps. Right after the Civil War, No. 129 also hosted weekly meetings of the Federal Council of Internationals, a Marxist group.

At about the same time, in 1869, the notorious well was rediscovered serendipitously during excavations for a flower garden at No. 129. "The old well was known to exist," the *Times* reported, "but its precise location had passed from the memory of the 'oldest inhabitant.'" The article, headlined nebulously only as OLD NEW-YORK, was similarly vague in describing the discovery: "It is of large diameter, and was covered over with large flat stones." By the 2010s, the exposed brick lining of the well, once buried beneath Lispenard's Meadows, stood incongruously amid trendy clothes and accessories in the basement of a branch of the COS clothing store chain, a mute and unmarked witness to a trial of the century. Visiting the site that had been discovered in 1869 and then forgotten again, Meyer Berger of the *Times* wrote in 1957, "Winds stir sooty papers in it and high walls hem it in. In twilight, it has a sinister, brooding air." Berger added: "The cab driver who had brought the reporter to that lonely spot wondered what it was that brought him to the alley. The reporter said, 'Just checking on a murder; a girl was killed here.' The cabby said, 'I think I read about it a coupla days ago.'"

That well is the only physical remnant of the murder of Elma Sands. Ezra Weeks's architectural legacy survives in New York in two charming country homes, Hamilton Grange and Gracie Mansion. But just as Levi was remembered either as an innocent man unjustly accused or a privileged defendant who got away with murder, so, too, Ezra remains an enigma. He had powerful friends, including Burr and Hamilton, who were literally in his debt. Was the judge somehow beholden to him, too? Why did he resort to bribery to keep Coleman from publishing the complete trial transcript, peppered with incriminating circumstantial testimony? Was Ezra the second man in the sleigh seen heading toward the Manhattan Well?

As New York boomed in the first half of the nineteenth century, Ezra Weeks prospered in local politics, society, and business. He became the president of the New York Dry-Dock Company, which, like Burr's Manhattan Company, was also endowed with "banking privileges." He bought the five-story, red-brick City Hotel, New York's grandest, designed by John McComb Jr., which occupied the full blockfront on the west side of Broadway between Thames and Cedar Streets. In 1846 he wrote his sister that "everything I touched seemed to turn to gold until I was just past 50 years of age," when an acquaintance defaulted on $120,000 that Weeks had loaned him, and he suffered catastrophic property losses in the Great Fire of 1835, which destroyed hundreds of buildings on a mid-December night when even the frozen East River was ablaze from turpentine that had seeped from a waterfront warehouse.

"This humbled me to the dust, and with the aid of my heavenly dream, which I think I related to, I was brought to my senses," he wrote. "That dream caused me to see my dependence upon my Saviour, and I rejoiced at my losses and felt grateful that I had enough left to make me comfortable." Quite comfortable, in fact. Three years later, on June 20, 1849, Ezra Weeks died in his house at 12 LeRoy Place, an esplanade on Bleecker Street between Mercer and Greene. It happened to be less than three blocks from the buried Manhattan Well, "the locality of which," the *Times* would later report, "had been forgotten."

Like Judge Lansing, Levi Weeks vanished, too, though more or less of his own volition. Not everyone, it seemed, was as certain of his innocence as the judge, and living in New York became unbearable. After about two years he returned home to Massachusetts, partnered in a general store until 1805, then headed west, and wound up in Natchez in the Mississippi Territory. There, thanks to a wealthy lawyer who was also Aaron Burr's army buddy, Levi became a prominent and prosperous architect. He designed the Briars, where Jefferson Davis was married, and which became a prototype for southern plantation mansions. He died in Mississippi in 1819 at the age of forty-three. The cause was yellow fever, the same disease that—spread by a contaminated water supply—had spurred New York's legislature to grant the Manhattan Company its charter to build its first well, the one in which Elma Sands's body was discovered, exactly two decades before.

7

Christian Harriot

The Original Road Hogs

B y 1800, thanks in part to its five-year spell as the nation's capital, New York's population exceeded Philadelphia's and Boston's combined. Within a decade or two the city was bemoaning another benchmark, though, one that was also defining New York to travelers from elsewhere in the United States and abroad: New York had more pigs than Washington, D.C., the new national capital, had people. To put it another way, as Gwynn Guilford wrote on *Quartz*, the estimated twelve thousand pigs in New York meant there was one for every five people, or slightly higher than the ratio of cars owned today by Manhattanites.

Charles Dickens would particularize the New York porcine as "in every respect a republican pig, going wherever he pleases, and mingling with the best society, on an equal, if not superior footing, for every one makes way when he appears, and the haughtiest give him the wall, if he prefers it." After a full day of scavenging, Dickens wrote, "just as evening is closing in, you will see them roaming toward bed by scores, eating their way to the last," with "perfect self-possession and self-reliance, and immovable composure, being their foremost attributes." Privately owned pigs got more benefit of the doubt than some people, particularly after Dickens toured the horrific slums of the Five Points, where many of the more feral four- and two-legged New Yorkers were concentrated. "Many of those pigs live here," Dickens wrote. "Do they ever wonder why their masters walk upright in lieu of going on all-fours? And why they talk instead of grunting?" Henry David Thoreau, no New York chauvinist to begin with, largely agreed, grunting to Ralph Waldo Emerson, "The pigs in the street are the most respectable part of the population."

Europeans generally associated their former colonies with Native Americans, Ted Steinberg wrote in *Down to Earth: Nature's Role in American History* (2002), "but when they pictured American cities, it was not Indians and buffaloes but pigs that came to mind. No animal loomed larger in their image of U.S. urban areas." Like most of the people living in New York, the pigs were imports—in their case, from Europe. New Yorkers of a certain class abided them the same way they regarded most needy immigrants, with whom they were lumped together metaphorically as the "swinish multitude." Efforts to contain the pig population date as far back as at least 1640, when the Dutch West India Company complained that unrestrained swine were digging up the company's crops indiscriminately. Peter Stuyvesant, as intolerant of pigs as of all other free spirits, threatened to shoot any that tunneled under Fort Amsterdam.

But until downtown became too dense, and the pigs too obtrusive, they were largely indulged as scavengers. They provided sustenance for the impoverished and kept the streets cleaner than they otherwise would have been, and more cheaply. Pigs roamed and rummaged with impunity—and, apparently, legally—in New York in the early 1800s, until Christian Harriot decided to defend their right to do so.

The hogs had grown emboldened as the city became less hospitable. They brazenly dug up gardens, endangered vehicular traffic by grubbing up unpaved streets and uprooting cobblestones with their stubby snouts, threatened and sometimes even killed people when provoked, frightened horses and overturned carriages, grunted disgustingly, and contributed mightily to the pervasive stench. "They were mean, dangerous, and uncontrollable beasts," Professor Hendrik Hartog of the University of Wisconsin Law School wrote in the *Wisconsin Law Review*, "hardly an urban amenity."

The diarists Philip Hone and George Templeton Strong both pronounced the city a "pigsty," just one of the many porcine metaphors, adjectives, or nouns with negative connotations (think *pigheaded, pork barrel, pig in a poke, squealer, pig in shit, high on the hog, porker*, and *sweating like a pig*—the last a dichotomy, since pigs have no sweat glands). Virtually everyone, except observant Muslims and Jews, ate ham, pork, and bacon, although delving into precisely what pigs raised in urban environments ate, much like questioning the making of sausage, was better left unasked. "People ate pigs, and pigs ate the human and animal wastes and garbage which lined the streets of the city," Hartog wrote.

"The Police, under the direction of Inspector Downing, clearing the piggeries of Bernard Riley," from Frank Leslie's Illustrated Newspaper, *August 13, 1859.*

The social division between the pig haves and the pig have-nots was chasmic. The upper class consumed pork to vary their diet. Less fortunate artisans (skilled handicrafters, from blacksmiths to wheelwrights), immigrants, and Black and poor people (a disproportionate number of them women) bred pigs for sustenance and sold them, too. They could raise them virtually without overhead. Breeding required no real estate because the pigs roamed free. They cost nothing to feed because they devoured the detritus of a population devoid of systematic sanitation services. The breeders constituted vocal constituencies, which the Common Council pandered to. (Black people were, in effect, disenfranchised when the state constitution was revised in 1821 to eliminate property qualifications for white men, while Black men who wanted to vote had to prove that they owned $250 worth of property.) The consequences were predictable: the council would pass legislation and then, under pressure, reverse itself; or enact regulations but fail to enforce them.

Piercing a pig's nose with a metal ring was supposed to protect the pavement from being uprooted, so the council imposed a fine in 1809 on any errant unringed pig's owner who could be identified. Implicit, though, was the presumption that ringed pigs could wander at will. In 1816 Abijah Hammond, a director of Alexander Hamilton's Bank of New York, mobilized two hundred fellow merchants and property owners to demand the council ban itinerant swine altogether. As Catherine McNeur wrote in *Taming Manhattan: Environmental Battles in the Antebellum City* (2014), the council actually went so far as to contemplate a pig prohibition but stopped short twice.

That fall, without notice, the council proposed and passed a law on the same day, to take effect January 1, 1818, that in effect imposed a bounty on stray pigs. This time the pig prohibition left enforcement to the private sector. Anyone whose stray pig was captured and delivered to the public pound would have to pay a whopping ten dollars to whoever had turned it in, plus twelve cents a day for its upkeep at the public trough. Undaunted, Adam Marshal, a Black chimney sweep and pig proponent, submitted a written appeal—strategically signed only by white petitioners—that prompted the pliable alderman to repeal the ban.

In June 1818, when two men whose carriage was overturned by hogs demanded that the council reconsider some form of antipig bill, the lawmakers punted. They drafted still another bill, delayed it, then buried it. City officials had to find some other means to stanch the pig plague, which they did with the unwitting help of Christian Harriot. Their strategy insulated the process from pure politics. It was undemocratic. But it would provide the legal basis for New York to displace pigs from the city limits over the next few decades. Stemming the swine scourge would also result in profound urban policy implications that Cadwallader Colden, the man who prosecuted Levi Weeks, could never have imagined in his vision of a pigless city.

Virtually all of the city's legal arrows in the nineteenth-century war on pigs were drawn from the quiver that Mayor Colden gathered in 1819 against Christian Harriot. Colden had been appointed—not elected, and therefore insulated from the electorate—by Governor DeWitt Clinton, like him an early proponent of the Erie Canal. Unlike the majority of aldermen, Colden was a Federalist, not an agrarian Jeffersonian Democratic-Republican, and while he favored ending slavery in the state, his overall views on liberation uncharitably did not extend to the pigs that many Black New Yorkers bred to feed their families. Shortly after he was named as mayor and judge of the sessions court in 1818, Colden empaneled a grand jury to investigate the pig proliferation. Even then, as a former district attorney who had argued the murder case against Levi Weeks, he knew full what New York's chief judge, Sol Wachtler, would publicly and poignantly acknowledge well into the next century: a prosecutor has so much sway over grand jurors, he could get them to indict a ham sandwich.

Taking no chances in his test case, Colden got the grand jury to lodge charges against *two* ham sandwiches—two butchers, actually. Both were accused of the common-law misdemeanor of "keeping and permitting to run hogs at large in the city of New York." The first defendant, Louis Lashine, went to trial in December 1818. Once it was firmly established that he indeed housed about forty hogs on Duane Street, he offered no defense and was fined. The second defendant was Christian Harriot, who at the time operated out of his home on Mulberry Street, near the city's northern boundary. Harriot figures so infrequently in most histories of New York that few chroniclers even agree on how he spelled his name, which also appears as Herriot, Herriott, and Harriott.

Harriot was born in 1780 in New York, the son of Israel Harriott, who hailed from a large clan of New Jersey progenitors, apparently descended from Scottish immigrants who arrived in the late seventeenth century. Christian's father, who fought in the Continental Army at the battles of Long Island and Yorktown and was the first independently elected constable of Scarsdale after the American Revolution, was a shipwright by profession. His mother, Charity Haviland, came from Purchase in Westchester County. In 1806 Christian wed Martha Howard in the Dutch Reformed Church. Their marriage didn't last. Only six months later, he placed an advertisement in the *New York Gazette* declaring that "Martha Harriot having absconded without provocation, I forbid any person trusting her on my account, as I will not pay any debts of her contracting after this date."

A little more than three years later, in February 1810, Christian couldn't pay his own debts either. The *Mercantile Advertiser* published a notice on February 12, 1810 from Pierre C. Van Wyck, the city recorder, advising Harriot's creditors that as "an insolvent debtor," his assets would soon be distributed. He was rescued from further insolvency, perhaps, by the War of 1812, during which he served as a corporal in the Third Artillery Regiment.

The war ended early in 1815. That same year, Harriot married Eliza Coddington in the Duane Street Methodist Church. They had a daughter, Sarah, and Christian adopted two sons from Eliza's first marriage. Although the New Jersey Harriots were engaged in various vocations, their New York flesh and blood seemed mostly into butchering. Christian returned to that trade, often advertising mutton and beef for sale from his stall at Washington Market. What lured the authorities to the piggery he maintained at his home were the hogs that foraged freely nearby on Mulberry, Spring, and Broome Streets and that he both owned and boarded for others. When the grand jury empaneled by Mayor Colden formally accused Harriot of maintaining a public nuisance, he insisted on challenging the charge.

Harriot's trial began on January 5, 1819, presumably in the new city hall. Mayor Colden presided. The same Pierre C. Van Wyck who had advertised Harriot as a debtor in 1810, now the New York County district attorney, prosecuted. Harriot hired two lawyers, John Rodman and Hugh Maxwell, to defend him. Thanks to the precedent set in the Levi Weeks murder case less than two decades earlier, the court maintained a transcript of the trial—not in case the facts were disputed or for a future appeal, but because the fundamental question of what constituted a public nuisance was at stake.

The first witness for the prosecution was a man identified only as Ames, a neighbor of Harriot's. He could just as well have testified for the defense. Ames affirmed that, yes, he had "seen hogs in the street about his house, a great many of them," and that "he kills hogs sometimes," and they did wander about.

"Do you think they have produced any inconvenience to the neighborhood?" Maxwell asked.

"No," Ames replied, "I don't know that they did."

"Do you keep hogs?"

"I dare not say," Ames replied. "I am afraid they will convict me if I confess in open court."

When District Attorney Van Wyck said he intended to prove that hogs running loose were a nuisance, prima facie, Maxwell interjected: "I trust that the prosecution will be held to prove that it was the defendant's hogs identically that did the mischief." Van Wyck called witnesses who recalled boys riding pigs roughshod, a sow biting a little girl, and other violent incidents, but none of them involved Harriot's hogs specifically.

The defense called no witnesses, relying instead on the strength of its summation. Harriot's lawyers argued that banning the pigs would remove "an essential source on the score of provisions" for the poor and less opulent, defending the hogs as "the best of scavengers." The lawyers acknowledged that, yes, while Harriot kept swine in the city, the prosecution had offered no proof that his hogs ran loose or created a nuisance. If the charges were upheld, Harriot's lawyers pleaded, "the dandies, who are too delicate to endure the sight, or even the idea of so odious a creature, might exult; but many poor families might experience far different sensations, and be driven to the Alms House." Moreover, the Common Council had passed and then repealed a law banning swine in the streets: "How then can the present defendant be charged with a breach of the laws?" The sessions court was empowered to enforce statutory misdemeanors defined by the council and the legislature—neither of which had banned free-roaming pigs.

Van Wyck began his closing argument on several conciliatory notes. He insisted that the prosecution was not vindictively targeting Harriot, but was merely making him an example to right a wrong; that while the practice he was accused of had been tolerated from time immemorial, it was long overdue for correction; and that even if the municipal corporation had expressly authorized swine to run at large in the street, city officials could not legally have done so because they would be violating and superseding common law. The prosecution could have called numerous witnesses, Van Wyck explained patiently, but the few who testified had demonstrated that Harriot "kept some hogs," which was prima facie proof in the matter of "whether it was lawful to keep hogs at large in the city or not."

Mayor Colden, summing up in his charge to the jury, took great pains to define a nuisance in practical and legal terms: "A nuisance is an offence against the public order and economical regimen of the state, and as annoyance to the public, such as produces disturbance in the reasonable enjoyment of life, property, or common comforts of life." He acknowledged that "what would be a nuisance in one place, might not in another—keeping hogs, for instance, in Broadway, might not be so at the eight mile stone," he said, referring to the more bucolic Village of Harlem. And, speaking of decency, he added, "is it so in this great and proud city, that our wives and daughters cannot walk abroad through the streets of the city without encountering the most disgusting spectacles of those animals indulging the propensities of nature."

Moreover, the mayor agreed with Van Wyck that the aldermen, in whatever they passed or repealed as it affected Harriot, had overstepped the boundaries of common law and state jurisdiction. "The corporation seems to have given him a license," the mayor said, "and that exonerates him from any immoral intent." He dismissed the last two arguments curtly: "It is said that if we restrain swine from running in the street, we shall injure the poor. Why, gentlemen! Must we feed the poor at the expense of human flesh?" And then, proposing an alternative solution that for one reason or another had eluded the mayor's predecessors, he concluded: "It is further said that they are a useful sort of scavengers; but I think our corporation will not employ brutal agency for that object when men can be got to do it." The jury found Harriot guilty. He was fined one dollar.

Mayor Colden's prosecutorial end run around the Common Council and the verdict in *People v. Harriot* didn't magically make pigs fly or flee. But, as Professor

Hartog emphatically concluded, "The point was to establish a principle that there was no legal right to keep swine in the streets of the city or, alternatively, that doing so constituted a public nuisance which left the perpetrator subject to criminal prosecution." Given that the decision was not appealed and that apparently the issue was never reargued, "it may well be that the case succeeded in establishing that principle," Hendrik Hartog wrote. "A distinctively bourgeois vision of a pig-free city had thus become a legal reality in New York City."

The legal decision—what amounted, in some wards, to a matter of minority rule—would not be definitive immediately. Its implementation would be impeded by financial constraints, prosecutorial prerogative, and bureaucratic entropy—and by hog riots organized by a brief collaboration between pig-owning immigrant Irish and African American women in the mid-1820s, 1830, and 1832, triggered by Common Council–mandated roundups that gave a whole new dimension to the correlation between reaping and sowing. Higher courts would also get in the way. They ruled in 1831 that confiscating stray pigs and donating them to the almshouse—a more permanent solution than allowing them to be reclaimed—amounted to an unconstitutional taking of property. In 1848, when a man sued the city after his son was killed by a pig running wild on Chatham Street, the superior court conceded that the fatality was unfortunate but inevitable and one, Chancellor Sanford (who had ruled in the Anneke Jans case) conceded, "which no legislation can prevent and which no system of laws can adequately redress."

What finally spurred a solution was the same impetus that had delivered pure water to the city decades earlier: a cholera epidemic, in 1849. Pigs were fingered as consumers and producers of filth; thousands were rounded up and either slaughtered or relocated to piggeries in northern precincts, which ended the problem, as a practical matter, for property owners and pedestrians downtown. Immigrants were singled out as biped brethren of the swinish multitude. When the site for Central Park was being acquired, the *Times* described the hundreds of acres as overrun by "shanties in which the pigs and the Patricks lie down together while little ones of Celtic and swinish origin lie miscellaneously, with billy-goats here and there interspersed."

But Hartog and other historians make the case that Christian Harriot's challenge to the grand jury's charge had seismic repercussions for New York that went well beyond questions of legality, safeguarding the public, gluttony, or gridlock. People won and pigs lost, albeit by fiat rather than majority rule, because even New York's still largely agrarian society was evolving into a publicly financed bureaucracy with communal responsibilities like street cleaning. Putting pedestrians first and evicting piggeries from vacant, undeveloped property redefined who and what was entitled to public space. The poor and vulnerable near poor, no longer able to keep pigs as a cushion against the vicissitudes of a market economy, would now have to depend on institutionalized public and private welfare.

The not-even-in-your-backyard bans on pigs in the nineteenth century would reverberate in the twentieth in exclusionary strategies like minimum one-acre residential zoning in the suburbs, widening class cleavages. "The modern—that is to say, 19th century—city springs from the text of Mayor Colden's charge to the jury in *People v. Harriot*," Hartog concluded. "The creation of a modern bureaucracy, the transformation of relatively self-sufficient artisans and mechanics into a working class, and the growth of a commercial rural agriculture dedicated to feeding urban residents are all commonly viewed as central features of modernity."

The war against the pigs eventually drove out pig owners, too. "They suddenly had to make ends meet or move to New Jersey," Catherine McNeur wrote in *Taming Manhattan*, which is precisely what they did. In 1859 city inspector Daniel Delavan banned piggeries south of Eighty-Sixth Street altogether, driving the biggest offender, local fire company foreman James McCormick, to dismantle his pens and move (where else?) to New Jersey. Plenty of pigless people remained in New York or migrated to the city, however, creating an urban working class that without crops, farm animals, wells, or wood for fuel, was no longer self-sufficient. After the verdict, Christian Harriot would sell the lease for Stall 21 to his daughter and open a grocery on Broome Street, finally leaving to join relatives in New Jersey, too. He died there in 1839. He was fifty-nine.

In 1962, after 150 years at the same location, the Washington Market was demolished. Its mostly family-owned businesses were relocated to the Bronx, victims of the density that had proven fatal to the pigs and the soaring value of real estate, which drove out a last vestige of agrarian society, only to replace it with multimillion-dollar apartments—some of whose occupants have lobbied the city council, so far unsuccessfully, to let them keep pigs as pets.

8

Jacob Hays

The Constant Constable

When Jacob Hays was named the city's high constable, New Yorkers were still unnerved by the unsolved murder of Elma Sands. Highwaymen stalked the unlit streets, petty crimes proliferated, and mini-riots would be triggered at the slightest provocation among gangs, political factions, rival fire companies, bereaved relatives furious at grave-robbing medical students, or drunken saloongoers. While the litany of Hays's official functions was dominated by ceremonial imperatives—serving as sergeant at arms of the board of aldermen and crier at the court of sessions, marching at the mayor's side during parades—he defined his duties more prosaically, as more or less a police chief. Embracing that role, he developed a mythical reputation as a prescient crime fighter, preventing and solving infractions, a reputation he redeemed and embellished time and again as his legend grew.

When the nineteenth century dawned, random murder was still a rarity, which was why Levi Weeks's acquittal struck many New Yorkers as not only shameful but also terrifying. If Weeks was actually innocent, then a murderer was still at large, perhaps prepared to strike again. Still, the murder rate during much of Hays's tenure, according to the urban historian Eric H. Monkkonen, remained under ten per one hundred thousand residents. It was only in the late 1960s that it markedly accelerated, rocketing to a peak of thirty per one hundred thousand in 1990.

"Hays was really a sort of medieval village constable," another scholar, Patrick Bringley, wrote, "except his village kept growing and growing." If nonfatal violent crime and lesser offenses proliferated during Hays's tenure, the pace still lagged the perception, especially with the advent of the penny press, which aggressively delivered its graphic accounts of crime to a broad audience. Statistics tell only part of a story, but in 1810 fewer than 5 percent of the cases dismissed in the Court of General Sessions involved violent assaults. By 1840, some 90 percent did, which presumably meant that only the most heinous attacks reported to the police were being prosecuted and that most were relatively minor or pursued on flimsy evidence. By the mid-1800s, as the city's population mushroomed and the onrush of new immigrants met a nativist backlash, more law prevailed than order. Newly enfranchised voters, gripped by several sensational murders, demanded a full-time, twenty-four-hour professional police force. While Hays was not the city's first high constable, he would be the last. Remarkably, though, with only brief lapses, he would hold office for nearly half a century. The Hayses were Sephardic Jews, their name said to have been derived from the Dutch De Haas, which in turn was a corruption of the Spanish Diaz. The family would spawn the owners of the *New York Times*, including a namesake, Arthur Hays Sulzberger, a twentieth century *Times* publisher.

Jacob's great-grandfather arrived in America from Holland early in the eighteenth century. His grandfather unsuccessfully mined silver in Westchester and became a ritual slaughterer for the Shearith Israel congregation in Manhattan, originally the city's sole synagogue. Jacob's father, David, may have fought under George Washington in the French and Indian War and opened an inn and general store in suburban Bedford in Westchester. "After the British took New York in 1776, David Hays, of Westchester County, drove into town and signed an address of loyalty to the English," Jacob Rader Marcus wrote in *United States Jewry* (1989). "The following year he swore allegiance to the new United States; two years later the English and the Loyalists raided and destroyed his home; his wife and children were compelled to take refuge in the woods." David Hays insinuated himself into local politics and was said to have befriended Aaron Burr during the Revolution.

Born in 1772 to Ester Etting Hays, Jacob was circumcised at Shearith Israel but apparently not bar mitzvahed. He married a Christian woman named Catherine in 1797 after moving to Manhattan from Westchester and was said to have joined a Scotch Presbyterian congregation, but he was never baptized and made a point, at least in his official capacity, of attending the dedication of the rebuilt Shearith Israel

NEW-YORK, SATURDAY, JANUARY 24, 1846.

JACOB HAYS, HIGH CONSTABLE OF NEW YORK.

It is with the most unfeigned pleasure that we present our readers with the above portrait of our venerable and renowned High Constable. We particularly commend the character of the original to the attention of all the police officers of the United States, as a distinguished and honorable example of the benefits which can be conferred upon society by an energetic and inflexibly honest man.

"Jacob Hays, 1846," from Sins of New York as "Exposed" by the *Police Gazette by Edward Van Every (New York: Frederick A. Stokes, 1930), 36.*

Synagogue on Mill Street in 1818. Hays lived with his family on Lispenard Street, about three blocks from the notorious Manhattan Well.

Jewish police officers, much less chiefs, were surely a rarity in the nineteenth century, but while Hays's career did not appear to have suffered from antisemitism, his ethnicity did not go unnoticed. "His features, of the Jewish type, were prominent and striking," Abram Child Dayton wrote in *Last Days of Knickerbocker Life in New York* (1882). "His sharp, deep set black eyes were almost hidden by heavy over-hanging eye-brows, which had the effect of imparting a forbidding, sinister aspect to a face which, if analyzed in detail, would have been pronounced intellectually fine." In *Sunshine and Shadow in New York* (1868), Matthew Hale Smith described Hays similarly: "He was a short, thick-set, stout-built man, looking as if nature intended him for a giant, and altered her mind. He had a round, stolid face, of the hue of mahogany—a genuine Jewish physiognomy."

Hays's career in law enforcement began in 1797, when he was twenty-six. He was named a city marshal by New York mayor Richard Varick, also presumably with the blessing of Burr, then a U.S. senator from New York. The job was unsalaried and largely akin to a process server for the courts, but the marshals and constables received fees for serving legal papers and, better still, collected rewards on items that had been lost or stolen. Hays took full advantage of the job's ancillary jurisdiction, which, according to the mayor's orders, empowered him to monitor the city for "riotous or tumultuous assembly," brothels, gambling dens, and "all idle Strollers, vagabonds, and disorderly persons whom you shall suppose would become chargeable to the city." He was elected a constable—the mixed blessing conferred on two candidates by the voters in each of the city's six wards, and four in the Out Ward, which covered the rest of Manhattan—and also worked as a night watchman, armed with a thirty-three-inch-long club and garbed in the signature hide cap that inspired the unflattering nickname "leatherheads."

In 1802 New York mayor Edward Livingston gave Hays the new title of high constable of New York, reporting to the high court. It was no surprise to relatives, colleagues, and acquaintances when Jacob and Catherine Hays named their second son, born barely two weeks later, Aaron Burr Hays: the boy's ubiquitous namesake had yet again furthered Hays's fortunes, calling in a favor from Mayor Livingston, Burr's political ally and confidante.

From that time on, Hays occupied the post of high constable whenever the Democratic-Republicans, his party, were in power. From 1813 to 1849 he was reappointed annually, and his duties were expanded to include rigorous enforcement of any violations of the Sunday laws restricting nonreligious activities on the Sabbath, assisting in the capture of runaway slaves, and harassing the homeless. By 1820 a justice of the peace could have vagrants confined for up to six months without a trial. As tenements overflowed with struggling immigrants, a dual system of justice was institutionalized. Ill-equipped to cope, police and the courts resorted to a reflexive targeting of the poor. Government and private capital formed an enduring partnership, protecting those who were better off and could afford to pay extra for the service.

Certainly Hays, his hangers-on, and, as he aged, his die-hard loyalists hyperbolized his reputation as a one-man police force, but the claim was not preposterous. In small-town early nineteenth-century New York, Hays needed no badge to strike fear into the clannish criminal underworld. "Wherever he goes his slightest action is watched and criticized," the essayist William Cox wrote in the *Cyclopedia of American Literature* (1881); "and if he happen carelessly to lay his hand upon a gentleman's shoulder and whisper something in his ear, even that man, as if there were contamination in his very touch, is seldom or never seen afterwards in decent society."

At fifty Hays was already famous, the name "Old Hays" (life expectancy being around forty then) used as a cudgel by frustrated parents, teachers, neighbors, and other adults. He evoked fear in the hearts of juvenile rapscallions and hardened miscreants alike. Hays had an uncanny photographic memory. He could recognize the faces of former defendants and suspects instinctively. Strangers he could not readily identify were suspect themselves by their very anonymity. If he were not endowed with supernatural powers to "see things that are hid from mortal ken," Cox asked, "how is it that when a store has been robbed, he, without step or hesitation, can march directly to the house where the goods are concealed, and say, 'there are they'—or, when a gentleman's pocket has been picked, that, from a crowd of unsavory miscreants he can, with unerring judgment, lay his hand upon one and exclaim 'you're wanted!'—or, how is it that he is gifted with that strange principle of ubiquity that makes him, 'here, and there, and everywhere' at the same moment?"

In the beginning, Hays's daytime police force comprised two constables per ward, typically in fixed posts (very fixed, if sleeping on a stoop or in a guard shack qualified), though he soon got them mobilized to patrol. He focused primarily on property crime, for two reasons: the victims were typically members of the political class that perpetuated his appointment and paid his salary; and one of the major perquisites of his job was all or part of the reward when the miscreant was caught or the merchandise recovered

Tipped off by a boardinghouse proprietor on the Bowery, Hays solved the spectacular 1831 robbery of $245,000 (somewhere around $100 million or more in today's dollars) from City Bank and recovered all the loot. When a suspect denied the particularly brutal murder of a ship captain, Hays force him to view the corpse, which was awaiting burial. "Look upon the body; have you ever seen that man before?" Hays demanded of the shaken suspect. "Yes, Mr. Hays," he blurted. "I murdered him." Despite the prevailing two-tiered system of justice, the high constable himself appeared to have enforced the law equitably. He once arrested twenty-four-year-old Cornelius Vanderbilt for ice skating on the Sabbath. Years later, when "Commodore" Vanderbilt was still a mere captain, violating the monopoly that the Livingston family was granted on Hudson River steamboats, Hays confronted him on board ship with a court order. "I didn't want to back down, however, too hurriedly," Vanderbilt recalled, "and I said that if they wanted to arrest me, they should carry me off the boat." Hays did.

Hays patrolled in plain clothes—which in his case constituted its own uniform: black pants, a frock coat, a stovepipe hat, and a white kerchief around his thick neck—and unarmed, except for his gold-tipped staff of office. He would strategically wield the staff during civil disturbances to knock the hats from rioters and then, when they bent down to retrieve their hats, shove them to the ground in a tangled pile and round up the ringleaders. He would also apply the staff liberally to the knuckles and shins of combative scoundrels with a vengeance that today would get him booted for police brutality. "As early as the mid-19th century, American police correctly understood themselves as actually administering justice, punishment as well as arrest," Eric Monkkonen wrote. "Given the arrested felon's likelihood of acquittal, one can see why." Deconstructing a rare daguerreotype of Hays, the police detective and novelist Edward Conlon wrote recently: "Aside from the owlish tufts of hair that stick out from his temples, his most distinctive features are his 'you-don't-fool-me' scowl and his 'don't-even-think-about-running' stare. Once you lock eyes with him, the past falls away: Jacob Hays is watching. He doesn't forget. He doesn't even blink. And nothing is likely to surprise him, no matter the miracles and miseries that attend the passage of the years."

Two sensational crimes committed in Manhattan changed everything, just as the death of Elma Sands had done decades before. In April 1836, twenty-two-year-old Dorcas Doyen of Temple, Maine, alias Helen Jewett, was discovered dead in the brothel where she worked on Thomas Street, struck in the head with a hatchet. One of her customers was charged with the murder. Presented with five days' worth of entirely circumstantial evidence and testimony mostly from other prostitutes, the all-male jury took fifteen minutes to acquit the suspect, touching off a public uproar like the one triggered by the verdict in favor of Levi Weeks.

Then, on July 28, 1841, the body of Mary Rogers, who hailed from Lyme, Connecticut, and worked as a salesclerk in a tobacco shop, was found floating in the Hudson River near Hoboken. The police were unsure of the cause or the perpetrator: it appeared that either she was the victim of gang violence or her corpse was dumped after a botched abortion. Complicating their search for a motive, a few months later, her grief-ridden fiancé killed himself. The Mary Rogers murder inspired Edgar Allan Poe (who transplanted the story to Paris), but even Jacob Hays, the bane of New York's netherworld, never progressed as far as Poe's fictional amateur sleuth,

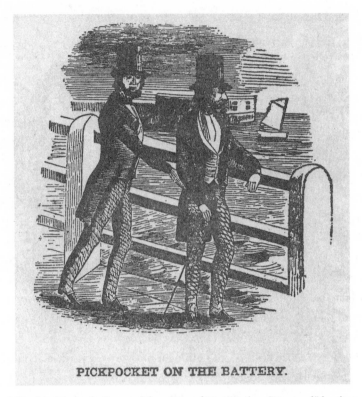

PICKPOCKET ON THE BATTERY.

"Pickpocket on the Battery," from Sins of New York as "Exposed" by the Police Gazette by Edward Van Every *(New York: Frederick A. Stokes, 1930), 8.*

C. Auguste Dupin, in "The Mystery of Marie Rogêt," the sequel to his pioneering detective story "The Murders in the Rue Morgue."

To red-blooded Americans, wanton criminality was a plague brought by poor, uneducated, and unskilled immigrants, especially Irish Catholics, who competed for work that demanded low-skilled labor and paid even lower wages. Mayor Philip Hone seized on the influx, comparing the Irish to locusts and lice and complaining that the city had become infested with gangs who "patrol the streets making night hideous and insulting all who are not strong enough to defend themselves." Those very same immigrants were simultaneously embraced as potential voters by the Democratic machine and harbored as vulnerable souls by Bishop Hughes of the Roman Catholic Diocese. Still, even Davy Crockett, descended from French Huguenots who migrated to America from Ireland, delivered what would prove a somewhat prophetic juxtaposition: "I thought I would rather risk myself in an Indian fight than venture among these creatures after night." (A year later Crockett was killed at the Alamo, though not by Native Americans.)

In 1844, rising crime catalyzed the election of James Harper—who with his siblings founded Harper & Brothers, the U.S. publisher of Charles Dickens's *Bleak House*, as well as of Poe and Washington Irving—as mayor on the newly minted American Republican Party ticket. The party's then-nativist platform, which heralded the upsurge of the anti-immigrant Know-Nothings, included a twenty-one-year wait—a generation, at that time—for citizenship, and repeal of the 1842 law that required nonsectarian public schools and supported a separate parochial school system. Harper privately pursued his personal agenda ("Trust in God, pay your bills, and keep your bowels open" was his motto) while purging foreigners from the municipal workforce. As part of reforming the police force, which was established while Hays was high constable, Harper outfitted them in blue frock uniforms, which they refused to wear, fearing that they would be singled out as targets by hooligans.

Police apparel was always problematic. In 1802, when Old Hays was the definitive face of the city's police force, no one had wanted to deploy a standing corps of uniformed officers—men in blue or any other cast—that would evoke the redcoats, who less than two decades before were subjugating ordinary New Yorkers with rifles and bayonets rather than batons. As late as 1839, envisioning an amorphous forerunner of community policing, Mayor Isaac Varian insisted that the police should be "but a part of the citizens."

Inspired by Sir Robert Peel of London, Mayor Harper introduced his uniformed, salaried, and expanded municipal police force. It proved short-lived: in 1845, Tammany Hall regained control of city hall and, abolishing marshals, inspectors, wardens, and other anachronistic positions, deployed as many as eight hundred full-time paramilitary police in plain clothes.

The *Times* offered another explanation for the officers' reluctance to be identifiable, one that went beyond the republican "prejudice against any distinctive badge of office." Rather, the paper grumped in 1853, "When they are wanted they are not to be found; where they should be seen most often, they are generally invisible." When uniforms finally became obligatory, almost overnight the officers would be distinguished by a new nickname: "copper," inspired by their glistening shields.

"By 1834, New York's constabulary was among the largest and most efficient in the United States," Mike Wallace and Edwin G. Burrows wrote in *Gotham*. The two dozen constables who patrolled by day were supplemented by as many as a thousand leatherheads. These night watchmen were mostly moonlighting, and only empowered to arrest criminals in the act, but their presence was still a deterrent. "Hays proposed innovative patrolling techniques as a watch captain, and went after audacious targets as a constable," Patrick Bringley wrote in his Hunter College master's thesis. "The cumulative effect of his competence was profound."

The creation of a formal police force made Hays more or less redundant, but he remained invulnerable. No mayor wanted to fire him, so, like great generals, he just faded away. When he died in 1850 at the age of seventy-eight, finally retiring the title of high constable after nearly fifty years, he had already outlived his reputation by a decade or two. "Such was the terror of his name in that day," the *Literary World* wrote in his obituary, "by reasons of his mighty prowess as a thief-taker and general detector of delinquency, that if he had died in 1830, his demise would have been regarded as a holiday, and the small boys and lawless 'prentices of the town would have thrown up their caps in a general jubilee."

In his final years, Hays limited himself largely to his ceremonial duties in the courts and on the board of aldermen. When, as the essayist William Cox put it, "the warrant arrives upon which no bail can be put in," Cox invoked Byron:

> *There was a laughing devil in his sneer*
> *that raised emotions both of hate and fear:*
> *And where his glance of "apprehension" fell,*
> *Hope withering fled, and mercy signed, farewell!*

But with the population expanding exponentially, crime was keeping pace. Hays's career would be bookended by the two challenges to policing that would cost many of his successors their jobs: politics and the press. In 1817 the ever-politic Hays had covered his political bases again by naming another newborn son after a potential Federalist patron, the new governor, DeWitt Clinton, whose Erie Canal would open the Port of New York to America's Great Lakes and Midwest. DeWitt Clinton Hays would grow up to become president of Aaron Burr's Bank of the Manhattan Company.

Crime was becoming a political football, in part, because the public's perception—fear, to be more precise—of randomly falling victim to a felon had been exploding in the fifty years since the death of Elma Sands produced the first verbatim transcript of a murder trial. Thanks to publishers like Benjamin Day and James Gordon Bennett, anyone with a penny to spare could now gain instant access to a new journalism. Bennett's son would prove to be an even wackier publisher than his father, but underneath the eccentricities the old man's agenda was deceptively simple: to make his newspaper irresistible to advertisers by promising them the eyeballs of a critical mass of readers lured by the unvarnished, and sometimes unverified, trials, tribulations, and triumphs of their fellow New Yorkers.

Typically Bennett gussied up that formula by quoting Samuel Johnson in the epigraph to his memoir:

Those familiar histories which draw the portraits of living manners, may perhaps be made of greater use than the solemnities of professed morality, and convey the knowledge of vice and virtue with more efficacy than axioms and definitions.

9

James Gordon Bennett

A Penny for His Thoughts

James Gordon Bennett's protocol for proper deportment was an unrepentant parody of personal propriety and of professional etiquette. After a rival editor, whom he had accused of stock manipulations, assaulted him on the street, Bennett cheerfully apologized in print to his readers for what he described as "the want of my usual life today." Then he elaborated on the editor's sneak attack in lurid detail. He described how his assailant "by going up behind me, cut a slash in my head about one and a half inch in length, and through the integuments of the skull. The fellow, no doubt, wanted to let out the never-failing supply of good humor and wit, which has created such a reputation for *The Herald* and appropriate the contents to supply the emptiness of his own thick skull."

Bennett's own skull was as thick as his skin. And, as a former colleague wrote when Bennett died, he "displayed his eccentricities in print, and for a purpose; personally, he was quiet, reticent and irreproachable." He was an outlander from birth, afflicted with strabismus, an ocular focusing disorder that affected his socialization because it meant that no one could ever look him straight in both eyes. He was raised by a Roman Catholic family, the son of a crofter, or prosperous tenant farmer, in Banffshire in the northeast of predominantly Protestant Scotland. At fifteen he enrolled in a seminary but rebelled at the uncompromising doctrine and the centuries of accrued pomp. When he was twenty-four, Bennett and a friend sailed for North America. He taught school in Halifax, Nova Scotia, and Portland, Maine, then worked as a proofreader, bookseller, freelance writer, and editor in Boston, New York, Philadelphia, and Charleston, South Carolina. Later, when critics questioned his credentials and disparaged him as a former peddler, he replied: "From my youth up I have been a peddler, not of tapes and laces, but of thoughts, feelings, lofty principles, and intellectual truths. I am now a wholesale dealer in the same line of business."

By 1826, while employed as an editorial assistant in New York, Bennett was hired as Albany and Washington correspondent for the *New York Enquirer.* He repaired to New York to launch the *Globe,* a journal that quickly failed, then to Philadelphia, where he edited the pro–Andrew Jackson Democratic-Republican Party's house organ until he was accused of placing his own ambition first. "I found out the hollow-heartedness and humbuggery of these political associations and political men," he later recalled in his autobiography, "but yet I was so fascinated with the hairbreadth

"Portrait of James Gordon Bennett Sr.," from The National Cyclopedia of American Biography, *vol. 7 (New York: James T. White & Co., 1897), 241.*

escapes and adventures that I could not disconnect myself from it until the revulsion took place between me and my partners."

Bennett learned his lesson: he would never permanently ally himself or his newspaper with power brokers again. "An editor," he wrote, "must always be with the people—think with them—feel with them—and he need fear nothing, he will always be right—always be strong—always popular—always free." He returned to New York and invited Horace Greeley, the publisher of a literary magazine called the *New-Yorker*, to join him in launching a newspaper. Greeley declined. On his own, investing five hundred dollars, Bennett rented a cellar office at 20 Wall Street, hired a printer at 34 Ann Street, and on May 6, 1835, virtually by himself, published the first edition of the *New York Herald*.

In 1933, the *New York Sun* had introduced two innovations that would radically reshape the news industry: the installation of steam-powered presses, which could print thousands of papers an hour, and the recruitment of an army of newsboys who, howling out the headlines, hawked the papers that they bought wholesale in one-hundred-copy bundles. Benjamin Day's *Sun* originated reality journalism by delivering to its readers news about crime, divorces, suicides, and, for the first time, extraordinary things that happened to ordinary people. Bennett went well beyond. He flaunted a profound irreverence for pretension and pomposity, reporting the occupancy of state prisons one year as 1,492 rogues, but adding irresistibly: "And God only knows how many out of prison, preying upon the community, in the shape of gamblers, blacklegs, speculators, and politicians." He and his son, to whom he bequeathed his newspaper to be published in perpetuity, would revolutionize journalism and mass communication, and help transform New York into America's media capital. The *Herald* pioneered financial news and analysis, stock listings, sports reporting, weather forecasts, extensive correspondence from Washington and abroad (he ran special trains from Long Island's East End to beat his competitors with news from European papers arriving by ship), the verbatim interview, and coverage of arts, society, theater, and local news. The *Herald*, like the *Sun*, cost a penny.

"Its distinction rested upon the fact that it embodied four original ideas in journalism," Allan Nevins wrote in *The Evening Post: A Century of Journalism* (1922). "The first, and most important, was the necessity of a thorough search for all the news. The second was that fixed principles are dangerous, and that it is most profitable to be on the winning side . . . The third was the value of editorial audacity—that is, of impudence, mockery and Mephistophelian persiflage." The fourth "was the value of audacity in the news; of unconventionality, vulgarity, and sensationalism. Above all, Bennett gave New York City the news with a comprehensiveness promptness, and accuracy till then undreamed of."

At the time, most contemporary papers were unabashed mouthpieces for one political party or another. Bennett declared that the *Herald* would be "equally intended for the great masses of the community—the merchant, mechanic, working people—the private family as well as the public hotel—the journeyman and his employer—the clerk and his principal." Also, for the winner of the presidential election, whom he managed to support in nearly every cycle. "Privately, he does not assume to control or mold public opinion," Junius Henri Browne wrote in *The Great Metropolis: A Mirror of New York* (1869), "but to follow it; and he generally manages to be about 24 hours behind it, that he may publicly declare he has anticipated and created it." As a journalist, he presaged in the nineteenth century the success of Fox News in the twentieth, as acutely expressed by the columnist Charles Krauthammer. "The genius of Rupert Murdoch and Roger Ailes," Krauthammer wrote, "was to have discovered a niche market in American broadcasting—half the American people."

Bennett relished rubbing powerful people the wrong way. He impudently dished out derision but could take it, too; he had no compunctions about mocking himself in the pages of his own newspaper. When John Kelly, a Tammany Hall leader, publicly attacked Bennett's character, the publisher cheekily replied: "The proprietor of *The Herald* lost his reputation long before Mr. Kelly was ever heard of." When the robber baron Jay Gould distributed a ten-thousand-word diatribe against Bennett to the entire press corps, the *Herald* published it in full.

The *Herald* surgically replaced priggish and ambiguous euphemisms for human physiology and for articles of clothing. It defied the contemporary convention that a woman's name should occur but twice in print, on the occasion of her marriage and in the announcement of her death. At the turn of the century, the murder of Elma Sands had transformed Levi Weeks into an outcast who finally fled New York. Another murder, one that would defy the bloodhound clairvoyance of Constable Jacob Hays, transformed James Gordon Bennett into a pariah among fellow publishers and patricians, but elevated the *Herald* into the city's largest circulation newspaper.

At three A.M. on April 10, 1836, barely a year after the paper's debut, the body of twenty-two-year-old Helen Jewett was discovered in bed in an upscale brothel on Thomas Street, a few blocks from New York City Hall. Making her rounds, the madam, Rosina Townsend, found smoke billowing from Jewett's room, the back door to the house ajar, and an unseasonably late snowfall flurrying in. A bloodstained hatchet was discovered in the backyard. A search began for Jewett's last customer, a man using the pseudonym Frank Rivers, who worked as a clerk for a dry goods store on Maiden Lane. His real name was Richard P. Robinson. Police found him at home at 42 Dey Street.

MOST ATROCIOUS MURDER, the *Herald* proclaimed on Monday, April 11, going on to report: "Our city was disgraced on Sunday by one of the most foul and premeditated murders that ever fell to our lot to record." Once the city was disgraced, Bennett apparently had no compunctions about amplifying the turpitude by recording it in grisly detail. Personally plunging into the demimonde by venturing to the scene himself, he interviewed Rosina Townsend and produced a florid eyewitness account of finding Jewett's body still on the floor next to the bed: "I could scarcely look at it for a second or two. Slowly I began to discover the lineaments of the corpse as one would the beauties of a statue of marble. It was the most remarkable sight I ever beheld."

Bennett also speculated about motive: that Jewett was jealous of Robinson's dalliances and threatened to expose him. Most rivals accused Bennett of skewing the coverage in Robinson's favor, though, of even accepting bribes to do so and of frequenting the very bordello where the murder occurred. He was unfazed. "I well remember the first and only time I ever entered a house of that kind was in Halifax, Nova Scotia," he revealed, delighting his readers and confounding his critics, "when the girls told me, 'You are too ugly a rascal to come among us.'" (Nor was he shy about publicly proclaiming the impact of his belated marriage, a blissful bond that he had declared earlier he would forever forsake all others to consummate his primary allegiance to journalism. The wedding announcement ran under the headline NEW MOMENT IN CIVILIZATION.)

His coverage of the Jewett case added an entirely new dimension to daily journalism. "Here was an occasion not only to whet readers' morbid curiosity but to lift the curtain on a forbidden aspect of the city's life," Richard Kluger wrote in *The Paper: The Life and Death of the* New York Herald Tribune (1986), "to explore the sociology of sin and report it more graphically and honestly than convention had permitted." Such sociology endowed the premeditated murder, still a rarity in the 1830s under Constable Hays, with a foreboding. Helen Jewett (or Ellen, another pseudonym, as the *Herald* referred to her) was a fallen woman—her "situation" was "ignoble," was how the paper put it—who had come from a good family in Maine but was apparently seduced as a teenager. The *Herald* again distinguished itself from its rivals initially by reminding its readers about the judicial system's presumption of innocence and that Robinson, guilty or not, had been employed full-time and had never before crossed paths with the police. Jewett and Robinson "brought out numerous sexual tensions of antebellum America," Timothy Gilfoyle wrote in *City of Eros: New York City, Prostitution, and the Commercialization of Sex* (1992), and Jewett, especially, embodied "middle class fears of downward mobility." The jury barely had time to leave the courtroom and return before delivering its verdict of not guilty. Meanwhile, the *Herald*'s daily circulation soared as high as 150,000. Two weeks later, the defense witness who had provided Robinson with his alibi for the night of the murder killed himself. Robinson left town and died two years later in Texas. The *Herald* raised its price to two cents. The murder was never solved, leaving the identity of the actual killer in doubt.

Nobody was ambivalent about Bennett, though. He was, a *New York Times* book reviewer wrote in 1942, "the most detested and hated man in America—and the most widely read." He was vindictive and vile, especially when he directed his bile at fellow publishers. His favorite target was his chief competitor, the *Sun* ("a small, decrepit, dying penny paper") and then Greeley's *New York Tribune*, both of which he ravaged with racial vitriol, partially because they favored abolition of slavery while Bennett was extending olive branches to the South and, after the Civil War, even hosting Jefferson Davis at his country home in Washington Heights.

Archbishop John Hughes of the Roman Catholic Archdiocese of New York incurred Bennett's wrath when he suggested that his coreligionists organize politically to lobby for parochial school subsidies from the state. Demanding an American pope instead of one "decrepit, licentious" Italian after another and ridiculing a clergy who had "mystified, brutalized and uncivilized the great truths" of Jesus, Bennett—a Roman Catholic himself—invoked what he described as the nation's deeply imbued division between church and state. "How, then," he asked, "in such a happy, and free, and positive condition of public opinion, could Bishop Hughes expect that if the Church of Rome had a favor to ask of a Protestant country, the best method to acquire it was to trample this holy principle under foot, and organize his church into a political club?" He did not discriminate in his blasphemy; he also belittled Moses, pointing out that "a man who would take forty years to get a party of young women through a desert is only a loafer."

In the run-up to the Civil War, Bennett was so fearful of a popular backlash to his sympathetic coverage of southern sentiments, slaveholders, and of their commercial bedfellows in New York that he stocked the *Herald* building with a supply of rifles. ("If Lincoln is elected," he warned his readers, "you will have to compete with the labor of four million emancipated negroes.") But when war finally broke out, he conspicuously bedecked the building in red-white-and-blue bunting.

After the war, Bennett built a new headquarters for the *Herald*, appropriately enough on the site of Barnum's American Museum downtown (Barnum bilked him on the lease). When ten wealthy New Yorkers formed a syndicate and offered $2 million (about $40 million in today's dollars) to purchase the *Herald*, Bennett refused to be bought. "What shall I do with the money?" he said. "More important yet, what shall I do with myself?" But in 1867, after more than three decades at the helm of the nation's most powerful newspaper, he relinquished control to his only son, James Gordon Bennett Jr., a European-bred yachtsman. Bennett Jr. commissioned a successor *New York Herald* Building, this one designed by Stanford White, on what would become Herald Square in midtown Manhattan. Junior had no children by the wife he married at seventy-three (an asteroid was named after him, though), so for once unpretentiously and without putting on heirs he leased the site of the new *Herald* Building for only three decades. Asked why, he alluded to the inevitable advance of development uptown, and replied: "Thirty years from now the *Herald* will be in Harlem, and I'll be in hell." (The *Herald* did move north, but only to West Fortieth Street, when it was bought by the *Tribune*; Bennett Jr., who died in 1918, left no forwarding address.)

New Yorkers who figured that Bennett Sr. could not be outdone in the idiosyncrasy department had another thing coming. One cause for incredulousness was Junior's obsession with owls. He commissioned White to design a 125-foot-high hollow granite owl-shaped mausoleum atop a seventy-five-foot pedestal on the family estate in Washington Heights. After White was murdered, however, Bennett Jr. settled for twenty-two bronze owls whose green glass eyes, illuminated at night by incandescent bulbs, glowered from the top of the new *Herald* Building, which opened in 1895. A rooftop clock, now at ground level opposite Macy's, was dominated by a statue of Minerva, the Roman goddess of craftsmen and professionals, accompanied by her signature owl and two animated bell ringers named Gog and Magog, figures from the Book of Revelation who portentously heralded the final battle with Satan.

Junior's behavior was so scandalous that merely sputtering his name—"Gordon Bennett!"—became a metaphor for stupefaction. At a New Year's Day party hosted by his fiancée's family in 1877, he put an end to his engagement (and his standing in the city) by urinating in the fireplace. Another Gordon Bennett moment was the paper's November 9, 1874, front-page exclusive: wild animals, the headlines screamed,

"*The 'New' Herald Building,*" *from* The Memorial History of the City of
New-York: From Its First Settlement to the Year 1892, *vol. 4, edited by*
James Grant Wilson (New-York History Co., 1893), 156.

had escaped from the Central Park Zoo. While the paper admitted that its account
was a "wild romance"—an homage to the *Sun*'s 1835 attempt to outdo the fledging
Herald by reporting that civilized life had been discovered on the Moon—it
attempted to reclaim a modicum of credibility by asking, "How is New York prepared
to meet such a catastrophe?" Junior also established the paper's international edition
in Paris, and recruited Henry M. Stanley to search Africa for the explorer and
missionary Dr. David Livingstone in 1871.

As Bennett Sr. prepared to hand the reins to his even zanier successor, the *Times*
delivered to him an unequivocal encomium: "He has built up the great newspaper
which he controls solely by his own genius, courage, and pertinacity. As a newspaper writer, he is perhaps more truly a man of genius than any other who has
risen to distinction in this country. His mind is characterized by originality of
thought and wit in equal proportions; and he has always appreciated the value of

news. These elements—independence, originality, wit, courage, and news—have made the success of the *Herald*; and this success there is now nobody to dispute." One measure of that success was, as the *Times* wrote, his facility as a writer. He had fulfilled a goal that he once described much more eloquently himself: "I have infused life, glowing eloquence, philosophy, taste, sentiment, wit, and humor into the daily newspaper. Shakespeare is the great genius of the drama—Scott of the novel—Milton and Byron of the poem—and I mean to be the genius of the daily newspaper press."

When the dynasty ended with Bennett Jr.'s death in 1918, the *Times* would write, "It is hardly too much to say that the first James Gordon Bennett, one of the most vigorous and cynical of the great figures on the personal stage of American journalism, was the founder of the modern newspaper." (The paper's name would live on. In 1924, the smaller *New York Tribune* acquired the *Herald*, but the *Herald*'s name came first in the new logo under the terms of Bennett Sr.'s will.) Another measure of Bennett Sr.'s success was his net worth. When he died in 1872, he left an estate valued at $5 million. The only person at his bedside, despite the impious diatribes he had hurled at the church, was a priest. The next morning's *Herald* carried news of his death, but no full-fledged biography. The following day, the paper reprinted obituaries by his competitors. For all the complaints about fabrications and fake news that they had leveled against the *Herald*, none got his date of birth right. The pallbearers included his fellow publishers Greeley of the *Tribune* and Charles A. Dana of the *Sun*. Joseph Pulitzer's *New York World* lionized him as "the Columbus, the Luther, the Napoleon, the what you will, of modern journalism."

Henry J. Raymond, who founded the *New York Times* in 1851 with George Jones, another of the pallbearers at Bennett's funeral, never offered to buy the *Herald* itself, but he did put a price once on his rival's journalistic acumen—a competitive gene that would haunt the *Times* until the *Herald Tribune* folded in 1966. "It would be worth my while," Raymond said, "to give a million dollars, if the Devil would come and tell me every evening, as he does Bennett, what the people of New York would like to read about next morning."

10

David F. Launy

The First Broken Windows Theory

Whoever originated the jaded adage "You can't fight city hall" never heard of David F. Launy. He fought city hall. Without a lawyer. And won. What's more remarkable is that he fought a city hall that hadn't even been built yet.

Since the earliest years of the Dutch, New Amsterdamers and New Yorkers have been a litigious lot. They have hauled each other to court for things they did or said or wrote or might have been thinking of doing. They have challenged virtually every regulation, ordinance, law, mandated and discretionary discharge of duty, and nonfeasance by appointed and elected officials and municipal employees. "Not in my backyard" has been the reflexive response to any municipal project, from the 1647 regulation of individual private pigpens and privies on public roads to the wholesale encroachment of the Manhattan street grid in 1811—when Manhattanites still had backyards (as well as afterward, when dense tenements precluded backyards altogether)—to chasmic expressways that uprooted entire neighborhoods.

New Amsterdam's first city hall was housed, fittingly, in the City Tavern downtown at Pearl Street and Coenties Slip. In 1641, it was renovated into the more formal Stadt Huys. In 1699, the British broke ground for a proper city hall, which they boldly placed at the northern boundary of what by then had become New York. This first structure erected specifically as a city hall abutted the rebuilt Dutch stockade on Wall Street and was constructed with some of the foundational stones from the actual wall. It was sited on a plot that included a historic garden generously donated by

Abraham de Peyster, a merchant and prominent former official. Perhaps inspired by the Bogardus heirs, de Peyster, the first mayor born in New Amsterdam, later fought city hall himself, claiming in 1713 that the newly constructed building infringed on his adjoining property. (De Peyster's bronze effigy suffered even greater indignity. The original was commissioned by a descendant and placed briefly in Bowling Green but was replaced by a smaller version after "political differences" with city officials. In 1976, the statue was booted to Hanover Square, where it remained until 2004, when it was moved again to make room for a garden dedicated to British nationals killed in the World Trade Center attack. Finally, it was placed in Thomas Paine Park.)

De Peyster's suit against the city, it was reported, "was successfully defended by the Recorder"—establishing a precedent that even a former treasurer, chief justice, and governor of the province and former mayor of New York could not successfully fight city hall. By 1800, after being renovated as Federal Hall to serve as the first capitol of the United States, the hundred-year-old building had become decrepit and was considered beyond repair. City officials selected a site for a new city hall, a peripheral, sodden plateau a full half-mile north known as the Commons. After an architectural design competition, twenty-five plans were rejected in favor of a joint effort by John McComb Jr., the city's first native-born architect, and Joseph-François Mangin, a French-born surveyor from Saint-Domingue. The sorest loser was Philadelphian Benjamin Latrobe, who would later design the U.S. Capitol in Washington. Latrobe bitterly dismissed his successful rivals as "a New York bricklayer and a St. Domingo Frenchman" and pronounced their proposed city hall as "a vile heterogenous composition."

By virtually every other standard, though, it remains a majestic jewel box, a miniature palace, again prophetically positioned at what was once the city's frontier. After two years of dithering, the Common Council finally approved the project on October 11, 1802. Even then, it would set a precedent for prolonged municipal public works as a result of ongoing disputes with and among city officials and architects about the cost, frequent design changes, epidemics, diversions to brace for another possible war with Britain, and delays in delivering materials. It inspired a song, "The Irish Rover," about a cargo of bricks from the Quay of Cork. (While there is no evidence that New York City Hall was built with Irish bricks, the song might not be apocryphal; according to the lyrics, the ship laden with the bricks sank before it reached New York.) Construction would not be completed for fully eight years—about five years longer than it took to build its perfectly respectable forerunner on Wall Street beginning in 1699.

"City Hall, 1826," aquatint colored and drawn by W. G. Wall, from As You Pass By *by Kenneth Holcomb Dunshee (New York: Hastings House, 1952), 138.*

Mayor DeWitt Clinton officially dedicated the new seat of city government on July 4, 1812. Given the project's longevity, the formalities were almost anticlimactic. The Common Council's minutes barely memorialized the belated event, merely squeezing in a reference between a notice of the appointment of a fire warden and another of a resolution that would require the city to share with private contractors hired to remove manure from public thoroughfares any fines collected from individuals who harvested the dung illegally. The relatively low-key ceremony was in marked contrast to the official laying of the cornerstone on May 26, 1803, which brings us back to David Launy.

Not much is known about Launy personally. An upscale jeweler and watchmaker who arrived in Boston from Brittany on the sloop Fair Lady on September 7, 1789 ("M. Friedel Launy, and lady, who purpose settling in America," according to the annotated news of incoming passengers), he probably embarked from France, opportunely, a few days before the July 14 storming of the Bastille in Paris. He appeared to have established himself in New York at 21 Hanover Square. As his personal promotional material put it, he was "formerly distinguished in several cities of Europe."

By 1792 he was advertising himself as "David Frederick Launy, watch-maker from Paris." He advised potential patrons that he had transplanted himself to New York on "the advice of several Gentlemen of this City" and was available to repair or custom-make watches of every kind and size, including "repeaters, horizontal, either of Granam or L'Epine's invention, wholly executed by his hand; likewise perpetual motions with running second hand, or dead bit for the use of physician and mariners, longitudinal time pieces, astronomical do, executed according to the plan either of Hariffon, or Ferdinand Berthoud's method." He warrantied all of his work and promised a one-year full-price guarantee for every watch he made and any he repaired, with a disclaimer that the device not be subsequently dropped or immersed in salt water.

By the mid-1790s Launy had become a naturalized American citizen. A prodigious advertiser, he ballyhooed his emporiums at 255 Broadway and 2 Maiden Lane. He sold prints and trumpery from 141 Pearl Street, too, although, perhaps overstocked by the Panic of 1796, he proclaimed in *Greenleaf's New Daily Advertiser* that a recent shipment from Europe that included timepieces, books, prints, telescopes, cutlery, pistols, spectacles, and "many other articles too tedious to enumerate" would be "sold cheap for cash or short credit."

The recession of 1797, which choked off deferred payment plans, left the most successful businessmen bankrupt but hit Launy especially hard. That his business deteriorated in the late 1790s was also suggested by the filing of a dozen lawsuits against him in the Court of Chancery, the state's highest jurisdiction. He was in such dire straits that on Valentine's Day in 1797, he appealed in desperation to the "impartial public" in an advertisement in the *New-York Gazette*, even invoking the melancholy of his German-born wife, Maria. During the previous September, October, and November, he explained, he had scarcely made a single sale, "although my store contained one of the finest assortments of articles of jewelry and other fancy goods." As a result, "in that disastrous period" he foundered after being exploited by creditors from whom he had borrowed at up to 4 percent a month (or as much as 50 percent annually). He recounted that after he summoned lenders to his home on December 2, 1796, and offered to repay them in installments over two years, they "were forced to acknowledge, that if I had not been an honest man, I might have adopted measures more prejudicial to their interest than that of a respite in payments."

"Would a generous public believe it?" Launy asked rhetorically but incredulously. "This proposition was rejected!" Instead, his creditors had him committed to debtors' prison by December 6, "leaving an unhappy wife to moan alone over my misfortunes, to do the daily drudgery of marketing and cooking for herself and us in prison, and to take charge of one of the most valuable stores in this city. Is it possible for her to guard against the pilfering hands of persons who frequent such stores, while she is engaged in the daily occupations of a cook and house maid? To the generous of her own sex I appeal, whether she can long maintain so heavy a burden."

Launy held nothing back in his public tearjerking confessional, although why he figured that his regular customers and potential purchasers would care one whit about his personal finances or his wife's household habits is anyone's guess. Still, he made a second overture to his creditors, offering to repay them in installments over three years without interest. Unmoved, they "insisted on my giving up all my effects"—an ultimatum to which he finally consented, on the condition that he could retain his "furniture, linen, and wearing apparel."

Still in jail after two months and stripped of his property, Launy thundered with all the considerable indignation he could muster: "Is it possible that so unjust and barbarous a proceeding, should be tolerated in any civilized country, as to permit creditors to deprive a man of his property at perhaps one quarter of its value, and then leave him to languish in jail for the residue of his life, without a single resource, or ray of hope?" His notice ended with an ambiguous declaration that he would stage a public sale of all his remaining assets to reimburse his creditors, but until then, he should "feel myself authorized to appropriate what may be necessary, for the comfortable maintenance of myself, associates and family, treating for my justification to this public declaration of my situation and motives."

By the following year, the courts were selling off a house at Broadway and Cedar apparently owned by two of Launy's partners, Samuel Guppy and John Warren Armstrong, to satisfy a judgment against all three men. In 1799, as Launy had predicted, the heavy burden of drudgery and moaning over the family's misfortunes took its toll on his wife, Maria. She died on July 6 at the age of forty-four, the *New-York Spectator* reported, "after a severe and painful illness, which she bore with her well-known fortitude."

By the end of 1801, Launy was proudly announcing in the *Evening Post* that he had recommended business, this time at 9 Warren Street, just west of Broadway, bordering the Commons, which would be transformed into City Hall Park once the new seat of government was finally finished. "The several thousands of Watches, sold and repaired by him in this city, to the satisfaction of his former employers," his advertisement proclaimed, "induces him to solicit and expect further favors." The *New*

York Daily Advertiser carried his notices for "a handsome assortment of gold and silver Repeating, Horizantal, Hunting, and plain Watches . . . any sort of Clock and Watch work, made and repaired on the shortest notice, and warranted for one year or more." Never shy about self-promotion, he proclaimed in another newspaper advertisement that he had just received from Europe "an extensive variety of fashionable Jewellery," "an elegant assortment of silver plate and plated ware," and "an extensive variety of ladies watches richly enameled and ornamented with fine pearls."

A regular advertiser on the front page of the *Evening Post*, Launy typically promoted his general merchandise to a broad audience while luring a more select clientele with extravagant items, including a clock designed by Charles Bertrand of the Royal Academy that he claimed was commissioned for the library of the king of France (the advertisement didn't specify which one, but the last ruling king, Louis XVI, had been beheaded in 1793) for a hefty five hundred dollars, a "finger ring watch" embellished with fifty diamonds for three hundred dollars, and "an excellent chronometer (or time-keeper)" that calculated longitude at sea and had been field-tested aboard ship in the East Indies.

While most jewelers were content to sell only products perfected by other craftsmen, Launy also made a name for himself as what might best be described as a creative dabbler whose expertise blurred the line between tinkerer and inventor. As 1803 dawned, the *New York Commercial Advertiser* reported that as "an artist well-known in this city, and formerly distinguished in several cities of Europe," Launy had made another IMPORTANT DISCOVERY, as the headline heralded it. Since Galileo invented the pendulum two centuries earlier, the article fretted, defects in time occurred because its constant speed was affected by temperature variations that caused the swinging metal rod to expand or contract. While some progress had been made by clockmakers in Britain and France, Launy had devised "a full and complete corrective of the defects," which, the newspaper predicted, "will carry to perfection, an art of so much use in society, will unquestionably gain the highest honor to its ingenious author." Honor aside, the article added that "with very little expense, Mr. Launy will affix his pendulum to any well made eight-day week clock, and to regulate it so correctly, that it will not vary more than two or three minutes in twelve months." *Boston Magazine* effused: "If this information is correct, America will be honored, while art is beautified, by Mr. Launy's invention."

At that time Launy had already moved from Warren Street around the corner to 255 Broadway between Warren and Murray Streets, directly opposite the Commons, where the official cornerstone-laying ceremony for the new city hall had belatedly been scheduled for Thursday, May 26, 1803. On this date, it would appear, nothing else happened in New York—nothing, at least, that would inspire an apothegm for the ages from any municipal muse. Even in the early nineteenth century, the Common Council was not a fount of imagination or erudition. Either bereft of inspiration or reluctant to commit themselves to words that might prove too controversial or beyond their ken, municipal officials chose an inscription for the building's cornerstone that could not have been less stirring: they merely listed the date and the names of worthies destined for immortality. On one side of the stone block was emblazoned EDWARD LIVINGSTON, ESQUIRE, MAYOR and JOHN B. PROVOST, RECORDER, followed by a litany of aldermen. The other side was inscribed with the names of the building committee members, the architect McComb Jr. (Mangin, who balked at revisions ordered by the Council, was deliberately excluded), and carpenters, masons, and stonecutters, for a total of twenty-nine craftsmen and political cronies.

If the inscription was numbingly leaden, the celebration itself was exuberant, perhaps excessively so. The Sixth Regiment mustered in midafternoon at the old city hall at Broad and Wall Streets, then marched to the new site, where the white marble slab foundation stone was laid at precisely six P.M. at the southeast corner of the building site. At that moment, a seventeen-cannon salute—one for each state, Ohio having been admitted to the Union on March 1—was fired by the First Brigade of Artillery of the Seventh Regiment. (The other claim to fame of the regiment's commander, Brigadier General Ebenezer Stevens, is that he is standing between George Washington and the British general Benjamin Lincoln in John Trumbull's painting *Surrender of Lord Cornwallis.*)

"The Mayor on laying the Stone," McComb recorded in his diary, "gave the workmen One Hundred Dollars—on which he had a handsome Collation provided for the workmen and plenty of drink given them. All the Builders supped with a part of the Corporation at the Alms House—had an excellent Supper and plenty of good wine." While they skimped on the size of New York City Hall and on its marble facade, the municipality munificently underwrote the festivities, which extended well past midnight. "We stayed until one o'clock A.M.," McComb wrote unapologetically.

Whether David Launy was on hand for the cornerstone ceremony is not known. What's certain is that by the time the revelry ended, he, for one, was not celebrating. The reverberations from one or more of General Stevens's cannon had shattered the bow window of his storefront across the street. Launy, never one to let even a single volley go unanswered, wasted no time in demanding indemnification. The current operating seat of government was still more than a half mile downtown, on Wall Street in the moldering, century-old retrofitted Federal Hall, but Launy's ire was directed at the newly turned earth and pile of stones across Broadway that would eventually become the new city hall. He immediately filed a claim for reparations, published in the Common Council's minutes on May 30, 1803, seeking reimbursement for a replacement window. His claim was referred to the city comptroller.

Fighting city hall was never easy, whether it was the decrepit one on Wall Street facing demolition (and which Abraham de Peyster sued for encroaching on his property) or the new one for which ground was only just being broken. What, if anything, transpired over the next six months in response to Launy's requisition is unclear. But that December, he impatiently filed "a renewed application" for compensation, which appeared on the Common Council's calendar, with no elaboration on what had happened to his original claim.

In January the council again ordered the comptroller to investigate the facts "respecting the manner in which the windows of David F. Launy became broken, and whether the same was in consequence of firing cannon on laying the corner stone of the new city hall so as to entitle him to a compensation from this board." Apparently, this time the claim was properly processed; the comptroller was persuaded that Launy's lien was legitimate. Finally, on February 7, 1804, more than eight months after Launy first filed his claim, the council ordered the mayor to withdraw $6.08 from the city treasury to compensate him for his pane (the same day, as it happened, an invoice was issued to pay Jacob Hays $119.56 as chief constable). It was a first step down a slippery slope into boundless liability. Nowadays, about thirteen thousand claims are filed each year against New York City, and about $1 billion in claims are doled out annually to companies, private individuals, and dismissed employees. The largest number still involve property damage, but by motor vehicle—not for wrongful firing, at least not by cannon.

Launy was lucky. Less than a year elapsed between the time he filed his claim and when it was adjudicated and, presumably, paid. (It's a good guess the $150 John Bogert, the local alderman, advanced for the cornerstone-laying jollification was reimbursed pronto; nowadays, about 10 percent of the $1 billion or so paid out annually nowadays is for claims that have been pending a decade or more.) By contrast, it would take fully eleven years to finish the construction of New York City Hall. And while the completed seat of city government would endure as an architectural gem and, ceremonially, as the centerpiece of municipal celebrations and the summit of Broadway's Canyon of Heroes, the building, and its occupants, except those who briefly lie in state, have rarely inspired the respect of ordinary New Yorkers to whom fighting city hall remains an inviting challenge, however futile.

Notwithstanding the precedent that Launy set, suing the city would always be simpler than winning. Still, in transplanting city hall from a site where it abutted the wall erected to bar outsiders to a convenient venue in the middle of a park, perhaps the municipality's nerve center was made a little too accessible to the public. Not long after the new city hall opened, an alderman introduced a resolution protesting "the indecent practice of persons making water against the walls" of the official seat of government.

Despite all the public hoopla at the 1803 ceremony, what remained inaccessible was the cornerstone. By the mid-twentieth century, when the building's original marble facade had eroded, preservationists made a startling discovery: the cornerstone laid by Mayor Livingston had gone missing.

New York City Hall curators cheerfully told me a few years ago that the cornerstone is on display in the basement of the building, which is the oldest continuously functioning (loosely defined, in this context) city hall in the United States. The nine-foot-long marble slabs displayed in the basement, though, were originally the coping on the front of the building, just above the roof level, not the cornerstone at the bottom.

Which begs the question: What happened to the cornerstone that was laid as the cannon boomed that broke David Launy's window? In 1916, the American Scenic and Historic Preservation Society reported without further explanation that the actual cornerstone was "not now discoverable." The reason was revealed by reconciling contemporary newspaper accounts and McComb's own diary. The *Evening Post* and *Morning Chronicle* reports on the groundbreaking stated that the building committee list was inscribed on the "upper-side" of the stone, while the names of the architect and others were on the "other"—or what McComb referred to as the "reverse"—side. It was left to I. N. Stokes in his monumental *Iconography of Manhattan Island* (1928) to conclude that "the 'slab,' thus cut on the 'upper' and on the 'reverse' sides, must have been entirely surrounded and covered by the foundation, as it does not now appear on the surface of the wall."

That the cornerstone of New York City's legally sanctioned government, the official corporate entity that Launy distinguished himself by successfully suing, had seemingly vanished into thin air would have struck even cynics benumbed by municipal sleight of hand like a bolt from the blue.

While city hall itself would remain a constant for centuries, 1803 was a turning point for Launy. Having survived debtor's prison in 1797; the death of his wife two years later; and convulsed, perhaps, by the reverberating cannon (or euphoric over the prospect of successfully suing the city), he reinvented himself—a recurring diversion among New Yorkers—from a craftsman in the mechanics of timekeeping to a self-styled authority in what makes people tick. Launy was not only litigious, he was ingenious. Given his uneven record as a retailer, he was determined not to be captive again to a capricious marketplace in jewelry and clocks.

Within a month or so after settling his case against the city government, he was already galvanized by a new venture. Launy not only proved that you *can* fight city hall. He also helped pioneer audacious hucksterism, the buncombe that became another New York contribution to American commercialism and popular culture. Launy's version presaged by several years the viral fake missing person notices that Washington Irving published to publicize his *Knickerbocker's History of New York* in 1809, another precursor of twentieth-century literary hoaxes, Madison Avenue's bodacious advertising campaigns and the lengths to which authors will go to promote their own books.

Precisely what inspired Launy to switch careers remains a mystery, but it's likely that his decision stemmed in part from the most unfortunate experience of George Forster on January 18, 1803, just a few months before the cornerstone ceremony at New York City Hall. Forster was hanged that day at Newgate Prison for drowning his wife and child in London's Paddington Canal. His body was delivered to the Royal College of Surgeons, where Giovanni Aldini conducted an experiment that stunned an audience of doctors. By generating electrical current through a chemical reaction in a battery and applying conducting rods to Forster's face and rectum, Aldini appeared to have revivified the dead man. Forster's jaw quivered, his left eye opened, his legs kicked, and his clenched fist punched the air. Aldini's macabre demonstration was grounded in the research of his uncle Luigi Galvani, the Italian physician whose research into bioelectromagnetics inspired the verb *to galvanize*. Presumably it also inspired the transformation of a European immigrant watchmaker into *Dr.* Launy of New York, who flirted with eternity by extending limb and life.

By April 1804, Launy announced in the *New-York Commercial Advertiser* that he had constructed a "large Medical Apparatus" in his chambers on Broadway which could bestow its salutary effects on twelve people simultaneously "without the painful shaking of galvanic operations, nor the dangerous shocks or sparks, without any or very little effect, or atmospheric electricity." The Apparatus (always capitalized) "pours unfeelingly the principle of life, and restores health without the help of medicine," he boasted, elaborating with an eighteen-line catalogue of diseases, injuries, aches, sores, bites, and chronic ailments that have baffled medical professionals for years, but for which effective treatment was now supposedly feasible. This was followed by a litany of endorsements that Launy not only published in the *Evening Post* and other newspapers regularly but also even bound in a small self-published book in May 1805.

By now identifying himself regularly as Dr. Launy, he explained in a preface signed by an otherwise vaguely unidentified "Alliot, M.D." that his Medico Condensed Air Apparatus was derived from the research of the ancient philosopher Aristeas. Misspelling Launy's name and dispensing with his medical honorific, Alliot assures readers that "with what he calls his medical apparatus, and having felt powerfully the cold air escaping out of his reservoirs, that the curing air, to which he cannot give a name, is the very condensed air of Aristea revived."

Launy's pamphlet then recounted case after case of miraculous correctives for these conditions: the London lady who suffered from daily stomach paroxysms for a decade; a rheumatic headache that for five years had inflicted pain in the jaws; a case of palsy, and paralysis on the right side, accompanied by speechlessness; incurable heart palpitations with a constant pulse rate of 105; dysentery; malignant ulcers; raving madness; scurvy; giddiness; and (n.b., the Common Council of New York City) "involuntary loss of urine in both sexes." How Launy contrived his apparatus from Aristea's amorphous prescription is open to question, as is whether the ancient philosopher from Proconnesus even existed.

Using electric current for medicinal purposes was hardly unheard of when Launy discovered it could cure his frequent lapses of liquidity. In 1811 newspaper articles about Launy's patent for an "agent of health, in natural and experimental philosophy" were leavened by only a modicum of incredulity. Dr. Launy also marketed his "elixir of health saturated with his Medico Condensed Air" in eight-ounce vials for one dollar each. He claimed they promised "a wonderful effect in fortifying dejective powers, promoting sound digestion" and "to drive the winds out of the stomach."

Launy left no memoir in which he might have revealed how his legal victory over city hall emboldened him to challenge other conventions. As the years went by, though, he harvested more and more laurels—but never rested on them. He even claimed that his indefatigable research produced a breakthrough that defied the laws of thermodynamics, although he never elaborated. On January 1, 1805, Launy breathlessly and audaciously wrote to President Thomas Jefferson himself from New York that at nine A.M. two days earlier, "I did Discover the Long wished for, principle of Reaction, and consequently, that of perpetual motion."

Perpetual motion drove Launy from upstate New York to Philadelphia, where he settled with his second wife and where he became more vainglorious and self-congratulatory, even going so far as to claim that he had cured a man who had been deafened by the thunder of ninety cannon being discharged continuously. By 1812 he was offering to make the apparatus available to "any other person animated with the wish of relieving their fellow citizens from chronic or other diseases which resist the power of physic" regardless of whether they held a medical degree—an offer suggesting that the blast of artillery fire that accompanied the new city hall's groundbreaking shattered not only Launy's store window but also his personal canon of ethics.

One year later, in May 1813, Launy himself resisted "the power of physic." He died in Philadelphia. His widow returned to New York after selling off his personal inventory, which included one original item undoubtedly crafted by Launy himself and, perhaps, inspired by his experience on the night of the cornerstone-laying in 1803: "One large elegantous Dial, suitable for a gentleman's country seat, or for a watch maker—a cannon is attached to it which fires at any hour when it is set by the attraction of the sun."

11

Thomas Downing

A Man for All Seasonings

On February 14, 1842, some three thousand New Yorkers feted Charles
Dickens at the Park Theater opposite New York City Hall in what the diarist
and former mayor Philip Hone gushed was "the greatest affair in modern times."
Regular-price tickets were going for a breathtaking $150 in today's dollars, but the
demand to see (and be seen with) the celebrated author was so high that even offers
of $1,000 and more to gain admission failed to seduce potential sellers. Hone hailed
the elaborately staged tribute to Dickens as "the tallest compliment ever paid to a
little man." To whatever degree Hone was scrupulously weighing his words, he
also paid what was probably the sincerest compliment that a white New Yorker
could bestow on a Black man in the mid-nineteenth century. Hone referred to
Thomas Downing, who catered the gala, as "the great man of oysters" (fifty thousand of them, plus two thousand mutton chops, seventy-five tongues, forty hams,
and fifty turkeys, and countless rounds of beef were served) without ever mentioning
his race.

Downing was an anomaly in New York in the mid-nineteenth century: a free,
proud Black man born to slaves in Virginia. His reputation as a restaurateur
had spread across the country and even to Europe, but he had not sacrificed his
personal principles to acquire considerable wealth. Despite Hone's unspoken
compliment, though, racial discrimination permeated most aspects of everyday
city life. Restaurants were segregated; all of Downing's customers were white

(although he sometimes joined them at their tables). He had been granted a rarefied gateway to the white world, but within the confines of a circumscribed profession. As early as 1810, more than half of the twenty-seven New Yorkers who listed themselves in the city directory as oystermen were Black.

Yes, he pioneered the respectable oyster eatery and "became the preeminent oyster caterer in the antebellum period," Cindy R. Lobel wrote in *Urban Appetites: Food and Culture in Nineteenth-Century New York* (2014). But, Lobel added, "Downing's example shows both the limits and possibilities for African American entrepreneurs in antebellum New York. By entering into a service occupation—cooking and waitering were acceptable jobs for African Americans within the white power structure— Downing found a niche for himself without upsetting racial conventions." His niche became a nexus for New York power brokers, offering him, as Lobel points out, "access—if not entry—to the highest political and social circles in the city."

THOMAS DOWNING

Portrait of Thomas Downing, 1860. (Illustration via the Schomburg Center at the New York Public Library)

Thomas D. Downing was born in 1791 to parents who had adopted the surname of their master, Captain John Downing, a wealthy landowner from tiny Oak Hall on the Delmarva Peninsula hugging the Eastern Shore of Virginia. The captain was descended from Sir George Downing, the English-born son of a Puritan missionary, one of nine students in the first graduating class of Harvard. The captain was the nephew, on his mother's side, of Massachusetts governor John Winthrop (and therefore kin to John Bowne's wife, Hannah Feake).

Sir George was also a trusted emissary of King Charles II, whose grandfather, James I, was credited by Thomas Fuller in his *The History of the Worthies of England* (1662) as proclaiming that "he was a very valiant man who first adventured on eating of oysters," as long as a century before Jonathan Swift did. More to the point, perhaps, Sir George was instrumental in arranging the lopsided swap that handed Surinam to the Dutch and rechristened New Amsterdam as New York, a deal memorialized in the name of Greenwich Village's Downing Street.

Around 1780, an itinerant evangelical preacher converted Captain Downing to Methodism, a Protestant denomination that required new congregants to manumit their slaves within a year. As a result, Thomas was born free. He was raised on Chincoteague, a barrier island on an Atlantic inlet in oyster country just south of the Maryland line. He attended school with Henry A. Wise, who would become governor of Virginia.

Thomas Downing headed north around 1812. Exactly why is unclear, but his departure might have been prompted by a violent confrontation with Captain Downing's heirs, who had overturned the captain's unilateral decision to abolish slavery at Oak Hall. (The Methodist Church, too, later revised its views on slavery—John Downing himself is on record buying a slave later in life—and the Haitian slave revolt of the 1790s sent plantation owners in the slave states of America into a punitive panic.) In any case, Thomas Downing apparently joined American troops resisting the British invasion in the War of 1812. After spending seven years in Philadelphia, where he worked as a housepainter and met his wife, Ruth West, he moved to New York around 1819.

Downing rented an apartment on Pell Street, bought a skiff, and rowed to the Jersey Flats every morning at two A.M. to harvest oysters, returning to Manhattan before dawn to sell them. He eventually opened a stand outside 5 Broad Street, at the corner of Wall Street and two blocks west of Pearl Street, named for the translucent oyster shells with which it was originally paved. "He knew no tire," Downing's son George said of his father. Since oysters were most popular from September to April (the months with the letter *R*), when they were neither spawning nor tainted by algae toxins, Downing's early newspaper advertisements informed readers that in the off-season he was also available as a "White-Washer, Water-Colourer and House-Cleaner."

By 1825 Downing had expanded his business by opening Downing's Refectory at 5 Broad Street, distinguishing his eatery in two ways. While the scores of other oyster cellars and saloons, as Dickens later wrote, were content to attract diners with signs shaped "like river buoys, or small balloons, hoisted by cords to poles," he offered them an opulent dining room, outfitted with mirrored arcades, curtains, and a chandelier—the only one specifically catering to New York's aristocracy and appealing to women (accompanied, of course, by their husbands or chaperones). His menu was also distinct. He served not only Blue Points and Saddle Rocks, raw, fried, and stewed, but also scalloped oysters, oyster pie, fish with oyster sauce, and poached turkey stuffed with oysters, and introduced Cold Spring, Mill Pond, and Oyster Bay oysters, "salt, fat and well-flavored, and fresh from the ponds" of Western Long Island. (His recipe for oyster pan roast with wine and chili is now on the café menu at the National Museum of African American History and Culture in Washington, D.C.)

"Ladies and gentlemen with towels in hand, and an English oyster knife made for the purpose, would open their own oysters, drop into the burning hot concaved shell a lump of sweet butter and other seasonings, and partake of a treat," Thomas's son George, who maintained the family's bivalve business until at least 1871, would recall. "Yes, there was a taste imparted by the saline and lime substances in which the juice of the oyster reached boiling heat that made it a delicate morsel. Truly, one worthy to be borne to the lips that sipped from the shell the nectareous mite."

Once the taste for oysters was acquired by European settlers from Native Americans in the seventeenth century, demand became unquenchable. When rumors spread in 1854 that raw mollusks might somehow be linked to the cholera epidemic that year, Downing slyly quashed the scuttlebutt by quipping: "If any gentleman can prove he died of the oysters I work in, I'll pay his expenses to Green-Wood"—referring to the final resting place of the famous and infamous in Brooklyn.

By 1835 Downing's Refectory had expanded to the neighboring buildings on either side. At 3 Broad Street, Downing constructed a storage vault in the basement, so deep that it was perpetually damp from the seeping saltwater tide, and at No. 7, he enlarged the dining room. Downing's Refectory thrived through 1857. In 1842 Downing expanded again, opening the Oyster Saloon at 245 Broadway. Here he sold fresh and pickled oysters (the latter packed in stoneware jars decorated in cobalt and

"Oyster Boats along West Street, 1880," from Valentine's Manual of Old New York: The Last Fifty Years of New York, *edited by Henry Collins Brown (New York: Valentine's Manual, 1925), 81.*

manufactured in Brooklyn) retail on the ground floor, served restaurant patrons on the second floor, and was available for private parties on the third. He shipped oysters overseas, including to Queen Victoria, who sent a gold chronometer as a thank-you gift. "He made a fortune," James Weldon Johnson wrote in *Black Manhattan* (1930).

Downing had listed himself as an oysterman in the city directory as early as 1823. Once he graduated from tonging for oysters on the Jersey shore himself, his geniality, shrewdness, and tirelessness served him well in fending off competitors. He would often greet oyster boats at the wharves as early as midnight to bargain for the best cargo and the lowest prices. Sometimes he would even intercept incoming vessels in the harbor before they docked. Then, to subsidize the oystermen who sold to him at bargain bulk rates, he might accompany them to the piers where other restaurateurs were waiting and, having already supplied himself, deliberately bid up the price of their lesser stock to compensate them for his discount.

Downing displayed the same gumption in public life. He endeared himself to fellow merchants and civic leaders for his quick-witted heroics during the great conflagration of December 1835. The fire began in a warehouse on what is now Beaver Street. City cisterns were almost empty at the time, and work on the Croton Aqueduct had not yet begun. Whipped up by gale force winds howling, the flames consumed more than five hundred buildings on seventeen city blocks in an area bounded roughly by the East River, Maiden Lane, and William Street. It would have done even more damage, as temperatures plunged into the teens and fire hoses froze solid, had Downing not commandeered barrels of vinegar from a basement on Garden Street (later renamed Exchange Place) and emptied their contents to contain the blaze.

Downing was governed by an uncompromising sense of civic responsibility, particularly as a crusader for civil rights in a city historically ambivalent at best about racial equality. New York was so intertwined financially with the cotton economy of the South that on the eve of the Civil War, Mayor Fernando Wood advocated secession from the Union and, as a congressman, opposed the abolition of slavery. In 1833 Downing became one of the founding members of the American Anti-Slavery Society; he opposed colonization in Africa, and harbored fugitive slaves in his cellars, which became a stop on the Underground Railroad. Downing lobbied not only for better schools for Black children but also for more Black teachers, too, and with other civic-minded parents helped establish the first Black high school in New York. In 1841 he was beaten after refusing to leave his seat in an unoccupied whites-only Harlem Railroad trolley car. He pressed charges, and his assailants were arrested. When he was subjected to a similar indignity in 1855—this time for sitting in a car already occupied by whites—he was recognized by fellow passengers, who rallied to his defense.

As vice president of the New York Association for the Political Evaluation and Improvement of the Colored People, Downing fought unsuccessfully for the right of Black people to vote for public officials. But he eventually won a bitter sectarian battle within the Episcopal Church over whether St. Philip's Episcopal Church on Mulberry Street, the Black elite congregation in the New York Episcopal Diocese, would be accorded equal voting rights at the annual diocesan convention. St. Philip's claim in 1845 was endorsed by relatively few abolitionists, including William Jay and John Jay II, son and grandson of the former governor and chief justice. Several of the Black congregation's delegates to the convention agreed to a devil's bargain, however: they would support the reinstatement of Benjamin T. Onderdonk, who had been convicted of immorality by an ecclesiastical court, in return for his influence on behalf of St. Philip's. Downing refused to go along on the grounds that Bishop Onderdonk was a racist. Onderdonk survived, but St. Philip's vestry would not be granted voting rights until 1853, and grudgingly at that.

Downing righteously—if tangentially—challenged the judicial system again in 1860, this time when he was summoned to a court proceeding in Brooklyn. Because the government categorized him as property and not a person according to the Supreme Court's 1857 Dred Scott decision, he argued, he was not eligible to testify. ("The Judge caved," the *Brooklyn Evening Star* reported.) He also refused to tell census takers the value of his property, since as property himself, he could not own any. His balkiness was reported by the *New York Herald*, which described him as "the most celebrated oysterman in America," without mentioning that he had rescued the newspaper with a ten-thousand-dollar loan to James Gordon Bennett years earlier.

Dissecting the 1860 census returns, the *Herald* found that fully half of the Black people in the city who listed their occupations identified themselves as servants or waiters. Only eighty-five out of the total ten thousand counted owned real estate, with a cumulative value of $356,000, which, given the property qualifications for Black enfranchisement, meant that only perhaps about seventy were entitled to vote. What its statistical analysis demonstrated unequivocally, the *Herald* concluded, was that "true philanthropy demands that we should assign to the negro that position for which nature, or nature's God, intended him which is one of servitude. His best and surest happiness is secured only in a state of slavery, under the care and authority of a superior race." Downing, according to James Gordon Bennett, was an exception to the premise that most Black men were not ambitious and woefully indisposed to work.

Some other whites who considered themselves well intentioned were blinkered by their condescension. Among them was John Van Buren, the former New York attorney general and son of the former president. Although opposed to slavery, John Van Buren quoted approvingly in 1866 in the *Raleigh (NC) Daily Standard* as saying, in a speech he delivered in Bridgeport, Connecticut, "I am one of those who have always entertained the most friendly feelings toward the black race. For instance, all the servants I have ever had occasion to employ have been blacks. So, if I want to go to a refectory in New York, I turn aside from the splendid palaces and have gone to Thomas Downing's, an honest, respectable old black man." And in 1862, a year before antidraft rioters (who spared Downing's Refectory) torched the Colored Orphan Asylum on Fifth Avenue and West Forty-Third Street, the *Herald* praised Downing's "practical philanthropy" in soliciting contributions for the asylum, editorializing: "Mr. Downing's bivalves are good; but his example is better. We recommend both to the digestion of our abolition friends."

Five children were born to Thomas and Ruth West Downing in New York. The family was so upwardly mobile that two of the children, George and Peter, would be schooled in Paris, and both became caterers in their own right. Peter had a concession at the new Custom House on Wall Street, and George managed a restaurant that served the House of Representatives in Washington, D.C.—where he successfully fought against the ban on Black people in the House gallery—and opened the Sea Girt Hotel in Newport, Rhode Island. Thomas's grandson, George's son Philip Bell Downing, would patent the ubiquitous street mailbox with its familiar secure hinged door, which obviated routine trips to the post office.

Sometime during the Civil War in the early 1860s, around the time that President Lincoln issued the Emancipation Proclamation, Thomas Downing was incapacitated by a stroke. He died in 1866. Recalling that the city's leading families had dined at his restaurant, the *New York Evening Post* wrote that "his name thus became a warrant for good living" and added: "He lived a useful, industrious and honorable life, and few of our citizens, in the humbler walks of life, have been more generally or justly respected." The *Herald* was laudatory, if a bit refractorily, again considering Downing's earlier bailout of Bennett: "The fact that he was of African descent," an editorialist wrote, "abated in no degree the regard in which he was held."

While Downing was a millionaire by any measure, he consistently declined to reveal his net worth. Instead, he would again invoke the Supreme Court's Dred Scott decision, which defined Black slaves as property. The greatest irony, though, was that the last day of Downing's life was the first day that he was entitled to his full rights of citizenship. He died on April 10, 1866. The Civil Rights Act of 1866, which Congress passed over President Andrew Johnson's veto, took effect on April 9.

12

John Randel Jr.

The Geek Who Invented Gridlock

In 1811, when New York officials dedicated the petit palais that still serves as city hall, they skimped by surfacing its backside in brownstone. The building's elegant marble facade faced downtown, where, at the turn of the century, most people still lived. "By the time the new city hall was completed in 1811," Hendrik Hartog wrote in *Public Property and Private Power* (1983), "the settled city was already on the verge of reaching behind Chambers Street back toward Canal Street, leaving the city government's brownstone rear end visible for all to see."

That same year, three commissioners chosen by the Common Council adopted a visionary plan to accommodate the city's growth. In theory, it would rationalize and speed development by imposing a predictable, block-by-block matrix that encompassed not only the five hundred or so acres south of New York City Hall but also most of Manhattan Island's other fourteen thousand acres, too. When it was completed, the Commissioners' Plan of 1811 would span nearly eight miles, beginning at Houston Street (formerly North Street, which Nicholas Bayard III, a descendant of Peter Stuyvesant and of a former mayor, had only recently renamed—and later misspelled—for his son-in-law, William Houstoun, a delegate from Georgia to the Continental Congress in New York) and stretching to what would become 155th Street. The map itself would be fully nine feet long.

Not until 1808 would the council pass the buck to the street commissioners, Gouverneur Morris, a vigorously antislavery Founding Father whose half-brother

Lewis had offered his Bronx estate as the site for the nation's capital; John Ruther-furd, a surveyor and former U.S. senator from New Jersey; and Simeon De Witt, the state's surveyor general and a cousin of New York mayor DeWitt Clinton. Morris suggested De Witt's twenty-year-old assistant John Randel Jr., a native of Albany whose father ran a brass foundry and had fought alongside De Witt's brother during the Revolution, as the surveyor who would conduct the fieldwork.

As the heirs of Anneke Jans belatedly learned, the very fact that the commis-sioners were overseeing a relatively finite amount of land was sufficient to rouse feverish speculation—the covert, cutthroat bidding wars that make real estate Manhattan's most valuable resource. Which was why, after more than one false start, they enlisted Randel, a temperamental and litigious surveyor, to superimpose a map of imaginary streets on the sparsely populated and heavily forested island. (Trinity Church, driven by the same spirit of speculation, had a half century earlier surveyed and imposed a rectilinear grid on its own holdings, including the disputed Bogardus tract, from Cortlandt Street to Christopher Street.)

"To some it may be a matter of surprise that the whole island has not been laid out as a city," the commissioners wrote. "To others it may be a subject of merriment

"John Randel in 1854." (Illustration via the Maryland Center for History and Culture)

that the Commissioners have provided space for a greater population than is collected at any spot on this side of China." Still, they insisted, to have done less might "have defeated just expectations; and to have gone further might have furnished materials to the pernicious spirit of speculation" (which is precisely what the map did below 155th Street).

Randel would draw heavily from a geographic survey begun by a Polish immigrant, Casimir Goerck, whose 1796 view was commissioned to enable the cash-strapped city to sell off some of the common lands west of Broadway. Goerck died in 1798, but his collaborator, Joseph Mangin, the uncredited coarchitect of New York City Hall, would present the Common Council in 1803 "not the plan of the city such as it is," he explained in what has been called the municipal government's first urban planning ground game, but "as it is to be." The council embraced the plan, but it was vetoed by none other than Dr. Joseph Browne, the Aaron Burr crony whose lack of expertise, already demonstrated in supplying water to the city, was now being tested again in his new role as the city's street commissioner. Browne's veto was another suspected payback from Burr, who had sponsored Benjamin Latrobe in the architectural competition for the new city hall that Mangin and John McComb Jr. won.

The council also rejected a "healthy, convenient, and beautiful" city punctuated by "squares, crescents and circuses" that would enhance the value of the land. That suggestion came unsolicited from Dr. James Jay, John's estranged brother, who had apparently faked his own capture by the British in the last days of the American Revolution, lived in England for a quarter century, and returned to New York in 1806 as an urban visionary who prophetically also proposed to tap the Croton River as a water supply.

Randel would not only draft the new map; he would spend thirteen years ducking invectives and more dangerous projectiles as he plotted out the projected intersections. He was, in effect, the commissioners' retainer. But he extended the configuration, perfected it, plotted it, and both figuratively and quite literally put it on the map. In the field, he became the face of the grid.

Randel's original role was to map the existing natural and man-made topography and to precisely chart Goerck north–south roads so a grid could accommodate them. (Two centuries later it's still uncertain, unless perhaps to complement the meanders of Broadway, why the wider crosstown streets were placed at such seemingly random intervals—at Fourteenth, Twenty-Third, Thirty-Fourth, Forty-Second, Fifty-Seventh, Seventy-Second, Seventy-Ninth, Eighty-Sixth, Ninety-Sixth, 106th, and 125th Streets—instead of, say, every ten blocks.) Randel's survey, said Simeon De

Witt, was executed with "an accuracy not exceeded by any work of the kind in America." New York's grid was linear and undeviating, much like Randel himself, "like batter flowing into the grooves of a waffle iron," as Marguerite Holloway put it in *The Measure of Manhattan* (2013).

Any layman could glean from a brief glimpse at Randel's template what the commissioners elaborated in fifty-four pages of annotations and explications: Manhattan's common lands, farms, forests, and estates above the former North Street were being divided from the intersection of First Avenue and First Street into roughly 2,000 rectangular blocks, hewn from the undulating soil and schist by 12 north–south avenues intersecting with 155 east–west streets. To replicate the angle of the rivers that flank the island and shape its shoreline, the grid veered about 29 degrees west of true north. (Which is why the phenomenon of "Manhattanhenge"—when, to an observer looking toward the Hudson on crosstown streets, the sun appears to lazily sink between skyscrapers—does not occur precisely on the solstice.)

Among the contemporary critics of the egalitarian grid was Clement Clarke Moore, the poet who claimed authorship of "A Visit from St. Nicholas" (better known as "'Twas the Night Before Christmas") and whose Chelsea estate would be doomed when a clatter arose from highwaymen on his lawn, armed with picks and shovels. Moore bewailed the destruction of "the natural inequities of the ground" and the reduction of "the surface of the earth as nearly as possible to dead level" by men "who would have cut down the seven hills of Rome." Jean-Paul Sartre later bemoaned the sheer uniformity of the matrix: "I am never astray, but always lost."

But the plan also proved to be surprisingly resilient. A century and a half later, the Dutch architect Rem Koolhaas deliriously endorsed the latticework of streets and avenues. Though it was deprecated as "a negative symbol of the shortsighted-ness of commercial interests," Koolhaas wrote, the commissioners' "apotheosis of the gridiron" was in fact "the most courageous act of prediction in Western civilization: the land it divides, unoccupied; the population it describes, conjectural; the build-ings it locates, phantoms; the activities it frames, nonexistent." Imagining the grid as "a paradigm for the exploitation of congestion," Koolhaas wrote that its "two-dimensional discipline also creates undreamt-of freedom for three-dimensional anarchy."

Where Koolhaas would divine New York's "poetic density," Randel meticulously recorded measurements, filling forty leather notebooks with field notes—among them a recipe for Irish butter and a twelve-dollar invoice for a horse—that prompted his patron Gouverneur Morris to describe him as "more ambitious of accuracy than profit." With his crew, he marked future intersections with three-foot-high marble markers—1,549 of them—or, where the ground was too rocky, drilled holes, filled them with molten lead, and installed instead six-inch-long iron bolts, ninety-eight of them, at least one of which still protrudes from a boulder in Central Park.

Randel's satisfactory surveying for the Commissioners' Plan of 1811 and the ninety-two watercolor maps of pre-grid Manhattan that constituted his Farm Map in 1820 were a great source of pride to him, though he would never get over the council's award to city surveyor William Bridges of a contract to publish and sell copies of what was in effect Randel's draft map. In that case he had reason to be aggrieved. But he also began to acquire a reputation as a sanctimonious malcontent. He was headstrong, but often turned out to be right. Four years after he finished the Farm Map, he was denounced as a "lying nincompoop" by a colleague with the Chesapeake and Delaware Canal Company and fired as chief engineer. After he sued for wrongful dismissal, a jury awarded him a mind-boggling $226,886.84 (about $5.7 million in today's dollars) in damages. The Randels invested their windfall in a 1,415-acre estate in northeastern Maryland, the modestly named Randelia. After settling in at this monument to his vindication, he worked as a surveyor and engineer on canals and railroads. In 1846 he returned to New York, still surging with imaginative public works projects. Shortsighted aldermen rejected his inventive scheme to erect a three-mile elevated line of cable cars to carry commuters between Bowling Green and Union Square.

In 1865 Randel died in Albany, along with his visionary mass transit dreams. He was seventy-four. He died broke, but his map would make others very rich. The assessed valuation of Manhattan's real estate soared from $25 million in 1807 to $1.225 billion eight decades later. Among those who profited was John Jacob Astor, though not as much as he would have liked. "Could I begin life again knowing what I now know and had money to invest," Astor was quoted as saying, "I would buy every foot of land on the island of Manhattan."

13

John Hughes

The Bully Pulpit

John Joseph Hughes was born on June 24, 1797, on a hardscrabble Irish farm in Annaloughan, county Tyrone. As he later wryly recalled, he spent the first five days of his life on a level of "social and civil equality with the most favored subjects of the British Empire." On the sixth day, however, he was at once freed from original sin and permanently banished from his short-lived parity: he was baptized as a Catholic.

Still subject to British law but no longer his Protestant neighbors' peer, Hughes could be denied an education according to his religious preference. When he grew up, he could neither own a house valued at more than five pounds nor hold a commission in the royal military. Regardless of how he had lived, when he died he could not legally be interred according to Catholic canons. Hughes would never forgive the English for denying one of his sisters a decent burial in Ireland. Instead a priest, barred from the cemetery, could only bless a handful of earth for a layman to toss on her grave.

If Hughes were born a Catholic in the United States barely a decade earlier, he would not have fared too much better. Only in 1784, after the War for Independence, was British colonial law barring Catholic priests from even entering New York State repealed. The first mass was celebrated in the first church only in 1786 at St. Peter's, a small Georgian house of worship of the first Roman Catholic parish in New York City, at Barclay and Church Streets, overseen by the French consul and underwritten by King Charles III of Spain. By 1808, as the growing influx of immigrants swelled New York's Catholic population, Pope Pius VII established the Roman Catholic Diocese of New York. A diocese demanded a cathedral, and a plot that had been purchased in 1801 on Mott and Prince Streets as a Catholic burial ground was chosen as the site.

Two years later, John Joseph Hughes immigrated to America. He arrived a year after his father, a farmer and weaver, and his brother. "Like some disjointed or feeble spur, no longer useful to the wrecked and stranded barque of which it had once been a portion," he recalled, "I voluntarily floated off from the shores of this island." He was twenty. He landed in Baltimore with only a satchel of clothes and a week's worth of money, but, he said, "I was made a freeman and an American citizen long before the Act of Catholic Emancipation was passed by the British Parliament" (twelve years before, in fact). Rather than join his father, who had settled in Pennsylvania, John Hughes got himself hired on Maryland's Eastern Shore as a gardener on a plantation, a role in which he oversaw the slaves who did the gardening work. In his mid-twenties, he encapsulated that experience in a poem printed in a local newspaper:

> *Hard is the life of him who's doomed to toil,*
> *Without one slender hope to soothe his pain,*
> *Whose sweat and labor are a master's spoil,*
> *Whose sad reward a master's proud disdain.*

With only a minimal education but a love of learning, Hughes moved to Emmitsburg, Maryland, where he applied to Mount St. Mary's College, founded and run by the Reverend John DuBois, a refugee from the French Revolution. Hughes applied to become a seminarian, doubling as a tutor, but DuBois rejected him. The best Hughes could do was get hired tenuously as a groundskeeper. Only after several of Hughes's supporters—including Sister Elizabeth Seton, who would become America's first saint—importuned the rector of the college was he allowed to even keep his job while being tutored in the coursework required should he be deemed eligible for the priesthood. In 1826 he was finally ordained and assigned to a church in Philadelphia.

Even as a parish priest, Hughes considered himself a defender of the faith. In 1830 he embarked on a surreptitious campaign to undermine the credibility of the *Protestant*, an anti-Catholic New York weekly. Hughes drafted and submitted a fake news blitz of nativist screeds, supposedly written by a Protestant, which were published verbatim even as they became more and more fanatical and virulent—until Hughes revealed himself as a Catholic priest, exposing the guile and gullibility of the weekly's editor. Apologists for the nation's founders ask modern Americans to understand their eighteenth-century support for or tolerance of slavery in the context of the times. Mid-nineteenth-century anti-Catholicism would also be rationalized by some of the most prominent and respected New Yorkers, including abolitionists. The xenophobic and ethnocentric nativists claimed to be proudly upholding the values and vocations of a demographic being anachronistically upgraded as "Native Americans."

"Portrait of John Hughes," engraving by George E. Perine, from History of New York: Embracing an Outline Sketch of Events from 1609 to 1830, and a Full Account of Its Development from 1830 to 1884 *by Benson John Lossing, 2 vols. (New York: A. S. Barnes, 1884).*

Hughes taunted John Breckinridge, a prominent Presbyterian minister, into a public exchange of letters on whether Catholicism or Protestantism was the true religion of Christ. The resulting dialogue was most unsaintly. "Before they were done, their scathing dislike for each other was impossible for readers to overlook," John Loughery wrote in *Dagger John: Archbishop John Hughes and the Making of Irish America* (2018), "with Breckinridge writing that he felt ashamed of Hughes for his 'diarrhoea verborum' and pomposity, and Hughes blasting Breckinridge as a willful twister of words without an ounce of gentleman about him."

In 1838 Hughes was appointed coadjutor to the bishop of New York, who by then was none other than John DuBois, the very man who had deemed Hughes too uneducated to enroll as a seminarian. Hughes never forgot the slight. His appointment, when he was barely forty years old, was also a bitter payback for the ailing Dubois, who in his mid-seventies had suffered a stroke two weeks after Hughes was named. In 1842 Hughes succeeded DuBois as bishop of the nearly bankrupt Diocese of New York; he would preside for more than two decades. He was, Charles R. Morris wrote in *American Catholic: The Saints and Sinners Who Built America's Most Powerful Church* (1998), "a visionary, a patriot, and a politician" with "a demagogue's flair" who "never lost his common touch despite a fierce self-education." Morris described him as "the embodied nightmare of nativists" whose "foibles, like the shameless patronizing of his relatives and the ill-fitting toupee he wore in his late years, only underscored his humanity." One overriding agenda would drive Hughes: to demonstrate that Roman Catholics were patriotic Americans, without dual loyalty to their birthplace abroad or, more to the point, to the dictates of the pope.

The challenge he faced was formidable. In 1844 anti-Catholic rioting reached a fiery frenzy in Philadelphia and spread to New York, where an anti-immigrant mob was poised to breach the ten-foot-high brick walls that flanked St. Patrick's downtown and storm the cathedral. Hughes recruited thousands of volunteers to guard it and other houses of worship. When the newly elected mayor James Harper, one of the book publishing brothers who had run on the anti-immigrant American Republican Party ticket, asked whether the bishop was worried that New York's Catholic churches would suffer the same fate as Philadelphia's, Hughes invoked the scorched-earth defense by Russians as Napoleon's troops approached in 1812. "If a single Catholic Church were burned in New York," he declared, "the city would come to a second Moscow." When asked by city officials to rein in the determined defenders of the faith whom he had mustered, Hughes replied, unwittingly portending his limp response to the draft riots two decades later, "I have not the power. You must take care that they are not provoked."

Hughes's victory in 1844 established him as a force to be reckoned with. Within the church hierarchy itself, he not only one-upped Bishop DuBois but also decisively defeated the diocese's lay trustees in a power struggle with wide-ranging implications. Institutionally, though, Hughes's greatest legacy to New York's immigrants was to provide for their education, guaranteeing them access to quality schools that would prepare them for futures not only as groundskeepers or stonemasons but also as seminarians or teachers, doctors, lawyers, public officials, politicians, or whatever else they wanted to be.

When Hughes became bishop, as many as half of the city's school-age Irish Catholic immigrant children were not enrolled in either public or parochial schools.

New York's public schools were run by a quasi-public organization of philanthropic Protestant laymen called the Public School Society. Immigrants faced overt discrimination there. The daily Bible reading was from the King James version. Teachers and texts, including history and even geography books, were blatantly biased. Hughes found an ally in William H. Seward, the Whig elected as governor of New York in 1838. To prevent Catholic illiteracy from accelerating, with lasting social and economic consequences, Seward favored public financing for parochial schools "in which their children shall enjoy advantages of education equal to our own, with free toleration of their peculiar creeds and instructions." Seward's rationale was straightforward: his goal was to make students not good Catholics, but good citizens.

In February 1840 the first Catholic schools in the city petitioned the Common Council for their fair share of the municipal education budget, which the Public School Society had all but monopolized. The council responded by invoking the principle of separation of church and state. Hughes maintained that the so-called public schools were themselves sectarian because they provided historical and religious instruction that was not objectively presented but grounded in the Protestant Bible. First aligning himself with the Democrats, he later founded a new political party known as the Carroll Hall Catholics, named for Charles Carroll of Maryland, the only Catholic signer of the Declaration of Independence. If candidates were "disposed to make infidels or Protestants of your children," he urged his followers, "let them receive no vote of yours." The Carroll Hall slate, Charles R. Morris wrote, was "arguably the only Catholic political party slate in American history." When the returns were counted, Hughes's party provided the margin of victory in a dozen New York City legislative districts.

Although his effort to funnel public funds to parochial schools was unsuccessful, Hughes helped persuade the legislature that the Public School Society had "failed to accomplish the great object of its establishment—the universal education of the children of the city of New York." In fact, a state report found that of the sixty-three thousand eligible children between the ages of five and sixteen in the city, the Public School Society was only regularly reaching—never mind educating—about one in five. By a single vote in the senate, the legislature passed a bill that barred religious education in publicly funded schools, placed these schools under the supervision of an elected board of education, and prohibited any public support for denominational instruction.

"St. Patrick's, the New Roman Catholic Cathedral," from Manual of the Corporation of the City of New York *by Joseph Shannon (New York: E. Jones, 1868), 461.*

Not surprisingly, Protestant nativists felt as if they had been fleeced. A mob ransacked Hughes's residence; the militia had to be mobilized to protect churches in the diocese, which was still bereft of an adequate educational system. "We shall have to build the schoolhouse first and the church afterward," Hughes said. "In our age the question of education is the question of the church." Having first favored publicly funded sectarian education, he helped establish a universal system of secular education instead. "Many Catholic authors have honored Hughes as the father of Catholic education in America," Vincent P. Lannie wrote in *Public Money and Parochial Education: Bishop Hughes, Governor Seward and the New York School Controversy* (1968). "If this be so, then it is paradoxical that the father of American Catholic education should also have acted as a catalyst in the eventual secularization of American public education."

Catholics also became mired in another immutable political struggle: slavery. Hughes was an incrementalist. He assumed that, as South Carolina senator John C. Calhoun put it, the "peculiar labor," which, after all, had not been banned in biblical times, eventually would be doomed by more compelling economic and social imperatives. Early on, he denounced bondage in theory, but by mid-century he had become persuaded that in practice, Black slaves provided with food and shelter on southern plantations were for the most part better off than the impoverished immigrants struggling to survive in northern cities. Before the Civil War, when New York City was so divided that the city fathers were even mulling secession from the mainland United States, he denounced extremist abolitionist propaganda so vigorously that his opposition to slavery was seriously called into question.

Once the war began in 1861, though, Hughes favored both symbolic and material support for the Union in his ongoing campaign to prove the patriotism of his Irish immigrant brethren. He confidentially enlisted as an adviser to William H. Seward, the former governor, who had become President Lincoln's secretary of state. Seward in turn recruited Hughes to dissuade Napoleon III of France, who was flexing his muscle as a Catholic regent, from granting diplomatic recognition to the Confederate States of America. Lincoln reciprocated by delivering a transparent appeal to the Vatican to promote the archbishop as America's first cardinal. Hughes ordered Catholic churches to prominently display the American flag and, more provocatively, heartily endorsed conscription. That a legally blind man was enlisted to choose the names of conscripts from a rotating drum did nothing to change the unfairness of the draft. Native-born and Protestant New Yorkers were more likely to have the three hundred dollars needed to hire a substitute and avoid the draft.

Just how much Hughes could have tempered the fury of the anti-draft mob is arguable. Without a doubt, though, his response was sluggish. Personally and politically, he was a shadow of the firebrand who in 1844 had threatened city officials with "a second Moscow" if nativists sacked Catholic churches. He publicly denounced the "reckless" ruffians who led the riots, and appealed to their Catholic fellow travelers to go home. But days passed before he summoned his parishioners to his residence on Madison Avenue. Too weak to stand, he delivered a personal appeal to the faithful from the balcony, a mealymouthed demurral. The draft rioters had "some real grievances," Hughes acknowledged, as well as "many imaginary ones." Without passing judgment on his listeners, be they reformed rioters or Catholics appalled by the behavior of their brethren, he ended with the vague stipulation that "I hope nothing will occur until you return home." "For an hour he rambled on," the Reverend Richard Shaw wrote in *Dagger John: The Unquiet Life and Times of Archbishop John Hughes of New York* (1977), "almost hesitantly, much like a parent attempting to make peace with a child after a deed too despicable to discuss and analyze openly." It would be his last public appearance.

As John Loughery wrote in his biography of Hughes, "The crowd then left, according to one reporter, after vociferous applause, but in a state of understandable confusion as to whether they had been exonerated for any wrongdoing, gently reprimanded, reminded that as Irishmen they were better than what they had been accused of doing that week, or simply instructed to see that the city return, if possible, to normal." By then federal troops had arrived from the battlefield, the city fathers were promising to borrow money so that any young man could afford to buy his way out of the draft, and the riots had pretty much sputtered out. Within six months, Archbishop Hughes was dead.

Hughes's physical imprint alone was enormous. By 1859, he estimated that he had dedicated ninety-seven churches in the previous two decades. He established one hundred grammar and high schools and was instrumental in founding Fordham University and Manhattan, Manhattanville, and Mount St. Vincent Colleges. "He was complicated: warm, impulsively charitable, vain (he wore a wig) and combative (he once admitted to 'a certain pungency of style' in argument)," William Bryk would write in *City of Smoke*, his anthology of newspaper columns early in the twenty-first century. Even James Gordon Bennett, the *New York Herald* publisher and the archbishop's implacable foil, would graciously acknowledge that "in his death the Catholic Church of America has lost its best friend" and "the country one of its purest patriots."

Hughes's most enduring visible legacy remains the glorious St. Patrick's Cathedral on Fifth Avenue. The new St. Patrick's Cathedral was "meant to be a statement in stone of the Catholic presence in a city that was then the capital of Protestant America," Monsignor Thomas J. Shelley writes in his *History of the Archdiocese of New York* (2016). The cornerstone that Hughes ceremonially laid in 1858 was sealed exactly two years later, on August 15, 1860, after remaining open to accommodate offerings from ordinary citizens as well as the names, Hughes said at the time, of the original 103 benefactors of the cathedral plus 73 additional donors. "Though unseen by men, they will ever be under the eyes and inspection of God, and may turn up for honor and mercy on the Day of Judgment," Hughes said. "The noble impulse that actuated the primary patrons of the new cathedral are entitled to the respect of being incorporated and recorded in the cornerstone, which, in all probability, will never be disturbed by human agency."

St. Patrick's Cathedral formally opened in 1879, two decades after Hughes laid the cornerstone and one year after the death of Boss Tweed, the corrupt Tammany tiger stripped of his stripes after an investigation by Charles O'Conor, an immigrant lawyer whose legal victory heralded the Irish hegemony in New York City politics. Hughes proved remarkably prescient about the cornerstone. Not only has it never been disturbed; like its city hall counterpart, it has never been found.

14

Charles O'Conor

Why Irish Eyes Were Smiling

The eventual decline of the Anglo-Saxon Protestant political imperium in New York was presaged by the influx of Catholic immigrants fleeing the potato famine in the mid-nineteenth century. Daniel Patrick Moynihan, the cerebral Harvard sociologist and U.S. senator from New York, dated the actual debut of the Irish ascendancy to the early 1870s. That was when Charles O'Conor initiated the prosecution of William Meager Tweed, the Tammany boss with a certain ring to his name. Tweed, Moynihan wrote in the *Reporter* in 1961, was "the last vulgar white Protestant to win a place in the city's life." By the end of Tweed's reign, New York's working class had become predominantly Catholic, and "the Irish promptly assumed the leadership of this class"—including, through "Honest John" Kelly, control of Tammany Hall. And who better to topple the old dominion, at least temporarily, than a descendant of the kings of Connaught, the son of an Irish rebel, and a lawyer whom the *Dictionary of American Biography* called "the ablest member of the New York bar"?

Charles O'Conor's Dublin-born father, Thomas O'Connor, had arrived in New York in 1801. Defying the usual chronology, after a stint in debtors' prison, Thomas O'Connor became a journalist. Charles was born in 1804 in a flat on Front Street in Lower Manhattan. He was named for his great-grandfather, the eighteenth-century Irish historian and defender of Catholic rights Charles O'Conor of Bellanagare. From this ancestor his great-grandson inherited a legacy that included the nimble intellect of a litigator and a burning passion for justice (as well as his surname, which the younger Charles later changed to conform to the original spelling).

The young Charles O'Conor was also precocious. His only formal education was crammed into one month in a school on Barclay Street. Years later, according to the *Century Magazine*, a young man sought O'Conor's advice about his own course of study, providing a lengthy enumeration of the books that he had already read. He had not even heard of half of those books, O'Conor replied, but he "could safely advise him to read less and to think more."

O'Conor began reading law in an attorney's office when he was twelve, and was admitted to the bar in 1824 before he was twenty-one. In 1843, of the twenty cases heard before the state's highest court in its June term, he personally argued four, including one estate ruling that affirmed "that mere imbecility of mind in a testator, however great, will not avail against his will, provided he be not an idiot or

"Portrait of Charles O'Conor," from The National Cyclopedia of American Biography, *vol. 3 (New York: James T. White & Co., 1893), 387.*

a lunatic." He would also become famous for representing the estate of Stephen Jumel, whose wife, Eliza, was briefly married to Aaron Burr, and Catharine Forrest in her divorce suit against Edwin Forrest, the American tragedian whose theatrical rivalry with the British Shakespearean William Charles Macready sparked the Astor Place riots in 1849. For all his reverence for the law, he was also plainspoken and practical. Asked once whether it was legal to shoot a burglar, he replied, "The law would hang you for it, but no jury would convict you, so shoot the burglar."

Like many New York Democrats, O'Conor was more intent on preserving the union than on risking civil war, which was just one reason that he had no compunctions about defending Jonathan Lemmon's right to transport his Black slaves from Virginia to Texas without New York interfering with his property rights. "Negroes, alone and unaided by the guardianship of another race," O'Conor argued, before the state's highest court in the 1850s, "cannot sustain a civilized state." (The lawyers opposing O'Conor included Chester A. Arthur and John Jay, grandson of the Founding Father, who argued that slavery was not a protected property right because the Constitution only referred to persons, not to slaves.) As a matter of principle and politics, after the Civil War O'Conor also jumped at the opportunity to defend Jefferson Davis, the president of the Confederacy, when he was tried for treason. His premise was that the southern states had a right to secede, and that Davis did not betray the United States because, once Mississippi left the union, he was no longer an American citizen. Davis, as the defendant, was less concerned about principle than about the practical results of a trial that could result in the death penalty. His pragmatism left O'Conor, as the *Times* later recalled, "immensely disgusted to find his client more solicitous not to be hanged than to have the validity of his position established, and willing to accept a compromise which illogically put him at liberty without giving his counsel an opportunity to argue the main question." President Andrew Johnson rendered the matter moot; on Christmas Day 1868, he pardoned Davis.

While O'Conor never sought or held elective office, he was an unwilling nominee for lieutenant governor of New York in 1848 on a Democratic ticket that, with the party split between regulars and antislavery Free Soilers, was handily defeated by Hamilton Fish, the Whig candidate. Except for his brief appointment in the early 1850s as the U.S. attorney for the Southern District of New York, O'Conor's political career was largely stunted by his prickly personality and impertinent and implacable convictions. In 1872, after refusing to support Horace Greeley as the presidential nominee of the liberal Republicans and Democrats, he was nominated for president by the maverick "Straight-Out Democratic Party," a conservative southern faction, with John Quincy Adams II as his running mate. O'Conor refused the nomination, but the party had no time to choose a substitute, which made him the first Catholic on an official presidential ballot. He received twenty-three thousand votes, or about 0.36 percent; Ulysses S. Grant, the incumbent Republican, was reelected.

O'Conor's lingering grudges against Grant only grew during his second term. In 1876 he scored an esoteric hat trick by invoking the general's home county in Ohio, the Canaanite god associated with child sacrifice, and Irvin McDowell, the Union commander who suffered a crushing defeat in his campaign to capture the Confederate capital in Richmond. He mocked Grant as that "drunken Democrat whom the Republicans dragged out of the Galena gutter besmeared with the blood of his countrymen slain in domestic broil, and lifted to a high pedestal as the Moloch of their worship."

In the contested 1876 presidential election, O'Conor unsuccessfully represented New York governor Samuel J. Tilden before a putatively bipartisan Federal Electoral Commission on which Republicans, with a one-seat plurality, delivered enough party-line rulings to hand Rutherford B. Hayes the presidency. (Ironically, Tilden's election would have been a victory over Confederate sympathizers and virulently anti-Black factions in the South.)

Appointed by the state attorney general as a special deputy in the early 1870s, O'Conor established what he christened as the Bureau of Municipal Correction. Its target was Tammany Hall, which Boss Tweed had weaponized into a finely tuned engine of corruption. The name was inspired by the Native American chief who signed a treaty with William Penn and who evolved into a fabled icon for peaceful negotiation. Real life did not mirror myth, however. Unlike the chief and his indigenous people, however, Tammany Democrats inevitably had the upper hand. No aboriginal getup could obscure the undisguised greed that motivated Tammany during the late nineteenth century. As a machine, its primary function was self-perpetuation. Once in power, Tammany's considerable record of public works was motivated not by a noble ambition to bequeath a civic legacy but by the need to placate the moguls who permanently wielded power in the rapidly expanding city—regardless of which political party happened to hold office—and to generate the spending that would guarantee the plunderers of the public purse a sufficient percentage of the take.

Bill Tweed's early vocation was as a chairmaker, which perhaps presaged the facility with which he would install his cronies in cushy seats of power that demanded almost no expertise. He traced his partisan roots to the fiercely competitive fire brigades that served as early political clubhouses. In 1852, when Tweed was only twenty-eight, he was elected to the New York City Board of Aldermen, a group universally known, for good reason, as the Forty Thieves. He served one term in Congress, then to the New York County Board of Supervisors. In 1863 he was elevated by his party's cronies to grand sachem of Tammany Hall, the omnipotent Democratic organization, which he controlled unilaterally from 1866 to 1871, with a further infusion of power after 1868, when he was elected to the state senate and gained unfettered access to what the Democratic machine's bard, the district leader George Washington Plunkitt, famously justified as "honest graft."

Tweed's jurisprudential experience had been limited to avoidance and evasion rather than compliance, but a friendly judge nonetheless certified him as a lawyer, allowing him to disguise bribes as legal fees. He took control of the New York Printing Company, which was fortuitously anointed the city's official engraver. After shepherding legislation through in Albany that validated Jay Gould and Jim Fisk's swindling of Erie Railroad founder Cornelius Vanderbilt with watered stock, he became a director of the railroad. He was also a director of and stockholder in the Brooklyn Bridge Company, the Third Avenue Railway Company, and the Harlem Gas Light Company; and a savvy real estate investor.

In 1850, the California city that would become the nation's second largest municipality was christened the City of Angels. Nobody would have bestowed any such spiritual appellation on New York. Decades earlier, New York ("York" derived from Old English for "town of wild boar") emerged as the City of *Angles* for Tweed and other politically savvy grifters, thanks to John Randel Jr. and the street commissioners who stamped their quadratic grid on Manhattan. Transforming the hand-drawn and engraved matrix into functioning thoroughfares made Manhattan's blocks playthings for well-placed politicians, another opportunity to seize before the oblivious public did.

The early nineteenth-century street commissioners set no timetable to implement their matrix. As Gerard Koeppel wrote in *City on a Grid* (2015), they also expanded the Common Council's prerogatives to include determining the grid's topographical, or surface, dimensions, a grant of discretion, to use the term loosely, that tempted lawmakers—unused to operating on the level—to profit from real estate options and purchases on the basis of inside information. As a result, the cognoscenti could invest in property that would suddenly appreciate in value as it became more accessible.

That corruption was epitomized in an 1884 C. S. Bush cartoon in *Harper's Weekly*. A clueless, neatly dressed couple asking a newsie for directions inquires: "If you please, sir, we want Broadway and Tenth Street." To which he replies: "Yez can't have Broadway. It's been giv'away." But if the couple hurries and corrals an amenable alderman, the newsie helpfully advises, they might still have a chance at getting Tenth Street.

The opportunities for patronage and graft were so great that, to circumvent the city's Democratic machine, Republicans in the state legislature resorted to their fail-safe defense and usurped home rule. They imposed a new city charter in 1857, which shifted responsibilities for policing and street openings to *metropolitan* boards whose membership, drawn from a broader regional political base beyond Manhattan, would disfavor Democrats. The result was chaotic. Competing police forces fostered rivalries that exploded in violence that June. New Yorkers were also saddled with dueling street commissioners, one appointed by the mayor and another by the governor. Mayor Fernando Wood, a Tammany Democrat, ordered his Municipals to forcibly remove the street commissioner appointed by Governor John King, a Republican. Augmented, as the diarist George Templeton Strong wrote, by a "miscellaneous assortment of suckers, soaplocks, Irishmen and plug uglies officiating in a guerrilla capacity," the Municipals succeeded in routing Governor King's Metropolitans. King's commissioner was finally freed after the governor summoned the Seventh Regiment of the National Guard. The jurisdictional battle of the badges was eventually settled by the state's highest court, which ruled that the governor's police powers superseded the mayor's—a ruling, Strong concluded cynically, that merely stipulated "which horde had the legal right to be supported by the public plunder."

There was plenty to go around. The Tweed ring perpetuated its power through other city agencies by catering to the party's constituents. The boodlers extracted their share, but at the same time they provided social services that poor immigrants appreciated. It's arguable whether Tweed actually boasted that "the ballots made no result; the counters made the result," but in his heyday he controlled both. Still, with all his prerogative, he ruled at the sufferance of the business elite, which willingly paid a surtax in return for more or less dependable government and civic order—until Tammany lost its leverage.

In July 1870, Irish Protestants provocatively marched up Eighth Avenue to celebrate the 1690 victory of William III over James II in the Battle of the Boyne. They taunted Irish residents of Hell's Kitchen, who followed the parade to Elm Park at Ninety-Second Street, where a bloody riot ensued. In 1871 Tweed hoped to head off a second riot by banning the parade altogether, but reversed himself under formidable pressure from the press and the city's Protestant elite. After National Guardsmen began shooting into the crowd blocking the route, more than sixty civilians, mostly Irish Catholic laborers, and three militiamen were killed. The melee was labeled the Tammany Riot, a branding opportunity that Tweed would happily have declined. Further evidence that he was losing his grip was provided daily by the *Times*, which detailed his "audacious swindling," and graphically by Thomas Nast, the *Harper's Weekly* cartoonist, whose scathing illustrations Tweed feared even more. Many of his constituents might not be able to read, he figured, but they couldn't help but notice the unvarnished caricatures of bloated, greedy Ring leaders stuffing their pockets with ill-gotten gains. Still, the day before the election, a blue-blooded mayoral commission chaired by John Jacob Astor III gingerly pronounced the city's books "faithfully kept."

Tweed was reelected to the state senate, but the handwriting was on the wall. With Tilden as Democratic state chairman and leading an anti-Tammany legislative slate as a special member of the assembly, Charles O'Conor was appointed, as a special state attorney general, to investigate and prosecute not only Tweed but also the rest of his ring on behalf of the Committee of Seventy, a group of fed-up do-gooders. "It was a master stroke to enlist the aid of the venerable O'Conor," the journalist and historian Denis Tilden (no relation) Lynch wrote in *"Boss" Tweed: The Story of a Grim Generation* (1927). "No one could ascribe other than the highest motives to any act of this great jurisconsult," Lynch wrote. "No one could question the motives of a gray-beard who came from an honorable retirement to be of unselfish service to the people. Not alone for his legal attainments was O'Conor selected, but because of his antecedents." Those antecedents, as a descendant of Irish kings, endowed him with a divine self-righteousness that, as one admirer put it, helped make him a great lawyer but prevented him from becoming a great man.

That intransigence set him apart from a number of other prominent reformers who, either because they owed Tammany for favors past or figured that they would need Democratic ward heelers in future campaigns, preferred to make Tweed the

THE LION'S SHARE.
They have all had their share, and it now seems to disagree with them.

"Thomas Nast's The Lion's Share," from Doomed by Cartoon: How
Cartoonist Thomas Nast and *The New-York Times* Brought Down
Boss Tweed and His Ring of Thieves *by John Adler with Draper
Hill (New York: Morgan James, 2008), 167.*

fall guy and leave the party machine and its cogs in place. Thomas Nast had magnified Tweed, Mayor A. Oakey Hall, comptroller Richard B. Connolly, and chamberlain Peter Sweeney as mythical miscreants. But of the rapacious quartet, only Tweed was tried, convicted, and imprisoned. Hall was acquitted three times; Sweeney fled to Canada, returned, and, blaming his dead brother for the scandal, paid modest restitution. O'Conor was so concerned that Connolly would flee (he was, after all, known as Slippery Dick) that when he met $1 million bail, O'Conor raised it to $1.5 million on the spot. Connolly's wife, who controlled the family finances, refused to pony up the difference, and her husband went to jail for a month, until bail was reduced to $500,000. Vindicating his moniker, Connolly slipped away to Europe, never to return. He died in France in 1880 as a fugitive.

No one will ever know precisely how much the Tweed Ring plundered, how many opportunities, in Plunkitt's words, it saw and took. Just the value of property levies and other revenue discounted for favored taxpayers is incalculable. And while a good deal was invested in essential and monumental public works, the city and county of New York's debt rose from $34 million to $101 million in the thirty months ending January 1, 1869, alone. On Friday, December 20, 1871, Tweed waited in his private office at the Department of Public Works to be arrested. When a *Times* reporter asked how he would respond, the Boss replied sanguinely, "I shall give bail here on the spot." He had already been told that bail was set at $1 million but was unfazed, because Jay Gould was on hand to post it. The chief defense strategy was to delay, with Tweed's lawyers feigning incredulity that he would be tried for fifty-five offenses, four counts on each, simultaneously. ("More counts than in a German Principality," Judge Noah Davis mused.)

Meticulously documented and corroborated by O'Conor's investigators, the case finally went to trial more than a year later, in January 1873. The jury was divided. Tweed walked. A second trial began in November 1873 and proceeded much like the first, but with one fewer prosecution witness: Andrew Garvey, the so-called Prince of Plasterers, who bilked the taxpayers for constructing the courthouse behind New York City Hall but who had turned against the ring, wasn't called. His absence caught the defense by surprise, depriving Tweed's lawyers of their already scripted takedown of a turncoat. Instead, the gist of the prosecution's case in the retrial was that Tweed and the other two members of the board of audit, Mayor Hall and Comptroller Connolly, hadn't done any auditing at all but had assigned their minions the job of rubber-stamping fraudulent vouchers. Justice Davis, none too pleased that defense lawyers had sought unsuccessfully to remove him from the case before the trial even began, minced no words in charging the jury. Where was Tweed when, on twenty-six occasions, he was supposed to be auditing the city's accounts? "If there is any evidence of that character," the judge said sarcastically, "of course it is your duty to recollect and apply it for the benefit of the defendant."

Among the transactions that the audit board members apparently overlooked, the judge said, was a claim for $16,240, mysteriously inflated to $49,000, most of which was transferred the same day into Tweed's account at the Broadway Bank. "What the reasonable conclusion to be drawn from that," the judge added archly, "is for you, and not for me, to say." Judge Davis didn't stop there, though. He pointed out that the suspect invoice was only one of 190 vouchers that empowered the board of audit to perfidiously funnel more than $6 million into accounts controlled by Tweed and his circle. The judge cautioned the jury not to infer sinister motives from the defendant's refusal to testify, except that had Tweed taken the stand in his own defense, he might have offered a reasonable accounting of the mysterious money trail.

This time, the jury took one day to reach its verdict: guilty on 204 counts. In pronouncing the sentence, Davis no longer felt bound by whatever judicial constraint he'd used in charging the jury. He left no doubt that he, for one, had been persuaded by the prosecution's ironclad case. Above all, Davis singled out O'Conor, whom he praised as a singular lawyer "who stands without stain upon a character as pure and noble as any man's in this great city."

Davis sentenced Tweed to twelve successive one-year terms and $12,500 in fines. Tweed would spend only a year in prison, though, before the New York State Court of Appeals, the state's highest court, would (mischievously citing a brief filed by O'Conor in a separate case) pare the penalty to one-year imprisonment and a single fine of $250. Prodded by Judge Davis, O'Conor published a scathing rebuttal, likening the court's reasoning to telling a man whose leg is severed by a train that only the leg can sue for damages. And he viciously lambasted the appeals court judges themselves, accusing two of owing their elections to Tweed and implying that two others were linked to associates who "could not have failed to see in Tweed's possible prostration the harbinger of their own." O'Conor concluded: "Thus a majority of the highest and the controlling judicial tribunal was found to occupy rather close relations with two powerful sets of official corruptionists."

"Had almost any other lawyer written and published such a letter," Henry Lauren Clinton, one of O'Conor's distinguished colleagues, remarked, "he would probably have been severely punished for contempt of court and might have been disbarred." "One is almost tempted to say that at one and the same time Charles O'Conor was the *greatest* lawyer in America and the *smallest* lawyer in Christendom," Clinton added. "This was by no means the only occasion on which Mr. O'Conor had shown that however much he might respect a lawyer who would *argue* against him, he would have no respect for a judge who would *decide* against him."

In any case, Tweed's legal victory was Pyrrhic. Released from the county penitentiary on Blackwell's Island (now Roosevelt Island) in January 1875, Tweed was immediately rearrested. He was confined to the Ludlow Street Jail on the Lower East Side as a result of the state's civil action to recover the $6 million he was accused of looting. This time, the grateful benefactors who posted bail when Tweed still seemed invulnerable had vanished. Before, he was awaiting trial for effectively stealing

$6 million. Now he was being interned as a debtor, unable to repay what he had plundered. Not surprisingly, though, Tweed was no ordinary prisoner. Almost every day around noon, he was allowed to leave the jail with two guards. They took a carriage uptown for a walk in the woods, sometimes with his son, and stopped on the way back for dinner at his mansion on the southeast corner of Fifth Avenue and Forty-Third Street for dinner. On December 4, 1875, Tweed's guards looked to retrieve him after dinner, but he was nowhere to be found. "If one escapes from criminal or civil process and desires to hide there is probably no place in the civilized world where he can be secreted with as much prospect of safety as in the City of New York," Henry Lauren Clinton wrote.

Meanwhile, the civil case to recover the stolen $6 million proceeded without Tweed. Most New Yorkers assumed that if he were acquitted, he would return from his hideaway, a bit chastened, perhaps, but vindicated and, at fifty-three, eager to reclaim the mantle of a power-brokering boss. The evidence against Tweed remained compelling. Still, as the trial approached, he appeared to be on the verge of a lucky break: O'Conor, who was seventy-one, suddenly became gravely ill. "No great man's sick bed was watched with more anxiety," Matthew P. Breen wrote in *Thirty Years of New York Politics* (1899). O'Conor's health was so precarious that on November 30, 1875, in the frenzy of competition, several newspapers published his complete obituary.

On February 7, 1876, the trial opened. Its two protagonists, the defendant and his Torquemada, were absent: Tweed in hiding, O'Conor bedridden. But the day after David Dudley Field, Tweed's lawyer, began presenting his counterargument, he suddenly halted his interrogation of a witness. Breen, who attended the trial, recalled: "The court officers were making way for somebody, the chairs were moved about, and with the shuffling of feet some noise was created. Mr. Field halted in his question, and turned round. Then I saw the tall form of Charles O'Conor, pale emaciated and feeble-looking, with the collar of his great coat raised about his neck, slowly and painfully walking forward toward the bench. Almost every man in the court room rose to his feet but maintained a respectful silence."

O'Conor's spectral appearance was deceiving. "Ten minutes did not elapse when he rose and said: 'If your Honor please,'" Breen recalled. "O'Conor slowly, and with the aid of some one near him, took off his great coat and began to speak, his words being drawn out and his manner extremely painful to witness." He rose to his full height and asked the judge to strike as irrelevant all the testimony presented until then by the defense. Swept up by the lawyer's argument—his "cold, severe, rasping and aggressive" manner, as Breen described it—the judge, completely in thrall to O'Conor, granted his motion.

The next morning Tweed, disguised as a laborer in the New Jersey Palisades, read in the newspapers that O'Conor had rallied sufficiently to appear in court and personally prosecute the case against him. Tweed instantly prepared to flee, first to Florida, then to Cuba and Spain. Just as he had feared, Tweed was recognized from Nast's cartoons and captured by the authorities aboard ship off the Spanish coast.

"This unconscious tribute of Tweed to the power of O'Conor was justified by the sequel," Breen wrote. On March 9, the jury returned its verdict: guilty. Tweed was returned to the Ludlow Street Jail, the debtors' prison that the Boss had doubtlessly commissioned with a bloated budget, as a member of the board of supervisors. (Tweed paid seventy-five dollars weekly to the warden for his two rooms, a bedroom and a sitting room, and was accompanied by Luke Grant, a servant, who still called him Boss.)

On December 5, 1876, Tweed wrote an impassioned plea to his nemesis, Charles O'Conor, at his home in Fort Washington: "All further resistance being hopeless, I have now to make and only seek the shortest and most efficient manner in which I may make unqualified surrender," he wrote. "I am an old man, greatly broken in health, and cut down in spirits and can no longer bear my burden, and to mitigate the prospects of hopeless imprisonment, which must speedily terminate my life, I should, it seems to me, make any sacrifice or effort."

Earlier, Tweed wrote, he had been prepared to make restitution. Now, he could no longer afford to do so. Instead, he appealed to O'Conor as a man of high reputation and character who was less concerned with the recovery of the city's money than with "the vindication of principle and the prospect of permanently purifying the public service." According to Tweed's legal emissary, John Drake Townsend, O'Conor was initially skeptical, but then remarked that "the spectacle of Tweed upon his knees asking for mercy and consenting to be a witness against his associates in crime would have more effect as a preventative against future associations of like nature, than would the recovery of all the money that had been stolen."

But O'Conor himself was about to get a bitter lesson in political principle and purity. He immediately presented Tweed's letter to Tilden. With only three weeks left in his term as governor, Tilden balked. He ordered O'Conor not to even suggest setting Tweed free until the boss delivered whatever evidence he had of the culpability of his cohorts and after it was verified. To O'Conor, who had refused any compensation while devoting five years at Tilden's request to surgically removing not only the tumor that Tweed embodied but the entire cancer of corruption that had metastasized through New York' government, Tilden's rejection of O'Conor's radical strategy was beyond a personal snub.

"When it was coupled with an admission of what O'Conor had long suspected, that the prosecutions of The Ring were to be limited to Tweed, and that the dying prisoner in Ludlow Street Jail was to be made the scapegoat of the sins of hundreds of equally guilty," author Denis Tilden Lynch concluded, "this strait-laced old man, took his hat, and with a formal good-evening, withdrew from Tilden's presence and further participation in the prosecution of The Ring frauds." Of the estimated $50 million stolen by the Tweed ring (about $1 billion in today's dollars), only about $1.1 million was recovered.

Three months after O'Conor quit the prosecution, in March 1877, attorney general Charles S. Fairchild visited Tweed at the Ludlow Street Jail. No record exists of what transpired, but Tweed, dispirited and perhaps driven by wishful thinking, believed after conferring with Fairchild that in return for his written and oral court testimony in the state's suit against Peter B. Sweeny, the former city chamberlain, he would be freed. Instead, Fairchild wielded Tweed's incriminating statement against Sweeny to extract a financial settlement of the state's $7 million claim against him. Sweeny ultimately agreed to pay restitution. He reimbursed the state for $400,000, but in the name of his recently deceased brother, a minor Tammany functionary, who he blamed for bilking the public.

On June 12 Fairchild wrote Tweed's attorneys: "After careful consideration I have come to the conclusion that the testimony which said Tweed could give, as shown by said statement, would not justify his release." Tweed would testify on the city's behalf in various suits when summoned, but by the following March, fed up with false hopes and broken promises, he left the witness stand abruptly in mid-testimony and, figuring that he could not be punished further for contempt of court while already incarcerated, returned to the Ludlow Street Jail. Just before noon on April 12, 1878, he sipped a cup of flaxseed tea and told the prison matron's daughter, "I have tried to do good to everybody, and if I have not, it was not my fault." A few moments later, he told one of his lawyers, "I hope Tilden and Fairchild are satisfied now." His darndest last words before dying, according to S. Foster Dewey, his private secretary, were a mixture of self-righteousness and magnanimity: "I have tried to right some great wrongs," Tweed supposedly said. "I have been forbearing with those who did not deserve it. I forgive all those who have ever done evil to me, and I want all those whom I have harmed to forgive me."

O'Conor would reflect on the corruption scandal sanguinely, but given his temperament and prior public outbursts, it is difficult to imagine that he mellowed much with age. "At a period not very remote certain trading politicians discovered that the City of New York might be made the Golconda of fraudulent cupidity," he wrote in an anonymous, annotated compendium of court rulings titled "Peculation Triumphant." He recounted the absolute power that Tammany's "quartette" exercised ("each of them was studiously protected, by the requirements of unanimity") over local officers and the judiciary.

As he argued to Governor Tilden, O'Conor was against singling out an individual—even one as notorious as Tweed—as a scapegoat. Instead, he preferred that greedy officeholders be spooked by the prospect of prosecution and imprisonment. "The aim was," he wrote, "by making examples and instituting safeguards, to deter from such evil practices as have obtained, and thereby to save from official rapacity the money which still remains in the possession of our citizens, as yet unstolen."

O'Conor acted, unlike Tilden, with "no political axes to grind, no revenges to gratify." Matthew Breen described him as "the master-spirit that guided the criminal as well as civil proceedings against the Ring; he, more than any other man, had contributed to their downfall, disgrace and punishment." But after he died in 1884 on Nantucket, he was overlooked by history, perhaps because of his defense of slavery or as retribution for his well-deserved reputation for antagonizing his foes.

In 1875, when O'Conor was believed to be on his deathbed and about to be given the last rites, he was told firmly by the attending clergy that he could not be granted absolution unless he forgave all his enemies. Inflexible as usual, he agreed to forgive all except one. He finally relented, but with a caveat: he would forgive that one adversary, but only if he himself should actually die first. That may be why O'Conor recovered, lived nearly another decade, and, in the interim, successfully prosecuted Boss Tweed.

15

Elizabeth Jennings

The Right to Ride

D espite New York's reputation for tolerance, from its very beginnings the city
was no stranger to racial discrimination, segregation, and slavery itself. Slaves
had been imported to New Amsterdam since 1626. They built Fort Amsterdam
and the stockade that defined Wall Street. In colonial times, as many as one in
five New Yorkers were enslaved Africans. About four in ten households owned
slaves—a proportion rivaled by only one other big city, Charleston, South Carolina
(although, typically, individual New Yorkers didn't own as many). Thanks to a
Quaker delegation, a deathbed appeal from Benjamin Franklin, and aggressive
lobbying by abolitionists, emancipation was briefly raised before the First Congress
at Federal Hall in New York. Lawmakers managed to defer a full-fledged debate,
however—instead implicitly perpetuating slavery by limiting naturalization to
"free White persons" and refusing to antagonize the southern states by imposing a
punitive tax on imported slaves. Moreover, slaves were counted separately in the
1790 census (and, in terms of Congressional representation, were worth only three
fifths as much as free people).

The city's mercantile economy depended on the slave trade and on the slave labor
that harvested sugar, tobacco, and cotton. Slaves were used as collateral for loans from
New York banks and insured by plantation owners under policies written by New
York companies. After kidnapping slaves for return to the South was legalized in
1850, Frederick Douglass declared that "Mason & Dixon's line has been obliterated;

New York has become as Virginia." (In 1860, though, in the habeas corpus case brought by Charles O'Conor on behalf of a Virginia slave-owning couple, Jonathan and Juliet Lemmon, New York's highest court freed eight slaves being transported to Texas.) The growing influx of immigrants, who competed with Black New Yorkers for low-skilled jobs, feared even greater conflict—and wage cuts—if millions of freed slaves migrated north.

New York is where P. T. Barnum audaciously—and surreptitiously—presented a blackface performer at the Vauxhall Theater who was actually Black—leading Thomas L. Nichols to warn in the *Herald* that "there was not an audience in America that would not have resented, in a very energetic fashion, the insult of being asked to look at the dancing of a real negro." New York was where "Dixie" was first performed (in blackface, of course). In 1860, New York was where Lincoln established his bona fides with the Republican Party in his "right makes might" speech at Cooper Union, but where he was swamped later that year in the presidential election against Stephen Douglas by nearly two to one.

Still, New York was, and had been since before the Revolution, also a hotbed of abolitionism—even if some of the very founders of the antislavery Manumission Society of New York, like John Jay, were slaveholders themselves. By 1800, for the first time, free Black people in the city outnumbered the enslaved by about 3,500 to 2,900. Whites predominated in the history books about abolitionism, but free Black New Yorkers were among the most effective advocates for the cause—and in organizing the Underground Railroad, which in 1838 transported an escaped slave named Frederick Douglass from Maryland to David Ruggles's safe house on Lispenard Street.

About a decade before Douglass fled the South in disguise, Elizabeth Jennings was born in New York, a state where slavery would still be legal for four more months. (Just after her birth, her father was named secretary of New York's Jubilee from Domestic Slavery celebration, scheduled for Emancipation Day, July 4, 1827.) Her mother, Elizabeth Cartwright Jennings, had been born into slavery in Delaware in 1798. She married Thomas L. Jennings, the son of free Black parents from New York. Jennings had dug trenches as a volunteer for the defense of the region during the War of 1812 and been apprenticed to a tailor as a young man. He opened a clothing store on Nassau and Chatham Streets (later Park Row) near what became Printing House Square, where most of the city's newspapers would be headquartered.

When he was only thirty, Thomas Jennings perfected a process to clean fabric that he called "dry scouring," an early version of dry-cleaning. He was issued Patent

No. 3306X in 1821 by the U.S. Patent Office, the first granted to a Black inventor. Slaves were not eligible to legally protect their innovations with the government's imprimatur, but as *Douglass' Monthly* reported in Thomas Jennings's 1859 obituary, the letters of patent signed by President John Quincy Adams hung in an antique gilded frame above Jennings's bed, and "although it was well known that he was a Black man of 'African descent,'" because he was a *free* Black man, they recognized him as a "'citizen of the United States.'" Fees from his patent enabled him to buy freedom for his wife, who was still considered an indentured servant.

Elizabeth's older sister, Matilda, would become a dressmaker. Her younger brother, James, would follow in Elizabeth's footsteps and become a teacher. When Elizabeth was only ten, she was said to have delivered from memory a lecture titled "On the Improvement of the Mind," although historians quite possibly miscredited her with writing the address. It was more likely written by her mother, who was a member of the Ladies' Literary Society of New York. When Elizabeth was ready to graduate from public school, parents of her white classmates pressured the board of education, headed by Andrew H. Green, to bar her from the commencement exercises. Board officials sanctioned a separate graduation ceremony where she received her diploma, which qualified her to teach in public school. In 1857, at the New York State Teachers Association convention, one of the delegates, a thirty-seven-year-old upstater, Susan B. Anthony, introduced a resolution declaring that the expulsion of Elizabeth Jennings and another student from the public diploma presentation "was a gross insult to their scholarship and their womanhood."

The Reverend Levin Tilmon, who was born into slavery in Maryland and became the pastor of the Colored Methodist Congregational Church, to which the Jennings family belonged, believed that "there are two positions which the colored people occupy in this country. First as slaves, and second, as nominal freemen." While slavery was legally abolished in New York in 1827, racial segregation—and, to a greater and more enduring degree, discrimination (to say nothing of prejudice)—survived. When the first horse-drawn bus and trolley service began in the 1830s, the *Colored American* cautioned its readers that rather than be "degraded and insulted," they should remember: "Brethren, you are Men—if you have not horses and vehicles of your own to travel with, stay at home, or travel on foot." For all his growing fame as a restaurateur, Thomas Downing was reminded of that in 1838 when, after refusing to leave a New York and Harlem Railroad train, he was beaten and ejected.

In addition to teaching, Jennings played the organ regularly during Sunday-morning services at the First Colored American Congregational Church on Sixth

"Portrait of Elizabeth Jennings Graham," from
the American Woman's Journal, *July 1895.*
(Illustration from the Museum of the City of
New York via Kansas State Historical Society)

Street near the Bowery in Lower Manhattan. On July 16, 1854, because she was
running behind, Elizabeth Jennings turned out to be a century ahead of her time.
Rushing from the home she shared with her parents at 167 Church Street to the stop
at Pearl and Chatham (now Park Row) Streets, she boarded the first horse-drawn
Third Avenue trolley that arrived. The conductor admonished her to wait for a car
reserved for Black passengers. This was how she described what happened next (a
passerby, who she identified as a German bookseller, also volunteered as a witness)
in a statement that was read the following day at a public protest at her church and
delivered to two sympathetic newspapers, *Frederick Douglass' Paper* (under the headline OUTRAGE UPON COLORED PERSONS) and the *New York Tribune*, whose anti-
slavery editor, Horace Greeley, reprinted the article in full:

Sarah E. Adams and myself walked down to the corner of Pearl and Chatham Sts. to take the Third-Av. cars. We got on the platform when the conductor told us to wait for the next car. I told him I could not wait, as I was in a hurry to go to church.

He then told me that the other car had my people in it, that it was appropriated for "my people." I told him I had no people. I wished to go to church and I did not wish to be detained. He still kept driving me off the car; said he had as much time as I had and could wait just as long. I replied, "Very well, we'll see." He waited some minutes, when the driver becoming impatient, he said, "Well, you may go in, but remember, if the passengers raise any objections you shall go out, whether or no, or I'll put you out."

I told him I was a respectable person, born and raised in New York, did not know where he was born, and that he was a good-for-nothing impudent fellow for insulting a decent person while on their way to church. He then said he would put me out. I told him not to lay hands on me. He took hold of me and I took hold of the window sash. He pulled me until he broke my grasp. I took hold of his coat and held onto that. He also broke my grasp from that. He then ordered the driver to fasten his horses and come and help him put me out of the cars. Both seized hold of me by the arms and pulled and dragged me down on the bottom of the platform, so that my feet hung one way and my head the other, nearly on the ground.

I screamed, "Murder," with all my voice and my companion screamed out, "You will kill her. Don't kill her." I went again in the car and the conductor said, "You shall sweat for this." Then told the driver to drive until he saw [a police] officer or a Station House. They get [a police] officer on the corner of Walker and Bower.

The officer without listening to anything I had to say thrust me out and then tauntingly told me to get redress if I could. This the conductor also told me. He wrote his name, Moss, and the car, No. 7, but I looked and saw No. 6 on the back of the car. After dragging me off the car, he drove me away like a dog, saying not to be talking there and raising a mob or fight.

When I told the conductor I did not know where he was born, he answered, "I was born in Ireland." I made answer it made no difference where a man was born, provided he behaved himself and did not insult genteel persons.

I would have come myself but am quite sore and stiff from the treatment
I received from those monsters in human form yesterday afternoon. This
statement I believe to be correct and it is respectfully submitted.

While Jennings's encounter with the conductor was unplanned, she had been
primed by temperament and family ties to seek retribution—as Rosa Parks was,
almost precisely a century later, when she rejected a Montgomery, Alabama, bus driver's order to give up her seat in the colored section for a white passenger after the
space reserved for whites was filled.

Jennings's father had helped found the New York African Society for Mutual
Relief, a charitable group for free Black people; he paraded for civil rights with a
banner that proclaimed AM I NOT A MAN AND A BROTHER? and was an early congre-
gant of the Abyssinian Baptist Church downtown, nearly a century before it would
leapfrog to Harlem. A vigorous opponent of the back-to-Africa colonization movement, he argued that "our claims are on America," which he described as "the land
of our nativity." Comparing Black and white Americans, Thomas Jennings said:
"Africa is as foreign to us as Europe is to them."

Moreover, Thomas Jennings's daughter's rude confrontation with the conductor
may not have been the first brush between a member of the Jennings family and the
mass transit system. A few years before, his son Thomas Jennings Jr. had been routed
from a segregated railroad car in Massachusetts. His father was not about to let a
second forced expulsion of one of his children go unchallenged. (Although, as Jerry
Mikorenda wrote in *America's First Freedom Rider* [2020], Jennings Sr. and Thomas
Downing, the restaurateur, were among those who, while they favored the right of
women to debate matters before the American Anti-Slavery Society, in 1840 drew
the line at their joining and fully participating.)

Elizabeth Jennings's ejection from the trolley presented an opportunity for a legal
challenge that Thomas Jennings and his fellow abolitionists immediately grasped.
He issued a public appeal for donations to underwrite an injunction against the
company, insisting that he was unaware "of any difference in the law of this state in
relation to persons of color, except the elective franchise." Thomas Jennings left no
doubt that the suit that he and his fellow civil rights leaders hoped to pursue was
not about physical injury as much as the psychic scars being inflicted on Black people
in New York, slave or free. They enlisted the law firm of Erastus D. Culver of Brooklyn,
an abolitionist former congressman from upstate, to sue the Third Avenue Railway
Company. Culver assigned the case to his very newly minted twenty-six-year-old

partner, the future president Chester A. Arthur, who had been admitted to the bar only two months before. Jennings sued the company for discrimination and for damages in State Supreme Court in Brooklyn, where it was headquartered.

Word of the incident and the backlash it generated spread well beyond New York in the volatile and ambivalent antebellum North. The grandees of the Young Men's Association in San Francisco passed a resolution, reflecting their own ethnic prejudices, condemning the brutal outrage on the "persons of intelligent and upright citizens" who were "violently ejected from a public conveyance into the street, by a ruffianly Irish driver in the city of New York solely on account of their color, while on their way to Church, upon the Sabbath." Nearly eight decades later, the *Brooklyn Eagle* would gratuitously recall, "The suit attracted great interest in all parts of the country. The colored people were something of a problem in those days, and all the large cities were particularly watchful of the case in the New York courts."

Jennings v. Third Avenue Railway went to trial on February 22, 1855. In his opening argument, Chester Arthur began by reminding the court that state law obligated common carriers like the trolley company and its agents to transport passengers regardless of race. Taking his cue from Arthur, Judge William Rockwell, a nativist who disliked Irish immigrants even more than Black people, further advised the jury that the company was specifically required to convey all respectable passengers, including "colored persons, if sober, well-behaved, and free from disease," and that it was liable if they were excluded.

Jennings demanded $500—about twice her annual salary as a teacher—in damages. The jurors ruled in her favor, but while a majority were willing to award Jennings the full $500, the *Tribune* reported, "others maintained some peculiar notions as to colored people's rights" and the jury settled on $225. The judge added 10 percent (for a total of about $7,000 in today's dollars) plus costs. Under the felicitous headline A WHOLESOME VERDICT, the *Tribune* article continued: "Railroads, steamboats, omnibuses, and ferry-boats will be admonished from this, as to the rights of respectable colored people," adding with its own affront at foreigners: "It is high time the rights of this class of citizens were ascertained, and that it should be known whether they are to be thrust from our public conveyances, while German or Irish women, with a quarter of mutton or a load of codfish, can be admitted."

Jennings's victory did not end segregation in New York. Hardly. But it galvanized what amounted then to a civil rights movement in the city, perpetuated Thomas Jennings's Legal Rights Association, and provided a juridical foundation on which subsequent legal victories would be constructed. Only a month after the jury decided in Jennings's favor, two similar struggles involving Black passengers were reported on the Eighth Avenue line in Manhattan, prompting this observation in the *Provincial Freeman* of Toronto: "Although Miss Jennings is said to be in every sense of the word a lady, being intelligent, refined in manners and of a very respectable appearance, the passengers in the car who saw the whole affair, and the crowd around, suffered a brutal conductor to push her off the platform. Could the circumstance of a white woman being treated in such a manner, without having given provocation, have occurred, some gentleman regardless of consequences, would have stepped forward as champion forthwith. But in this case, the sympathy was about as observable and effectual as one may imagine expressed around an auction block, when some 'likely negroes' are about to change owners."

Thanks to the Legal Rights Association, the Reverend James Pennington, a former slave and the pastor of the First Colored Presbyterian Church of New York, won another case against the Eighth Avenue Railroad on appeal. In 1859 Peter Porter, the Legal Rights Association's treasurer and the Sunday-school superintendent at Union Methodist Church, sued the recalcitrant Eighth Avenue Railroad Company for discrimination as a result of a similar altercation. The company settled out of court.

That same year, Elizabeth Jennings married Charles Graham, an apprentice tailor born in St. Croix who, according to one listing, was also a caterer. For teachers at the time, getting married usually meant getting fired; instead, the principal of her school gave her a raise. The couple moved to 541 Broome Street near Varick Street in what a century later would be rechristened as SoHo. In July 1863, their sickly one-year-old son, Thomas, died there of convulsions during the draft riots, the bloody three-day orgy in which largely immigrant mobs vented their frustrations on innocent Black people who, as noncitizens, were exempt from conscription. Through a contact at a local chapel, the Grahams enlisted the Reverend Morgan Dix of Trinity Church, who presided at a graveside service for their son at Cypress Hills Cemetery in Brooklyn.

The Grahams appear to have left the city temporarily not long after the riots for Eatonville, New Jersey, near Long Branch, joining an exodus that would pare New York's Black population by 20 percent, to its lowest level since 1820. (It would not decline again numerically until after 2010, when gentrification, more opportunities in the suburbs, and a return to the South contributed to the decline.) By the time the Civil War ended, though, most of the city's public transport system had been desegregated—at least legally—after a final challenge by the widow of a Black soldier who had fought and died to preserve the Union.

Charles Graham died in 1867. Jennings returned to Manhattan in 1871. In all, she would teach in New York for thirty-five years. She had been hired initially in 1849 by the New York Society for the Promotion of Education Among Colored Children at its School No. 2, an elementary school at 19 Thomas Street. The principal was Charles L. Reason, who would become the first Black professor to teach at a predominantly white college (Free Mission College, founded by anti-slavery Baptists in Cortland County, New York, southeast of the Finger Lakes). She continued to teach at School No. 2 after it was placed under the jurisdiction of the city's board of education, which kept it segregated and merely changed its name to Colored School No. 5.

Whatever high hopes Jennings may have harbored for Chester Arthur as president did not appear to have been redeemed. By 1890 she had moved to Midtown West in Manhattan. Now in her sixties, she plunged into a contemporary controversy as a favor to T. Thomas Fortune, the militant civil rights leader who had been born into slavery in Florida and rose to become the editor of the *New York Age*, the nation's leading Black newspaper at the time. Jennings had politely declined a decade earlier when Fortune had asked her to join in denouncing President Arthur for betraying Black Republicans in the South. But when Fortune himself was a victim of discrimination, she rose to his defense.

It happened one evening in June, when Fortune walked into Trainor's Hotel on Sixth Avenue and West Thirty-Third Street and ordered a beer. Told that the hotel didn't serve Black people and that he would have to leave, Fortune refused. A police officer was summoned but said he was helpless because no crime had been committed. Finally, after the hotel's manager physically ejected him, Fortune was arrested for disorderly conduct. The case was dismissed, but Fortune sued the hotel for $10,000 and, in a nineteenth-century version of crowdfunding, appealed to the Afro-American League that he had cofounded for help. In a letter to the *Age*, Jennings evoked her own lawsuit, revealing for the first time that despite the public outcry at the time, her father had succeeded in raising only $7 from the public for her defense. This time, she decried "the lack of public spirit" because only $87 had been contributed to subsidize Fortune's lawsuit. Nonetheless, a jury awarded Fortune $1,016.23.

Nearing seventy, Jennings was still the treasurer of the Sunday school at St. Philip's Episcopal Church, which also had been transplanted uptown to West Twenty-Fifth Street. In 1895 she founded what was described as the first kindergarten for Black children at her home, 237 West Forty-First Street, in Manhattan. She died there on June 5, 1901.

When Rosa Parks died in 2005, her body would lie in state in the Capitol Rotunda in Washington to memorialize her role in the Montgomery bus boycott. After Jennings died, her memory was swept away even by Black historians. In *Black Manhattan* (1930), James Weldon Johnson alluded only to a "courageous colored woman, a teacher in one of the Negro public schools, who on being ordered out of a car clung to her seat until she was dragged out." Without naming Jennings, Johnson wrote that her stubborn, principled refusal to step off the trolley ended "this particular humiliation" and produced a legacy that included the 1873 civil rights law passed by New York, the third state (after Massachusetts and Pennsylvania) beyond the Reconstruction legislatures of the South to do so.

In 2007 Jennings was finally immortalized—to a degree. Third- and fourth-grade students at P.S. 361 on the Lower East Side successfully lobbied to name the street corner at Park Row and Spruce Street, where she had boarded the Third Avenue trolley a century and a half before, in her honor.

16

The Bradley-Martins

After the Ball Was Over

I t must have seemed like a good idea at the time. By 1897 New York was beginning to recover from the Panic of 1893, a dysphemism for what is now called a
crisis or, better yet, a recession or a correction. The lingering economic slump, already
nearly a decade long, had been building even before the London banking house of
Baring and Brothers stunned financial markets by suspending business in
November 1890, the same year that Bradley and Cornelia Martin hosted an ostentatious dinner for a hundred guests at Delmonico's. There was good reason, therefore, during garden-variety gossip over breakfast in 1897, for the Martins to invent
some guise to lift the city's spirits, to find a pretext to celebrate and to put the best
face on it.

Manhattan was poised to grow into Greater New York—if Brooklynites could
be persuaded. Electric taxis had been introduced, which, with pigs pretty much no
longer befouling the public thoroughfares, held the promise of ridding the streets of
mounds of horse manure. Sanitation commissioner George Waring's "white wings,"
his uniformed brigade of street sweepers, promised a spotless city despite the surge
of immigrants. And the *New York Sun* editorial page was assuring an eight-year-old
named Virginia O'Hanlon on the Upper West Side that her little friends were wrong,
that they had been "affected by the skepticism of a skeptical age," and that, yes, there
is a Santa Claus who exists "as certainly as love and generosity and devotion exist."

Still, in retrospect, you have to wonder what Bradley Martin, a New York lawyer whose wife, Cornelia, had inherited a fortune when her father died, was thinking—or if he was thinking at all—when at breakfast at the family's West Twentieth Street and Fifth Avenue mansion he had a brainstorm.

"There seems to be a great deal of depression in trade," his brother Frederick remembers Bradley saying. "Suppose we sent out invitations for a concert?"

"And pray, what good will that do?" Cornelia Martin broke in. "The money would only benefit foreigners. No, I've a far better idea; let us give a costume ball at so short notice that our guests won't have time to get their dresses from Paris. That will give an impetus to trade that nothing else will."

Which was how the Bradley-Martin ball began. And how New York's Gilded Age ended. With an embarrassing bash.

Mark Twain and Charles Dudley Warner had popularized the term *Gilded Age* as the title of their 1873 satirical novel. It stuck and became an indelible epithet. Its legacy was great libraries, museums, and universities. But it also branded an era characterized by vulgar oligarchs, plutocrats, and robber barons extravagantly flaunting and squandering their material wealth on foolish flings and fripperies. Many of the buccaneer businessmen were well schooled if not well educated, and therefore remarkably oblivious to the outcry in more compassionate quarters over Jacob Riis's evocative 1890s contrast between the one half of the world that doesn't know how the other half lives. Riis's vivid (if primitive) flash photographs and commiserative (if often bigoted) accounts in newspaper articles and books about economic inequality that isolated New York into a tale of two cities, resonated into the twentieth century and the twenty-first. "Strangers coming to New York are struck with the fact that there are but two classes in the city—the poor and the rich," James Dabney McCabe wrote even earlier in *The Secrets of the Great City* (1868). "The middle class, which is so numerous in other cities, hardly exists at all here."

Bradley Martin was born in 1841 in Albany, a scion of the Townsend family, which originally built its fortune on iron and salt, and the son of a banker and merchant. He graduated from Union College in Schenectady, and was an aide to New York governor Reuben E. Fenton, a lawyer and founder of the Republican Party. Cornelia Sherman was born in 1845 in Buffalo. Her father, Isaac, a cooper who bought and exported barrel staves, was another founding Republican who established Sherman & Romaine, a dealer in fancy woods and leathers, in New York City. By 1865 he had retired to devote himself to study in taxation, international law, political economy, and French literature. Bradley and Cornelia met at the 1868 wedding

Cornelia Bradley-Martin, as Mary Stuart,
Queen of Scots, at the Bradley-Martin ball,
1897. (Photo © New-York Historical
Society/Bridgeman Images)

of Margaret Louise Vanderbilt, granddaughter of Cornelius. He was best man to Elliott F. Shepard, owner of the Mail and Express newspaper and a president of the state bar association. She was a bridesmaid. The Martins married the following year.

The couple lived well but not flamboyantly by late nineteenth-century New York high society standards—until 1881, when Isaac Sherman died. He had not flaunted his wealth either, but he had profited well and invested wisely, as would his son-in-law, and left virtually all his fortune—variously estimated between $4 million and $10 million (roughly $100 million to $250 million in today's dollars)—to his only daughter. The couple combined the inherited properties 20 and 22 West Twentieth Street into a fifty-two-foot-wide mansion where they would winter. In summers, they leased the sixteenth-century Balmacaan House in Scotland (which came with a staff of forty) and its sixty-five-thousand-acre game preserve overlooking Loch Ness. (They wanted to buy the place, but Lady Seafield refused to sell.) The property had been bestowed by King James IV of Scotland in 1509, a full century before Henry Hudson reached America's East Coast.

In 1885, the couple returned from summering in Scotland and built an elaborate sixty-eight-by-twenty-five-foot temporary supper room over their backyards for, the

Times rhapsodized, "the most superb dance that has ever been given in New York, or in America for that matter," which "placed Mr. and Mrs. Martin in the front rank of New York society leaders and entertainers." Party favors for the women included mother-of-pearl fans.

Five years later, the Martins invited three hundred of their closest acquaintances to that dinner at Delmonico's. Having blazed a trail into New York society, they bored their way into British royalty in 1893 when their sixteen-year-old daughter, also named Cornelia, became engaged to William George Robert, the fourth Earl of Craven. Cornelia returned to New York from Scotland for the wedding on the White Star liner *Teutonic* with 128 trunks. The *Times*, which featured the wedding at Grace Church on Broadway as its lead front-page story on April 19, reported: "The British lion captured another American prize yesterday and $1,000,000 more of Yankee money"—referring to the bride's personal fortune (exclusive of the fifty-thousand-dollar pearl necklace she received from her grandmother as a wedding gift, and the diamond tiara once worn by the Empress Josephine, from her mother)—"has gone to swell English exchequers." Perhaps already seized by the hometown spirit, Bradley Martin overruled his daughter's in-laws, who had wanted to hold the wedding in London. Without elaborating, the *Times* reported: "It has been said on good authority that the choosing of his native city as the place for the wedding was with Bradley Martin a matter of conscience and not of wish."

As a meteoric heiress, the mother-in-law wasted no time in putting on airs. Surely, she hypothesized, her inheritance entitled her to a hyphen, so she rebranded herself as Cornelia Bradley-Martin, more or less leaving her husband, Bradley, without a first name at all (or at least, rendering it redundant, as Bradley Bradley-Martin). By the following year, the newly minted *Life* magazine was being spoon-fed a gold mine of parody. Alerted by a news item in the *Herald* that the couple was returning to New York, *Life* dutifully informed the dilettantes among its readers, tongue firmly in cheek, that "Mr. and Mrs. Bradley Martin are two very quiet New Yorkers, of scientific and literary tastes, whose limited means prevent their indulging in vulgar show even if so inclined."

The couple didn't get the hint. Their dozen years of grandiloquence, as it turned out, were mere overtures to the fancy dress ball that Bradley-Martin proposed over their metamorphic breakfast in 1897. No one whispered a warning. Nor, apparently, was the couple familiar with the French (probably postrevolutionary) maxim *Vivre caché pour bien vivre*—"Live hidden to live well." Ward McAllister, the self-appointed arbiter of social status in New York, was already dead, assuming even he would have noticed (or cared by then) that the age's gilt was being alchemized into guilt as the Progressive Era of a new century dawned. McAllister had written his *Society as I Have Found It* in 1890, the same year that Jacob Riis published *How the Other Half Lives*. Two years later, McAllister unabashedly compiled a list of the chimerical Four Hundred who, he proclaimed, were the only ones who mattered in fashionable society and also happened to be the number who could be accommodated in Caroline Schermerhorn Astor's ballroom. The Martins (as they were known at the time) were not among them. (O'Henry responded a decade later with his anthology titled *The Four Million*, New York's population at the time, suggesting implicitly that everybody counted.)

Cornelia Bradley-Martin undoubtedly felt inoculated from criticism because she was unblushing about her beneficent motivation for the fancy dress ball: to provide a collateral quick buck for New York's couturiers, hoteliers, florists, and caterers and their employees. "Mrs. Martin is credited with two separate ambitions, which, it is said, induced her to give the coming ball," the *Times* reported. "They are, first, a desire to round off her society career in New York with the most superb entertainment the city has ever seen, and, second, a wish to have her ball surpass the famous Vanderbilt one of 1883." That costume party was said to have shifted the New York social world's center of gravity from the wife of William Backhouse Astor Jr.—*the* Mrs. Astor—to William Kissam Vanderbilt's wife, the former Alva Erskine Smith Belmont.

Cornelia Bradley-Martin unapologetically intended to set a precedent in opulence. The press happily obliged. Dixon Wecter called it "the greatest society news-story in American history" in his *The Saga of American Society: A Record of Social Aspiration, 1607–1937* (1937). Twelve hundred guests were invited. They were given only three weeks' notice for the February 10 gala, forcing them to purchase their attire and accoutrements from local firms. Invitees were instructed to arrive at eleven P.M. at the Waldorf wearing costumes evoking characters from the sixteenth, seventeenth, and eighteenth centuries. The *Brooklyn Eagle* heralded the fete as "the most elaborate private entertainment that has ever taken place in the history of the metropolis."

Too elaborate for some tastes. "Directly Mrs. Martin's plan became known," her brother-in-law Frederick later recalled, "there was a regular storm of comment, which arose in the first instance from the remarks made by a clergyman who denounced the costume ball from the pulpit." Not just any clergyman, but the Reverend William Stephen Rainsford, rector of St. George's Protestant Episcopal, the Romanesque

Revival sanctuary on Stuyvesant Square that was popularly known as "Morgan's Church" after its senior warden, the financier J. Pierpont Morgan.

Rainsford declined to say whether he had advised his parishioners to attend, but he was unequivocal that a fancy costume ball estimated to cost the Bradley-Martins at least $370,000 (some $12 million in today's dollars, not counting the guests' costumes) was "ill-advised." Regardless of Cornelia Bradley-Martin's motivation, Rainsford considered her gesture to be a case of bad timing at best, given the level of joblessness and the chord struck by the redoubtable William Jennings Bryan among Populists in the previous year's presidential election. (Bryan polled 44 percent of the vote in Manhattan, more than any other New York county except for Schoharie, which he carried.)

"Such a display now will furnish additional texts for sermons by the socialist agitators," Rainsford cautioned. "New York is now credited by outsiders with being ostentatious, luxurious and unpatriotic. I think such charges are untrue, and I think the bringing of them is injurious to the entire country and to New York. The offering of any excuse to bring them should be avoided, especially not when there is so much suffering and so great a tendency to distinguish between the masses and the classes." (Rainsford's homily preoccupied the city's chattering classes for weeks. Among those caught in the crossfire were Charles Schwab, who was berated by J. P. Morgan, his associate at U.S. Steel, over his indiscreet gambling spree in Monte Carlo. When Schwab replied that he had nothing to hide—at least what he did was not behind closed doors—Morgan supposedly replied, "That's what doors are for.")

While the minister's moralizing fed the media frenzy, it did not trigger much of a backlash among the invited guests to the Bradley-Martin ball. Few became so consumed by guilt or distracted that they considered whether to come costumed in sackcloth and ashes or to toss their tickets into a bonfire of the vanities. "New York is now convulsed over the Bradley Martin ball, owing to that fool Rainsford having denounced it," police commissioner Theodore Roosevelt said. "I shall have to protect it by as many police as if it were a strike."

In its society pages, the *Times* dissed Rainsford's critique as "a grandstand play." The *Illustrated American*, a weekly journal, indignantly complained that the reverend, in seeming to concern himself more with image than injustice, hadn't gone far enough: "Not a word has he to say against the causes that are broadening the gulf between the rich and the poor. He does not look upon it as an evil. Indeed, it would appear that he looks upon the enrichment of his parishioners at the expense of the toiling millions as an unmixed blessing. His plea to his parishioners is: for Heaven's

"The Bradley-Martin Ball, February 10, 1897" by Harry McVickar. (Illustration via the Museum of the City of New York)

sake do not jeopardize, for the enjoyment of a few hours' wanton waste of wealth, the permanence of the system that has made possible and makes possible the accumulation of this wealth. By the display of your wealth you will cause those whom you have despoiled to rise up and unhorse you." William Cowper Brann, the icono-clastic Waco, Texas, editor whose many categorical targets included Episcopalians, bleated, "Dr. Rainsford would not abolish Belshazzar's feast—he would but close the door and draw the blinds, that God's eye may not look upon the iniquity."

The *London Daily News*, already familiar with the Martin family and its eccen-tricities, fulminated that the party epitomized the gap between the "upper class and dangerous classes" that rapid industrialization had manifested in the growing number of strikes in America. "With some, Mr. Bradley Martin is a philanthropist, not to say a patriot, whose luxury furnishes employment to the poor," the newspaper opined. "With others, he is little short of a madman not to wait for better times." That dichotomy, if not unique to America, would never have simmered to the boiling point in Britain. "There is one of the greatest dangers of the United States," the *Daily News* added. "With the positive lust of the good things of life that prevails among all classes, nobody accepts poverty as a condition." William d'Alton Mann, the acerbic editor of the gossipmongering *Town Topics*, churlishly allowed that the Reverend Rainsford was wasting his breath because whatever deprivation they were suffering at the moment in Manhattan, "the poor are to be very happy in heaven."

Most of the sarcasm was directed at the hosts, who, if they were *un*happy, didn't let on, even after their extravagance provoked angry letters, bomb threats, and a burlesque by Oscar Hammerstein ("The Bradley Radley Ball") on the New York stage. "My brother and his wife invariably refused to discuss the matter," Frederick Martin wrote. He let his own feelings be known, however. "I was highly indignant about my sister-in-law being so cruelly attacked," he said, "seeing that her object in giving the ball was to stimulate trade, and, indeed she was perfectly right, for, owing to the short notice, many New York shops sold out brocades and silks which had been lying in their stock-rooms for years." (However, even Frederick was overwhelmed if not mortified that, as he put it, "the power of wealth with its refinement and vulgarity was everywhere.")

To be sure, some were at least willing to give the Bradley-Martins the benefit of the doubt: Rabbi Gustav Gottheil of Temple Emanu-El reminded critics that "the life of business depends upon the confidence in the existing order of things" and challenging it "means the drying up of the sources from which the laborer derives his living." *Munsey's Magazine* argued that ostentatious displays by the wealthy did not anger other Americans because they all aspired to be rich someday. "The working people do not read the accounts of great fetes like this with bitterness in their hearts," *Munsey's* wrote. "The Country is still young enough for any American to believe that he or his son has the possibility to achieve anything." George C. Gunton, the president of the School of Social Economics, acknowledged, too, at the time that common sense dictates that it's better to "spend $300,000 on a ball than to distribute the money among the poor and thereby encourage pauperism."

On Wednesday, February 10, 1897, some two hundred police officers cordoned off West Thirty-Third Street at Fifth Avenue and flanked the Waldorf Hotel, whose first- and second-floor windows had been boarded up to keep prying neighbors and sightseers from catching much more than a glimpse of the goings-on inside. Scores of carriages began arriving at ten fifteen P.M.; Cornelia and Bradley Martin alighted first. Beginning at eleven P.M., guests left their second-floor dressing rooms and descended a white-and-gold stairway where they were greeted by the host and hostess perched on a crimson dais beneath an undulating canopy of priceless tapestries.

Bradley Martin was costumed in pink-and-white satin brocade not as Louis, the Sun King who built Versailles, but as his great-grandson Louis XV, the Beloved, to whom was attributed the prophetic "Après mois, le deluge" (by which, it was said, he meant not the French Revolution, but the impending reappearance of Halley's Comet, which was blamed for the Great Flood in the Bible). Cornelia Bradley-Martin prophetically came as Mary Queen of Scots (who was forced to abdicate and later beheaded) in a black velvet gown lined with cerise satin. Appropriately enough, she wore a ruby necklace that once belonged to Marie Antoinette—an ensemble that was estimated to have set the couple back millions of dollars by today's count for jewelry alone and which, one wag couldn't help but note, meant that she dressed as one doomed queen and was accessorized by another.

"For weeks," the *Times* reported, "an army of costumers, perruquiers, milliners, dressmakers, caterers, florists and bootmakers have been busily employed in the arrangements for the dressing and reception of the guests, and for weeks past the American public has been stirred by discussions as to the ball and its object lessons." The entourage entered a corridor lined with mirrors and festooned with Souzet garlands entwined with plemousa vine, then stepped into the Grand Ballroom, which was bedecked with thirty-five thousand succulent galax leaves, five thousand roses, and three thousand orchids. As the Hungarian Band played Nevins's "Narcissus," the guests were led to one of the 125 tables for six. "The first impression on entering the room," a *Times* reporter wrote, "was that some fairy god-mother, in a dream, had revived the glories of the past for one's special enjoyment."

As many as fifty other guests, oblivious to inevitable comparisons, were also garbed as the last queen of France, including Ava Astor, the wife of John Jacob IV (who in a bow to numerical symmetry came as Henry IV of France). His mother, Caroline, making a rare appearance at a hotel reception, sported a gown adorned with $250,000 in diamonds from nape to navel, prompting the *London Daily News* to exclaim: "The jewels alone are enough to revive the Populist agitation." August Belmont sported gold-inlaid armor valued at $10,000. Stanford White wore a court costume of black velvet and white satin. Otto Cushing, the budding illustrator from Boston, scandalized some puritanical guests with his sixteenth-century falconer's tights, which left little to the imagination. (Anne Morgan, J. P.'s daughter, also defied convention, as was her wont, by appearing as Pocahontas.)

Bradley Martin's brother Frederick proclaimed the ball "one of the most lavish and expensive—probably the most expensive—dinners ever given in America," describing it as "a hyphenated feast": every dish on the menu punctuated as an amalgam of exotic ingredients, "the record of which is writ large upon the annals of metropolitan society." Plates overflowed with Poularde Farce aux Truffles, Filet de Boeuf Jardiniere, Terrapene Desossee a la Baltimore, Canard Canvasback, Galantine a la Victoria, and dozens of other delectables to keep the diners sated until the party petered out around dawn. The *New York Press*, which devoted its entire front page to the event, concluded: "For lavish expenditure, for artistic decorations and surroundings, for a reflection of the most picturesque episodes in Old World history, and a gathering of the fairest and bravest in New World life, last night's ball marked an epoch." The Bradley-Martins finally decamped for home around six A.M.

William Cowper Brann savaged the ball. "Of the 350 male revelers more than 100 were costumed as Louis XV, while but three considered Washington worthy of imitation," he noted. Brann also disparaged the proliferation of aspiring Madame Pompadours. "And what is the difference, pray, between a Pompadour and a Five Points nymph du pave?" Brann asked. "Simply this: The one rustles in silks for diamonds, the other hustles in rags for bread, their occupation being identical."

The historians Charles and Mary Beard were more tempered but no less condemnatory in labeling the costume party "the climax of lavish expenditure." They would write several decades later: "This ball of the plutocrats astounded the country, then in the grip of a prolonged business depression with its attendant unemployment, misery and starvation." The *Times* had devoted full pages to the affair in advance, including alphabetical lists of the guests and their costumes, the shocking news that one of the Waldorf's servants had misguidedly applied Lima oil to polish the furniture and the rotten egg odor had still not dissipated, and, again, the consolation that the party was providing employment to the masses. "A great army of poor folks in Alabama have been engaged in gathering clematis vines for the affair," readers were informed. On February 11, the Bradley-Martin ball was the lead story on the *Times*'s front page, bumping news of the escalating Cuban revolution and the death of Armand Castelmary, the French bass who received a boisterous ovation from the oblivious audience as he collapsed on the stage of the Metropolitan Opera while singing Tristano in *Martha*.

Finley Peter Dunne's Chicago *Times-Herald* editorialized against the "popular wealth-hating fad in this country," but as Charles Fanning wrote in *Finley Peter Dunne and Mr. Dooley* (1978), in Dunne's column the Bradley-Martins infused at least a fictional defender in Hennessy, Dooley the bartender's hapless patron, who observed: "If these people didn't let go iv their coin here, they'd take it away with them to Paris, or West Baden, Indiana, an' spind it instid iv puttin' it in circulation amongst th' florists an' dressmakers an' hackmen they'll have to hire. I believe in encouragin' th' rich to walk away fr'm their change."

The Bradley-Martin ball mocked Oscar Wilde's maxim that nothing succeeds like excess. Even more than the maxim itself, it evoked the title of Wilde's play from which that proverb was popularized: *A Woman of No Importance*. Ethan Mordden wrote in *The Guest List: How Manhattan Defined American Sophistication—from the Algonquin Round Table to Truman Capote's Ball* (2010): "Suddenly, the notion of who was elite and how elitism worked underwent evolution, and the grid of power was unlocked. One may date it from . . . well, the Bradley-Martin Ball, perhaps, in the public's rejection of its values." Mordden described the affair as "the kind of thing that inspires French Revolutions." Frederick Martin, as much as he would bemoan the profligacy of the very rich, gave a pass to his brother and sister-in-law. "I cannot see," he would still write in 1913, "why this entertainment should have been condemned."

But it was. And it became a touchstone for how the Gilded Age, which, while it imbued the nation with priceless cultural, academic, scientific, and spiritual resources, imploded in an orgy of gluttonous greed. The Bradley-Martins may have been billed as little as $10,000 by the Waldorf, but the costumes, catering, sixty cases of champagne, Victor Herbert's band, decorations, props, party favors, security, and other expenses inflated the total outlay to as much as $500,000, or perhaps $16 million in today's dollars. It might just as well have been a going-away party for the Gilded Age, or, for that matter, a prelude to the insinuation of arrivistes of various persuasions into what passed for society but had been superseded by celebrity. The Bradley-Martins left town with their hyphen intact, but escaping the country could not spare them a question mark, too. By then, you might say, the court was in their ball.

"The great event had proved to be so blatant and heartless in its abdication of taste and social conscience," Justin Kaplan wrote in *When the Astors Owned New York* (2006), "that public opinion, along with a punitive doubling of their tax assessment, eventually pushed the Bradley-Martins into exile or, as they thought of it, preferred residence in England." When the city's Tax Commission slapped that higher assessment on their property (punitively or not), the family refused to pay and sued. They claimed that because they had settled abroad after 1898, they should be classified as nonresidents, immune from local levies. Yes, Bradley Martin acknowledged that the house on West Twentieth Street was always kept ready for occupancy, that he was still a member of the Metropolitan, Union, Downtown, and Tuxedo Clubs in New York, maintained a pew at Grace Church, and kept accounts in New York banks; but he and his wife and mother-in-law lived full-time in Balmacaan House, which they leased, and owned a permanent residence in Chesterfield Gardens in Mayfair.

The courts ultimately rejected their challenge. The *World* listed Martin among the "millionaire tax dodgers." The *Tribune*'s front page blared: BRADLEY MARTIN MUST PAY. Eventually, after the ruling that "it appears that he still retains his citizenship and that there has been no change in his habits of life since 1882," Bradley Martin abandoned his appeals. He delivered a check to the city for $37,000 he owed for the $650,000 assessment that had been levied for 1898 and 1899.

The couple returned to New York again in April 1899 on the liner *Teutonic*— this time with only forty trunks—to sell their New York residence and dispose of some furniture before decamping permanently to Britain with the rest. They checked into the newly merged Waldorf-Astoria, which had also developed an affinity for hyphens to end a feud among Astor cousins. The following month, they hosted a farewell dinner at the hotel for only about eighty of their closest friends—perhaps, the only ones left. The Bradley-Martins sat on opposite sides of an elongated fifty-foot table as the hotel orchestra performed from the couple's prescribed playlist. Two years away had not taught them much about empathy for the American public. Among the favorite tunes that evening was the minstrel hard luck song, "When You Ain't Got No Money, Then You Needn't Come Around."

17

Charles Dowd

The Day of Two Noons

O ur columns groan again with reports of wholesale slaughter by Railroad trains," the *Times* lamented in 1853 after the latest fatal collision of two expresses speeding toward each other on a single track. Concluding dryly that "the variation of a *time-piece* is assigned as the immediate occasion of the meeting," the newspaper's editorial brooded: "Has human ingenuity been exhausted, in devising the means—or has the power of Society proved unable to enforce by law such regulations as will prevent these horrible holocausts to the Railway demon?"

That same year, Charles Ferdinand Dowd, an eighth-generation New Englander whose ancestors arrived in America in 1639, was scheduled to graduate from Yale. The son of a shoemaker, his schooling was delayed because he was short of cash, but he finally managed to earn both a bachelor's and a master's degree when he was thirty-one in 1853. (In 1888 he also would receive a doctorate in theology from New York University.) Yale's class of '53 included such notables as Andrew Dickson White, a staunch abolitionist who would become the first president of Cornell University; George Shiras Jr., a future Supreme Court justice; and various cabinet members and ambassadors. But no less an arbiter of primacy than Chauncey Depew, Yale class of 1856, who would become a U.S. senator from New York and the president of the New York Central Railroad, would later say that rated by achievement, "Dr. Charles Ferdinand Dowd was not only the most famous member of his class, but entitled to the distinction of being the most famous Yale graduate."

For Charles Dowd, though, fame was ephemeral. His renown would come as the result of an avocation rather than a livelihood. Unlike David F. Launy, he did not make or sell clocks and cures. Instead, he would envisage a commonsensical solution to an inconvenient and injurious conundrum and give it away for free. And even when he achieved visibility, two decades after the *Times* sought to conjure up "human ingenuity" in some fertile scientific mind, the fame Dowd received was tangential, at best. For someone who made time stand still, Dowd barely got his fifteen minutes.

Around 1860, Dowd and his wife, Harriet Miriam North, a graduate of Mount Holyoke Seminary, bought the North Granville Ladies Seminary in upstate New York, where they both taught. About 1865 the couple relocated to Saratoga Springs, the spa town where they would run the Temple Grove Seminary together for the next thirty-five years. Dowd taught philosophy, his wife history.

"Portrait of Charles Dowd," from Charles F. Dowd: A Narrative of His Services in Originating and Promoting the System of Standard Time *by Charles F. Dowd (New York: Knickerbocker Press, 1930).*

Like every other train traveler, Dowd was fully cognizant of the inconvenient and sometimes fatal disconnect between local time and railroad time. "He liked order, he disliked confusion," a Dowd biographer wrote. Confusion was the order of the day in mid-nineteenth-century train timetables, however. In virtually every locality in the country, noon was determined astronomically, by the hour when the sun was at its midpoint in the sky, which meant that twelve P.M. varied from place to place, minute by minute. Each railroad line would operate independently, by its own sweet time. Synchronizing timetables to accommodate transfers from one train to another was the passengers' problem. Reconciling schedules to keep trains from colliding, as worthy a goal as it was, would become a mind-boggling exercise in establishing order from chaos.

A passenger taking a train from Portland, Maine, to Buffalo, New York, would pass through four time zones. He would leave at twelve fifteen on his own watch, which was noon on New York Central time, and eleven twenty-five on the Lake Shore Railway. He would arrive in Buffalo at eleven forty local time. At noon in New York City, it was eleven fifty-nine in Albany, eleven fifty-five in Philadelphia, eleven forty-seven in Washington, and eleven thirty-five in Pittsburgh. In Connecticut, local town clocks varied eight minutes between the New York and Rhode Island borders. "The traveler's watch was to him but a delusion," Dowd wrote in frustration. The mutinous minute hands proved so discordant, the *Times* observed, that "had there stretched across the Continent a line of clocks extending from the extreme eastern point of Maine to the extreme western point on the Pacific Coast, and had each clock sounded an alarm at the hour of noon, local time, there would have been a continuous ringing from the east to the west lasting three-and-a-quarter hours."

New Yorkers were still largely dependent on rudimentary sundials until as late as 1877, when Western Union revolutionized timekeeping with what today seems like an equally primitive device. At exactly noon a telegraph operator in the U.S. Naval Observatory in Washington sent a signal that activated an electromagnet, which tripped a lever that released a three-and-a-half-foot diameter copper ball down a twenty-three-foot-tall pole atop the newly completed ten-story Western Union Telegraph Building at 195 Broadway in Lower Manhattan.

Just a few decades earlier, sundials sufficed. Time hadn't mattered as much. In 1825, when the Erie Canal opened, one reason for its stupendous if short-lived success was its monopoly; railroads had laid perhaps a hundred miles of track in the entire country. By the Civil War, thirty-five years later, though, some thirty thousand miles of track crisscrossed the nation and its territories. In 1869, after Leland Stanford of the

Central Pacific Railroad and the Union Pacific's Thomas Durant swung and missed, a lowly railroad worker drove the ceremonial Golden Spike into a wooden tie in northern Utah that signaled the beginning of transcontinental mass transportation—a marathon journey that made timely connections even more imperative.

Other technological advances demanded a synchronous system to integrate who and what was where precisely when. The completion of the first transcontinental telegraph even earlier, in 1861, connecting New York and California, made it even more imperative that timetables correspond. So did scientific experimentation—coinciding astronomical and seismological observations, for example. Fortunes could be made or lost on Wall Street depending on the share price at the very moment that the transaction took place. The industrial age demanded that what John Milton inscrutably described as a "two-handed engine" be defined unambiguously. Charles Dowd, an amateur with no vested stake in the outcome whatsoever, took it upon himself to do just that, and on his own time.

After conducting some eight thousand calculations along five hundred rail lines, Dowd first conceived a uniform national time. That proved impractical; the United States was simply too vast. The sun took some 231 minutes, or nearly four hours, to move east to west across the country. Eventually, he devised a system of four time zones, each 15 degrees longitude wide, a formula that he first broached to his seminary students in 1863. Six years later, in 1869, Dowd formally presented his proposal to a convention of railway executives in New York City. He would spend the next fourteen years lobbying engineers, astronomers, college professors, civil engineers, newspaper and magazine editors, and the military.

Among Dowd's earliest champions was John M. Toucey, the general manager of the New York Central and Hudson River Railroad. Its Grand Central Depot on East Forty-Second Street in Manhattan was the busiest in the nation. Toucey endorsed Dowd's four-zone proposal when it was originally presented in 1869 and formally introduced a virtually identical protocol before the General Railway Time Convention in 1883. His resolution slashed what by then had already been pared to a mere fifty different time zones nationally to four, effective Sunday, November 18. "No crisis forced the railroads to alter the way the railroads kept time, no federal legislation mandated the change, no public demand had precipitated it," Carlene Stephens, the curator of time at the National Museum of American History, wrote. "The railroads voluntarily rearranged the entire country's timekeeping, albeit under the threat of government interference if they did nothing. The country, for the most part, went along without too much reluctance."

"Workmen reinstall ball clock at information booth, Grand Central Terminal, 1954." (Photo by Neal Boenzi via the *New York Times*)

The New York Central Railroad, seeking to minimize any disruption, took the lead. It embraced Eastern Standard Time before anyone else, at ten A.M. that Sunday at Grand Central—a first that would be perpetually celebrated after 1913 in one of the majestic new terminal's pedestrian passages to Lexington Avenue. The words "Eastern Standard Time" are imperiously etched into the marble under a clock just off the Main Concourse (even though, of course, for nearly two thirds of the year the hour hand accurately conveys daylight saving time). Mayor Franklin Edson ordered that all clocks comply with the new railway time. On November 18, in room 48 of the Western Union Telegraph Building on lower Broadway, James Hamblet, the superintendent of the company's Time Telegraph subsidiary, stopped the pendulum of his regulator clock at nine A.M. New York time.

Time stood still for an obligatory 3 minutes, 58.38 seconds, until the cylindrical pendulum was activated again. Jewelers, stock tickers, and police and fire stations

linked to Western Union in New York by thirty miles of wire also adopted standard
time at ten A.M., but the rest of the city waited anxiously for two hours. The Bible
proclaims that God's timing is "always and forever." Who knows what might happen
if mere mortals are presumptuous enough to tinker with it? A crowd gathered
on Lower Broadway at New York City Hall for the horological geste that became
known as the Day of Two Noons, when the Western Union time ball dropped
twice—first to signal local time and then, four minutes later, the new Eastern Standard Time. (The clock in the hall's cupola stopped twelve minutes late because
Martin J. Keese, the city's official timekeeper, was stuck in the crowd on Broadway
watching the Western Union ball drop so that he could set his own chronometer.)
"All intelligent persons will ask why the change was not made years ago," the *Times*
said. Regardless, it was made none too soon. While the change was featured on page 5
of the newspaper, the front page displayed a headline about a TERRIBLE RAILWAY
COLLISION in Illinois.

In Washington, U.S. attorney general Benjamin H. Brewster balked, insisting
that so momentous a revision in the nation's culture required congressional approval.
The superintendent of the Naval Observatory ignored Brewster's legal interpreta-
tion, adopting the new railroad standard as the country's official timekeeper. Dire
predictions from the pulpit of divine disfavor in response to human trifling with
time proved unfounded. ("There was no convulsion of nature," the *Times* sniffed,
"and no signs have been discovered of political or social revolution.")

There was no sign, either, of Charles F. Dowd. His offstage role as Father Time
had been largely preempted in the public mind by William F. Allen, an engineer
by training and the editor of the *Travelers' Official Railway Guide for the United
States* who suited the narrative more convincingly than a Presbyterian elder who
presided over a school for girls. Allen was also secretary of the railroads' General Time
Convention, which, fourteen years after Dowd originally published his concept,
had adopted it nearly intact. In a report to the American Meteorological Society in
1883, Allen would characterize Dowd's 1870 pamphlet on time zones as "the first
published proposition of which I have any knowledge." Moreover, the *Wall Street
Daily News* pointed out that Dowd, "in recognition of his claim of inventorship,
received annual passes over every great railway and its branches."

Dowd retired as principal of the liberal arts seminary in 1898 when he was seventy-
three. Sometime past five thirty P.M. on Saturday, November 12, 1904, a full hour
after sunset, Dowd, by then nearly eighty, was walking back to his home on Spring
Street in Saratoga Springs after visiting a critically ill friend. Thanks to the voracious

Delaware & Hudson, which billed itself as North America's oldest continually operated transportation company, the village had become a thriving railway hub. Thirteen tracks dissected downtown at street-level, and at some of them, like the one at Van Dam where Dowd was crossing North Broadway, the sidewalk was unguarded by protective gates. The engineer of the regularly scheduled No. 6 train, which had been due to arrive at five twenty-five from Montreal en route to Albany with a connection to Grand Central, did not see Dowd. Nor, with the Waverly Hotel blocking his view, did Dowd see the train barreling along the tracks rounding a curve at thirty miles per hour about two blocks from the station. The engineer applied the brakes but was unable to stop before fatally striking him. An investigation determined that the train was going faster than normal. Running late, the engineer was making up for lost time.

The city fathers would belatedly celebrate Dowd's feat of "human ingenuity" at a site near his fatal accident. In his memory, though, they unwittingly added insult to injury by erecting a six-foot spherical sundial.

18

Annie Moore

Coming to America

Like many immigrants who left so much heritage behind, the lineage of Ellis Island in Upper New York Bay is ambiguous. The Dutch figured they bought it from the Native Americans in 1630 as a gift for Michiel Reyniersz Pauw, the *burgemeester* of Amsterdam and a director of the West India Company. The last private owners of what was originally known by Europeans as Little Oyster Island were the family of Samuel Ellis, a Welshman who lived in Lower Manhattan and ran a tavern for fishermen on the island.

Ellis died in 1794—four years, as it happened, after Congress, convening at Federal Hall in New York, passed the nation's first Naturalization Act, which granted citizenship to any white male who had lived in the United States for at least two years, resided for one year in the state from which he was applying, was "of good character" (not otherwise defined), and swore to support the Constitution. A century later, those standards would become more selective, involve the federal government in processing newcomers and forever link Ellis and his island in the public mind with immigration. Ellis's death triggered a protracted legal dispute with his heirs, which appeared to have finally ended in 1808. After they sold it, the state condemned it, and ceded it to the federal government for ten thousand dollars.

New York City's first official debarkation point for foreigners had opened in 1855 at the southern tip of Manhattan. Initially, it was built not to welcome foreigners but to keep them out. The ring-shaped sandstone redoubt designed by John

McComb Jr. on a tiny artificial island was christened Fort Clinton in 1811. It was equipped with a self-protective battery of twenty-nine cannons that could lob a ball up to 1.5 miles but, as military history unfolded, never needed to be fired in the city's defense. It was transformed into New York State's immigration reception station.

By the time Castle Garden, as it became known, grew obsolete and was shuttered in 1890, some eight million immigrants had been processed there. As Congress began closing the golden door, the federal government assumed jurisdiction over immigration. While a complex was being built on Ellis Island solely for the purpose of processing arrivals from abroad, immigrants were more or less welcomed temporarily at the Barge Office at the Battery. By 1875, Congress had barred convicts and prostitutes. In 1882, Chinese immigrants and, separately, any "lunatic, idiot, or any person unable to take care of himself or herself without becoming a public charge," were excluded. In 1891 those categories were augmented to weed out anyone "convicted of a felony or other infamous crime or misdemeanor involving moral turpitude, and polygamists." In 1903, a year and a half after the assassination of President William

A picture believed to be of Annie Moore, the first immigrant to set foot on Ellis Island when it opened on January 1, 1892. (Courtesy of the Family of Annie Moore)

McKinley, persons "opposed to organized government" were also barred. In all of 1891, 555,617 passenger arrivals were recorded. Among the 444,209 steerage passengers, fully 428,618 were immigrants, including 80,000 from Germany, 65,000 from Italy, 50,000 from Russia, and 36,000 from Ireland.

Most ships from overseas actually docked in Manhattan, where first- and second-class passengers disembarked. Many others had traveled in steerage—the cheapest accommodations, such as they were, just above the cargo hold (originally nearest the rudder, or steering machinery); they were ferried by steamboat or barge to Ellis Island where, between 1892 and 1954, over 12 million immigrants entered the United States. More than 120,000 were excluded, or about 1 percent; another 3,500 died there while they were being temporarily detained on the island for one reason or another.

On December 20, just before Christmas of 1891, the SS *Nevada*, a 3,150-ton steamer operated by the Guion Line, left Queenstown (now Cobh) on the south coast of county Cork, Ireland, for New York. The *Nevada* arrived in New York on New Year's Eve, in time to disembark the first- and second-class passengers, who were ferried directly to Pier 38 at West Houston Street. At ten thirty the next morning, after a signal flag on Ellis Island was dipped three times, the bulk of the passengers, who were traveling steerage, glided on bunting-festooned transfer boats from the *Nevada* to the new immigration station, just north of the Statue of Liberty, which itself had been dedicated only six years before. Despite its later symbolism as an immigrant beacon, the statue was actually conceived as a celebration of Civil War emancipation. (In Frédéric Auguste Bartholdi's original design, "Liberty Enlightening the World" is holding a broken chain and shackle in her left hand.) The statue's ultimate legacy would finally be defined by a testimonial from Emma Lazarus, a fourth-generation American whose father was a wealthy sugar refiner and whose great-great-uncle welcomed George Washington to the Jewish congregation in Newport, Rhode Island, in 1790. Her poem "The New Colossus," commissioned during a fund-raising campaign for the pedestal in 1883, was only engraved on the base twenty years later.

On January 1, 1892, Anna Moore disembarked from the side-wheeler ferryboat *John E. Moore* and officially became the first foreigner to land on the federal government's new Ellis Island immigration station. A ROSY-CHEEKED IRISH GIRL THE FIRST REGISTERED, the *Times* reported on Saturday, January 2. "Hustled ahead of a burly German by her two younger brothers and by an Irish longshoreman who shouted 'Ladies first,' Annie from County Cork was officially registered by Charles M. Hendley, the former private secretary to secretary of the treasury Windom." (The *World* identified Herman Zipki as the German and Mike Tierney as the fellow passenger who pulled him aside in the "spirit of Celtic gallantry" so that Annie could alight as the immigrant vanguard.) Curiously, the *Sun* described her more cynically as the first of the *Nevada*'s 107 passengers to enter through Ellis Island "into the land of the hustler." She was presented with a ten-dollar gold eagle by the commissioner of immigration, Colonel John B. Weber. "Is this for me to keep, sir?" she was quoted in the *Herald* as saying. She was assured that it was. "She says she will never part with it, but will always keep it as a pleasant memento of the occasion," the *Times* wrote. (How long she kept it is anyone's guess. The gold eagle, worth about three hundred in today's dollars, could easily have covered a month's rent or more.) Annie was escorted downstairs from the registration hall, where she and her brothers were greeted by her father, Matt, and their mother, Julia, whom they had not seen in three years while they were living with their father's sister in Cork.

Annie would be remembered in Brendan Graham's maudlin ballad, "Isle of Hope, Isle of Tears"—the tears conjuring up both Ireland, where immigrants, often

A picture said to be of Annie Moore, holding a child, found in a scrapbook. (Courtesy of the Family of Annie Moore)

apprehensively, left hungry family members and generations of forebears behind, and Ellis Island, where some of the tired, poor, and "wretched refuse" in particular were turned away and sent back home because of some real or perceived physical or mental incapacity or other disqualification that inspectors decided in split-second suppositions would pollute the American gene pool.

> *On the first day of January,*
> *Eighteen ninety-two,*
> *They opened Ellis Island and they let*
> *The people through.*
> *And first to cross the threshold*
> *Of that isle of hope and tears,*
> *Was Annie Moore from Ireland*
> *Who was all of fifteen years.*

Annie was described in the ballad as fifteen, one of many inaccuracies (she was seventeen) that would dog her in life and, for well over a century, in death, too. That New Year's Day, she was one of some seven hundred steerage passengers from three steamships who disembarked at Ellis Island. Those destined for local addresses were transported to a slip alongside the Barge Office in Manhattan on the ferryboat *J. H. Brinckerhoff,* where they were left to proceed on their own. In Annie's case, she headed to her parents' already cramped apartment in a five-story tenement at 32 Monroe Street on the Lower East Side.

What appeared to have happened next would become the stuff of legend. Like most legends, especially those that seem at first blush to be plausible, compelling, and indisputable, this one took on a life of its own. Supposedly, Annie and her family heeded Horace Greeley's advice and went west. She reached Texas, married a descendant of the Irish liberator Daniel O'Connell, and then died tragically in 1923, at forty-six, in an accident under the wheels of a streetcar near Fort Worth. "It's a classic 'go-West-young-woman' tale riddled with tragedy," the genealogist Megan Smolenyak said. "If only it were true."

In 2006, though, Smolenyak determined that historians had arrogated the wrong Annie Moore. The Annie who died instantly in the streetcar accident was not the first immigrant to set foot on Ellis Island. She was not an immigrant at all; she had been born in Illinois, and with her family moved to Texas as early as 1880. But the tale had been implanted so solidly in the folkloric firmament that descendants of the Texan Annie Moore came to believe it themselves. They were even recruited as props for commemorations on Ellis Island and in Ireland.

Debunking the foundational myth of Annie Moore, the immigrant, was just the first step. Finding the genuine Annie took some tenacious genealogical detective work. Smolenyak teamed up with New York City's commissioner of records, Brian G. Andersson, to retrace the real Annie's route from the Ellis Island ferry. First Andersson located the naturalization certificate belonging to Annie's brother Philip, who arrived with her on the *Nevada*. Philip was also listed in the 1930 census with a daughter, Anna. That identification led to Anna's son, who is Annie Moore's great-nephew. "As soon as I said 'Annie Moore,' he knew instantly—'That's us,'" Smolenyak said. "They had been overlooked, but they had sort of resigned themselves."

The real Annie Moore initially joined her parents in a row of squalid tenements where mortality from natural causes far exceeded the combined total inflicted by vehicles of any sort. The death rate for residents with Irish-born mothers was about three times higher than for those whose mothers were born in America. Her brother Anthony, who also arrived on the *Nevada*, died in his twenties in the Bronx. He was temporarily buried in Potter's Field, the resting place for the anonymous poor on Hart Island in Long Island Sound. Annie's father was a longshoreman. In 1895 Annie married Joseph Schayer, the son of a German-born baker. With her husband, variously identified as an engineer and salesman at the Fulton Fish Market, she had at least eleven children. Five of them survived to adulthood.

For three decades Annie struggled like other poor immigrants within a few congested square blocks on the Lower East Side's notorious Fourth Ward. In *Al Smith and His America* (1958), the historian Oscar Handlin described the slums sandwiched between New York City Hall and the East River as "a motley array of tenements, of converted warehouses, of dwellings in every stage of repair and decay, and of shacks and shanties." Health Department maps would pinpoint offensive privies, uninhabitable buildings, houses where typhoid fever or smallpox had been discovered. In *New York* magazine Jesse Green recited a roll call of locations, some since vanished, where Annie and her family searched within severely circumscribed boundaries for what James Truslow Adams, at the start of the Great Depression, would call the American Dream. They moved from place to place on the Lower East Side: "*Rutgers Street*, where the couple set up home and where their first known child, William, died at age 20 months in 1898. *New Chambers Street*, where the 1900 census found them living with daughter Catherine and son Joseph Jr. *Oliver Street*, their home for more than a decade, where Theodore and Julia were born and Winifred, Walter, and Edward died at, respectively, three months, three years, and three days of age. Finally, *Cherry Street*, where Mary Anne was born; where Henry, Annie's last known child, died in 1919; and where Annie herself died in 1924—so fat, says a family story, that firemen could not carry her down the stairs. They had to haul her out the window."

Annie Moore died of heart failure at 99 Cherry Street. She was fifty, having lived eight years longer than the average for someone born in Ireland the same year she was, and four years longer than the Texas Annie. One of her granddaughters remained in the neighborhood as a public housing project tenant until she died in 2001. Today, two blocks away, apartments in a new condominium tower sell for an average price of $2.5 million and rent for $8,800 monthly. Annie was buried near six of her eleven children in an unmarked grave in Calvary Cemetery in Woodside, Queens. In 2008, with contributions from her newfound relatives and from Commissioner Andersson, a limestone Celtic cross, imported from Ireland, was dedicated during a ceremony at which the tenor Ronan Tynan sang "Isle of Hope, Isle of Tears."

Rectifying the legend of Annie Moore after more than a century turned out to be a rare case in which historical revisionism enhanced a legacy instead of subverting it. As one guidebook says: "Annie Moore came to America bearing little more than her dreams; she stayed to help build a country enriched by diversity." Annie and her brothers "truly became prototypical New Yorkers, with lives and families inextricably linked to the New York immigrant experience," Tyler Anbinder wrote in *City of Dreams: The 400-Year Epic History of Immigrant New York* (2016). She may not have fulfilled the American dream, but many of her progeny did. Today, her descendants and her brothers include representatives from many other leading New York City immigrant groups—Italian, Eastern European Jew, Chinese, Dominican. "It's an all-American family," Megan Smolenyak said. "Annie would have been proud."

19

Andrew H. Green

Brooklyn's Great Mistake

B y the end of 1868, fifteen years after construction of Central Park began, the
park's commissioners proudly quantified their progress on the still uncom-
pleted urban sanctuary. In the preceding twelve months alone, the commissioners
boasted in their annual report, the park had hosted almost 7 million visitors (3.1
million pedestrians, 71,000 on horseback, and two each on 1.3 million carriage
rides). Construction had been completed on the Children's Cottage and on two
additional birdhouses. The assessed valuation of private property adjoining the
park had soared 15 percent (and had nearly quadrupled in a decade). George
Armstrong Custer's Seventh Cavalry Regiment had donated an American buffalo
to the zoo, eight years before the Battle of the Little Bighorn. Wool sheared from
the eponymous inhabitants of the Sheep Meadow had generated $207.74 in
revenue; 4,286 cartloads of manure had been collected; 6,876 trees had been
planted; and the most arrests by far were merely for speeding.

Those factoids may have been gripping to anyone farsighted enough to figure that
the 840 acres that the city fathers had presciently reserved for the public in the middle
of John Randel Jr.'s grid would become the most heavily used park in the country.
Chances are, though, few readers would have been riveted enough to reach appendix
H on page 148 of the report. Had they gotten that far, they would have happened
upon just a hint of the visionary strategy that would guarantee the growing city's
hegemony through the twentieth century and into the twenty-first. But appendix

H, innocuously titled "Communication of the Comptroller of the Park," could easily have been overlooked. Perhaps it was deliberately intended to be soft-pedaled at the time, so as to place its modest proposal irradicably on the record without triggering too great a backlash or implying that its author was overstepping his mandate.

Containing its author's conceit was another matter, though, when New York City—largely meaning Manhattan at the time—emerged from the Civil War with a booming manufacturing and commercial economy and as a magnet for immigrants. Its population remained preeminent (closing in on one million in 1870, with Philadelphia second at about 675,000 and Brooklyn, a proudly separate city, ranked third with 400,000). If, as early as the 1830s, the *Tribune*'s Horace Greeley had advised ambitious young men to "Go West," by the late 1860s he was championing New York as the place to succeed instead. The city, Greeley predicted, was becoming the center, "as it should be, of industrial as well as commercial greatness in the New World and ultimately in the whole world." New York and London had just been connected by cable. Appendix H hinted at connections closer to home, to links that would bind Manhattan physically and legally to mainland America, to Brooklyn, to the burgeoning villages in Queens County and even across the bay to Staten Island so that New York City would have ample room and resources to grow and to fulfill Greeley's hometown version of manifest destiny.

Appendix H received virtually no press coverage; it was largely disregarded by the public and even by most government officials. Yet the very first sentence should have alerted any reader who had persevered to that point that this appendix was the opposite of a vestigial tangent. Certain matters had "come to be practically important, and call for distinct notice and specific consideration," appendix H stated plainly enough. And while the man who was calling for "distinct notice" to those matters, the comptroller of the park, had never been elevated to high office by the voters and had no discernible constituency of his own, he was nobody to be trifled with. Not when he was declaring that he had something "practically important" to say.

That man, Andrew Haswell Green, was born in Worcester, Massachusetts, in 1820, a seventh-generation American descended from the Pilgrims and supposedly with ancestral links to Shakespeare, Milton, and Benjamin Woodbridge, the first graduate of Harvard College. He was the fifth of nine children by his father's third wife.

A diligent reader, he had only a few months of formal education and couldn't afford college. When he was barely a teenager, in 1835, he and his older sister embarked for New York by steamboat from the family home at Green Hill, not so much to make his fortune as to make a living. He was hired as an errand boy and worked his

"Portrait of Andrew H. Green," from A Volume Commemorating the Creation of the Second City of the World *(New York: Republic Press, 1898), 23.*

way up to clerk for a linen importer. Thanks to a family friend, he was deployed to Trinidad as deputy overseer on a sugar plantation. Thwarted after a year in his efforts to improve production and to uplift the recently emancipated Black population by instilling Christianity, he returned to New York frustrated by the resistance of local planters and priests, but more fundamentally by the attitude of newly emancipated Trinidadian Black people. Green invoked a revealing adjective to denigrate their nature: "indolent," which means not easily aroused to work or to action, a racist characterization that years later—at least in the case of one impassioned Black man—he would come to regret.

"I like New York much better than I thought before I came," Green wrote his father in 1838. He taught at the voguish girls' school run by two of his sisters at 1 Fifth Avenue, then read law with an attorney who was another family friend, and soon partnered with Samuel J. Tilden, the lawyer son of a manufacturer of medicinal cannabis, and a future governor and presidential candidate, in what would become a lifelong professional, personal, and political association. While Green's own brief classroom experience ended when he was only thirteen, his commitment to public education was manifest. Perhaps inspired by Tilden, whose Democratic political connections had already led to the job of city corporation counsel and his election as a state legislator, Green rose in rapid succession from a school trustee in the Fourth Ward downtown to a member of the newly empowered board of education in 1855, and to presidency of the board less than three years later.

As board president, Green would seek to insulate the public school system from Protestant parochialism and Tammany politics and to protect teachers' tenure. He also pioneered a refrain that would become a perennial battle cry when city officials ritually traipsed, hat in hand, to Albany: that New York City taxpayers routinely contribute more to the state's tax coffers than they get back in school aid. The presidency of the board also endowed Green, given his responsibility for school building, with the beginnings of what he would develop into a pharaonic stewardship over public works in the late nineteenth century, which he performed with the gusto and gamut that evokes the power-brokering of Robert Moses in the twentieth.

In 1857, when Green was only thirty-seven, he was named a commissioner of what was still referred to as *the* Central Park. Its area (about eight hundred acres) and grid-blotting boundaries had only just been decided. While some feared that the park would be overrun by rowdies and rabble, others bemoaned the prospect of it winding up as a gated playground reserved for boulevardiers and carriage travelers. A coalition of Common Council members, apparently seeking to bridge the class divide (and perhaps inspiring the patina of noblesse oblige perpetrated most conspicuously a generation later by the Bradley-Martin family), wrote, "It is useless to raise the cry, that by surrounding the park with magnificent dwellings, we thereby array the wealthy against the poorer classes; that beautiful drives, so inviting to the carriage of the wealthy, inspires ought else than pleasing thoughts to the more humble, they delight in viewing magnificent and imposing structures, and in being employed in their construction. We should, therefore, not only present but encourage the affluent to expend their surplus funds in the erection of villas, and giving employment to the poor, and induce the opulent to surround the park, that will be the pride of the city, with their superb edifices."

The *Real Estate Record*, inspired by Napoleon III's two-decade reinvention of the French capital, had demanded "a Haussmann who will do for New York what that great re-constructor did for Paris." Green (an apt surname for a parks planner) was not only against suggestions to shrink Central Park so as to squeeze more property tax revenue and profit from developing the real estate adjoining it, he enlarged it. Frederick Law Olmsted, the landscape architect, groused that Green was a micromanager who literally left no stone unturned in constructing the park, which, while calculated to look natural, was largely man-made. Olmsted was awed, though, by what he called the "politico-commercial alliances" that Green forged to hurdle what had seemed like insurmountable obstructions to getting the greensward approved, funded, and finished. "No one but Green," Olmsted acknowledged, "knows, or will take the trouble to inform himself, of the facts bearing on any question of policy sufficiently to argue on it effectually."

As if serving variously as president, treasurer, and comptroller of the Central Park Commission weren't enough, Green was also drafted into the war against municipal corruption in 1871 thanks to Tilden, Charles O'Conor, and former mayor William Havemeyer. Reformers were playing a perilous game: they wanted to rid New York City of the unscrupulous Democratic machine run by Tammany Hall without besmirching other Democratic Party candidates for state and federal office. First, they insinuated Green by appointment as a deputy city comptroller, then promoted him over his ostensible boss, the machine-made Richard B. Connolly, who finally resigned as comptroller on November 18, 1871 and was arrested a week later.

To the colleagues that Connolly left behind, the threat suddenly posed by scrupulous bookkeeping was clear. Green had to be escorted to work by a phalanx of mounted police officers. Naturally, he made enemies just by accepting the job, but he courted more by his attitude—imperious, impatient, and sanctimonious. "He kept few friends while gaining many admirers," Thomas Kessner wrote in *Capital City* (2003). Self-deprecation was so alien to his nature that his audience was stunned when he once humorously recalled his first case as a "young and bumptious" defense lawyer. With utmost confidence, he recalled jokingly, he rose to make several motions. "Each was overruled by the judge as soon as made, and on entirely just grounds, as I have since come to see. I then began a laboriously-prepared address.

" 'Your honor,' I commenced, 'my unfortunate client—'

" 'There the court is with you,' the judge interjected."

Green was relentless. He systematically exposed graft and installed safeguards against what he preferred to call "peculation." Invoices that had been blindly approved were suddenly rejected wholesale. Bills were presumed fraudulent unless proven otherwise. Green disallowed a $72,000 claim from James Gordon Bennett for printing official city notices in the *New York Herald* after discovering that the bill included $18,398 for publishing one of Mayor Hall's speeches verbatim as news, but charged for it as advertising at $1 a line, $0.60 more than the going commercial rate. He refused to honor a street paving bill at $6 per square yard that the same contractor had bid at $4.07 in Newark and which was won by another firm for $2.87.

Green disallowed a claim of nearly $1 million for water meters "not used, but alleged to have been furnished to the city under special contract" with commissioner of public works William M. Tweed. He slashed the street lighting bill from $841,036.41 to $237,234.44 for ten months in 1871 after conducting his own inventory, which found that 235 of the lights that the city had been paying for didn't exist, and another 339 were illuminating the homes of politicians, political clubs, saloons, and other private properties. He also stumbled upon what appeared to be another perversion of the city's personnel requirements: a sewer inspector who met most of the job qualifications—except that he was legally blind.

By the early 1870s Green's power in municipal government had transcended even his two official titles, as formidable as they were. As comptroller, he ranked second to the mayor but wielded absolute discretion over the city's purse strings, subject only to judicial second-guessing by injunction and protracted appeals. Other officials could appropriate all the money they wanted for pet projects; Green decided whether it actually got spent and who got paid for past performance. He withheld the salaries of the board of aldermen, arguing successfully that they were not entitled to double-dip and collect separate pay as county supervisors just because New York was uniquely both a city and a county.

His notorious tight-fistedness, after the Tweed ring's unbridled profligacy, delayed reimbursements to exasperated legitimate contractors and clogged the court system but saved the city government a fortune. "Two rules guided his public priorities," Thomas Kessner wrote. "The first was to hold on to every penny of public money as if it were an only child ('extravagantly penurious' wrote the *Times*). Incongruously, his second rule was to cast New York as an expansive, efficiently designed and majestically arranged commercial metropolis." Even Olmsted, who tangled with Green over his punctiliousness, grudgingly admitted, "Not a cent is got from under his paw that is not wet with his blood and sweat."

Despite all the money that Green spared New York taxpayers, he meticulously dissected the municipality's expenses as if it were solely a legal corporation and not a body politic. "What is perhaps most amazing, in view of his deep interest and participation in the cause of municipal reform," George A. Mazaraki wrote in *The Public Career of Andrew Haswell Green* (1966), "is his total silence on such issues as tenements, slums, sweatshops or any other of the many human problems created by the

city." Barry J. Kaplan, in *Andrew H. Green and the Creation of a Planning Rationale*
(1996) described him as "essentially a 'structural reformer' concerned with institutions, procedures, and moral abstractions rather than social needs."

Green's titles at the Central Park Commission (which by 1870 had been renamed
the Department of Public Parks) belied his broad mandate, much as Robert Moses
would later transcend his official role, putatively confined to a solely recreational
agenda. Even before the boundaries of the Central Park were finally ratified, the
commission's authority extended well beyond its geographic borders. In 1865, as
the commission's comptroller, Green visualized the development of the entire
Upper West Side, beginning from Fifty-Ninth Street. His conceit stretched to
Washington Heights and the very northern tip of Manhattan to cleave crosstown
streets through the bluffs that bordered the Harlem River. "Green, viewing the park
board's mission as analogous to that of the 1811 Street Commission that laid out

The
Second City of the World

New York

January 1
1898

Title page to A Volume Commemorating the
Creation of the Second City of the World
(New York: Republic Press, 1898), 1.

Manhattan's grid," Roy Rosenzweig and Elizabeth Blackmar wrote in *The Park and the People* (1992), "had little doubt that a well-planned city required the overarching intelligence of 'a single mind or a single interest'—his own."

Green's power as comptroller peaked in 1874. John Kelly, the fiscally conservative former congressman and sheriff, had succeeded Tweed to become the first Catholic boss of Tammany, having earned the sobriquet "Honest John" by comparison. (He nonetheless left an estate valued at about $500,000, although his defenders said much of that originated in fees he collected legally as sheriff.) Kelly revived the machine by wooing Irish workingmen while continuing to placate the business establishment, and with labor's support regained the trust of immigrants by restoring the city's most reliable relief program: regular distribution of holiday turkeys and buckets of coal.

In March 1876 the state assembly rejected an appeal from a group of merchants and bankers to extend Green's term as comptroller for another five years. The following October, though, he accepted the nomination for mayor on the Reform ticket offered by delegates of the Independent Citizens' Party and the German-American Independent Organization. But hopes for a fusion candidacy collapsed when the Republicans decided to go their own way. With the election less than a week away, on November 1, Reform Democrats feared that an independent candidacy might jeopardize New York governor Samuel J. Tilden's presidential campaign. Persuaded that the Republican alternatives for municipal offices were even worse than Tammany's, they urged Green to withdraw. He did so, with characteristic humility. He could not imagine a "more flattering recognition of my success in vindicating the independence which Municipal administration ought to sustain to party politics," he wrote the short-lived coalition, than his nomination by a venerable group divided in their opinions on issues but "thoroughly agreed as to the vital necessity of selecting municipal officers solely on grounds of capacity, experience, and honesty."

Green, the visionary, somehow could not see beyond the detritus the bosses had left to cultivate some of the ambitious if Tammany-tainted projects he had seeded with the Central Park commissioners in the late 1860s. Still, he indisputably endowed a legacy of institutional reform that elevated the city government's financial and ethical values. "In the city government, as Mr. Green left it," wrote John Foord, who was instrumental in the *New York Times*'s exposé of the Tweed ring, in 1913, "there were at least the beginnings of new standards of public responsibility, and new conceptions of civic virtue, that in spite of manifold disappointments and reverses have, in the last 37 years, grown from more to more."

Though Green might be faulted for placing moral bromides ahead of pragmatic responses to social demands, his Central Park would be nonetheless a people's park, if accessible only to those who comported themselves according to the commissioners' definition of acceptable behavior. Anyone deemed to be "in a filthy condition" would be removed. Fortune-telling, indecent language, and throwing stones were prohibited. Again presaging Moses in the twentieth century, Green envisioned something much greater than any individual project, whether it was the repaving of a street downtown crudely surfaced by a Tammany contractor in wooden planks that had already rotted in less than three years, or blasting through granite to create his eight hundred acre, man-made park in the middle of Manhattan that would be almost twice the size of Monaco.

Unlike Moses, as Kessner wrote in *Capital City*, Green had the advantage of working "on a nearly empty canvas," so he could fulfill his dreams without doing much harm. Georges-Eugène Haussmann bulldozed a city to build his Paris, and Chicago created a vibrant downtown thanks, in part, to Mrs. O'Leary's cow. "New York had no Napoleon, had suffered no transforming conflagration," Kessner wrote. "What it had was Andrew Haswell Green, and over the 40-year period following the Civil War, no New Yorker gave more serious or more systematic thought to the direction of urban development than he did."

On the surface, Green's appendix H, the "practically important" communication to the Central Park Commission in 1868, was a meticulous analysis of the number of bridges that eventually would be needed to span the Harlem River and connect New York County with southern Westchester in what is now the Bronx. Reading between the lines, though, Green's analysis was presumptuous on two grounds: geographically, it leapt miles beyond the northern boundaries of Central Park itself; and politically, it implied that the process of dredging the river and building the bridges linking northern Manhattan with the Westchester towns that would become the Bronx be conducted jointly by a single jurisdiction, auguring the consolidation of New York County (Manhattan) and what was then southern Westchester into Greater New York. As subtle as it was, Green was sounding his first lonely cry for what would come to be called consolidation and would define his career. How could any master plan be complete, Green asked incredulously, without extending Manhattan's major arteries across the Harlem River (which shriveled in places to a muddy ditch and was navigable end-to-end only by rowboat) and the Spuyten Duyvil Creek (like the river itself, an estuary) into lower Westchester, and without linking New York with Brooklyn and Queens on Long Island?

Green even calculated that to match the number of links that existed across the Thames in London and the Seine in Paris, New York would need twenty-two to thirty bridges respectively, connecting the two shorelines between the Battery on the south and Wards Island on the north, although the East River at its narrowest is as wide as the Thames at its broadest. Rather than barriers, he viewed the rivers as "the means by which communities meet and mingle," arteries of an indissoluble natural network. In 1883, Emma Lazarus's poem "The New Colossus" would describe "the air-bridged harbor that twin cities frame." Brooklyn and Manhattan were fraternal twins, of course, not identical. Green wanted them to be conjoined retroactively.

"It is not intended now," Green wrote in 1868, "to do more than direct attention to the important subject of bringing the City of New York and the County of Kings, a part of Westchester County and a part of Queens and Richmond . . . under one common municipal government, to be arranged in departments under a single executive head." (Kings included the City of Brooklyn and several towns, which it annexed by 1896; Queens was comprised of Long Island City and other local jurisdictions; Richmond was contiguous with Staten Island; New York County included part of what became the Bronx borough in 1898 and county in 1914.) Still, he added, "can anyone doubt that this question will force itself upon the public attention at no very distant period?" He unambiguously volunteered what he considered the obvious answer: "All progress points towards eventual consolidation and unity of administration," he wrote. "The disadvantage of an incongruous and disjointed authority over communities that are striving by all material methods that the skill of man can devise to become one, will be more and more apparent, and the small jealousies and petty interests that seek to keep them separated will be less and less effectual."

The process was jump-started just a year later when the legislature expanded the commission's planning authority to what would become the Bronx. In 1874, after a referendum in Westchester and Green's prediction that the Harlem River might even emerge as New York City's geographic center, Albany lawmakers approved the city's annexation of the Towns of Morrisania, West Farms, and Kingsbridge west of the Bronx River. (The Town of Westchester and part of Eastchester, east of the river, were annexed in 1895.) Annexation integrated the city politically with the American continent for the first time. Legally grafting the city's boundaries to include mainland America increased New York's size by about half, from fourteen thousand acres to twenty-one thousand, and its population by forty thousand.

In 1869, a year after Green issued appendix H, construction began on another project that would inevitably lead to the creation of Greater New York. Green was one of the original incorporators of the private New York Bridge Company, chartered in 1867. He was also one of the eight pallbearers two years later when John A. Roebling, the chief engineer, died, and his wife and son inherited the monumental challenge to redeem his legacy. In 1884, the first full year that the Brooklyn Bridge was operating, twelve million people crossed the span. "Only Connect!" became Green's credo decades before it was embraced by E. M. Forster.

Events leisurely but ineluctably advanced Green's agenda. In 1886 Henry George's second-place finish for mayor on his radical reform platform terrified the New York business community, which now saw that its salvation lay in broadening the voter pool by enlisting more conservative Brooklynites. In 1888, just in time to celebrate the centennial of the first president's inauguration, Green established another littoral link between Manhattan and the expanded municipality on the mainland with the opening of the 2,375-foot-long Washington Bridge across the Harlem River, connecting Washington Heights in Manhattan and the continental United States. By the early 1890s, New York ranked third in population among world cities, behind only London and Paris. Consolidation would have put New York in second place. Bragging rights, and the concomitant impact on economic development and culture, was one goal of numerical superiority; necessity was another. London in 1890 had a density of eleven people per acre. In Philadelphia, it was twelve. In New York, it was about fifty-nine. "New-York is full to-day, with no allowance for the demands of to-morrow," the *Times* concluded. That same year, the city's ego would be dealt a giant psychological blow. Dreams of a Greater New York were suddenly punctured by a lesser reality: Chicago, having just supplanted Philadelphia in population to become the nation's proverbial Second City, was selected by Congress as the site of the World's Columbian Exhibition to celebrate the quadricentennial of the explorer's voyage.

In 1889, when Chicago began lobbying for the World's Columbian Exposition (and gaining on New York for first place), Green devised a seemingly innocuous new vehicle to advance his grail of a Greater New York. A March 11 *New York Times* editorial outlined what looked like a baby step but was in fact Green's first official footfall on the course to municipal consolidation. It landed in the state legislature in the guise of a bill to create a twelve-member "inquiry commission" to determine whether consolidation was a practical means of generating economic growth in the region, or merely Green's personal hobbyhorse.

The commission would be made up of the state engineer; one member each designated by the mayors of Brooklyn and New York and the board of supervisors of Westchester, Kings, Queens, and Richmond Counties; and five specifically named individuals: Frederic W. Devoe, New York City's commissioner of public schools; John Foord, the former *Times* editor who was also a founder of India House, the club for promoters of foreign commerce; J. S. T. Stranahan, a former congressman and champion of Prospect Park, the Brooklyn Bridge, and consolidation; Calvert Vaux, the landscape designer and Olmsted's mentor; and Green himself. The legislation breezed through the assembly but died in the senate at the hands of Brooklynites, abetted by an Upper Manhattan real estate lobby that feared the competition from large tracts of undeveloped property in Kings County that consolidation would necessarily deliver.

In 1890, the legislation was resurrected, to vigorous opposition. "Not only is the consolidation bill fatally defective from the point of view of local self-government," the *Brooklyn Eagle* thundered, "but it commits the question to a packed commission." Sparing no sarcasm, its editors wrote that while the consolidation advocates "do not go so far with the divine assurance of celestial felicity as to tell us in the words of the scriptures, that, 'there shall be no more night there,' they seek by implication at least, to persuade us that under the new conditions our happiness will be complete. What more, to be sure, could Brooklyn ask than to be taken under the sheltering wing of Tammany Hall; to be brought into wholesome juxtaposition with the uplifting influences of the Bowery, Mott Street and Mulberry Bend." The paper saw right through Green's claim that the inquiry commission was merely satisfying its curiosity about consolidation. And indeed, although it would take nearly a decade of legislative jujitsu, Green had figured out how to sidestep a direct, binding referendum by the voters on combining the two cities along with other nearby unincorporated areas, villages, towns, cities, and the County of Richmond.

Green portrayed the bill as merely a technical ratification of geography. "The first step towards union of our peoples here," he wrote in a thirty-two-page brief to the legislature, "was taken when nature grouped together in close indissoluble relation, at the mouth of a great river, our three islands, Manhattan, Long and Staten, making them buttresses and breakwaters of a capacious harbor." (Actually, tapping into New York City's potable water supply was one real incentive for Brooklynites.) If natural law were not persuasive enough, Green appealed to people's pocketbooks and to the optimism epitomized by progress, rallying consolidationists in what he framed as an encounter "between the retreating forces of the tribal system and the competing forces of the cooperative system, between barbaric tradition and educated aspiration."

This time the bill passed. On June 3, 1890, the new commission elected Green as its president. It couched its stated mission carefully: Manhattan would not annex its neighbors, but unite them. Thus, after conducting its preliminary inquiry, it put the question to the voters in 1894 in what it claimed was "nothing more than a simple expression of opinion." It was true that the results were not legally binding, but, as the *Eagle* predicted, they would belie the commission's pretense that "if every ballot in a city or town were cast in favor of consolidation there would be no finality about it." The vote galvanized both sides of the debate, particularly in Brooklyn, where the state legislature was accused by local loyalists of a new kind of crime, "civicide," its intended victim a distinct municipality "in which the native-born population is distinctly in the majority, with American notions and American principles and institutions reigning."

The consolidation vote coincided with the November 1894 municipal elections, which swept out the Tammany mayor Hugh Grant in New York and elevated William L. Strong, a millionaire Republican dry goods merchant and banker topping the Fusion Party ticket. Consolidation carried in Manhattan by 96,938 to 59,959; in Queens, by 7,712 to 4,741; in Richmond (Staten Island) by 7,041 to 5,531; and in East Chester and Pelham. The referendum failed only in Flushing and in the Town of Westchester, where it was defeated by a single vote, 620 to 621. The big question mark, of course, was Brooklyn, where the initial returns strained credulity. The referendum was defeated within the City of Brooklyn itself, exclusive of the Kings County towns, by 61,443 to 62,477, but passed overall in Kings County by a suspiciously small margin of 277 (64,744 in favor of consolidation; 64,467 against).

The Reverend Richard S. Storrs, pastor of the Church of the Pilgrims in Brooklyn, wondered aloud whether good government would be possible within a vast, heterogenous population—an incongruous commingling of Brooklyn, where, he said, two thirds of the residents were "born on American soil and trained from childhood in American traditions," and Manhattan, which was distinguished by a disproportionate number of immigrants who epitomize "the political sewage of Europe" and are "profoundly ignorant of our customs and laws or profoundly opposed to both" and a government "in the hands of crafty and mercenary leaders of the ignorant or unscrupulous rabble."

In Albany, the craftiest leader of them all at the time was Thomas C. Platt, the Republican boss and former (and future) U.S. senator. But even Platt was unable to ram through Green's version of consolidation during the 1895 legislative session. The bill was doomed by a telegram from Brooklyn mayor Charles A. Schieren, vowing a veto.

As the 1896 session approached, with Republicans in control of both Brooklyn and Queens, Platt was more primed than ever. Green, too, was getting impatient, going so far as to accuse Brooklynites who placed their local civic pride ahead of the greater good of being guilty of "senile sentimentalism." Pleading not guilty, William C. Redfield, a steel and iron manufacturer and secretary of the League of Loyal Citizens of Brooklyn reminded Green that the 1894 vote was supposed to have been "a simple expression of opinion," and that in any case, those results were inconclusive at best.

In March 1896, ignoring pleas for another popular vote, the legislature disingenuously seized on the results of the nonbinding 1894 referendum as a license to officially proclaim Greater New York. Dreaming of a Republican-dominated city to check Tammany's hegemony, Platt rammed through a consolidation bill that passed the state senate 38–8 and the assembly 91–56. Mayors Strong of New York and Frederick W. Wurster of Brooklyn, both vetoed the bill. Strong believed that consolidation was inevitable but quibbled over the particulars. Wurster, a Republican, was unequivocal: "Until a bill shall be prepared defining the terms and conditions of consolidation, which shall be submitted to the people for approval or rejection, I cannot feel that justice will be done to this city."

Platt engineered a legislative override (by 34 to 14 in the Senate; and by 78 to 69, only two votes more than needed and thanks for them to Tammany, in the Assembly). The bill was signed by the newly minted Republican governor Levi P. Morton of Manhattan. Green, who was naturally named to the commission responsible for drafting a charter for the consolidated city, immediately sought out the Republican boss. "Bubbling over with joy, that venerable patriot grasped me by the hand," Platt recalled in his memoir, "and exclaimed: 'I came in to express my gratitude to the Father of the Greater New York.' As I returned his grip, I could not refrain from saying: 'And I desire to express my appreciation of the marvelous devotion and work of the Grandfather of the Greater New York.'" Were it not for Green, the *New York Sun* declared, "it is not too much to say, there would have been no Greater New York in this generation." The *Sun* went so far as to suggest at the beginning of 1897 that Green was "the fittest man" to be Greater New York's first mayor.

The mayoral boomlet was short-lived. Green was ailing, too ill even to attend a boisterous combined New Year's Eve and consolidation celebration at New York City Hall in Lower Manhattan. In Brooklyn, at the fifty-year-old Greek Revival monument to civic pride that, beginning the next day, would be demoted from city hall of the nation's fourth largest municipality to just another borough hall, a subdued observance marked what already was being mocked in Brooklyn as the Great Mistake.

"Calmly and with dignity," the *Eagle* reported, "Brooklyn passed from the state as an independent city into Greater New York." The main orator, St. Clair McKelway, whose editorials in the *Eagle* had raged against consolidation, made the best of it. He forecast "the Brooklynization of New York," rather than vice versa, and noted that at least the imperial borough had retained its own name, unlike its bridegroom across the East River. "If we are its annex, it is our suburb," McKelway said. "It is no longer New York. It is Manhattan and the Bronx" (meaning that Manhattan would no longer have a monopoly on the name New York, although even Brooklynites would still refer to it augustly as "the City"). The ceremonies in Brooklyn ended with a somber elegy written and delivered by its adopted son, the poet Will Carleton. Titled "The Passing of Brooklyn," it concluded more upbeat than it began:

> *Thousands of cities have stood in my seeing,*
> *Never a one had more right to its being:*
> *None in my heart has e'er clambered above you;*
> *Both for your faults and your virtues I love you.*
> *This is not death; though a life-link be broken,*
> *Still, shall your sweet name forever be spoken.*
> *This not death, but a second creation:*
> *Greater New York is your new incarnation!*

Just across the river, Manhattanites caroused unambivalently (revelry that the *Eagle* relegated to page 5). The stinging December rain by no means dampened the rapturous prose of a *Times* reporter who ended his 190-word lead sentence on the January 1, 1888, front page by describing the "many flash lights throwing their long shafts of white everywhere, intersecting each other, making eccentric evolutions in the darkness, and finally concentrating in one great glare" as "the flag of Greater New York was officially unfurled over the New York City Hall at midnight by a touch of a button by the Mayor of San Francisco, 3,700 miles away, and the second city of the world"—behind London, that is—"came into existence."

The ten-week war with Spain was over, but since a formal peace treaty still had not been signed by October 6, 1898, Green's seventy-eighth birthday was celebrated with a more subdued ceremony at city hall. "It may be appropriately be said," Municipal Council president Randolph Guggenheimer declared, "in the words of the familiar quotation, 'Si monumentum quaeris, circumspice'—if you seek his monument, look about you." General Stewart L. Woodford, a former congressman and colleague of Green's on the Charter Commission, declared that "to this dream of the greater city he adhered so resolutely and for its realization he labored so wisely and so untiringly that now, the first autumn of its completion, it is just to salute our friend, as we do this day, as 'The Father of Greater New York.'"

Consolidation had been augured inauspiciously with the 1897 election of Robert Van Wyck, a Tammany stalwart and former judge, as the first mayor of Greater New York. Two years later Van Wyck was disgraced by revelations that he'd managed to acquire some $700,000 worth of stock in the American Ice Company, which, granted a monopoly over ice in the city by Tammany appointees, planned to double its price to consumers.

By 1903, five years after consolidation, the total population of Greater New York (which combined Manhattan and the Bronx with the City of Brooklyn, Long Island City, and the towns and villages of western Queens and Staten Island to form the five boroughs) topped 3.6 million. As immigrants flooded the city, density grew to roughly two hundred people per acre in Manhattan—well beyond the fifty-nine that the *Times* had estimated a decade earlier. The gap between rich and poor was widening; violent crime also began to register an uptick. Precise comparative statistics on murders were hard to come by, but according to one measure, arrests for homicide were higher than in any of the other ten largest cities in the United States, at 13.9 per 100,000. In April 1903, even with eight months still left on the calendar, it seemed as if nothing would outrank the so-called Barrel Murder—a dismembered body stabbed eighteen times was found stuffed inside a wooden sugar drum in Manhattan's Little Italy—as the most horrific crime of the year. On the seismic scale of sensational murders, no crime had come close—until Friday, November 13, 1903.

By his ninth decade, Andrew H. Green had become largely an éminence grise of municipal government, confining himself to largely personal and his own professional affairs. He still commuted between his office at 214 Broadway at the southern tip of City Hall Park and his home at 91 Park Avenue, a three-and-a-half story town house between East Thirty-Ninth and Fortieth Streets, just south of the French Renaissance Grand Central Depot. On that Friday afternoon, November 13, Green left his office opposite St. Paul's Chapel around one P.M. He boarded an uptown Fourth Avenue streetcar to East Thirty-Eighth Street to join two of the three nieces and one nephew who lived with him. It was sunny and in the fifties, slightly warmer than average for mid-November. At one thirty-five P.M., as he reached the iron railing that defined the front of his town house, a neatly dressed mustachioed stranger, about five foot eight, confronted him and demanded to know the whereabouts of Bessie Davis, a woman who, the man claimed, had him dispossessed from his West Side apartment a year before.

"Who are you, anyway?" Green demanded. "I don't know you. Get away from me." Anne Bray, who worked as a servant for Green, overheard the conversation as she passed. By the time Bray reached the front door of the town house, she heard a shot. Then the man fired four more. Three struck Green. He lay mortally wounded in front of the house, just inside the iron railing. His assailant, who later identified himself as Cornelius M. Williams, made no attempt to flee. Completely calm and self-possessed, he stood over the body, still gripping the revolver. "He deserved it," Williams told a police officer who rushed to the scene. "He forced me to do it." Green was carried into the house, but by the time a doctor arrived, the Father of Greater New York, as he would be described in every news account of the murder, was dead. He was eighty-three.

Before Williams was known by name, he was universally described by two characteristics: he was identified as a Black man and he was assumed to be insane. The acting captain in charge of the East Thirty-Fifth Street police station asked Williams directly whether he had ever been certified as mentally ill. "I have been called foolish sometimes," Williams replied sensibly, "but never insane." Reporters on the scene made their own diagnoses. "While he was telling his story, however," the *Times* wrote, "he kept twitching nervously at his moustache, and his eyes, which were spoken of by everybody who saw them as being queer, rolled continuously."

But Williams's delusions, such as they were, were not completely unfounded. In 1895 he had fallen in love with Bessie Davis, a former cook and massage therapist who, before she was married, was known as Hannah Elias. Elias, who also was Black, was by then running a boardinghouse on the West Side, where Williams lived. Spurned, his love unrequited, Williams moved away. But he soon started stalking Elias at her home at 236 Central Park West. Her next-door neighbor, coincidentally, was Richard Henry Green, Andrew's cousin, whom Andrew visited regularly. One day Williams followed Green home, mistaking him for John R. Platt, a wealthy glass manufacturer and, with the same full white beard, a Green look-alike. Platt was in fact Elias's lover (though he described her as his masseuse). After Williams was arrested, he claimed that Elias had identified her visitor not as Platt but as

Green. (The irony that one man named Platt, the Republican legislator, had helped make Green's reputation for probity, and another equally nontransparent glass manufacturer named Platt had almost ruined it, seemed to have escaped most people.)

On November 16, 1903, district attorney Leonard Jerome said he was satisfied that Elias and Andrew Green had never met. Recalling that he answered the door once when Platt called for Elias, Williams himself would say, "I am not sure the man I shot was the one who called at the house, but he looked something like him." Though a lifelong bachelor (and, therefore, unconcerned about an adultery scandal), the lingering unanswered questions besmirched Green's legacy. More definitive evidence to salvage Green's reputation finally came some seven months later in June 1904 when Platt filed suit against Elias. He demanded the return of $684,000 (nearly $20 million in today's dollars), which he claimed "the little octoroon" had extorted from him during their two-decade affair. The story made the *Times*'s front page (ANDREW H. GREEN'S MEMORY IS CLEARED, the headline reassured readers), but the outcome was inconclusive: Platt's suit was dismissed. And that, pretty much, became the last that most New Yorkers heard of Andrew Haswell Green.

Announcing Green's death to the board of aldermen, New York mayor Seth Low had declared: "It may truthfully be said that to no one man who has labored in and for the city during the last fifty years is the city under greater and more lasting obligation than to Andrew Haswell Green." A century later, the Columbia University historian Kenneth T. Jackson would go even further: "Green is arguably the most important leader in Gotham's long history, more important than Peter Stuyvesant, Alexander Hamilton, Frederick Law Olmsted, Robert Moses and Fiorello La Guardia."

Yet a proposal to name a roadway after Green at the northern boundary of Central Park was never ratified; nor were sufficient funds raised for a semicircular columned court of honor and a heroic bronze statue in his memory at the entrance to Central Park at Seventh Avenue (now Adam Clayton Powell Jr. Boulevard) and 110th Street. About all Green got were five unmarked elm trees and a marble bench on a knoll overlooking a ravine near 106th Street that was not dedicated until 1929, when sufficient funds had finally been collected. In the 1980s the bench was moved two blocks south to make room for a compost pile. In 2008, Green was ignominiously eternalized as the namesake of a vest-pocket Upper East Side park, on the site of a former heliport and pier where garbage had been loaded onto barges and transported from Greater New York.

20

William J. Wilgus

The Making of Midtown

While die-hard Brooklynites still lament consolidation with New York as "the Great Mistake," the technological marvel that elevated the merger from Andrew H. Green's decades-long dream of a single legal and political entity into reality began not in Manhattan but in Brooklyn.

In 1898, the year that the two cities were joined in their marriage of convenience, the Brooklyn Rapid Transit Company began converting its elevated trains to electric power, thanks to Frank J. Sprague. His vision for a "Dynamo Electric Machine" catalyzed urban development by perfecting both mass transit and elevators (and leaving a legacy to scientific progress through electricity much greater than David F. Launy's earlier in the nineteenth century).

The switch to electricity from steam could potentially save New York City tons of coal and millions of gallons of water annually. Sprague's invention also transfigured the cityscape. Now the proposed subways and commuter lines linking four of the boroughs of Greater New York (the Bronx, Brooklyn, Manhattan, and Queens) together and New York City with New Jersey could be safely placed in tunnels under rivers and city streets when necessary, without asphyxiating their passengers.

Burrowing underground was exactly what William J. Wilgus decided to do in 1902, to spare his bosses from prosecution.

Barely one week after the year began, on the morning of Wednesday, January 8, Train 118, the New York Central and Hudson River Railroad's Manhattan-bound

local from White Plains, was due at Grand Central Depot at eight fifteen A.M.
Like the Delaware & Hudson train that would strike Charles Dowd in Saratoga
Springs two years later, No. 118 was running late. It was further delayed at
110th Street, near the mouth of the congested Park Avenue Tunnel, to let another
southbound local pass. When it finally emerged into Manhattan's vast open-air
train yard at Fifty-Eighth Street and Park Avenue, the engineer saw a red light
but was going too fast to stop. No. 118 smashed into the rear of a Danbury
commuter train, instantly killing fifteen passengers. The engineer was charged
with manslaughter; a state commission accused the railroad of gross negligence. But
the New York Central's officers and stockholders escaped prosecution. This time.

To insulate them legally and aggrandize their properties, Wilgus, chief engineer
of the New York Central Railroad, suggested a presumptuous and pricey solution:
Raze the depot, which had opened only a generation earlier, had recently been
renovated, and was the largest indoor space in the nation but already outmoded.
Electrify the rails to make the tunnels smoke-free. Carpet the cavernous belowground train yards south of Fifty-Eighth Street by decking over the yawning valley
of tracks with a luxuriant boulevard flanked by office buildings, hotels, and a civic
center that would shift Manhattan's cultural and commercial center of gravity from
downtown to Midtown.

William John Wilgus was born in Buffalo in 1865, where his grandparents had
transplanted themselves from Albany by way of the early nineteenth century's greatest
engineering feat in New York, the Erie Canal. As Kurt C. Schlichting noted in *Grand
Central's Engineer* (2012), Wilgus was influenced by two of his father's affirmative
initiatives: Frank Wilgus got himself hired as a freight agent for the newly formed
New York Central Railroad, which provided his son with one foot in the door; and,
to survey the family farm upstate, Frank recruited Marsden Davey, an English-born
civil engineer. Trailing Davey as he took his measurements, young William was captivated by what he later described as engineering's "mathematical exactitude" and
"aesthetic charm."

The Wilgus family couldn't afford college, so William was largely self-taught until
he was apprenticed to Davey from 1883 to 1885. His formal academic training
amounted to a correspondence course in mechanical drafting from Cornell. He left
home for a twenty-two-year stint railroading in the Midwest, during which he fortuitously met a young architect, Charles A. Reed; in 1892 he married Reed's sister
May. A year later he returned to New York, where he was hired by the New York
Central. By 1899 Wilgus had been promoted to the line's chief engineer. In 1902,

"Portrait of William J. Wilgus, the Central RR's chief engineer."

Reed, who was related by marriage to the president of the railroad, was hired with his partner, Allen H. Stem, to design the new Grand Central Terminal.

Wilgus had suggested electrification to railroad officials even before the fatal rear-end collision in 1902, and well before New York State mandated the elimination of steam-powered locomotives. Construction would take ten years and cost almost $2 billion in today's dollars. Bedrock Manhattan schist and thousands of cubic yards of earth would have to be excavated to build a subbasement as deep as ninety feet, the lowest man-made bunker in the city. Moreover, rail service would have to be maintained while the old depot was being demolished. But Vanderbilt and the rest of the board of directors validated Wilgus's audacious vision.

The number of passengers using the terminal would more than double between 1906 and 1930, from nineteen million to nearly fifty-one million. Real estate values in New York City and Westchester County would explode during the same period. Wilgus literally and figuratively inflated property values by developing the legal concept of air rights—then roofing over the giant belowground train yard in Midtown East with a deck supported by fifteen hundred columns, and leasing the empty space above it to developers. "Thus from the air would be taken wealth," Wilgus declared. The formula he concocted to lucratively monetize an invisible, elemental, and ubiquitous gaseous mixture would be replicated and embroidered to generate billions for property owners and developers and spare otherwise endangered landmarks from demolition in New York and around the nation.

Wilgus also guaranteed that Grand Central Terminal (a terminal because, unlike, say, Penn Station, the tracks end there), while interrupting the street grid, would be fully integrated into its surroundings. ("If Penn Station was built mainly to send a message about the splendor of arrival," the architecture critic Paul Goldberger wrote, "Grand Central was conceived to make clear the choreography of connection.")

While Wilgus was not an architect, he was keen on imposing his idiosyncratic protocol on Grand Central. After Reed & Stem, a St. Paul, Minnesota, firm that had designed other stations for the New York Central, won the architectural competition to design the new terminal, another firm, Warren & Wetmore, muscled itself into an acrimonious and costly partnership (it didn't hurt that Whitney Warren was William Vanderbilt's cousin). Their duel over design and credit would culminate after two decades in a $13 million legal settlement (in today's dollars) to Reed & Stem. Somehow, though, in spite of the ongoing conflict over ego, glory, legalities, and the actual design of Grand Central, the result was incredibly and classically seamless. The terminal, Wilgus argued, "marked the opening of a remarkable opportunity for the accomplishment of a public good with considerations of private gain on behalf of the corporation involved." Grand Central would be surrounded by a circumferential roadway, while passengers and pedestrians would navigate interconnected underground passages, corridors, and ramps, and be linked to the spanking new subway system. The terminal would boast every amenity, including a separate women's waiting room and a ladies' shoe-polishing salon staffed by "colored girls in neat blue liveries," and a barbershop where men could be shaved "in any one of 30 languages."

But the big draw in Grand Central Terminal was electricity—so much so that for all the marble and granite and brass all of the lighting fixtures were festooned with bare bulbs to flaunt how they were (and still are) illuminated. Trains powered by electricity could accelerate more quickly, a major advantage for stop-and-go commuter service. They didn't need to generate their own locomotion or carry the fuel to do so. The railroad had tested the first of its electric locomotives in Schenectady on the very same November weekend in 1904 that Charles F. Dowd, the father of

"Construction of Grand Central Terminal," circa 1905–1915. (Photo via the New-York Historical Society)

Standard Time, was killed in Saratoga. In 1906, beating by two years a state-imposed deadline, the first electrically powered train departed from Grand Central—with William Wilgus at the throttle.

While Andrew H. Green had missed the New Year's Eve celebration of consolidation on December 31, 1897, because he was convalescing at the family home in Massachusetts, his name nonetheless reverberated in numerous testimonials. When Grand Central formally opened in 1913, though, William Wilgus wasn't mentioned. He wasn't even invited. If he would share credit for saving the railroad in 1902, he would also be singled out for blame as the father of a failure—design, mechanical, or human—that resulted in another fatal accident in 1907.

Regular electrified service was finally initiated that February 15, between Grand Central and White Plains. The very next evening, during the rush hour, a Brewster-bound local left the terminal, rounded a curve in the Woodlawn section of the Bronx, and jumped the tracks. Twenty-four people died in the wreck, which a coroner's jury blamed on the electric locomotive's excessive weight and speed. The jury didn't fix individual blame, but A. F. Schwannecke, the Bronx coroner, held the entire board of directors of the New York Central Railroad responsible for failing to "take safe and proper precautions"—a sweeping indictment that was narrowed to manslaughter charges against one of the company's vice presidents, ...Fred H. Smith, and Ira McCormack, the Central's general manager.

McCormack was acquitted and the other cases were eventually dismissed, but the railroad would be held liable for hefty civil damage claims. *Engineering Record-News* concluded that "the investigation of this accident has shown not the slightest reason for charging the new type of motive power with any causative relation to the disastrous derailment." Nonetheless, five months after the accident, Wilgus became convinced that in the internecine search for scapegoats he had been betrayed by the railroad's officers and directors. He resigned as vice president, effective September 30, 1907—one year to the day after the first electric engine arrived at Grand Central—and left with thank-you notes from his colleagues which, he modestly suggested later, "that I measured up to some degree to the opportunities generously given me to serve the company that employed me and, in so doing, also contributed to the public welfare."

Wilgus was only forty-one. His reputation in the industry remained largely intact. The new Public Service Commission immediately enlisted him to tackle a challenging and dangerous nightmare that had been plaguing Manhattan's Lower West Side for decades: the hundreds of fatalities and injuries caused by the Central's street-level freight trains serving the docks, warehouses, and markets along Tenth and Eleventh Avenues, which together became known as "Death Alley."

Wilgus went on to audaciously suggest a circumferential freight subway system carrying versions of today's shipping containers on electrified flatcars serving all of Manhattan below Forty-Second Street, connecting with the West Sixtieth Street yard and railroad terminals in the Bronx and providing for future links to Long Island City, Brooklyn, and the New Jersey waterfront. The system would be versatile enough to not only deliver freight and mail but also to remove trash and snow. "His proposals, grounded in a vision of the city's future, received the support of engineers and of civic and commercial leaders," the historian Josef W. Konvitz wrote, but they were never executed. Wilgus argued against the prosaic patchwork solution that was ultimately approved: an elevated line that would operate from 1933 until the 1980s, when it would lie derelict until it was transformed into the luxuriant High Line.

Wilgus never gave up on his vision for a regional rail system, but he took a well-earned break from battling the city's bureaucracy to become deputy director-general of transportation for the American Expeditionary Forces during World War I.

Returning home, he suggested that the existing tracks on rights-of-way be double-decked to accommodate higher-speed express and commuter trains on an upper level. He proposed presciently that to maximize the system's twenty-four-hour capacity, a form of congestion pricing should be imposed "through a graduated range of fares for the different hours of the day, so as to stimulate travel during the hours when movements are now light."

As chairman of a board of consulting engineers, Wilgus and colleagues oversaw construction of the Holland Tunnel, connecting Lower Manhattan and New Jersey, which began in 1920. A year later, the long-aborning bistate Port of New York Authority was finally established as the first such joint agency with a metropolitan mandate, which both Andrew Green and William Wilgus had envisioned, to fulfill a regional agenda. But mass transit for passengers and freight was stymied by the railroads themselves when competition among them trumped consensus. Frustrated with their lack of coordination and cooperation, the Port Authority turned its attention to vehicular traffic instead. Wilgus joined urbanists at the Regional Plan Association, which would compensate with expertise, imagination, and relentless lobbying for what it sorely lacked in financial resources and political muscle.

Wilgus would direct the New Deal's Emergency Relief Bureau during the Depression, being responsible for mitigating the hardship faced by 130,000 New Yorkers on work relief administered by the city's welfare department. He retired to his farm in rural Vermont, two hundred miles north of New York but accessible to the Windsor–Mt. Ascutney railroad station. He died there on October 24, 1949. The *Times* relegated his greatest achievement to the midpoint of his thirteen-paragraph obituary. Incompletely and unsentimentally, it said only that Wilgus "assisted in the rehabilitation, improvement and expansion of the Central, the electrification of its suburban zone, and the design and construction of Grand Central Terminal."

21

Rudolph Aronson

"Remember Me to Union Square"

Rudolph Aronson would have been the first to admit that from the moment of his birth, he craved an audience. "I had my first opportunity to see the world in New York City on April 8, 1856," he began his autobiography. "I am credibly informed," he added, a little crestfallen, "that, aside from those directly interested in the affair, my arrival caused no unusual excitement." Even so, Aronson was ungrudgingly willing to indulge the city of his birth in a do-over. "Despite this rather quiet reception I remained in New York," he wrote. He began piano lessons at the age of six and embarked on a theatrical career that helped expand the frontiers of live entertainment in New York and transform the face of Midtown Manhattan.

Aronson and his siblings would play leading roles in the rialto's cultural and geographic metamorphosis at the end of the nineteenth and the dawn of the twentieth centuries, which, curiously enough, was driven by three sets of three brothers, each of whom had gravitated to New York. The best known were the Shuberts, Eastern European immigrants from upstate Syracuse, whose dynasty was preceded by the Frohmans, who migrated to New York from the Midwest to became managers, producers, and theater owners. (Charles Frohman's dominance ended melodramatically. He was vetting the manuscript of a new French play aboard the *Lusitania* when it was sunk by a German U-boat. Frohman's last words were reported to have been "Why fear death? Death is only a beautiful adventure." The French play he had been perusing aboard ship was titled *La belle aventure*.)

The third set of brothers, the trailblazers, were the Aronsons, Rudolph, Edward, and Albert. Rudolph, the nobby youngest brother who directed the trio, is mostly recalled as a composer if he is remembered at all. Albert, the oldest, had immigrated with his parents from Prussia to New York, where Edward and Rudolph were born. After attending Grammar School No. 35 on West Thirteenth Street, presided over by Dr. Thomas Hunter, who would go on to found the eponymous college, Rudolph prepared for a business career. But his commitment to music, kindled early through piano lessons, was secured by a surprising connection he made at the Academy of Music, a few blocks from the family's home on Fourteenth Street. "I, in company with my brother Edward, soon managed to form an acquaintance with the janitor of that then famous 'Temple of Art,'" Rudolph wrote in his 1913 memoir, "and two and sometimes three times a week the good-natured janitor smuggled us in through the stage, and, ascending the emergency staircase leading to the gallery, we heard there to our hearts' content the works of Bellini, Donizetti, Verdi, Rossini, Gounod, and Ambroise Thomas."

By the time he was seventeen, Rudolph had already composed, published, and performed his first waltz and was off to the Vienna Conservatory and the Paris Conservatoire. Gallivanting at music festivals in Austria, Germany, and France, he audaciously introduced himself to the most celebrated artists and insinuated himself into Europe's cliquish cultural circles. In 1877, when he was only twenty-one, he returned to New York, where he self-confidently performed and conducted the compositions of others as well as a repertoire of his own works that would eventually include some 150 dances and other orchestral scores, including the official presidential campaign marches for Teddy Roosevelt in 1904 and William Howard Taft in 1908.

Endowed with "a rather handsome face of decidedly foreign cast, and a gorgeous moustache," Aronson, the *Theatre* magazine gratuitously added, "belongs, we believe, to the great family of Israel, which has given so many distinguished and able men to the world." To those who knew him only by reputation, the adjectives invoked to characterize this dapper figure unencumbered by self-doubt were typically opaque. "Mr. Aronson made himself known to the public," the magazine hinted, "by means of bold experiments, quarrels, and lawsuits."

One of his first bold experiments was executed at what became Madison Square Garden on an off night for the Barnum Circus. The wild animals roared on cue when he conducted performances of Johann Strauss's "Tales from the Vienna Woods" and Anton de Kontski's "Awakening of the Lion." The verisimilar accompaniment was

"Rudolph Aronson." (Photo via the Billy Rose
Theatre Division at the New York Public Library)

transformative and, Aronson recalled, "convinced me that environment was one of
the essentials for proper concert entertainments." Yet Aronson's first effort to create
an innovative environment in which to flaunt his musical virtuosity in an unfamiliar
venue was largely a flop. He lured Wall Street financiers to invest in the Metropolitan Concert Hall at the southwest corner of Broadway and West Forty-First Street,
where audiences were entertained by the debut of Aronson's enduring waltz "Sweet
Sixteen" in 1880.

The concert hall's stockholders preferred more classical fare in a more convenient
locale. Since earlier in the nineteenth century, Manhattan's Theater District had been
periodically leapfrogging from downtown, most recently from Union Square at Fourteenth Street to Madison Square at Twenty-Third Street. Aronson persuaded investors to gamble on another vault uptown when he unveiled his Casino Theatre, a
Moorish brick-and-terra-cotta confection on the southeast corner of Broadway and
West Thirty-Ninth Street. The arabesque auditorium was so incomplete that the roof

leaked when it opened on October 21, 1882, with Strauss's operetta *The Queen's Lace Handkerchief*. When it was finally finished two months later, though, the Casino would become the capital of light opera. "The New York Casino may be fairly regarded as the birthplace of the most popular form of stage entertainment at the present time, musical comedy," M. B. Leavitt wrote in *Fifty Years in Theatrical Management* (1912).

Built on the site of a former coal yard, the Casino was New York's first all-electric theater. Aronson's other most visible innovation was the roof garden, designed to extend the theatrical season into the blistering summer months. "He may justly be regarded as the originator of that popular summer institution in this country," according to *Who's Who on the Stage* (1908). "There is a good deal of flirting going on in this 'castle in the air,' for the surroundings seem conducive to love-making," the *New York World* fussed.

While Aronson's financial and managerial control of the Casino was intermittent, he generally prospered as a producer. He introduced Gilbert and Sullivan operettas, showcased Lillian Russell, Sarah Bernhardt, and Marie Dressler, and, perhaps most famously, imported the longest-running—if now largely forgotten—comic opera of its time, Edward Jakobowski's *Erminie*, the saga of a star-crossed criminal duo. The Casino also staged the New York premiere of Pietro Mascagni's *Cavalleria rusticana*, in a legally questionable coup that magnified his rank as an impresario (which, by one definition, is an accomplished producer who promotes himself as scrupulously as his highest-paid performers). The opera debuted at the Casino in a special Thursday matinee—scheduled at that offbeat time slot deliberately to upstage a performance of the same opera that night directed by Oscar Hammerstein at the Lenox Lyceum. Aronson scored the publicity coup, but not the commercial one. He was barred from charging admission, since litigation by the rival producers over rights was still pending.

The following year, Aronson audaciously broadened his repertoire so that he and the Casino found themselves in familiar circumstances: the latter drawing full houses, and the former in court. He was charged with indecency for what was billed as an exhibit of "Living Statues," a thinly veiled display of figures in close-fitting flesh-colored tights and leotards. Several self-styled guardians of morality protested, but after the leading lady created a sensation by appearing on the witness stand in costume, Aronson was acquitted to thunderous courtroom applause.

Under the producer Edward E. Rice, the Casino Theatre also introduced *Clorindy, or The Origin of the Cake Walk* by composer Will Marion Cook and librettist Paul Laurence Dunbar in 1898. The groundbreaking one-act musical was billed as the first

"Casino Theater, Southeast corner of Broadway and 39th St., built 1882," from New York 1880: Architecture and Urbanism in the Gilded Age *by Robert A. M. Stern, Thomas Mellins, and David Fishman (New York: Monacelli Press, 2009).* (Photo via the New-York Historical Society)

all-Black production to open in a highbrow Broadway theater that catered to white audiences. Two years later the Casino imported the Edwardian musical comedy *Florodora*, which debuted the leggy sextet that would include Evelyn Nesbit, the chorine whose jealous husband, Harry K. Thaw, fatally shot architect Stanford White in the roof garden of Madison Square Garden in 1906. (Purportedly, after being released from an asylum and beholding an eccentric Florida villa designed by Addison Mizner, Thaw confessed, "I shot the wrong architect.")

As befitted the rialto, even more melodramatic than what the professional actors performed before the footlights were the backstage theatrics that Aronson inspired. He played the protagonist in scores of suits over abrogated contracts, the case of a discharged machinist's attempt to burn down the Casino during a performance, and the venerable partnership that ended after what he glossed as "a veritable merry war." Jessy Brodsky, a novelist, and Michael Green, who founded the Fullerton Cultural

Center in Newburgh, New York, dubbed the business relationship between Aronson, an immigrant Jew of Prussian ancestry, and John A. McCaull, a Scottish-born former Confederate soldier and lawyer who managed an eponymous opera company, that of "the odd couple who paved the way for modern Broadway."

Modern Broadway would doom the Casino, although it would outlast Aronson himself by more than a decade. He died in 1919 on the Upper West Side of Manhattan, where he lived with his three single sisters (all of whom he supported) after losing control of the theater, which eventually was taken over by the Shubert Organization. The Casino was razed after a final performance of *Faust*, Charles Gounod's operatic version of the legendary devilish bargain. While trained as a serious musician, in trading a classical repertoire for popular musical comedy Aronson probably would not have regarded *Faust* as autobiographical. He might just as well have been characterizing himself as his audiences when he wrote in his memoir that "the public had tired of the terror and melancholy conveyed to its mind by the plays that had enthralled it, and was eager to exchange tears for laughter."

Time passed the Casino by. Air conditioning began to obviate roof gardens. A nondescript office building was constructed on the Casino's site to house garment district workshops and showrooms before they, too, became anachronisms. The subway had elevated Times Square from the vanguard of Manhattan's theater district to its hub. "What was once the northernmost theater in New York," Ken Bloom's *Broadway: An Encyclopedia* (1991), concluded, "ended its life as the southernmost."

22

Philip A. Payton Jr.

Harlem on His Mind

W hen Philip A. Payton Jr. arrived in Manhattan in April 1899, nobody, at first glance, would have guessed that he would have made it *to* New York, much less that he would make it once he got there. He was twenty-four, jobless, and a high school dropout. Payton arrived in New York City with another indelible handicap: he was Black.

The Upper Manhattan that Philip Payton contemplated for the first time that spring, though, was fertile ground for a young man on the make. As Andrew H. Green had predicted, only a few months after the consolidation of Greater New York Harlem's proximity to the Bronx and what had been part of Westchester multiplied property values in what only a generation before was just a village. And, as William Wilgus had envisioned, a building boom was erupting in Central and West Harlem where work was poised to begin on a new subway that would be speedier than the clattering elevated lines that had deflated property values in the ear-splitting penumbra beneath their tracks. Developers also were rushing to beat the effective date of a more onerous construction code for tenement housing.

Within four years, the concurrence of those tides would alter the complexion of Manhattan and transform Philip Payton from a janitor who couldn't afford the nickel transit fare to and from downtown into a pioneering entrepreneur, not yet thirty, living in a row house he owned on West 131st Street and well on his way to making his fortune.

Born in 1876 in Westfield, near Springfield, Massachusetts, the grandson of slaves from North Carolina, Philip Payton Jr. was the second of four children. His father, a southerner, graduated from Wayland Seminary in Washington, D.C., headed north in 1873, and worked as a barber and sometime tea merchant. The family lived above the barbershop. Philip Jr.'s mother, who was from Baltimore, was a hairdresser and wigmaker. Whatever else he learned growing up, he inherited two affinities from his enterprising father. First, Philip Sr. bought land; in fact, he was the only Black property owner in the town of Westfield. And second, he was proficient at self-promotion, aggressively advertising his Ladies and Gents' Hairdressing and Bathing Emporium on Elm Street.

"In the fall of 1893, during my junior year in high school," Philip Jr. recalled without elaboration, "my father conceived the idea that I was forming some undesirable associations and decided to send me away from home." The elder Payton contacted the great orator Joseph C. Price, who in 1882 had founded Livingstone College, an African Methodist Episcopal Zion Church institution named for David Livingstone, the doctor, missionary, explorer, and abolitionist who, after having lost contact with the outside world for six years, was "found" in the African bush by Henry M. Stanley, a reporter for James Gordon Bennett Jr.'s *Herald*. After entering Livingstone as a high school junior, Philip Jr. remained there only one year, then apparently re-enrolled in high school but broke his wrist playing football during the fall of junior year. "Thus ended my education, much to the disgust of my father," he said.

His two brothers would graduate from Yale; one would be promoted to professor of Greek and Latin. Armed with a degree from what would evolve into Westfield State University in Massachusetts, his sister would become a teacher. Philip Payton Jr. would blaze a discrete career path as a disciple of Booker T. Washington, who preached accommodationist Black self-help through a practical, vocational education and entrepreneurship. They met through Washington's doctor, Samuel Courtney, who also lived in Westfield, Massachusetts, and over time they developed a fruitful personal and professional affinity: the leading Black moderate who had cultivated presidents, and the scrappy pragmatist battling block by block to materialize his mentor's agenda. In 1901, Payton was present when Washington formed his National Negro Business League in Courtney's home. (They would become so close that when Washington bought a summer home on Long Island sight unseen, he asked the Paytons to advise his wife on the interior decorating.) Payton also would organize the Negro Business League's conference in New York in 1905. "The story of his life," Washington would write, "would read like a romance."

"Portrait of Philip Payton," from The National Cyclopedia of the Colored Race, *edited by Clement Richardson (Montgomery, AL: National Publishing Co. 1919), 259.*

That story began inauspiciously, though. Payton worked in his father's shop, where he was home-schooled in barbering, a profession that his mother repeatedly warned would make lazy men of him and his brothers. "My father would invariably reply, 'Never mind, I'm going to teach them the trade,'" Payton later recalled. "'The knowledge of it won't be a burden to carry, and when they become men they won't be compelled to follow it, if they have sense enough to do anything else.'" In April 1899, "realizing that I was not making much of myself, and that I was not growing any younger, and that if I intended to do anything in this life it was time I started," Payton "decided to try a new field."

He arrived in New York, where he dabbled in several odd jobs, working in a Manhattan department store as an attendant at a photo booth and a standing scale where customers could weigh themselves for a penny. He learned one occupational lesson immediately: he was not indispensable. While he was on vacation, he was replaced. "I was up against it," he recalled. "What to do, I didn't know. One thing I did know, however, was that I was not going home for the boys to laugh at me." He briefly supported himself by doing what he knew best: barbering.

In February 1900, Payton literally entered the real estate business on the ground floor—the basement, actually, as a porter. One month later, August Belmont Jr. began building the Interborough Rapid Transit subway system. Payton shrewdly intuited the possibilities. After sustaining himself by sweeping floors for eight months and having saved enough to marry Maggie Ryans, a servant from Westfield, he quit his custodial job and opened a real estate office with a partner on West Thirty-Second Street near Eighth Avenue. During the entire winter of 1900–1901, they took in a total of $125. Rent alone was costing them $20 a month.

"I don't think it would require an expert to judge the condition of the firm of Brown & Payton after it had been running six months," he recalled. When the business flopped, Payton struck out on his own. That second real estate venture failed, too. "One time I remember walking from Nassau Street to 134th Street where I was living for the want of a five cent piece," he said. "I just simply was not making any money. My wife was doing sewing, a day's work or anything else she could get to do to help me along. Had it not been for her help, I fear I would have given up."

In *A Ten Years' War: An Account of the Battle with the Slum in New York* (1900), Jacob Riis wrote of African Americans for whom "perpetual eviction is their destiny." The Paytons learned that firsthand. They were dispossessed three times and once evicted for nonpayment of rent. "Our entire scanty belongings were set out on the sidewalk," Payton recalled. Booker T. Washington would later write, though, that Payton was better off for the experience: "He has thus been able to see how an ejectment suit looked from both the point of view of the tenant and the landlord." So far, however, their view was entirely one-sided. "All my friends discouraged me," he remembered. "All of them told me how I couldn't make it. They tried to convince me that there was no show for a colored man in such a business in New York."

Payton refused to succumb. Instead, methodically, apartment by apartment, building by building, he turned the tables on white landlords and real estate agents. He weaponized racial discrimination. Engaging in a strategy that, when whites wielded it, would be denounced as unscrupulous fearmongering and blockbusting, Payton transformed the sparsely populated swath of Manhattan north of 110th Street into a fertile destination for mass migration by Black people. (Italians and Jews had already flooded East Harlem where they were initially unwelcome, too.)

In 1900, at Eighth Avenue and West Forty-First Street, a Black man fatally stabbed a white police officer who was said to have propositioned his girlfriend. A race riot ensued. The uproar "woke Negro New York and stirred the old fighting spirit," James Weldon Johnson, the poet, novelist, and NAACP leader, wrote. But rather than fight, most Black New Yorkers fled. They abandoned neighborhoods like the Tenderloin (comprised, NAACP founder Mary Ovington wrote, of "human hives, honeycombed with little rooms thick with human beings"), Hell's Kitchen, and San Juan Hill on the West Side, roughly between West Twenty-Third and Sixtieth Streets, that they had shared with poor whites. (Some of those, too, would be displaced before long when tenements were demolished to build Pennsylvania Station.)

One magnet that beckoned was Harlem. (The storied neighborhood has no formal boundaries, but is generally considered to encompass the area west of Fifth Avenue to Morningside Avenue and north of Central Park.) West Harlem had been envisioned as recently as the 1890s as another ward for wealthy whites, with the inauguration of Oscar Hammerstein's elegant opera house, the opening of Columbia University's new campus, and the beginning of construction of the St. John the Divine, the world's largest Gothic cathedral. But within a decade or two the neighborhood was poised to outpace virtually every other section of the city in a racial demographic upheaval that diehards who refused to flee, or lacked the means to do so, euphemistically minimized as a "changing neighborhood."

A glut of residential construction in anticipation of the subway, coupled with repeated delays in the opening of the new transit routes, temporarily gave Black people seeking apartments a tenuous upper hand in both getting in the door and negotiating rents. Demand would grow again, this time forged by a more predictable migratory pattern driven by coursing streams from Manhattan's West Side, the Caribbean, and the Deep South. (Of the sixty thousand Black people in Manhattan in 1910, fewer than fifteen thousand had been born in New York.)

Several incidents in Harlem itself accelerated an exodus of whites and the influx of Black New Yorkers. A murder at 31 West 133rd Street terrified white tenants into departing. Undeterred, Payton and his wife tapped into cash they had accumulated from successive deals to buy an 1887 Victorian Gothic three-story, eleven-room town house that had been occupied by Ernest Rothschild, the white manager of a cracker factory, and his family down the block at No. 13. (The Paytons, who integrated the block, were briefly listed at that address in *Phillips' Elite Directory of Private Families and Ladies' Visiting and Shopping Guide* until the persnickety register dropped residential addresses where Black families were moving.) Nearby, on West 134th Street between Fifth and Lenox Avenue (now Malcolm X Boulevard), Payton would open his Afro-American Realty Company in a newly built apartment house.

In 1905, Payton turned adversity to his advantage again, or, as *The National Cyclopedia of the Colored Race* (1919) put it, "a grim sort of fortune held out her hand." A white landlord feuding with another property owner on the same block of West 134th Street figured to get even by renting his building to Black tenants— thereby making his antagonist's apartments unrentable to whites. Payton was just the man for the job. "I was able to induce other landlords to make the change and give me their houses to manage," Payton told the *New York Age*, a Black weekly, in 1912. "By opening for colored tenants first a house in one block and then a house in another I have finally succeeded in securing for the colored people of New York over 250 first-class flats and private dwellings, conveniently located as to transportation facilities, etc." Still, even Philip Payton expressed surprise that for the very same apartments in Harlem row houses, Black tenants were willing to pay more than whites and that "in order to rent to white tenants the apartments on the side next to the Negro tenement it was necessary to reduce the rent $4 a month less than on the opposite side, although the apartments were exactly alike."

"The white residents of the section," James Weldon Johnson wrote in *Black Manhattan* (1930), "showed very little concern about the movement until it began to spread to the west and across Lenox Avenue." White property owners coalesced to protect their investments, alliances that many outsiders cast as enlightened financial judgments rather than as racially motivated barriers to housing integration. "These organizations are not likely to cause race riots," the *Boston Globe* opined in 1906, "as their formation will not be due to a dislike or hatred for negro persons, but to a conviction among white owners that in any section of the city especially attractive to white people the leasing of flats in the section to negroes will not tend to enhance but to weaken values."

Among those self-interested organizations was Hudson Realty. The president of Hudson, a conglomerate, was Maximilian Morgenthau, whose brother Henry would become Woodrow Wilson's ambassador to Turkey and patriarch of a family of public servants. Hudson's board members included Joseph Bloomingdale, the department store magnate. Hudson Realty bought 40, 42, and 44 West 135th Street and evicted the Black tenants in a desperate, last-ditch plot to stymie Payton's incursions in Harlem with an all-white firewall. Payton adroitly retaliated by having his Afro-American Realty Company buy the buildings flanking Hudson's acquisitions and dispossessing the white tenants. Those occupants, who typically rented by the week or month, were notified unequivocally that "on and after July the house in which you are now living will be rented to colored tenants only, and you are hereby notified to vacate the apartment now occupied by you between now and that time."

By December 17, 1905, even the *Times* fretted, feverishly headlining its reporting: REAL ESTATE RACE WAR IS STARTED IN HARLEM. The article went on to say that "white folks, hat in hand," had filed into Payton's office on the eve of the Christmas holidays pleading to remain in their apartments rather than being dispossessed by their buildings' new owner, the Afro-American Realty Company.

"Changing neighborhood" was far too phlegmatic a term to apply to the housing revolution, unique in its application of reverse discrimination and unprecedented in scale. The wholesale churn transformed the neighborhood and elevated Payton into the role of Father of Black Harlem. Competing landlords and brokers waged virtual door-to-door combat, occupancy seesawed between Black and white tenants, and the magnitude of the displacement kindled a kinetic convulsion. Payton's advertising campaign in the *New York Age* and other papers with predominantly Black readership was direct and to the point: "Colored Tenants, Attention! After much effort I am now able to offer to my people for rent" several apartment houses "of a class never before rented to our people."

White refugees fled while Black people from other places flooded into the promised land of Harlem. "A constant stream of furniture trucks loaded with the household effects of a new colony of colored people who are invading the choice locality is pouring into the street," a *Times* reporter observed. "Another equally long procession, moving in the other direction, is carrying away the household goods of the whites from their homes of years."

"In the eyes of the whites who were antagonistic, the whole movement took on the aspect of an 'invasion'—an invasion of both their economic and social rights," James Weldon Johnson wrote. "They felt that Negroes as neighbors not only lowered the values of their property, but also lowered their social status. Seeing that they could not stop the movement, they began to flee. They took fright, they became panic-stricken, they ran amok. Their conduct could be compared to that of a community in the Middle Ages fleeing before an epidemic of the black plague, except for the fact that here the reasons were not so sound. But these people did not stop to reason, they did not stop to ask why they did what they were doing, or what would happen if they didn't do it. The presence of a single colored family in a block, regardless of the fact that they might be well-bred people, with sufficient means to buy a new home, was a signal for precipitate flight. The stampeded whites actually deserted house after house and block after block." A letter to the editor published in the *Times* in 1912 observed that, when riding the Sixth and Ninth Avenue El, "now you invariably have a colored person sitting either beside you or in front of you," asking plaintively: "Why cannot we have Jim Crow cars for these people?"

In the place of the white departees came well-to-do and aspirational Black people who could afford town houses in enclaves like Strivers' Row on West 138th Street (built for whites at the end of the nineteenth century and grudgingly sold to enterprising Blacks during the 1920s Harlem Renaissance) as well as those less wealthy who, because of rent gouging by Black and white property owners, had to double up with relatives or take in boarders. Even the white mainstream press, for the most part, acknowledged that Harlem's newcomers were in the main employed, hardworking, and law-abiding (an imprimatur that might have seemed even more gratuitous had the tenants been white).

Except for a few historic tracts (nineteenth-century hamlets, really, like Weeksville in Brooklyn and Seneca Village in Manhattan), Harlem was the first New York City neighborhood that Black people, typically relegated to poor mixed-race neighborhoods, could finally call their own. "He has proven that a Negro who knows his own people, is better able to deal with them as tenants than one who does not know them," Booker T. Washington wrote of Payton in *The Negro in Business* (1907). "He is able to discriminate between the good and bad tenants where a white man would treat them all as belonging to the same class." Harlem would become the world's largest Black enclave outside of Africa. "Philip A. Payton, a Negro and a wealthy real estate operator, may be rightly termed the father of this Negro community," E. F. Dyckoff wrote in the weekly opinion magazine the *Outlook* in 1914, "since it was he who, despite violent opposition, first installed his people in tenement property in this section 10 or 12 years ago. It was Payton's theory that living conditions equal to those available for the white man were what the Negro needed to give him the realization of white progress and white standards." White businessmen and property owners pressured banks not to grant Black patrons new mortgages or renew existing ones. But the 1904 opening of the subways on Broadway and Lenox Avenue accelerated the breach of what had been a short-lived boundary between East and West Harlem. The all-white firewall, like every other wall that New Yorkers had erected for centuries to exclude one group of outsiders or another, began to crumble. By 1908, Payton claimed that Afro-American Realty controlled thirty-four apartment buildings housing thirty-five hundred Black tenants.

"After a series of shrewd business dealings in which the syndicate was worsted," Dyckoff wrote, "the Negroes were left in possession of the nucleus of their future community, and Payton's dream of progress among his people had begun to be realized." In May 1904, Booker T. Washington wrote Payton, "I have read in yesterday's *World* how you turned the tables on those who desired to injure the race, and wish to congratulate you on this instance of business enterprise and race loyalty combined." Whites, not surprisingly, defined success differently. In July 1906, Afro-American Realty Company took a five-year lease on a fifteen-apartment building at 525 West 151st Street between Broadway and Amsterdam Avenue and gave white tenants until August 1 to vacate. NEGRO INVASION THREAT ANGERS FLAT DWELLERS, the *Times* bellowed, while quoting Payton as saying that his objective was to end the "forced colonization" of Blacks into completely segregated neighborhoods, much less racially mixed apartment buildings. He added: "We intend to have negro families in that apartment house. Of course there is a prejudice against them, but there was once similar prejudice against the Jews and the Italians. They overcame it and we should be able to do so."

To what degree money, racial justice, or revenge motivated Payton, we can never know. But he publicly appealed to investors in his company's prospectus (printed unselfconsciously in brown ink) by explicitly invoking the first two, couched as financial gain and integration. The third motive, of revenge—evening the score after decades of race-baiting by whites and, most recently, the evictions inflicted by Morgenthau's all-white syndicate—was, at the very least, implicit. "The reason for the present condition of the colored tenancy in New York City today is because of the race prejudice of the white owner and his white agent," the sociology lesson in Payton's prospectus argued, but he expressly added an economic caveat: "Race prejudice is a luxury, and like all other luxuries can be made very expensive in New York City."

Cynical or commonsensical, condescending or reciprocating, the prospectus unambiguously and brazenly stated that "the Afro-American Realty Company can turn race prejudice into dollars and cents. The very prejudice which has heretofore worked against us can be turned and used to our profit. A respectable, law-abiding, negro will find conditions so changed that he will be able to rent wherever his means will permit him to live." It stated unequivocally that its "avowed object is to make it possible for a negro to live anywhere he desires, if he has the money with which to pay rent." That didn't necessarily mean cheaper rents, though. As Kevin McGruder wrote in *Race and Real Estate: Conflict and Cooperation in Harlem, 1890–1920* (2015),

"While the blacks replaced some of the white apartment owners, the structure of the real estate market remained the same, with black owners benefitting from the limited choices available to black renters in the same manner that their white predecessors had benefitted."

Payton didn't have to be an economic genius to know that even bigoted landlords might opt for "profit over prejudice," anticipating by decades the arguments advanced in Gary Becker's *The Economics of Discrimination* (1957) and Milton Friedman's *Capitalism and Freedom* (1962), as Jim Epstein of the libertarian Reason Foundation wrote in 2018. "Just as a refusal to hire Blacks means that an employer must forgo worthy employees and pay higher salaries, refusal to rent to Blacks means that a landlord must forgo worthy tenants and accept less in rent," Epstein wrote. "Payton understood that he could exploit this market reality to buy buildings at a discount, and to sway even bigoted landlords to rent to Blacks to maximize their incomes. In a racist society, with fewer options open to them in the housing market, Blacks tended to pay higher rents for equivalent properties. Payton recognized he could use this regrettable fact to undermine racial covenants."

Buying Afro-American Realty Company stock, Payton exhorted Black investors, meant doing well *and* doing good. "Today is the time to buy," he proclaimed, "if you want to be numbered among those of the race who are doing something toward trying to solve the so-called 'Race Problem.'" The company's directors included Charles W. Anderson, the confidant of Booker T. Washington and Theodore Roosevelt's appointee as internal revenue collector for Lower Manhattan; the Reverend William H. Brooks; James C. Garner, a contracting and housecleaning mogul; Fred R. Moore, the publisher of the *New York Age*; Wilford H. Smith, the first Black lawyer to win a case before the Supreme Court; and James C. Thomas, a mortician. "All of the personalities in or around the Afro-American Realty Company were proteges of Washington and members of his business league," Harold Cruse wrote in *The Crisis of the Negro Intellectual* (1967).

Washington's name was the most prominent, but he was no figurehead or absentee director. "Behind them all stood the guiding mind of Booker T. Washington and his National Negro Business League," according to Cruse. "Black New York was a Booker T. Washington town," Louis R. Harlan wrote in his 1983 biography of Washington. The city "was in transition, as the scattered blacks of lower Manhattan moved uptown and the population pressure of southern migrants and the entrepreneurship of black realtors such as Washington's friend Philip Payton began to create black Harlem . . . In Harlem the spirit of business enterprise was more congenial to

Washington's social philosophy, and the arrival of southern migrants to Harlem tempered its urban attitudes with first-generation rural ones."

John H. Adkins, the president of the Negro Business League of New York City, observed at the time that while a number of Black entrepreneurs had succeeded, especially in the real estate business, "the name of a young man who came to New York City many years ago, stands out perhaps more prominently than any of them; his rise, his ascendancy, his remarkable achievement in so short a time has been Napoleonic. I refer to Mr. Philip A. Payton Jr. He has outstripped them all."

But Payton's dignified pince-nez glasses belied a swashbuckling ambition. Before falling victim to his overextended investing, Afro-American Realty was renting apartments to Black tenants in about two dozen buildings that it had leased from white landlords at high rents or purchased with hefty mortgages. When it was reported in 1910 that Payton planned to visit Liberia, Charles W. Anderson teased his friend Booker T. Washington, "You had better cause the Liberians to be notified of his approach that they might get out their padlocks, and nail down everything that's lying around loose." Washington would add a demurrer, though: "He has dignified for the colored man a business in which he was formerly a joke."

For all its promise, though, Payton's company oversold its vow to deliver a 10 percent profit to investors. A farcical exchange of civil lawsuits by disgruntled stockholders also claiming that Payton inflated the company's assets even triggered his brief arrest. Combined with an ongoing recession that crested with the Panic of 1907, the judgments against Payton for overstating Afro-American Realty Company's assets doomed the company. It ceased operations in 1908. That the promise in its prospectus—"The idea that Negroes must be confined to certain localities can be done away with"—remained unfulfilled was obvious when in 1912 Payton considered purchasing a six-acre shorefront mansion on Oyster Bay, abutting an estate belonging to Jennie K. Stafford, owner of Manhattan's Hotel Imperial. "Just what effect the introduction of a colored family will have upon the exclusive Lloyd Neck section is as yet a matter of speculation," the *Brooklyn Times* reported dryly.

Still, a little more than a decade after Philip and Maggie Payton had moved into 13 West 131st Street as the first Black family between Fifth and Lenox Avenues, according to the 1915 state census, nearly every household on the block was occupied by Black housekeepers, cooks, valets, porters, and elevator operators whose roots were in the Caribbean or the South. (The Paytons were raising Maggie's teenage niece and nephew there after their parents were killed in North Carolina.) Four of five Black New Yorkers lived in Harlem, to which they also transplanted the city's Black institutions like Elizabeth Jennings's church, St. Philips Episcopal, which moved there from downtown in 1910. By 1930, Black residents would account for 70 percent of Central Harlem's population (compared to about 10 percent in 1910). The efforts of Payton and his colleagues, Kevin McGruder wrote in the *Encyclopedia of African American Business* (2017), "would create in New York for the first time a large, cohesive African American community, from which the 1920s cultural movement that became known as the Harlem Renaissance was able to grow."

While the Afro-American Realty Company collapsed, Payton's personal reputation as a cocksure pioneer survived. He continued to conduct transactions through his Philip A. Payton Jr. & Company, which closed what was said to be its largest deal, the purchase of six apartment houses for more than $1.5 million, in July 1917. He named the buildings for Black heroes: Crispus Attucks, Frederick Douglass, Paul Laurence Dunbar, Toussaint L'Ouverture, Booker T. Washington, and Phyllis Wheatley. Payton died several weeks later of liver or kidney cancer at his summer home on the shore in Allenhurst, New Jersey. He was forty-one. He bequeathed a demographic legacy that would outlast the red-and-black PAP monogram that he placed on the gateways to his Harlem properties. *The National Cyclopedia of the Colored Race* would refer to him at the end of the decade as "without a doubt the greatest Negro real estate dealer that ever lived."

Maggie Payton sold the couple's Harlem home in 1919. By the 1940s the house next door had deteriorated from a vacant shell to an empty lot. No. 13 itself was being rented out as a furnished rooming house. As the twenty-first century dawned, though, Central Harlem was beginning to rebound. The Paytons' home was eventually converted into condominiums. In 2003 the asking price for a two-bedroom apartment was $420,000; it sold for $344,500. In 2017, the owners placed the same apartment on the market for $599,000. They sold it for $645,000.

Payton never lived to see the Harlem Renaissance, but he created its constituency. "The move to Harlem, in the beginning and for a long time, was fathered and engineered by Philip A. Payton," James Weldon Jones wrote in *Black Manhattan*. "When Negro New Yorkers evaluate their benefactors in their own race, they must find that not many have done more than Phil Payton; for much of what has made Harlem the intellectual and artistic capital of the Negro world is in good part due to this fundamental advantage: Harlem has provided New York Negroes with better, cleaner, more modern, more airy, more sunny houses than they ever lived in before. And this is due to the efforts made first by Mr. Payton."

23

Audrey Munson

The Limitations of Statues

By embossing his initials on his buildings and harnessing the power of advertising, hidden talent, and enterprising hustle, Philip A. Payton Jr. transformed
himself at the height of his exploits into a household name. He changed the face of
Harlem, though outside his own community he died nearly unnoticed.

So would Audrey Munson, the small-town teenager whose porcelain features and
sublime figure recast America's mores and catapulted her to instant recognition after
her own more visible talents were discovered fortuitously, if randomly, in Midtown.
For more than a century she has reigned as New York City's loftiest effigy, *Civic Fame*,
the gilded, three-times-life-size statue that crowns McKim, Mead & White's massive
Manhattan Municipal Building, across the street from New York City Hall. From
a dozen or more granite, marble, bronze, and copper monuments all over Manhattan,
Munson's face still stares inscrutably, but incognito—her name and her own ephemeral fame all but forgotten.

Audrey Marie Munson was born on June 8, 1891, in Rochester, New York, to
Edgar Munson, a descendant of English Puritans who had founded New Haven,
Connecticut, and Catherine Mahoney, a daughter of Irish immigrants who for
reasons unknown later spelled her name Katherine Mahaney. (She was called Kittie,
anyway, by everyone who knew her.) Audrey's Christian name, too, was misspelled
on the baptismal register in Rochester as Audrie, an inauspicious debut for a young

woman who would later claim publicly, without offering any evidence, that she was descended on her father's side from a seventeenth-century English baronet and on her mother's from the eighteenth-century Irish patriot Robert Emmet (whose brother became a close associate of the lawyer Charles O'Conor's father).

Audrey's parents were also big dreamers, but as James Bone wrote in *The Curse of Beauty* (2016), their individual dreams collided. Edgar made a killing in the Midwest, buying farmland on the cheap. Kittie was lonely there; she remained so even back in Rochester when Edgar returned home. While working as a streetcar conductor, he started an affair with a passenger who would become his second wife and the mother of his five other children. When Audrey was eight, the couple divorced.

"It was her mother who talked the stage into her from the time she was a baby," Edgar said years later. "I can remember taking her to the theater and she'd get so

"Portrait of Audrey Munson," 1922. (Photo from Bettmann via Corbis—Getty Images)

excited and so she'd stand through the whole thing." Kittie and Audrey moved to a boardinghouse in Providence, Rhode Island. Kittie sold corsets—an artificial corporeal constraint that her grown daughter would later rail against as a physical culturist and a feminist—while Audrey attended Catholic school. In 1908, when she was seventeen, Audrey made her stage debut at Rocky Point Amusement Park in Warwick, Rhode Island, as one of Gerald Hampton's five Dancing Dolls. She later toured with a musical called *Marrying Mary* before settling in Manhattan in a Washington Heights apartment house around 1909. Kittie worked as a nurse while Audrey appeared briefly on Broadway as a footman in *The Boy and the Girl*, a musical comedy starring Marie Dressler at the New Amsterdam Theatre in June 1909.

According to legend, though, Audrey's first big break in New York was totally uncalculated (and also open to multiple-choice versions). Still a teenager, she was window-shopping on Fifth Avenue (or Broadway) with her mother (or a fellow chorine) when she was stalked by a photographer later identified as Felix Benedict Herzog. Herzog was not just any photographer, but the one whose *Tale of Isolde* set a precedent at the Architectural League of New York by being displayed on parity with the works of painters—as well as an inventor, engineer, and patent lawyer. Herzog worked from a studio in the Lincoln Arcade Building, a fledgling cultural colony in the West Sixties. Beguiled by Audrey's perfect figure, he insisted on immortalizing her on film and flaunting her in the flesh to his circle of fellow artists, including the muralist William de Leftwich Dodge, who introduced her to the Vienna-born sculptor Isidore Konti.

Audrey's mother chaperoned her meeting with Konti and was initially shocked when he perfunctorily demanded that, in the parlance of the time, Audrey pose in the "altogether," and in no fewer than three positions. Konti calmly explained: "You don't know the meaning, Mrs. Munson, of posing for an artist. To us it makes no difference if our model is draped or clothed in furs. We only see the work we are doing." (Apparently, it did make a difference to Herzog; though thirty-two years older than Audrey, he hoped to marry her and become her guardian. He died suddenly after surgery in 1912, before he could propose.) In the meantime, Audrey became Konti's muse for *The Three Graces*, his marble sculpture of the daughters of Zeus who personified beauty, mirth, and abundance, which garnished the grand ballroom of the Hotel Astor in Times Square from September 1909 until the hotel was razed in 1967 and the statue was installed in the Metropolitan Museum. Audrey would describe *The Three Graces* as "a souvenir of my mother's consent."

Audrey quickly came around to the artists' perspective, abandoning her probity so painlessly that her alacrity became the stuff of legend ("the face that launched a thousand quips"). According to one such account, the humorist P. G. Wodehouse and his wife had recently moved into a Manhattan apartment previously occupied by a sculptor. One day, as his wife was leaving, she told Wodehouse to expect a decorator who was coming by to redo their couch. Audrey Munson, who did not know that the sculptor had moved, knocked on the door and asked if there was any work for her. Wodehouse assured her that there was, but asked first, "How much would it be altogether?" Without missing a beat, Munson replied, "You want the altogether?" then ducked into a bedroom and emerged nearly naked. (Wodehouse, Guy Bolton, and Jerome Kern incorporated the scene into their 1918 musical *Oh, Lady! Lady!!*)

No other artists' model in America before or since would achieve Munson's celebrity. She worked herself to the bone for it. She joined the Art Workers' Club for Women, a union of sorts established in 1898 by Helen Sargent, and was sought after to pose for artists, sculptors, and photographers in the Lincoln Arcade, the Tenth Street Studio Building, and MacDougal Alley, where Gertrude Vanderbilt Whitney, the commodore's great-granddaughter, invited Munson to model for her monumental works.

Munson's alabaster countenance and curvaceous figure personified the neoclassicism of the École des Beaux-Arts in Paris. Sculptors became infatuated with her physiognomy—including body parts even she had never noticed, particularly a pair of dimples on the small of her back. "They are nature's rarest and most attractive beauty spots," the American artist Salvatore Scarpitta enthused.

She was also the muse for Attilio Piccirilli, one of six Italian immigrant brothers who worked in marble in their Bronx studio. He used Munson as his model for his sculptural groups *Duty* and *Sacrifice* at the Firemen's Memorial on Riverside Drive, and, at the USS *Maine* Monument at the southwest corner of Central Park, for figures representing Columbia Triumphant, who rides a gilded chariot atop the elaborate cenotaph, and Peace, at its base.

Munson posed for Henry Augustus Lukeman's bronze *Memory* on West End Avenue and 106th Street to honor Isidor Straus, an owner of Macy's whose wife, Ida, declined to leave him when he refused a seat in a lifeboat on the RMS *Titanic*; Frederick MacMonnies's *Beauty* at the New York Public Library; Daniel Chester French's final marble sculpture of *Memory* and his *Mourning Victory* at the Metropolitan Museum; and a bronze reduction of Adolph Alexander Weinman's winged figure *Descending Night*, which was featured in the Court of the Universe at the

Panama-Pacific Exposition in San Francisco. Munson's head, at least, was the model for Pomona, the Roman goddess of fruitful abundance, conceived by Karl Bitter atop the Pulitzer Fountain at Grand Army Plaza, the Fifth Avenue gateway to Central Park. She posed for *Peace*, atop the Appellate Division Courthouse on Madison Square; *The Spirit of the Waters* at Saratoga; and, in Boston, *Suffering Humanity*, a memorial to General William Booth, who, with his wife, founded the Salvation Army.

Munson said her arms substituted for the ancient Greek original when Queen Wilhelmina of the Netherlands commissioned Bitter to replicate an intact, four-limbed version of the Venus de Milo—the "American Venus." She also claimed to have modeled for Francis Picabia, the French-Cuban modernist who was represented at the transcendent 1913 Armory Show in New York (although Munson pronounced Picabia's work as "an incongruous collection of color splotches"). As someone who would later be judged herself—and certified—by professionals, she pronounced Picabia's fellow modern artists with subjective foresight as "just crazy persons capitalizing on their insanities."

In several respects, though, *Civic Fame* symbolized the height of her career. Charles H. Dorr described the Municipal Building in the *Architectural Record* as "a modern Colossus of Rhodes," a 648,000-square-foot modified Italian Renaissance steel-and-granite office building—the world's largest at the time—that soars nearly six hundred feet above Chambers Street.

In crowning the Municipal Building, the architects were inspired by the Giralda Tower, which was completed in 1198 as a minaret for the Great Mosque of Seville. Poised on a copper globe atop the highest parapet, surrounded by dolphins, in deference to the city's maritime roots, stands the twenty-foot-tall figure *Civic Fame*. In one hand she holds a crown with five crenellations, for each of Greater New York's boroughs; in the other a circular shield emblazoned with the city's seal and a laurel sprig—"the symbol of Apollonian self-discipline," the architectural historian Francis Morrone wrote in *City Journal*, "the *sine qua non* of civic virtue, or civic fame, which in this context means something more like honor, not mere celebrity."

The barefoot figure and her accoutrements weigh 5,000 pounds. She was pretty much taken for granted—out of sight *and* out of mind—until 1935, when her corroded 150-pound right arm plunged eight stories, stopped from crashing through a skylight above the kitchen servicing a restaurant for municipal employees only because the glass had been fortified with wire mesh. The *Times* cracked wise that *Civic Fame* was "possibly envious of the attention" focused on *Civic Virtue*, which, though a humbler sculpture and fountain, stood more prominently across the street in front of New York City Hall (whose cupola is capped by a figure of Justice, for reasons unknown without her traditional blindfold).

"She was known for being able to evoke a complete mood with her posture and expression—she was also known for being able to hold a pose for a really long time," the *Sun* wrote of Munson. "This model's very public body had come to represent truth, memory, civic fame, the stars and even the universe." That was a lot for anybody to personify for long.

Munson soon learned that fame was fleeting, that truth could be manipulated, that memories were short, that even streetlights could obscure the stars, and that in a universe eternally expanding, some other resource was required not only to surmount one's chosen pedestal but also to remain lodged in the firmament indefinitely. "Of all the rewards of virtue," Cicero wrote, "the most splendid is fame, for it is fame alone that can offer us the memory of posterity."

In 1913, when she was twenty-two, the *Sun* proclaimed Munson "Miss Manhattan" after she modeled for *Spirit of Commerce*, the winged relief that Carl Augustus Heber crafted in her image in a former stable on West Twenty-Fourth Street near Eighth Avenue. "Yes, she is the real Miss Manhattan now," Heber told the *Sun* in 1913. "She has grit, determination and, best of all, a sense of humor." Her *Spirit* decorated one of two pylons supporting the Carrere & Hastings arch added to the Canal Street gateway to the Manhattan Bridge (which was almost lopped off in the early 1960s for Robert Moses's proposed Lower Manhattan Expressway).

Munson also posed for Daniel Chester French, whose twenty-ton granite maidens representing the two boroughs guarded the opposite entrance to the Manhattan Bridge across the East River. Installed in 1916, Miss Brooklyn graciously posed holding a tablet bearing the inscription EIN DRACH MACKT MAGHT (a Dutch-German conflation meaning "In union there is strength," a reference to the consolidation of Greater New York). Befittingly, Miss Manhattan's persona is an altogether different portrait of hubris. Her right foot defends a treasure chest; she holds an orb emblematic of authority. The tableau she is part of includes the bows of three ships, hinting at Manhattan's dominion in maritime trade, as well as a peacock representing luxury and immortality. French, who described Munson as "just such a type as many of the early painters would have selected for a Madonna," was captivated by "the certain ethereal atmosphere around her" and her "decidedly expressive face, always changing." (Some accounts, however, attribute the statue's face to the architect Cass Gilbert's daughter Julia.)

Munson never lived lavishly, typically sharing a rented apartment with her mother on Manhattan's West Side. Perhaps to compensate for what she considered a disconnect between her celebrated talent and her measly renumeration, though, she inflated her job title. Though she initially described herself as an "art worker," by 1915 the R. L. Polk & Co.'s Trow General Directory would list her on West Seventieth Street as nothing less than an artist. That same year, Munson demonstrated her bona fides on an incredible scale. Her visage dominated the Panama-Pacific International Exposition which opened on February 20, 1915 in San Francisco and celebrated both the completion of the Panama Canal and the city's resurgence from the 1906 earthquake. Munson was the model for something like 75 percent of the 1,500 statues which were stationed like a battalion of terra-cotta warriors between the Presidio and Fort Mason. They were commissioned and coordinated from New York by A. Stirling Calder, father of the kinetic sculptor. The completed statues were lauded by most critics, but Munson herself was vilified by the self-appointed arbiters of morality because she had allowed herself to be replicated stark naked.

Less than eight weeks after the world's fair opened, Munson embarked on what, for a former chorine, amounted to star billing in what was literally her Broadway debut, but actually a heavily promoted early version of what today might be branded as commercial live infotainment. Unpropitiously, the *New York Tribune* referred to her as "Adelaide" Munson, but an advertisement in the *Times* accurately proclaimed that the twenty "handsomest women in the world" would be joined by Audrey Munson, the "Panama-Pacific Exposition Girl" and the "world's most famous figure model" in "striking poses" at a Grand Spring Fashion Show at the Palace Theater. Starring as "the Spirit of Fashion," Munson modeled a Bonwit Teller chiffon negligee and two bathing suits (one in yellow taffeta gussied up with a ribboned Greek border and the other skintight with zebra stripes). If the swimsuits were ogled by male audiences, they left Djuna Barnes, the acerbic avant garde journalist who interviewed Munson backstage for the *New York Press*, singularly unimpressed. Recapitulating the fashion show, Barnes managed to belittle Munson and her entire career in three words. "Poor little ninny," she wrote.

Ninny or not (and her ghostwritten memoirs suggested otherwise, despite her lack of formal education), Munson was, at five foot four, arguably little and, if not abjectly poor, then rarely financially secure. For exhibiting the latest creations by Fifth Avenue's most exclusive modistes and milliners, she earned a bigger paycheck than ever before—one hundred dollars a week. But she sued for twenty thousand dollars when the fashion show opened in Brooklyn while still capitalizing on her name after dropping her from the cast, and further doomed her Broadway career after she accused a major theatrical producer of making sexual overtures backstage.

Seven months after the Grand Spring Fashion Show opened at the Palace in April 1915, Edwin Thanhouser premiered his groundbreaking film *Inspiration*, just in time to promote Munson into a marquee name. She was the first American leading lady to appear nude in a mainstream movie. She earned five hundred dollars a week for making the five-reeler (about fifty minutes) filmed in a suburban New Rochelle, New York, roller skating rink. While it passed muster to be filmed in New Rochelle, it was banned from being shown at the North Avenue Theater there because of concerns that it would embolden otherwise responsible but susceptible moviegoers to do God knows what.

The plot, such as it was, revolves around an artist's search for the perfect model. The hunt is conducted by three loyal friends, one of whom rescues Munson after she is struck by a taxi and takes her to the artist's studio where they fall in love until she discovers that he is already engaged to another woman. She vanishes, but he finds her at the Merchants' Gate to Central Park, slumped on the steps of the Maine Monument at Columbus Circle. Above her, the figure of Audrey Munson, representing Columbia Triumphant cast in gilded bronze (supposedly from gunmetal salvaged from the sunken battleship), commands a seashell chariot drawn by three hippocampi atop a marble pylon inscribed prophetically: BY FATE UNWARNED, IN DEATH UNAFRAID.

The tangential history lesson may have embellished the film's verities and offered the censors some justification to overlook the visuals. Verisimilitude was also provided by the casting of Munson herself as the ideal model, although she sorely tested artistic license when she appeared nude covered head to foot in wet plaster (which, once it dried, was gingerly chipped away as audiences swooned). The *Houston Post* concluded that "there is a splendid education value to the production." The *Nashville Tennessean*, while allowing that "Inspiration" depicted life in a sculptor's studio "hinted at in books not to be found in school libraries," quoted Thanhouser as acknowledging that "only under such occasions as to feature such a perfect beauty as Audrey Munson would even he, the most daring of all producers, advise the recommending" of nude figures in films.

Thanhouser couldn't help himself, irresistibly daring only eight months later to share Munson's perfect beauty with the public again in a second film that he anointed with an even cheekier title: *Purity*. In this seven-reeler filmed in Santa Barbara,

Statue of Audrey Munson at the top of the Municipal building at One Centre Street in Manhattan, New York, 2007. (Photo by Hiroko Masuike via the *New York Times*)

California, the screenplay fantasized that the model was posing nude in order to raise money to publish her boyfriend's poetry. The *Tampa Tribune* described the raven-haired, gray-eyed five-foot-four Munson with a thirty-three-inch chest, twenty-five-inch waist, and thirty-seven-inch hips as the personification of the flowing line, "the purity and the limpid clarity of beauty." The *Times* reviewer concluded that Munson's figure was "systematically and thoroughly exploited" on behalf of "a bad and extraordinarily funereal looking poet," and concluded: "From the sample of his verse flashed on the screen you fear the end did not justify the means."

Munson returned to New York, where, having achieved fame, she claimed to seek romance. She dated Hermann Oelrichs Jr., son of the multimillionaire American agent for the North German Lloyd shipping line and owner of the Rosecliff mansion in Newport and nephew of Virginia Fair Vanderbilt, whose husband was president of the New York Central Railroad. Kittie Munson later referred to Oelrichs as Audrey's husband. Whatever their actual relationship, it ended poorly. On January 29, 1919, in a letter from New York to the State Department in Washington, Munson vilified Oelrichs (who was Catholic) and a cabal of German Jews in the film industry and beyond who, she wrote, had sabotaged her vocation.

Munson's irrefutably career-ending catastrophe struck one month later, when she was twenty-seven, as a consequence of what was being billed as another love affair gone horribly wrong. On February 27, 1919, Dr. Walter Keene Wilkins and his wife, Julia, had just returned to Long Beach on Long Island from visiting friends in Manhattan when he noticed that the door to the garage of their home was open. Wilkins said when he went inside to check, he was struck on the head by an assailant. After the assailant and two accomplices fled, Wilkins, sixty-five, said he found his wife lying in a pool of blood with a machinist's hammer by her side. She died later that night.

Since the middle of 1918, Audrey and Kittie Munson had boarded at the Wilkins's home at 164 West Sixty-Fifth Street in Manhattan. They had moved out a few weeks before the murder. The doctor stood to inherit his wife's estate. Clues emerged suggesting a love triangle: the doctor maintained what neighbors described as a secret love nest just down the block from No. 164; police discovered among his belongings what was variously described as an advertising photograph of his boarder, Audrey Munson, in a bathing suit, but was more likely a calling card; his stepdaughter swore that her mother had warned her husband against flirting with Munson after the doctor once had cautioned the model indelicately: "Don't you ever get married because if you do you'll lose your symmetrical figure."

On March 24, 1919, the Nassau County district attorney appealed to the public for help in finding Audrey and Kittie Munson who, after moving from the West Side, left no forwarding address. The William J. Burns Detective Agency was enlisted in the search. Terrified at being implicated in a murder investigation, Munson would have been even more heartbroken to discover, based on the account in the *Times* of the prosecutor's appeal for her whereabouts, just how provisional her fame had been. The *Times* article spelled her name correctly, at least, but began supercil- iously by describing her as "Audrey Munson, said to be a motion picture actress and artists' model . . ." Burns detectives finally found the mother and daughter in Toronto, Canada. Audrey refused to return to New York to testify against her former landlord, whom she also characterized as her "medical advisor." Without Munson's testimony, after deliberating for twenty-three hours, the jury pronounced Doctor Wilkins guilty, but recommended clemency. The only possible sentence was death. He cheated the electric chair, though, by hanging himself in the Nassau County Jail.

Munson never recovered professionally or emotionally. A year after the trial, she tried to one-up Doctor Wilkins by feigning suicide. She sought to expunge her past by placing an obituary in her own name in a Syracuse newspaper but was thwarted by an alert clerk who immediately recognized her as the local girl who had become America's first supermodel. "I thought that if poor Audrey Munson were out of the way some of those who had cared for her and for her work in the past might remember her and be sorry and that her old self, under another name, might have a chance to work and to be happy again," she later told the *Evening World*.

To make ends meet, while Kittie sold kitchen utensils door-to-door, Audrey pawned her jewelry, taught dancing, waited tables and, according to one account, was so desperate that she briefly accepted an apprenticeship at the Syracuse Public Library at $0.15 an hour. Finally, sob stories in the press about her plight inspired her third and final autobiographical film, a cautionary tale aptly titled *Heedless Moths*. Perry Play Films promoted the promised movie in display advertisements that brandished replicas of a $27,500 check, which it described as Munson's down payment for the movie rights. That amount was never mentioned in the actual contract, though, which granted the press agent Allen Rock rights for a total of $7,500. How much Munson actually got is anyone's guess, but the prospect prompted a front page, banner headline in Albany's Knickerbocker Press, which proclaimed, prematurely, MUNSON EMERGES FROM POVERTY.

Heedless Moths opened in late May 1921 at the Greenwich Village Theater following a barrage of publicity—including a twenty-part weekly series titled the Queen of the Artists' Studios under Munson's own byline. Her proto-feminist plea for equality in the workplace, which offered suggestions as to how women could look their best by chucking corsets, garter belts, and high heels specifically (and, teasing presumably, clothes altogether), was syndicated by Hearst's *New York American*. Her perspective on modeling nude was, in a way, more revealing than the undraped frames the censors had snipped from her films. Testifying in St. Louis in favor of releasing the film, she declared: "A girl sitting on the edge of a table, wearing fine silk hosiery, abbreviated skirts and her legs crossed is what I consider immoral posing."

As for the film itself, the *Times* grumped that "Miss Munson may have inspired all of the artists whose names are lined up in the announcements of the film and in the story of the picture itself, but she failed to inspire those who made the picture." Worse still, except for the modeling scenes, the part of Munson was played by someone else. (Hedda Hopper, before becoming a columnist, played the sculptor's wife.) Munson, the eponymous heedless moth, bitterly raised a more fundamental grievance. She compared unfavorably the role of artists' models with that of actors who are considered part of a collaborative process: when a show is financially successful, the actors, playwright, director, and other principals are rewarded with "increases in salary and a step at least one notch higher on the road to fame and prosperity. Not so with the artist's model," Munson wrote. "She remains ever anonymous. She is the tool with which the artist works, though she provides the inspiration for a master-piece and is the direct cause of enriching the painter or sculptor."

Anonymous. Lost and lonely. Miss Manhattan missed Manhattan. She returned upstate, where she mounted what she would insist lamely was a private search for "the perfect man" to marry. Whatever her original motivation, thanks to her insa-tiable craving for publicity and the avid complicity of the *United Press*, the quest escalated into a very public stunt. The publicity helped popularize her poisonous eugenics apologies and anti-Semitic delusions in which she blamed Jews in Holly-wood and elsewhere for sabotaging her career and singling out several targets who were not, in fact, even Jewish. Her search generated hundreds of marriage proposals, but also one apparent high-profile rejection.

Munson had endured enough good and bad luck to have been haunted by the prophecy, or curse, supposedly delivered by a soothsayer who read her fortune at a Roma encampment that Kittie took her to in East Syracuse when she was five: *When you think that happiness is yours, its Dead Sea fruit shall turn to ashes in your mouth . . . You, who shall mock at love, shall seek love without finding one. Seven times you shall be led by the man who loves you to the steps of the altar, but never shall you wed.*

Munson led people to believe that the seventh man was a Joseph A. Stevenson of Ann Arbor, Michigan, who had responded to her perfect man pursuit. After prom-ising to marry her, according to the most widely circulated account, Stevenson changed his mind at the last minute. Instead of arriving for their nuptials in Mexico, New York, he sent a telegram that prompted her to swallow a glass of water containing four tablets of highly toxic mercury bichloride on May 27, 1922, less than two weeks before her thirty-first birthday (only one of the tablets dissolved and an antidote was quickly administered). "When I had read it, I knew that the end of life had come for me," she confided to *Movie Weekly*. Except that nobody was able to confirm that any such Joseph A. Stevenson actually existed. Like the contents of the telegram he supposedly sent, Stevenson himself forever remained a mystery.

So did the identity of the theatrical producer whose backstage sexual advances she said she had rebuffed. Also never revealed was the text of her affidavit in the Wilkins murder-suicide case, which Munson blamed for obliterating what was left of her professional prospects. Conjuring up just the right weapon, the *Washington Post* sermonized: "It surely seemed as if fate, wielding a mighty hammer, had brought down upon this model a blow that shattered."

Munson's behavior became increasingly erratic. When her father's second wife—her stepmother—died in 1926, she declined to attend the funeral. "Haggard in appearance and broken in spirit, Audrey, according to villagers, is merely existing these days," the *Republican-Journal* of Ogdensburg, New York reported. "She is penniless and only recently had to give up all of her dogs to the authorities when they found out that she was unable to feed them."

In 1931, Kittie Munson petitioned a New York court to commit her daughter to an insane asylum. Two doctors concurred. A judge signed the certificate of lunacy on June 8, Audrey's fortieth birthday. He ordered her confined to St. Lawrence State Hospital for the insane in Ogdensburg. While St. Lawrence was considered a progressive institution (it happened to be the first such asylum in the country that installed an on-site beauty salon to boost the self-esteem of female patients), Andrea Geyer, another Munson biographer, wrote: "It is unclear whether she was in fact mentally ill or a tragically misunderstood artist and feminist."

In her prime, Munson had embodied Manhattan in the raucous decade between the Gilded Age and the Roaring Twenties. "She is the real Miss Manhattan," the sculptor C. A. Heber had said. And who better to have personified the city than a pioneering adult-film star figured as the other woman in a love-triangle murder, tried to have herself declared dead, attempted suicide, was committed on her fortieth birthday to a lunatic asylum, where she lived until 1996 when she was 104, and was then buried in 1996 in an unmarked grave. (Her descendants and devotees who rediscovered Munson finally installed a headstone in 2016.)

Norman Rose, a journalist who interviewed her in 1915, could never have guessed her fate or whether she would be remembered as the befitting personification of Manhattan. But he predicted that her seductiveness, just like the city's, would be perpetuated. He described Munson as "a slender, graceful girl who will live in marble and bronze and canvas, in the art centers of the world, long, long after she and everyone else of this generation shall have become dust!"

Munson, who was born when the average life expectancy for an American white woman was forty-five, would not only outlive virtually every one of her contemporaries but also even outlast the vast majority of statues cast in her image (especially considering that most of the hundreds of plaster saints she modeled for at the San Francisco exposition were not preserved). Recalling her reign as Queen of the Artists' Studios, Munson was less concerned about the durability of the dozens of marble and bronze and canvas effigies that did survive or even in the promise of "going down in history" versus the verifiable evanescence of fame.

"What becomes of the artists' models?" Munson once asked purposefully. "I am wondering if many of my readers have not stood before a masterpiece of lovely sculpture or a remarkable painting of a young girl, her very abandonment of draperies accentuating rather than diminishing her modesty and purity, and asked themselves the question, 'Where is she now, this model who was so beautiful? What has been her reward? Is she happy and prosperous or is she sad and forlorn, her beauty gone, leaving only memories in the wake!'"

24

Clara Lemlich

The Little Lady Who Could

The four-paragraph article appeared on page 2 of the *New York Call* on Monday, November 22, 1909. It was sandwiched between a feature story headlined UNEMPLOYED FACE MISERY OF WINTER and a modest advertisement that proclaimed GOOD SOCIALISTS SHOULD SMOKE GOOD CIGARS—specifically Liberty Torch cigars, hand-rolled by union workers at a factory in Brooklyn. (The torch, not coincidentally, happened to be the logo of the Socialist Party, which published the *Call*.)

GOMPERS TO SPEAK, the article announced. It referred, of course, to Samuel Gompers, the man who had organized the cigar workers in New York and headed the American Federation of Labor since it was founded in 1886. The AFL had marginalized radical socialists by isolating their most vociferous adherents in local unions representing mine and garment workers. As he was poised to hold forth that night, Gompers himself was facing a one-year jail sentence stemming from the union boycott of a stove manufacturer. (He deferred, at the time, to the Supreme Court as the final arbiter, declaring, "We protest against the notion that a law is broken till it is finally and fully decided what is the law.") The announcement appeared in type smaller than the cigar ad, but it was large enough to draw thousands of angry garment workers. That evening they would jam the Great Hall in the basement of Cooper Union and overflow that fabled auditorium to be exhorted by other lions of labor at the Manhattan Lyceum, Beethoven Hall, and Clinton Hall.

Local 25 of the International Ladies' Garment Workers' Union (ILGWU), a fledgling coalition of female Jewish and Italian immigrants, had been picketing several manufacturers, including the Leiserson Company, Rosen Brothers, and the Triangle Shirtwaist Company, for months, demanding raises, shorter workweeks, and recognition of the union—rather than compliant company-created labor collaborators—as their bargaining agent.

For two hours, the crowd at Cooper Union was harangued by speakers including the socialist lawyer and future congressman Meyer London; Mary Dreier, president of the New York Women's Trade Union League; and Abraham Cahan, editor of the *Forward*, a daily socialist newspaper published in Yiddish. Gompers then admonished the volcanic crowd that he had never specifically instigated a formal job action, like a strike or slowdown, until every alternative had been exhausted. He hinted that Local 25, organized by Clara Lemlich and other women and deprecated by their male union counterparts, was not yet strong enough to survive on its own, much less win, a general strike. "The history of labor is littered with the skeletons of organizations done to death because of hasty strikes gone into for the best of reasons but unprepared," he cautioned.

Jacob Panken, a lawyer and early organizer for the Purse and Bag Workers' Union, was about to begin speaking next when Clara Lemlich interjected from the floor of the Great Hall. Lemlich could easily have been taken for a teenager—"the frail little girl, with flashing black eyes," the *Call* portrayed her through prisms of pity and pluck. But she was around twenty-three and, having only five years earlier fled the government-sponsored antirevolutionary pogroms in czarist Russia, already a battle-hardened veteran of the garment workers' picket lines. As soon as she stood up to interrupt the procession of labor and political luminaries diplomatically chosen to speak by the meeting's organizers, she commanded the attention of more than two thousand union members.

"I want to say a few words," Lemlich began in Yiddish. Those few words alone were enough for her to be swept from her seat to the stage. She needed no prepared text. She needed no interpretor. She had not rehearsed her remarks, but they flowed effortlessly. "I have listened to all the speakers," she said. "I would not have further patience for talk, as I am one of those who feels and suffers from the things pictured. I move that we go on a general strike."

Her listeners, too, had lost their patience with wasted weeks and months of talk. The few hundred workers who walked out of a handful of shops earlier had been replaced by scabs. Police abused strikers on the picket line. Union action had barely

"Portrait of Clara Lemlich, circa 1910." (Photo via the
Kheel Center at Cornell University)

dented the output and supply of blouses and dresses or budged the factory owners.
The only way to win the industrywide concessions demanded by the union was to
exert organized labor's last recourse: shut down all the shops, strangle production
entirely, and negotiate agreements with the hundreds of highly competitive bosses
one by one.

So thunderous was the response to Lemlich's brief but blunt exhortation that this
time the *Call*'s reporter needed no thesaurus to eclipse the mainstream press. "As
the tremulous voice of the girl died away," the newspaper reported the next day, "the
audience rose en masse and cheered her to the echo. A grim sea of faces, with high
purpose and resolve, they shouted and cheered the deliberation of war for living
conditions hoarsely." Everyone, the *New York World* concurred, shouted "an emphatic
affirmative, waving hats, canes, handkerchiefs, anything that came handy. For five
minutes, perhaps, the tumult continued."

Benjamin Feigenbaum, the associate editor of the *Forward* chairing the meeting, called for order, asking for a final moment of reflection. Don't be ashamed to vote no, he warned those who feared hunger and cold with winter coming. Those in favor, he said, should be prepared to struggle—and suffer—until the end. Then Feigenbaum, an irreligious socialist, histrionically raised his right hand and led Lemlich and the rest of the mesmerized audience in a biblical pledge. "Do you have faith?" he demanded. "Will you take the old Jewish oath?" As a sea of hands rose, the eager strikers declared: "If I turn traitor to the cause I now pledge, may this hand wither from the arm I now raise." Finally, Feigenbaum put Lemlich's motion to a voice vote. "There was a resounding roar of ayes throughout the hall," the *Call* reported, "and once again the vast crowd broke into roars of applause."

What became known as the Uprising of 20,000 might well have happened eventually without Clara Lemlich—perhaps when the union had grown stronger and going on strike was less risky. But there is little argument that, while the garment workers were moving toward open revolt at some point, Lemlich was the chief instigator of the massive walkout that November night in 1909.

Halfway around the world, the *Sydney Morning Herald* reported that "this girl jumped upon the platform where aimless speakers were wasting time, and in her native Yiddish spoke with such force and feeling that even those who did not know her language could understand her. She urged them to waste no more time in futile speech, but to decide there and then to strike or not to strike. It was the match that fired the pile, and the girls struck."

Clara Lemlich was born on March 28, 1886, in western Ukraine, about fifteen miles from Lviv, in a shtetl named Gorodok where nearly one third of the residents were Jewish. She was raised in a patriarchal, Yiddish-speaking household, which meant that as a young girl, she was denied the education her brothers received. Barred from the village's sole public school because she was Jewish, she was forbidden by her parents to learn Russian. Clara defied them. Older acquaintances tutored her in the language and loaned her books by Tolstoy, Gorky, and Turgenev. A neighbor exposed her to anti-czarist screeds and Socialism. She earned money by sewing buttonholes and writing letters for illiterate villagers to relatives who had emigrated to America.

In 1903, when Clara was seventeen, the bloody Kishinev pogroms in Moldova finally provoked her parents to escape with her and her four brothers. They arrived in December 1904 on the American Line's SS *New York*. According to the manifest, her father, Schimschan (Simon) Lumback, described his occupation as a bookbinder. He had been living in London, he said, had thirty dollars in his pocket, was neither a polygamist nor an anarchist, and was joining a cousin who lived on Stanton Street on the Lower East Side. Clara, listed as Cheise, identified herself to immigration authorities as a nineteen-year-old tailoress.

By the beginning of the twentieth century, more than half of the clothes manufactured in the United States were made in New York City, with most women's wear produced by immigrant girls who confronted gender inequality, sexual harassment, squalid and unsafe working conditions, low wages, and long hours. In a job market defined by volatile turnover and seasonal demand, Clara was hired within a few weeks after she arrived in New York in 1904. She rapidly advanced to a handsome sixteen-dollar-a-week salary as a draper, creating the patterns for mass production of specific blouse and dress designs by meticulously placing fabric over a mannequin. But, she later recalled, "the hissing of the machines, the yelling of the foreman made life unbearable"—even worse, she told the *New York Evening Journal*, "than I would imagine slaves were in the South." She and her colleagues worked sixty-five, sometimes seventy-five-hour weeks. They often had to supply their own needles and thread.

Determined to improve her lot, Clara began by enrolling in the Educational League on Madison Street to learn English. She studied Marxist theory at the Socialist Party's Rand School of Social Science, and educated herself at the East Broadway branch of the New York Public Library.

"We're human, all of us girls, and we're young," Lemlich told readers of *Good Housekeeping* magazine. "We like new hats as well as any other young women. Why shouldn't we? And if one of us gets a new one, even if it hasn't cost more than 50 cents, that means that we have gone for weeks on two-cent lunches—dry cakes and nothing else." A beautiful building on Fifth Avenue was a Potemkin facade, she said, for a factory where three hundred workers competed for one sink and two toilets, where the office clock was draped to prevent them from even glancing up to check the hour and cheat the bosses on overtime. The girls walked out "to prevent themselves from being starved out," she said. "The manufacturer has a vote; the bosses have votes; the foremen have votes; the inspectors have votes. The working girl has no vote."

Jews—including housewives, who already had a history of protest in rent strikes and kosher meat boycotts—and Italians, leery of organized labor in the beginning, edged warily into blue-collar alliances. These coalitions would spur the rise of politicians like future congressman and mayor Fiorello La Guardia, who at the time was finishing law school at New York University while working as an interpreter on Ellis Island. Among the first hundred immigrant girls Lemlich canvassed, only five agreed to join the union. "What did I know about trade unionism?" she said later of her fortitude. "Audacity—that was all I had—audacity." Her swagger, her refusal to be relegated to a cog, was what made her stand up to the bosses: "Girls, to them," she said, "are part of the machines they are manning."

Rose Schneiderman and Pauline Newman, who would later be universally celebrated as labor heroines, served as Lemlich's mentors. When she began working at Leiserson's, Annelise Orleck wrote in *Common Sense and a Little Fire* (2017), Lemlich brazenly "marched uninvited into a strike meeting that had been called by the shop's older male elite—the skilled cutters and drapers—warning them that they would lose if they attempted to strike without organizing the shop's unskilled women."

On August 12, 1909, five self-styled detectives hired by Rosen Brothers to protect Italian girls unwilling to jeopardize their jobs for union solidarity physically beat Lemlich and several other pickets during an altercation that left her hospitalized. She hid her broken ribs and bruises from her parents. The "detectives"—a prizefighter and several ex-convicts—were miraculously arrested, but a month later, even as Lemlich remained hospitalized, they were released from jail. The strikers were fined ten dollars each for disorderly conduct. But then wealthy women like Anne Morgan, J. P.'s maverick daughter, and Alva Belmont, whose father-in-law, August Belmont, was investment banker to the Rothschilds, provided more than money and moral support. They put their bodies on the line. The arrests of middle- and upper-class picketers made the manufacturers squirm.

Having been arrested seventeen times while organizing or picketing, Lemlich, barely five feet tall, had no compunctions about challenging her union's male leadership. Asked later how she managed to organize twenty thousand largely uneducated workers, Lemlich replied: "Well, to be honest, I didn't really organize them; I really just motivated them." She went on to recount how she felt that night at Cooper Union, listening to the speeches: "They just made me so mad because they talked in such general terms about the need for solidarity and preparedness and all that." Instead, "I demanded action . . . I was just saying what all the workers were thinking, but they were just too afraid to say."

Lemlich's role didn't end with her words at Cooper Union. "A committee of men is handling the strike, but Clara Lemlich, a pretty East Sider of 19 years, is the Joan of Arc who is recognized as the sentimental leader," the *Evening Republican* of Meadville, Pennsyvania, reported. "She went about everywhere encouraging her

"Garment workers in New York City, picketing circa 1915,"
from American Labor: A Pictorial Social History *by*
M. B. Schnapper (Washington, D.C.: Public Affairs
Press, 1972), 361.

companions and kept enthusiasm at high pitch." A Jewish weekly in Chicago, the *Reform Advocate*, declared: "The soul of this young woman's revolution is Clara Lemlich, a spirit of fire and tears, devoid of egotism, unable to tolerate the thought of human suffering." On the picket lines, the *New York Sun* reported, "The girls, headed by teenage Clara Lemlich, described by union organizers as a 'pint of trouble for the bosses,' began singing Italian and Russian working-class songs as they paced in twos before the factory door."

Many of the smaller shops met most of the union's demands early on, but the larger factories held out longer, defying the pickets by hiring scabs and even shifting production out-of-town. Wage increases were negotiable. So was reducing the work-week from as much as seventy-five hours in high season to fifty-two. What Triangle and the other biggest owners absolutely refused to budge on was recognizing the union and negotiating an industrywide collective bargaining agreement. As the walkout dragged on, the strikers' stamina was sorely tested, as Gompers had predicted. But as pickets paced in temperatures that averaged below freezing, a number of them suffered from malnutrition, and some seven hundred were arrested, public opinion began to shift. Even the *Times* was edging toward the view that responsible unionism, leading to constructive partnerships with management—what was being described under the broad umbrella of industrial democracy—was a necessary evil to fend off more radical and even revolutionary alternatives.

When the strike finally ended in mid-February 1910, after nearly three months, the union had won the battle, if not the war. Of the 353 member firms of the Associated Waist and Dress Manufacturers, representing the factory owners, 339 signed contracts that provided for a fifty-two-hour week, four paid holidays annually, provision of tools without fee, and job safeguards for union members. Within a few years, the so-called needle trades became a model of industrial unionism in America.

These labor victories must have gratified Clara Lemlich, but they didn't help her much professionally. Because her father (who, like his wife, had arrived from Russia illiterate) had difficulty keeping a full-time job, she often had to be the family's main breadwinner. She applied for work under aliases but was hounded out of the garment business.

On March 25, 1911, thirteen months after the shirtwaist workers' strike ended, a fire in the Triangle plant on Washington Place killed 146 workers, mostly young immigrant girls working late on a Saturday and unable to escape because exits were barred to prevent theft. The fire galvanized garment workers, progressives, labor organizers, and Democratic politicians into a muscular coalition that would shape social policy for decades. "If it had been a union shop," Lemlich said, "there would not have been any locked doors, and the girls would have been on the street almost an hour before the fire started."

Consumer advocate Frances Perkins was having tea at the Washington Square town house of Margaret Norris, a descendant of Alexander Hamilton, when she was stirred by steady wail of sirens and raced to the scene. At former president Theodore Roosevelt's recommendation, Perkins was named to head a committee on safety, which led to the appointment of a commission to investigate the factory. Its staff of inspectors—apparently at Perkins's suggestion—included Clara Lemlich. (Workplace owners were outraged. "It would seem," said one, "that in view of what Miss Lemlich says she has suffered at the hands of manufacturers she would be rather a prejudiced person to entrust to factory inspections.") In *The Triangle Fire, the*

Protocols of Peace, and Industrial Democracy in Progressive Era New York (2005), Richard A. Greenwald wrote that the commission "not only transformed working conditions in New York, it invented urban liberalism and forged the first working alliance between middle-class experts and reformers and machine politicians."

In 1911, Lemlich would also help found the Wage-Earners Suffrage League with Leonora O'Reilly and Rose Schneiderman. She married Joseph Shavelson, a printers' union activist, in 1913 (becoming a U.S. citizen as a result), moved in with his sister in Brooklyn, and devoted much of her time to raising three children. (Her two daughters both became social crusaders. Her son, Irving Charles Shavelson, a machinist in the Brooklyn Navy Yard, abbreviated his surname to Velson. He was later identified as a Soviet military intelligence agent in the Panama Canal Zone and who in New York collaborated with Bernard Schuster, the American Communist Party official who recruited Julius Rosenberg to steal American military secrets.)

By the mid-1920s, Lemlich was organizing boycotts of kosher butchers to protest high prices, leading rent strikes, and challenging evictions. Around 1926, she joined the Communist Party; she was the party's nominee for alderman in 1933 and for the state assembly from Brooklyn in 1936. She helped establish the nationwide United Council of Working Class Women, and during the Depression she mobilized a boycott that managed to shut down an estimated 4,500 butcher shops in New York City in protest against meat shortages and price gouging.

In 1944, after her husband got sick (he died in 1951), Lemlich returned to work in the garment industry. She retired three years later, beginning a protracted struggle with the ILGWU, which denied her a pension because she lacked fifteen years of consecutive service, though its venerable president David Dubinsky eventually intervened and awarded her a modest stipend.

Lemlich remained unapologetic and unreconstructed, protesting a broad range of what struck her as injustices. In 1960 she married Abe Goldman, an old acquaintance from the labor movement. When he died in 1967, she moved into the Jewish Home for the Aged in Los Angeles. (Her daughter Martha Schaffer lived in California, where she, too, was an advocate for social justice; her other daughter, Rita Margules, was in New York.) Even in her eighties, she successfully lobbied the administrators of the retirement home to honor the United Farm Workers boycott of nonunion grapes and lettuce, and even helped the orderlies there to form a union.

In *World of Our Fathers* (1976), Irving Howe invokes the memories of "our wonderful fervent girls" in the garment industry who had the guts to defy their bosses. But by the time Lemlich died at the nursing home at the age of ninety-six, in 1982, the ILGWU's membership, which had peaked in 1969 at 450,000, was already plummeting despite several mergers. It would eventually dwindle to some 80,000 nationally as garment industry jobs were lost to automation and to nonunion shops out of town and in Asia. Her role in the 1909 strike was invoked in the mid-1980s and early 1990s in the play and film version of Herb Gardner's *I'm Not Rappaport* but the newspapers that had lionized Lemlich in 1909 either no longer existed or had forgotten who she was. In 2018, fully thirty-six years after she died, the *Times* finally carried her obituary, in a series called Overlooked.

Some critics considered Lemlich a fanatic, on the fringes of what the author Mildred Moore defined in 1915 as "industrial feminism." She was also utilitarian, though. She knew instinctively that revolutionaries succeed by rallying followers to the right cause at the right time, by sacrifice, but also by sustaining themselves emotionally and materially. "Lemlich was perturbed when her grandson announced that he was going to follow in Clara's footsteps," she told the labor journalist Pauline Newman. " 'I'm going to be a radical,' her grandson, Joel Schaffer, said proudly. 'That's nice,' Clara answered from painful experience. 'A radical what? You can't just be a radical. You have to have a trade.' "

He chose one, as a mediator. "I am neutral; I am certainly not neutered," Schaffer said recently. "I certainly continue to ask myself when faced with a difficult problem, what would Clara do?"

25

Charles F. Murphy

The Benevolent Boss

Clara Lemlich and Charles Murphy both hailed from Manhattan's Lower East Side, and while their political priorities would improbably merge after 1909, chances are they never met face-to-face. They would be linked by an equally implausible intermediary, an Episcopalian woman born in Boston to a family rooted in mid-eighteenth-century colonial America. She was descended from James Otis Jr., the patriot who popularized the battle cry, "Taxation without representation is tyranny," and who had graduated from Mount Holyoke, where she majored in physics, and later earned advanced degrees in sociology and economics at Columbia University.

Given Frances Perkins's background and credentials, perhaps it was not astonishing that she would become the first woman member of a presidential cabinet, as Franklin Roosevelt's secretary of labor. But that she would play the go-between to Lemlich and Murphy, in retrospect, seems just as far-fetched as either of them emerging to fulfill their own defining roles in the city's history. The Triangle Shirtwaist fire catalyzed Perkins to transform the fury of immigrant workers, the conscience of society women, and the self-interest of urban politicians and their patrons into ground-breaking New York State legislation that, she would later proclaim, heralded the social welfare objectives of Governor Al Smith and his successor, Franklin Roosevelt, when FDR promulgated the New Deal in Washington.

Jacob Riis, the reformer who proved that photojournalism was not just a flash in the pan, sagaciously concluded that his battle with the slums "was a losing fight until conscience joined forces with fear and self-interest against it." Charles Murphy would distinguish himself by longevity—presiding over Tammany Hall for 22 of its 128-year existence by the time he died, longer than any predecessor. Yet while some of his contemporaries and even some historians would capriciously dismiss him as just another political boss on the make and on the take, Murphy was singularized by another unique characteristic: In the aftermath of the Triangle fire in 1911, he infused Riis's winning strategy of conscience, fear, and self-interest in his acolytes in the Albany legislature, driving them to produce among the first protections and other reforms for factory workers in the nation.

Several years later, Frances Perkins made a personal pilgrimage to Tammany Hall to seek Murphy's support for another round of legal safeguards for New York laborers. As George W. Martin recounted in *Madam Secretary: Frances Perkins* (1976), Murphy patiently allowed Perkins to make her case. Then he posed a question to which he already knew full well the answer. "You are the young lady, aren't you," he asked, "who managed to get the 54-hour bill passed?"

Perkins confessed that she was (she got the bill limiting the workweek for women and children passed in 1912, three years after Clara Lemlich's strike), knowing that Murphy had flatly opposed it. She also remembered that the bill had endeared the Democratic Party to an army of overworked immigrants, a ramification that Murphy had not forgotten. "It is my observation that the bill made us many votes," Murphy responded, then surprised her by volunteering, "I will tell the boys to give all the help they can to this new bill." As Perkins, both grateful and flabbergasted, expressed her thanks, Murphy posed another question: "Are you one of these women suffragists?" When she acknowledged that yes, she certainly was, Murphy replied, "Well, I am not, but if anyone ever gives them the vote, I hope you will remember that you would make a good Democrat."

Charles Francis Murphy, a staunch Catholic, had been born just before the Civil War, in 1858, which also happened to be the year that the Roman Catholic Archdiocese of New York poked its finger in the eye of the Protestant establishment by beginning construction of St. Patrick's Cathedral on Fifth Avenue in Midtown. The glorious cathedral would rise well beyond the immigrant ghettos of the Lower East Side and, just to the north, of the Gas House District, where Charlie's father Dennis had arrived from county Kildare in 1848 at the height of the Great Potato Famine.

The second of nine children, Charlie quit school at fourteen to help support his family, first at John Roach's Morgan Iron Works, shipbuilders on the East River, then as a driver—probably thanks to the patronage of a local Democratic leader—for the Blue Line, which operated a crosstown horsecar between the East Side and the Hoboken Ferry. After eight years, at the age of twenty-two, he had saved enough to open his first saloon, Charlie's Place, followed by three more, including one at East Twentieth Street and Second Avenue that would become the headquarters of his Anawanda Democratic Club.

Murphy's Anawanda Club became an integral cog in the Tammany machine, its idiomatic Native American insignia emblazoned prominently even on the club's signature poker chips. (The logo was discreetly erased from the building's facade during World War II because of its resemblance to the Nazi swastika.)

"Ready for a day with his lieutenants, Charles F. Murphy, the Boss at the office, Tammany Hall," 1913. (Photo by Underwood & Underwood)

Tweed was a charlatan who grounded his transactional bargaining in the swamps of personal expediency. Richard Croker, who commanded Tammany between John Kelly and Charles Murphy, was more calculating, politically savvy, and sufficiently scrupulous to avoid imprisonment. Croker enriched himself and, New York senator Daniel Patrick Moynihan said, "did the thing rich people in Ireland did: He bought a manor house in England, bred horses, and won the Derby." To which Moynihan coyly added a coda: "The king did not ask him to the Derby dinner." Murphy did Croker one better. He played his cards so close to the vest that while he raised suspicions by empowering surrogates as influence peddlers and living well beyond his visible means, he was never formally accused of corruption or other crimes.

Before Murphy, the bosses often squandered the power bestowed upon them through a subtle accommodations, which simultaneously allowed the city's elite to pursue its self-interested policy priorities and the politicians to exact their own rake-off. "The Irish leaders did for the Protestant establishment what it could not do for itself, and could not do without," Moynihan wrote. "But the Irish just didn't know what to do with their opportunity. They never thought of politics as an instrument of social change."

Charlie Murphy's quid was typically not meant to compensate for some past quo, but a down payment on a future one. In the Great Blizzard of 1888, New Yorkers of every rank, dependent solely on surface transportation and overhead power and telephone lines for communication, were paralyzed by two-story-high snowdrifts. Murphy steered $1,500 from the Democratic organization's relief fund to the Avenue A Mission run by St. George's Church, whose parishioners included J. P. Morgan. Remarkably, St. George's Anglican rector, the William S. Rainsford, a fierce critic of the party machine (and of the extravagance of the Bradley-Martin costume party ball at the old Waldorf-Astoria, which doomed the Gilded Age), proclaimed from the pulpit that Tammany in general would go a long way toward redeeming its reputation if it would follow Murphy's example.

"The politicians who make a lastin' success in politics," counseled Tammany's sage, George Washington Plunkitt, "are the men who are always loyal to their friends, even up to the gate of state prison, if necessary." Murphy had been fiercely loyal to Eddie Hagan, the Democratic party leader in the state assembly district dominated by the Anawanda Club. His loyalty was rewarded by Hagan on his deathbed. In what was said to have been his final breath, he delivered the exhortation: "Elect Murphy." The Anawandans complied. In 1892 Murphy succeeded Hagan, which also elevated him to the executive committee of Tammany Hall.

As a district leader, Murphy held court each evening at a lamppost at the northwest corner of Twentieth Street and Second Avenue, as plaintive constituents queued up to complain about their landlords, a court summons, an injustice by the municipal bureaucracy, or a grievance against a storekeeper, or to beg a favor that could run the gamut from advancement on the waiting list for a new apartment to a no-show sinecure. "A dictator in fact, yet preserving all of the tokens of democratic accessibility," Gustavus Myers wrote in *The History of Tammany Hall* (1901). By the early twentieth century, Murphy had cultivated a new ally, Big Tim Sullivan (officially, Timothy D. Sullivan, topping six feet and 200 pounds; the moniker distinguished him from fellow district leader Timothy P., known as Little Tim, although at 150 pounds he was diminutive only by comparison). Sullivan held citywide leverage over gambling and other illegalities, coupled with an enlightened political agenda (gun control, support for organized labor, and votes for women), allowing him to expand his ambit from the Bowery and Lower East Side to Tammany's inner sanctum.

By the turn of the twentieth century, Murphy had outmaneuvered his rivals and supplanted the brief interim triumvirate that ruled Tammany after Croker retired. In 1902 he inherited control of a countywide party organization that, as a result of the city's consolidation, was now first among the five ostensibly equal boroughs. Quietly, almost unnoticed, Murphy more than any of his predecessors managed to do well for the party organization and do good for New Yorkers, too. His strategy was commonsensical: identify and promote candidates whose progressive agenda not only appealed to the party's immigrant base but could also win over social-minded converts like Frances Perkins.

Did the tiger change his stripes, or did he succumb to political expediency? Whether giving the appearance of leading or merely getting out of the way of inevitable progress, Murphy supported the direct election of U.S. senators, women's suffrage, factory safety legislation, and the primary system for choosing party nominees. He mentored Al Smith, Robert F. Wagner, Jimmy Walker, and Franklin D. Roosevelt in the legislature. His handpicked chairman of the transportation board, John H. Delaney, who was building the Independent Subway, was a Murphy protégé considered to be a brilliant, irreproachable administrator. Recognizing the growing potential of Black defectors from the Republican Party, Murphy encouraged Ferdinand Q. Morton, the grandson of slaves, to lead the United Colored Democracy (in 1922, Morton was named the first Black member of the city's Civil Service Commission).

Murphy would be characterized by Isabel Paterson of the *Herald Tribune* after his death as the "political equivalent of the Forgotten Man," the personification of the American middle-class stereotype who, as defined by the social scientist William Graham Sumner, "is never taken into account because he cannot be definitely classified, although the social structure pivots on him."

It was easier to be forgotten, of course, if you were faceless in the first place. What Murphy was most famous for was being inconspicuous and, even more so, laconic. "If silence can be flamboyant, then Mr. Murphy was an exhibitionist," William Bryk wrote in 1998. "Asked by a passerby for the time, Mr. Murphy would gaze back

"Democratic Convention, Madison Square Garden, New York, July 1924."

benignly, pull out his pocket watch, and simply hold it up to the questioner's eyes. He left no records, formal speeches, or letters and granted no interviews of consequence. He once murmured, 'Never write when you can speak; never speak when you can nod; never nod when you can blink.'" (In the 1950s New York mayor Robert F. Wagner, another resilient political survivor, would, when prodded, reveal his own version of Murphy's formula for longevity: "When in danger, ponder; when in trouble, delegate; when in doubt, mumble.") That Murphy stood mute during the singing of the national anthem at one of Tammany's traditional Fourth of July celebrations clinched the closemouthed mythology.

"What's the matter with the Boss—can't he sing?" a reporter asked Tammany secretary Tom Smith, according to W. Axel Warn, who covered politics for the *Times*.

"Sure, he can. Why, the chief used to sing with a quartet in his younger days. He can yodel some, take it from me."

"Why didn't he join in 'The Star-Spangled Banner' then?"

"Perhaps," Smith replied, "he didn't want to commit himself."

Murphy never elaborated on his taciturnity, not in so many words. But Jimmy Walker, who rarely had an unspoken thought, supplied one answer. "Mr. Murphy once told me," Mayor Walker said, "that most of the troubles of the world could be avoided if men opened their minds instead of their mouths."

"It was the cards he was holding back that gave him command of the situation," M. A. Werner wrote in *Tammany Hall* (1968). If he was "Silent Charley" behind his back to lowly Tammany braves, he would be greeted by virtually every New Yorker as "Mister Murphy"—an honorific regularly reserved at the time for only one other worthy, John McGraw, the Giants manager. (Both deserved it. Murphy elected three governors, three mayors, and two U.S. senators and, had he lived, might have made Al Smith president in 1928 and spared Jimmy Walker the ignominy of resigning in 1932; during the same period under McGraw, the Giants won nine National League pennants and three World Series.) Murphy also never objected to being called "commissioner," a sobriquet bestowed by his appointment in 1897 as treasurer of the three-member dock board, the omnipotent overseer of the waterfront and the only official government job he ever held.

While the title of commissioner coincided with his appointment to the board, the praenomen Mister had to be earned. Murphy methodically worked to do so under the belated tutelage of an unlikely mentor with a Dickensian name, John Sergeant Cram, the dock board president. Cram, a Harvard Law graduate, was a scion of English immigrants who arrived in 1640 and whose family tree was overgrown with congressmen, governors, and Vanderbilts. "The fashionable attire and courteous manner of Mr. Cram were reported to have made a deep impression on Mr. Murphy," the *Times* reported, "and it was Mr. Cram who was said to have introduced Mr. Murphy to a Fifth Avenue tailor and to have given him hints which later were to make his manner easy in any company."

The dock board was a patronage plum, a prime example of the low-hanging fruit that George Washington Plunkitt, Murphy's fellow Democratic district leader, was referring to when he defined honest graft as the outgrowth of someone like himself more or less innocently seeing his opportunities and taking them. Murphy was no naïf. He conscientiously covered his tracks, but obviously he was presented with, contrived, and managed to seize enough opportunities to make himself a millionaire. Appearances counted in politics, too, but Fifth Avenue tailors and hints on good manners that would ease his way into any company couldn't presume to shroud the dock board's blatant shenanigans.

Apparently stung by criticism that the board played favorites in renting out wharves, Murphy went so far as to issue a defensive public statement in which he warned that competitive bidding in the leasing of piers "would open the way to endless blackmail" because "a man might build up a big coal business and then when his lease was expiring a rival might come along and threaten to outbid him for his pier. That would not be fair." Regardless of the potential for profit or for patronage, he decided unilaterally, and declared publicly, that "the city should not, in my opinion, make more than five percent on its property." That might explain why the board, under Murphy, leased a city pier to a favored company for thirty years at $750 annually. Under the successor Republican administration, an adjacent pier was rented out for only five years at $12,000 annually. Civic watchdogs collectively raised their eyebrows while individuals and privileged private companies, like New York Contracting and Trucking, benefited handsomely from Murphy's Law.

Only three of New York Contracting and Trucking's incorporators were publicly identified, but they alone provided grist for investigators. Alderman James E. Gaffney hailed from Murphy's district (and later bought the Boston baseball team and named it the Braves in deference to Tammany). Richard J. Crouch was one of Murphy's functionaries in the Anawanda Club. Murphy's own brother John was a former alderman and acting district leader, too. Together, Gaffney, Crouch, and John Murphy owned 15 percent of New York Contracting and Trucking. Who held the other 85 percent was never proven, but Charles Murphy (who at one point personally loaned the company $150,000) was always suspected of being a silent partner, a role that, given his pithiness, he was well versed to play.

In 1901 the company leased two West Side docks, at Seventy-Ninth and Ninety-Sixth Streets, from the city for ten years at barely over three thousand dollars. Under contract with the Department of Sanitation, ash and the detritus of subway excavations dumped on those docks was transferred to barges that would be towed to the Atlantic, where their contents were jettisoned. The contract netted the company about two hundred dollars a day, or about a 5,000 percent profit—a thousand times more than Murphy figured was a fair return for the government. One week's worth of profits was enough to pay nearly a half year's rent bill from the city.

Call it another coincidence, but in December 1902, three months after Murphy became the Tammany boss, the board of aldermen ended a three-year stalemate and finally approved a franchise for the Pennsylvania Railroad to provide direct train service to and from its majestic station in Manhattan through tunnels under the Hudson and East Rivers. For several years, the project had been delayed, inexplicably and interminably, it seemed, until the railroad was bullied into rejecting a bid that was some $400,000 lower and awarded a $5 million excavation contract to the New York Contracting and Trucking Company. Leading the belated charge for the railroad's franchise to build its station was James E. Gaffney. Excavation began in the summer of 1904.

If coincidence is always suspect in a world of cause and effect, then regulators' eyebrows were raised once again that same year when the board of estimate granted an adjunct of the New York, New Haven and Hartford Railroad a franchise to operate sixteen miles of trackage in the Bronx and Manhattan after the contract for the $5 million project was awarded to New York Contracting and Trucking. "By 1905, it was estimated that the New York Contracting and Trucking Company or its offshoots had received contracts aggregating $15 million from corporations and interests benefiting from the city government or depending upon favors from it," Gustavas Myers wrote. "Yet two years previously this very company was a nonentity as far as securing large contracts were concerned, and none of its heads had any experience in the contracting business. Now in a certain well-understood field, it was virtually free from competition." Just how much the company's political connections were worth compared to its contracting expertise became clear after John J. Murphy died. An audit of his estate placed no value whatsoever on New York Contracting's future goodwill because, the appraisers said, the business had depended largely on "personality."

Unlike his predecessors and some of his contemporaries, Charles Murphy flatly refused to taint Tammany's coffers with kickbacks or protection payoffs for prostitution and other vices that he personally considered iniquitous. His definition of immorality was transactional, however. "He wouldn't protect a criminal and get the money for that," Arthur Krock of the *Times* later recalled, "but he would take money from concessions on taxation. If your taxes should be five thousand, he's made them three, and you'd put up one. That was all right." New Yorkers could take some comfort in the fact that, on a scale published in 2006 by Rebecca Menes of the National Bureau of Economic Research, their city had dropped from most corrupt municipality in America during the 1850–1880 reign of the Forty Thieves and Boss Tweed to fourth place, behind Chicago, Philadelphia, and New Orleans, during the fifty years that followed.

Silent Charley never said so, but that he concurred in Plunkitt's criterion of opportunities to be taken is self-evident. Somehow, as a saloonkeeper, he was frugal enough to leave an estate valued at $30 million in today's dollars. Among his assets were a four-story town house on Stuyvesant Square, real estate that included the entire west-side blockfront of Lexington Avenue between East Twenty-Sixth and Twenty-Seventh Streets, and a fifty-acre estate in what is now Hampton Bays, Long Island, gussied up by a nine-hole golf course.

Still, Murphy seemed to distinguish between official corruption and what Plunkitt euphemized as honest graft, going by what he supposedly said to Al Smith in 1915: "Al, I'm making you sheriff, so you can make some money. Then you can afford to be an honest man." (As sheriff, he was legally entitled to keep 5 percent of all the judgments he executed.) Frances Perkins added: "I remember hearing Roosevelt tell people later on, 'You know Murphy always made it a point to keep Al honest. He never let Al Smith get smeared or tangled up with any of the dirty deals. He took great pains that they should never involve Al in any of these things, because he thought he was a capable fellow and he could go far.'"

As Murphy himself ascended from the district leadership to become the Tammany boss, he transplanted himself to the Tammany Hall headquarters at 141 East Fourteenth Street, the three-story marble-and-red-brick "wigwam," its façade dominated by a twelve-foot-high white marble effigy of the machine's namesake, Tamanend. As befitted a newly minted gentleman who had grown accustomed to being addressed as Mister, Murphy would gravitate after noon to Delmonico's at Fifth Avenue and Forty-Fourth Street. He secreted himself in what became known as the Scarlet Room (for the hue of its furnishings) on the second floor. But woe to the party functionary who mistook Murphy's newly acquired courtliness for effeteness. Velvet gloves masked iron fists. In 1910 the Democrats won control of the governorship with John Dix, and of the legislature for the first time in two decades. Two years later Dix lost the party nomination to William Sulzer, a maverick who was elected but who lasted barely nine months. After Sulzer balked at Murphy's implacable demands for patronage, the state legislature, loyally goose-stepping to Tammany's unforgiving injunctions, slapped Sulzer with valid but flimsy campaign finance violations. "When Governor William Sulzer refused to consult the 'ahrganization' on appointments," Daniel Patrick Moynihan wrote, "Murphy did not argue; he impeached and removed him." His victory was pyrrhic, though. In exorcising Sulzer, Murphy demonized himself to good-government groups.

Cynics would never be convinced that Tammany had reformed—or that it could. Presbyterian minister and six-time Socialist Party candidate for president Norman Thomas and apostate and muckraker Paul Blanshard would later suggest that Murphy's progressive agenda was less a road-to-Damascus conversion than a detour. Tammany hadn't altered its ends; it had merely adjusted its means. "The new Tammany is the old Tammany with the wisdom of age and experience added," Thomas and Blanshard argued in *What's the Matter With New York: A National Problem* (1932). "Today it has a legal device for every possible type of looting and a moral explanation for every bribe."

In 1903 the muckraking journalist Lincoln Steffens expressed concern about the apparently newly minted reformist platform that the Democratic machine had synthesized from self-interest and conscience. "As a New Yorker," Steffens warned, "I fear Murphy will prove sagacious enough to stop the scandals, put all the graft in the hands of a few tried and true men, and give the city what it would call good government. Murphy says he will nominate for mayor a man so 'good' that his goodness will astonish New York. I don't fear a bad Tammany mayor. I dread the election of a good one."

Putting his countywide leadership to the test for the first time, Murphy did just that. He recruited as Tammany's candidate George B. McClellan Jr., an East Side congressman and son of the Civil War general. Francis S. Barry, in his book *The Scandal of Reform* (2009), described McClellan as "a society elite with a dynastic Democratic name." Murphy also outmaneuvered the Reformers and the incumbent, Seth Low, by endorsing their nominees for comptroller and president of the board of aldermen, an act that burnished Tammany's reputation, doomed the Republican-Fusion ticket, and ensured a Democratic sweep of city hall. Murphy and McClellan triumphed, but two years later faced a challenge from newspaper magnate William Randolph Hearst, who, running on a third-party platform advocating municipal ownership of public utilities, forged a coalition of immigrants, organized labor, progressives, and disaffected members of the two major parties. Hearst punctuated his campaign with venomous slogans and speeches and vivid print advertisements, screeds, and cartoons, prominently caricaturing Murphy in prison (not tiger) stripes above the caption "It's a short lock-step from Delmonico's to Sing Sing." As the film critic Pauline Kael later wrote in the *New Yorker* (1972), "That reckless cartoon was the turning point in Hearst's political career."

Decades later Orson Welles would recall Hearst's campaign in his classic film *Citizen Kane* (the subject of Kael's *New Yorker* essay), combining several real-life

CHARLES F. MURPHY 259

episodes into a fictional narrative. Murphy is reincarnated as Hearst's thinly veiled doppelgänger, the villainous Boss Jim W. Gettys (played by Ray Collins). Furious because of a cartoon showing Murphy in prison stripes, Gettys threatens to expose publisher Charles Foster Kane as an adulterer unless Kane withdraws his mayoral challenge to Tammany's candidate. "In case you don't know," Kane explains by way of introducing his wife to Gettys, "this gentleman . . ." Gettys interjects: "I'm not a gentleman. Your husband is only trying to be funny calling me one. I don't even know what a gentleman is. Mrs. Kane, if I owned a newspaper and if I didn't like the way somebody was doing things, some politician, say, I'd fight them with everything I had. Only I wouldn't show him in a convict suit with stripes, so his children could see the picture in the paper. Or his mother."

The movie mirrored the outcome of Hearst's campaign. Murphy extracted revenge by disposing of enough Hearst ballots to reelect McClellan by a mere three thousand of the six hundred thousand votes cast. The following year, though, he turned around and handed Hearst the gubernatorial nomination in a display of statewide political muscularity, a small price for shutting down the Hearst newspapers' vitriolic mudslinging. By doing so, Murphy cloaked Tammany in Hearst's good-government mantle of municipal ownership of public utilities in return for what was estimated to have been a secret down payment of $500,000. Hearst conveniently lost the election to the incumbent, Charles Evans Hughes, and in 1909 Murphy replaced the ungrateful McClellan as mayor with a surprisingly respectable and independent successor, William J. Gaynor of Brooklyn.

Tammany supported Governor Hughes's progressive agenda, including the establishment of a public utilities commission. Murphy and his acolytes were also in the vanguard of enacting legislation that imposed standards for tenement housing and provided old-age pensions and compensation for incapacitated workers. Robert F. Wagner, who with Smith would spearhead the social welfare canon in Albany as a state senator and later as a United States Senator during Roosevelt's New Deal, would lionize Murphy's Tammany as "the cradle of American liberalism." And FDR himself, reversing his original antipathy toward Tammany, hailed Murphy as "a genius who kept harmony" and a strong and wise leader who "had helped to accomplish much in the way of progressive and social welfare legislation in our state." (In 1920, Murphy obliged in FDR's selection as James M. Cox's running mate after Cox was finally nominated for president on the 44th ballot.)

From 1854, when Irish immigrants heralded Tammany's hegemony, to the inauguration of Fiorello H. La Guardia eight decades later in 1934, reformers ran city hall for only ten years. Charles Murphy ruled for twenty-two, longer than any other Tammany leader. "By whatever definition, the machine system in New York was certainly more democratic than any of the alternative governments proposed by the reform groups that from time to time, with unhappy results, were voted into power," John F. Davenport wrote in the journal *New York Affairs* in 1975. "Tiger's milk nourished the early careers of some of the most enlightened public figures of the era, and Murphy was instrumental in easing their passage up and out."

Murphy died at his home on East Seventeenth Street on April 25, 1924, two months before the longest continuous presidential nominating convention opened at Madison Square Garden. The convention was the first in New York since 1868, a tribute, in part, to the Democrats' spectacular gain of thirteen seats in the state's congressional delegation in 1922. Al Smith claimed more delegates pledged to his presidential nomination than any other candidate. His selection would have been the capstone of Murphy's career. Instead, the convention deadlocked between Smith and William G. McAdoo of California; on the 103d ballot, the Democrats finally nominated John W. Davis of West Virginia. (Davis was swamped that November by the Republican incumbent, Calvin Coolidge. His reputation for pithiness rivaled Murphy's; when a dinner companion claimed to have bet she could get three words out of him, Coolidge supposedly replied: "You lose.")

In retrospect, even some of Murphy's most self-righteous critics grudgingly granted him a modicum of credit. The *Times* admitted that he "did not openly affront the moral sense" of most New Yorkers, but added this caveat: "Nothing of this should make us forget he was the exemplar and beneficiary of the system which without official responsibility degrades our official life, and which condemns New York City to suffer from maladministration and the lowest moral standards in public office." Still, nobody doubted the influence that Murphy wielded for more than two decades, much less the talent he nurtured—talent that arguably shaped the social policies in New York that would usher in the New Deal from Washington and help the nation survive the Great Depression. His death was reported under a three-column headline that led the *Times* the next morning, accompanied by two other front-page articles. The *World*, which had spearheaded exposés of municipal corruption, characterized Murphy as an individual who could "grow from unpromising beginnings, as a typical city boss over men strangely varied from the corrupt to the frantically partisan, into a better sense of public responsibility."

Jimmy Walker bluntly concluded that with Murphy's death, "the brains of Tammany Hall lie in Calvary Cemetery." Ed Flynn, Murphy's protégé and his cerebral successor as the Democratic boss of the Bronx from 1922 to 1953, said of his mentor: "You have to remember that none of the progressive legislation in Albany could have been passed unless he urged it and permitted it to be passed." Even Fiorello La Guardia, a nominal Republican who defeated Tammany after Walker's inglorious departure but expediently enlisted as an ardent booster and beneficiary of Roosevelt's New Deal, graciously acknowledged that Murphy had "granted the reforms that he could afford."

In *Bosses, Machines, and Urban Voters* (1977), John M. Allswang distinguished between Murphy as "a real professional politician, whose interests were in the obtaining and retention of political power" and Tweed, who "was an opportunist whose arena just happened to be politics." What matters less than why he embraced progressive candidates and platforms, Allswang wrote, was that "he did these things, and they not only perpetuated his machine, but also affected the nature of the government." The fact was, Allswang concluded, that "Murphy's Tammany Hall served the needs of more people better—as they saw it—than any alternatives offered them in New York City in the first quarter of the 20th century. There is a reason, after all, why Tweed's machine, and Seth Low's also, lasted only a few years, whereas Murphy's lasted a generation."

Murphy volunteered his own answer why, not long before he died. It was self-serving but statistically accurate. "When Tammany can elect its candidate so often in a city of 6,000,000, in a city of intelligence, in a city dotted all over by the church spire and the school house," he told an interviewer, "it seems silly to use the time-worn campaign cry that there is nothing good but everything corrupt in Tammany."

Still, the party organization was growing obsolete. With the deliberate closing of the Golden Door to immigrants—by 1920, foreign-born New Yorkers and their children made up three quarters of the city's population—and the institutionalization of Tammany's welfare largesse as a government entitlement, the clubhouse had become a victim of its own success. Ed Flynn of the Bronx would survive to become the Democratic national chairman in the early 1940s, and Carmine De Sapio of Greenwich Village would emerge a decade later from behind the tinted glasses that stamped him as the final incarnation of the crooked Tammany caricature. But the Democratic machine would be doomed by demographics, by reapportionment, and, in Murphy's own district, by urban renewal, which supplanted the nineteenth-century tenements with middle-class post–World War II housing complexes like Stuyvesant Town and Peter Cooper Village, whose tenants were better equipped to fend for themselves independent of political party patronage.

Political scientists have their favorite dates for when the Democratic machine ground to a halt. Some would say it was in 1924, after Murphy died suddenly and some sixty thousand New Yorkers lined the streets to pay their respects. Pat Moynihan traced the end of the Irish hegemony in New York City to Jimmy Walker's ignoble self-exile to Europe in the early 1930s. Still others single out 1973, when the sixty-three surviving members of the 104-year-old Anawanda Club voted to disband, selling the building that housed Boss Charlie Murphy's saloon with barely a scintilla of sentiment, as the point when the party was over.

Silent Charlie's last words went unrecorded, but his demise evoked two other deathbed scenes played by laconic politicians. One was district leader Eddie Hagan's imperative to "Elect Murphy." The other, pure fiction, reverberated with the ring of authenticity. Silent Charlie's last words, ambiguity and all, could have been conjured up by Mayor Frank Skeffington near the finale to Edwin O'Connor's *The Last Hurrah*, just before one of his cronies, John Gorman, grasps his hands in a goodbye grip. "Ah, Frank," Gorman says softly. "You've done grand things. Grand, grand things." To which Mayor Skeffington replies softly: "Among others."

26

Ciro Terranova

The Mayor and the Mobster

In 1639, only six years after they had emigrated to New Netherland from Amsterdam, Anthony Janszoon van Salee and his wife, Grietje Reiners, had already distinguished themselves as ungodly roustabouts and slanderers. Worse still, Janszoon, who had lived in the Moroccan port of Salee as a boy, whose mother was Moorish and who was commonly belittled as "the Turk," had brazenly badmouthed none other than the Dutch Reformed minister Everardus Bogardus. To make matters even worse, Reiners had defamed Bogardus's wife, Anneke Jans.

New Amsterdamers were infamously litigious and gossipmongering, traits that would endure through the generations to characterize many modern-day New Yorkers, too. Even in the seventeenth century, the civil docket was crammed with suits and countersuits that Anthony Janszoon either had filed or was forced to defend. Finally, a court was convened to weigh the totality of the couple's misbehavior. In a belated and grudging public repentance, Jansen declared that he considered Anneke Jans an honorable and virtuous woman, and promised to say nothing prejudicial about her or her choleric husband again. That apology, such as it was, spared Janszoon imprisonment. Nonetheless, in 1639 the couple was exiled from New Amsterdam—only to define the bounds of their banishment so narrowly that they managed to resettle across the East River in Brooklyn (which was also part of New Netherland). Within four years Janszoon had reinvented himself as a mini patroon. Defying the court order, he invested in Manhattan real estate and became the patriarch of an extended family who was said to have encompassed Whitneys, Vanderbilts, and Jacqueline Kennedy Onassis. (Supposedly, Janszoon's brother fathered a son whose descendants included Serena Downing, the wife of the restaurateur George Downing.)

Few cases of officially sanctioned ostracism would be sensationalized to the same degree as Janszoon's over the next three centuries, until New York's chief magistrate barred another notorious immigrant from the city proper. In neither instance, though, did fellow ethnics rally to the target's defense. In Janszoon case, there weren't any; he was widely believed to be the only self-identified Muslim in New Amsterdam at the time. The twentieth-century exile of Ciro Terranova from New York three hundred years later, in 1935, was something else entirely. Terranova had victimized his fellow Italians twice over: he forced them to spend more of their meager income on food, and he sabotaged their backbreaking struggle to become accepted as decorous, productive, and patriotic Americans.

Notwithstanding the city's foundational diversity and dependence on trade and the reputation it developed for tolerance, to one extent or another virtually every arriving ethnic and racial immigrant group suffered vitriolic, violent, and even fatal *us vs. them* collisions, beginning with Native Americans, who were accused (in their case, by the immigrants who supplanted them) of committing the first recorded murder. The original wall of Wall Street was built to keep them (and New Englanders) out.

The lyrics of Tom Lehrer's satiric 1959 song, acerbically titled "National Brotherhood Week," tracked that succession of ethnic, racial, and religious animosity through the nineteenth and twentieth centuries, inevitably concluding that "everybody hates the Jews"—even other Jews. For all Jacob Riis's success in battling the slums in the late eighteenth and early nineteenth centuries, his biases against their occupants from abroad were abiding. Prejudice against the Jews was all but officially justified in 1908 when police commissioner Theodore Bingham declared in a magazine article "that with a million Hebrews, mostly Russians, in the city (one fourth of the population) perhaps half of the criminals should be of that race." (He later publicly apologized, since the actual proportion, on the basis of arrests, was more like one fifth, considerable enough.) By the end of the twentieth century, one of Bingham's successors, Benjamin Ward, the city's first Black police commissioner, was blaming most of the city's crime on young Black men. He, too, courted condemnation, but he didn't backtrack. "I'm sorry that I had to say what I said last night," he told a group of Baptist ministers the next day, "that our little secret is out of the house."

If Ward shamed Blacks into sharing what he called "our little secret," Italians (when they dominated organized crime) were often too terrified to publicly acknowledge theirs. Before Prohibition cast bootleggers as good guys and *The Godfather* romanticized the Mafia, the Black Hand cabal and similar criminal enterprises transplanted from the Old World preyed covertly and violently on fellow Italian Americans. Even as more and more immigrants and their descendants were hurdling the barriers that Anglo-Saxon Protestant society placed in their way professionally and socially, they still bore the scars of corrosive discrimination.

"A proverb popular in the late 19th century in Sicily divided a peasant's opportunities into two categories: immigrate, or become a criminal," Justin Cascio writes on MafiaGenealogy.com. "Of course, some managed doing neither, and others did both." The Terranovas were among the multitaskers.

Ciro Terranova was six years old when he arrived in New York with his parents and four siblings at Ellis Island. They traveled from Sicily by way of Naples on the twelve-hundred-passenger SS *Alsatia* on March 8, 1893, barely a year after the immigration station opened. Most steerage passengers brought with them with two pieces of luggage; the Terranovas disembarked with sixteen. They reunited with Ciro's half brother, who had left posthaste for New York six months earlier because he was suspected of murdering a police official in Italy. Ciro's father, Bernardo, was a member of the Corleone clan called the Fratuzzi, or the Little Brothers. The family's surname, Terranova, literally translated as New Land, but their Old World traditions would die hard.

Bernardo and his household would become well connected by blood or marriage to a dodgy web of mobsters, including the Morellos, the Lupos, Giuseppe "Joe the Baker" Catania of the Bronx, and Santo Calamia of Louisiana, which was where the Terranovas migrated from New York in the mid-1890s when Bernardo got a job there sowing sugarcane. They then transplanted to Texas and picked cotton until a malaria outbreak sent them back to New York in 1896. There, Ciro attended school during the day. He worked weekends and evenings as a waiter in his stepbrother's Prince Street Saloon and part-time in the family's plastering business. He would later complain that the police had been harassing his family since he was fifteen. Not without reason—Ciro, his brothers Vincenzo and Nicolo, and his half brother Giuseppe Morello (known as "the Clutch Hand" for his disfigured, clawlike single finger) organized a criminal enterprise based in East Harlem with Ignazio Lupo, the boss of Little Italy, who would later marry Ciro's sister.

"Portrait of Ciro Terranova," from a morgue clipping file in Times Wide World, *1930.*

The Morellos would evolve into the Genovese crime family, the oldest of New York's five mob dynasties. They were implicated in counterfeiting, for the so-called Barrel Murders, in which rivals' bodies were stuffed into wooden drums for efficient and faceless disposal, and for years of internecine warfare, which ended temporarily in 1917 with Ciro and Nick Terranova triumphant. One year later, the same year he became a naturalized American citizen, having just turned thirty, Ciro was accused of murdering two gambling bosses. The only testimony prosecutors could marshal against him came from coconspirators and alleged accomplices, so he was acquitted.

By the 1925 New York census, Ciro no longer listed himself as a plasterer but as the proprietor of a vegetable market. Just shy of forty, he had so successfully fulfilled the American dream that he could afford to move in 1929 from East Harlem, where he was also thriving as a junior partner to Dutch Schultz in the numbers racket. He bought a twenty-four-room, 3,500-square-foot Spanish-style pink stucco mansion—on Peace Street, no less—in verdant Pelham Manor, just across the city line in Westchester.

The weekly *Pelham Sun* breathlessly informed villagers that their neighbor, who they knew only as a wealthy "artichoke importer," had previously been detained by New York City police in connection with the murders of gangsters Frankie Yale and Frank Marlow in 1928 and 1929, respectively. "He was not arrested, but his detention by the police brought to light interesting information which has had the Pelhams agog for two days," the *Sun* reported. Residents were aflutter not only that "within the limits of the tranquil Pelhams was a man suspected of being associated with the mystery gang murder of the day" but also that he was ferried around in a bulletproof automobile, he had an arrest record for offenses ranging from disorderly conduct to other homicides, his two brothers had been slain by rival mobsters, and he had paid cash for the $52,000 house (about $1 million in today's dollars), with a fountain on its luxuriant front lawn and a piazza in the rear.

If Italian Americans were becoming less vulnerable to outright coercion by their own countrymen, they remained susceptible to embarrassment by collective degradation. No wonder that in 1936 Fiorello La Guardia—whose parents were Italian immigrants, Catholic and Jewish—banned organ grinders from New York City. The mayor's pretext was that the street-corner performers had been rendered superfluous by music performed live at outdoor concerts and on radio. La Guardia was more likely to have been motivated by hurtful words that reverberated in his memory; as an army brat living in Arizona, he'd been subjected after an Italian organ grinder visited town to ethnic slurs by neighborhood children asking "Where's your monkey?"

La Guardia's simmering umbrage also may help explain the multiyear grudge match he waged against Ciro Terranova. In fact, the mayor should have been deeply indebted: arguably, Terronova helped elect him. When La Guardia first ran in 1929, he cast himself as a Republican anticorruption candidate. Since the death of Charles F. Murphy in 1924 he had condemned the Democratic machine as a tool of organized crime, exposing Tammany's links with Arnold Rothstein, the notorious gambler accused of fixing the 1919 World Series and who had loaned $19,600 to city magistrate Albert H. Vitale of the Bronx. In 1928 Rothstein was shot dead during a showdown with creditors at Manhattan's Park Central Hotel. When La Guardia ran for mayor the following year, he was dispatched at the polls almost as decisively by Jimmy Walker.

La Guardia's specific allegations of corruption against Tammany during that campaign might well have been forgotten by the next election, but for a testimonial dinner that the Tepecano Democratic Club hosted in Vitale's honor in November 1929, a month after Walker won, to welcome the magistrate home from his vacation in Virginia. Nobody in the upstairs private room at the Roman Gardens restaurant on Southern Boulevard in the Bronx was questioning why a judge was being honored by politicians in the first place. While no guest list was published in advance, the sixty partygoers themselves would not have been surprised that among those also invited was Ciro Terranova, not a name a judge would want leaked to gossip columnists. Seven *un*invited guests turned the fete into a surprise party and a public spectacle, however. They burst in after midnight (only one was masked) and robbed the invitees at gunpoint of two thousand dollars in cash and three thousand dollars in jewelry and other possessions. They also took an embarrassed police detective's revolver. Vitale at first seemed vexed mostly because the robbers had interrupted his thank-you speech; he had to be assured that the heist was not just a practical joke. The judge was relieved of forty-one dollars, but he managed to secrete a four-and-a-half-carat diamond pinkie ring in his waistband.

According to the cops, Terranova had engineered the bungled and bizarre robbery. His supposed motive: to retrieve a contract to murder Yale and Marlow that he had signed with a Chicago hit man, who claimed that he had been paid only five thousand of the twenty thousand dollars promised. The hit man had threatened to extort Terranova by anonymously surrendering the contract to the cops. (Why Terranova would have committed so incriminating an agreement to paper is anybody's guess.) During the aborted robbery, Terranova supposedly retrieved the contract. And thanks to a few discreet phone calls made by Magistrate Vitale, presumably fulfilling his oath to see justice done, within a few hours the guests' stolen loot—including the detective's gun—was also retrieved from the phony robbers Terranova had recruited.

Police commissioner Grover Whelan denounced Terranova—who would be played by Jack Weston in the TV series *The Untouchables*—as "the Al Capone of New York." But until La Guardia elevated him from midlevel mobster to racketeer royalty by expelling him, Terranova was so inconspicuous that eighteen of the guests at the Bronx dinner claimed they didn't remember seeing him there, according to their statements. After protesting, "I am a peace-loving man," he was released.

The investigation of Vitale didn't end with this fait n'accompli. The revelations triggered a marathon inquiry led by former court of appeals judge Samuel S. Seabury, a tenacious, priggish interrogator who was descended from the first Episcopal bishop of New York, the Loyalist clergyman whom Isaac Sears imprisoned in 1775. The investigation spread to the entire criminal justice system and the municipal government. Vitale would later be disrobed for failing to justify his accumulation of $165,000 (about $2.8 million today) over four years on an annual salary of $12,000. Evidence of municipal corruption would prompt Jimmy Walker to resign as mayor in 1932 rather than be removed by New York governor Franklin D. Roosevelt, who was in the midst of his presidential campaign. La Guardia, his allegations from 1929 vindicated, was elected the following year.

Other mobsters who made bad became known as capos or bosses. Ciro Terranova was the only one crowned a king—no longer *an* owner of a vegetable market or *an* importer, but *the* importer, having cornered the market, particularly in completely edible baby artichokes. "In its galaxy of leaders," the *Daily News* wrote in 1938, "the racket boasted no more singular figure than Ciro Terranova, who exploited the meek and lowly artichoke, lifting it from humble membership in the vegetable family to the rank of beer and booze as a gun-controlled commodity."

By the early 1930s public support for Prohibition was evaporating, and racketeers were already finding other legal commodities to monopolize. In this case, the targets were the farmers of Santa Cruz and Monterey Counties in California. As much as half the acreage of those two counties was devoted to cultivating artichokes, which were shipped east by rail in some 475,000 boxes annually to New York and a few other cities where a disproportionately large Italian American population made demand profitable. Unfortunately for the farmers, though, their profits were being diverted to Ciro Terranova's Union Pacific Produce Company, which monopolized the supply. Union Pacific offered the growers a nonnegotiable price of roughly six dollars a crate, then sold the contents at a markup of 40 percent or more. Some growers resisted. Most capitulated, though, after Terranova's thugs sprayed their artichoke plants with coal oil, dropped gasoline bombs on them from small planes, hijacked loaded trucks on their way to freight depots, or invaded the salty, sandy fields, wielding machetes.

"Who is this fellow, Terranova?" John L. McClellan of Arkansas, chairman of the Senate's Permanent Subcommittee on Investigations, asked the mob turncoat Joe Valachi during riveting televised hearings in 1963. "What was he known as?"

"The Artichoke King," Valachi replied on cue.

"What gave him that designation?"

"The way I understand it, he had the artichokes tied up," Valachi explained. "He would buy all the artichokes that came into New York. I didn't know where they came from, but I understand he was buying them all out. Being artichokes, they hold, they can keep. Then he would make his own price. In other words, an artichoke is something that Italians must have as a dessert. For instance, if he bought them for $5, then he would make his own price, say like $15 a case. You could not get an artichoke nowhere else."

"He was the king?"

"He was the king."

"He earned his name as the Artichoke King," Valachi would later elaborate, "because he was in a position to make his own price so the public had to pay 20 cents for a vegetable that should cost five cents."

Undaunted by the failure of gun-toting western sheriffs to break Terranova's stranglehold on the market, New York's gladiatorial mayor took matters into his own hands. La Guardia had vowed during his successful 1933 mayoral campaign to stifle corruption that forced the public to pay higher taxes and higher prices. Ciro Terranova was the perfect vehicle through which to redeem the mayor's promise. Unlike his brothers, Terranova had been remarkably bulletproof. He was arrested twelve times, including for the Yale and Marlow contract murders, but acquitted every time but once, in 1910, when at twenty-two he was convicted of a gun violation. In 1933, when his Union Pacific Produce, whose headquarters was on West Street (not far from where Christian Harriot rented his stall in the Washington Market), and several of his officers were charged with violating the Sherman Antitrust Act, Terranova wasn't named personally.

On December 21, 1935, the mayor was finally fed up. He declared war. La Guardia being La Guardia, he did so with all the flair demanded to depose a king. Heralded by two police trumpeters, he delivered his predawn pronunciamento at six fifty A.M. from the back of a truck at the Bronx Terminal Market. Proclaiming a state of emergency, he issued an unprecedented ban on the sale of baby artichokes within the five boroughs. The scene, the *Daily News* reported, suggested "a medieval burgomaster's appearance." La Guardia was returning in full cry to the newly built marketplace that he had dedicated not long before to revitalize the wholesale food trade, proclaiming to the vendors, "I found you pushcart peddlers; I have made you merchants." No way some gangster, especially an Italian American gangster, would undermine his accomplishment. "I want it clearly understood," La Guardia thundered that morning, "no thugs, racketeers or punks are going to be allowed to intimidate you as long as I am mayor of the City of New York."

La Guardia justified the ban on the sale, display, and possession of baby artichokes (prudently timed to take effect the day *after* Christmas) on the grounds that "nearly all, if not the entire sale of such artichokes within the public markets of the city has been under the control of a group of individuals now under indictment by the federal government." He said it would remain in effect "until such time as it is possible to purchase such artichokes freely and in the regular course of trade without unlawful restraint, restriction or racketeering coercion or duress."

The next day's *Herald Tribune* scoffed that the mayor was issuing imperatives for the "protection of the virtue of artichokes." For all the derision, though, after two days five wholesalers agreed to boycott Union Pacific and distribute to retailers on "a decent and honorable basis." Prices declined, sales increased, and within a few days La Guardia himself returned to his favorite dish of baby artichokes dipped in mayonnaise (or, as he told some interviewers, hollandaise sauce). La Guardia's histrionics not only fractured Terranova's monopoly, at least for the time being, but also inspired Bertolt Brecht in 1941 to write *The Resistible Rise of Arturo Ui*, an allegorical play about the rise of Hitler in which a gangster named Arturo Ui (rhymes with phooey) strong-arms the Cauliflower Trust through a protection racket.

La Guardia on the back of a truck, reading his proclamation to city-controlled markets while on a visit to the Bronx, with District Attorney Foley of the Bronx at the right, December 21, 1935. (Photo from Wide World Photos via the *New York Times*)

By the mid-1930s Ciro was the last survivor of the Terranova clan. Succumbing to a coup by junior partners from other families, Terranova was largely defenseless when the mayor targeted him again, overreaching for another flimsy arrow from his juridical quiver. Less than two weeks after announcing his artichoke ban, La Guardia, as the city's chief magistrate, banished Terranova himself from the City of New York. The city might have a reputation for tolerance, but La Guardia did not. Nor was the mayor's legal prerogative, to say the least, unambiguous. Nonetheless, La Guardia ordered police to arrest Terranova for vagrancy if he ventured one block south from his house on 989 Peace Street and crossed Split Rock Road from Westchester County into Bronx Manor. A police car was parked nearby Terranova's house, poised to apprehend him.

A decade earlier, Terranova might have marshaled a battery of lawyers and demonstrated, as David F. Launy did, that with proof, principle, and perseverance you can fight city hall. By now, though, the closest he could come to mustering a challenge was to have a friend or relative don his hat and overcoat, get into his bulletproof car, and drive off, leading the police on a wild goose chase while Terranova slipped away in another vehicle.

On January 3, 1936, Terranova was arrested while seated in his limousine in the West Bronx near the Alexander Hamilton Bridge. The charge of vagrancy lodged against him was undermined, though, by the fact that, as the *Daily News* reported, he was removed from his limousine "flashing diamonds and dressed in the height of what racketeers consider good taste." (His lawyers also pointed out that he was a legal resident of Westchester and to be guilty of vagrancy a defendant must have lived for at least six months in the county where he was arrested.) Terranova was detained at least twice more, including again that August, when he described himself as a baker on his way to the city for business. "I have to come down here sometimes," he pleaded on one occasion. After failing to produce his driver's license and the car's registration, he was held overnight at the White Plains Avenue station house in the Bronx, then released to his lawyer's custody the next morning. The charges were dropped after a witness testified that the overzealous New York City cops had seized him beyond their jurisdiction, five hundred feet north of the Bronx border.

By June 1937 Terranova was down to his last artichoke, pleading poverty in court to explain why he couldn't pay an eighteen-month-old bill of $542.87 for a new oil burner. That the seller dared to sue this potentially murderous once-powerful mobster in the first place suggested how far Terranova had fallen. The bank had seized his mansion; he was merely storing the armored car for a friend, he claimed, and it was out of gas anyway; he had lost his commission job with the bakery and had only $4 cash in his pocket; and his few remaining assets included a still unresolved claim against the city for false arrest. This time, he wasn't even wearing a watch in court.

While La Guardia never formally lifted his deportation fiat, by the end of 1937 police commissioner Lewis J. Valentine graciously considered it moot. This reprieve was not publicized, but reporters learned of it when in February 1938, admitted to Columbus Hospital with a stroke, Terranova listed his home address as 338 East 116th Street. He had been permitted to move back to East Harlem, Valentine said, because the former gangster was "now criminally and financially impotent."

Two days later, Terranova died. On his deathbed, according to a grandnephew, "*Guys and Dolls* characters were screaming at Ciro for his Swiss bank account password." If there ever was one, he never gave it up. Ciro was, as Mike Dash wrote in *The First Family* (2009), the only one of the four brothers to die in bed, more or less peacefully. He was forty-nine.

27

Tex and Jinx

The Birth of Celebrity

That Audrey Munson would have been queen of the tabloids in her prime as a model and movie star in the 1910s is incontrovertible—if there had been any tabloids. The first New York tabloid, the *Daily News*, didn't make its debut until mid-1919, after Joseph Patterson returned from the Great War. Paterson, its publisher, had been inspired by London's flashy magazine-format newspapers dominated by illustrations and distinguished by their cheeky disrespect for everything and everyone they covered. (The word *tabloid*, originally a brand name for compressed pills, came to be used for other condensed, digestible things, like the stories in tabloids.)

By the late 1910s, Munson's star was dimming. So was the idealized female physique epitomized by the classical hourglass-shaped Gibson Girl, eclipsed as the twenties roared in by the more androgynous flapper. Munson's first front-page headline in the *Daily News* ballyhooed her riches-to-rags sob story: an erstwhile beauty who had struggled against beasts in the guise of a lecherous Broadway producer and a libidinous doctor.

In June 1924, five years after Patterson founded the *Daily News*, William Randolph Hearst, who already published the *Evening Journal* and the *New York American*, launched his own New York tabloid, the *Daily Mirror*. Hearst plucked Arthur Brisbane from the *Journal* to run it. Brisbane had followed his father, Albert, into journalism, but with one major difference. The elder Brisbane, an outspoken socialist, paid Horace Greeley the standard advertising rate to print his column on the front page of the *Tribune*. His prolific son was said to have earned more than $250,000 a year (about $4.5 million in today's dollars), which easily would have made him the highest-paid print journalist in America.

In 1932 Brisbane hired John R. McCrary, a recent Yale graduate who not only became Brisbane's acolyte but also his son-in-law and his successor on the *Mirror*'s editorial page. McCrary, too, would groom a generation of journalists. With his wife, the actress and model Jinx Falkenburg, he would all but invent political talk radio and celebrity television interviews. He also would play supporting if largely backstage roles in some of the most consequential political events of the mid-twentieth century. McCrary would have a hand in cementing New York's post–World War II preeminence as a global capital by helping to replace a slaughterhouse on Manhattan's East Side with the United Nations headquarters.

John Reagan McCrary was born in 1910, the son of a cotton farmer in Calvert, Texas, a speck of a city in the east-central part of the state whose population had already peaked at about 3,300 at the turn of the century. John's father, who would become the head of the Cotton Growers Association, was struggling during the Great Depression to make ends meet. In stepped the Taylors, his mother's sister and her husband, Tom, childless Texas transplants to New York. Tom Taylor, a well-oiled lawyer, agreed to finance his nephew's education at Phillips Exeter Academy and Yale (where his classmates included Jack Howard, an heir to the Scripps-Howard newspaper chain).

After graduating from Yale in 1932, McCrary got his first job as a nineteen-dollar-a-week copy boy on the *New York World-Telegram*, which been born a year earlier from the sale of Joseph Pulitzer's *World* and the *Telegram*, which began as the evening edition of James Gordon Bennett's *New York Herald*, to Scripps-Howard. McCrary rose from a cub reporter there to feature writer at the weekly *Literary Digest*. After meeting Brisbane's daughter Sara at a party and being invited to her father's New Jersey estate, he seized the chance and jumped to the *Daily Mirror*. The *Mirror* sold more copies than any newspaper in the nation except one: its chief rival, the *Daily News*. The Hearst tabloid achieved "what ordinarily would be considered a splendid circulation" of five hundred thousand, Stanley Walker wrote in *City Editor* (1934), but "except for the fact that it carries Walter Winchell's daily treasure house of gossip and flabbergasting information, and the sports comment of Dan Parker, it has little in it that isn't done better in *The News*."

In 1935 McCrary married the boss's daughter. The couple moved into a suite in her parents' Fifth Avenue triplex, and when Brisbane died on Christmas Day 1936,

McCrary succeeded his father-in-law as the *Mirror*'s chief editorial writer. He was only twenty-five but armed with some valuable advice that Brisbane had conveyed as a wedding present, accompanied by a Leica camera with a 135 mm lens. "If you get a shot of a human face at the right moment, you'll never have to use an adjective in the caption," Brisbane counseled. "The adjective, dear boy, is the mortal enemy of the noun." He included this linguistic caveat: "Learn to write for people who follow the words with their finger and move their lips as they read. If you can learn that, then you can reach all people, including presidents and kings."

McCrary fully integrated Brisbane's tutorial on writing. As a Hearst editorialist, he also learned to palliate his personal opinions just enough to get by in an organization where talent was valued but decisions about whom to endorse or what viewpoint to embrace were not arrived at democratically. "Writing good editorials is chiefly telling the people what they think, not what you think," Brisbane once said.

"Portrait of Tex and Jinx." Jinx Falkenburg and Tex McCrary on CBS TV's Preview *in 1949.* (Photo by CBS)

Typically, though, the editorials reflected what the publisher's people were thinking—Hearst himself and his hangers-on. "We had a very simple understanding in the *Daily Mirror*," McCrary later explained. "There were a lot of things that I wanted to say that I was not permitted to say, but I was never made to say anything I didn't believe."

By 1939 McCrary had divorced Sara and begun writing the *Mirror*'s Only Human column under the byline of J. Reagan (Tex) McCrary, which was how he met Jinx Falkenburg. The column, like many Hearst fixtures, was formulaic: three days during the week it was devoted to amply illustrated profiles of attractive women; on two other days, the columns were virtually monetized as advertorials, promoting the virtues of potential advertisers or flattering existing ones. For the *Mirror*, that was no mean feat. The *Daily News* consistently surpassed it in circulation, so why buy ads in both? Moreover, most readers of the *News* and the *Mirror* were not the customers that the big department stores were trying to attract. "Part of my job was to help Mr. Brisbane get Macy's and Gimbels into the paper," McCrary explained. "Somebody at Gimbels said, 'The people who read the *Mirror* are our shoplifters,' so you see what we were up against." (The same retort was said to have been defensively hurled decades later by another department store owner at the *Post*'s Rupert Murdoch.) The title Only Human suggested a sheepish apologia for the five days of flackery, which left only the remaining two columns of the seven-day week for more or less serious subjects.

As a model and actress, Jinx Falkenburg fell into the first category, the columns about attractive women. Measured by the number of magazine covers and advertisements that featured her photograph, Jinx might have been the most attractive woman in the world in 1940, when she was twenty-one and Tex McCrary was twenty-nine. She was born in Barcelona as Eugenia Lincoln Falkenburg. Her father was an American electrical engineer working there for Westinghouse, her mother a Brazilian tennis champion who nicknamed her Jinx for good luck. Reared in South America and Los Angeles, she was discovered as a model by Paul Hesse, the self-taught Sunset Strip photographer of the glitterati who got his start as a voracious reader of photo books at the New York Public Library. Jinx's gigs in perfume and cigarette advertisements led to a contract in New York as the first Miss Rheingold, kicking off the annual beer promotional contest that was held from 1941 to 1964 and drew more voters than any election except for the presidency. No less an authority than the *New Yorker* adjudged that she "possessed one of the most photogenic faces and frames in the Western world." Jinx neither smoked nor drank beer, but the Rheingold campaign

produced an unexpected bonus: her physiognomy beguiled Al Jolson, who was convalescing in the same hospital as Jinx was after she fell from a hotel balcony in Hawaii
and landed on a dining room table. Jolson cast Jinx as a cowgirl in *Hold On to Your
Hats*, a musical comedy at the Shubert Theater.

As rehearsals began in June 1940 for the Yip Harburg and Burton Lane production starring Jolson and Martha Raye—some accounts say on the very first day—
Tex McCrary turned up, seeking fodder for one of that week's attractive-women
columns. He was immediately smitten with Jinx. "We went to Rockefeller Center
for a lemonade that night, after rehearsal," she said, "after a slight interview which
was work, and he advised me to be very careful in New York, it was a big city and it
was a dangerous city, and, uh, he would sort of look after me, which is what he did
for about three years." Tex made an immediate impression. "My mother still remembers my writing home to California," Jinx recalled, "and saying 'today I met the
nicest newspaper man I've ever met.' Of course, I'd never met a newspaper man before
either."

Yale notwithstanding, Tex was a tabloid newsman, a characteristic that, for better
and worse, would emerge in his many incarnations: as a press agent, celebrity talk-
show host, process broker (intuiting which gears needed greasing to leverage the
prerogatives of bona fide power brokers), and journalist. At the *Mirror* he searched
futilely for an inconspicuous half-blind citizen who he could hire, outfit with a glass
eye containing a concealed camera, and insinuate as a witness to the execution of
Bruno Hauptmann, the convicted kidnapper of the Lindbergh baby. Andy Rooney,
one of his many acolytes in the early days of press agentry and later a curmudgeonly
commentator on *60 Minutes*, called Tex "one of the great public relations experts
and con artists of all times."

Gabe Pressman, a pioneer of local radio and television news in New York who
also began as a novitiate to McCrary, recalled that Tex "respected reporters, but was
not above frustrating them in their mission to tell the truth"—most notably after
the U.S. Air Force assigned him as a public relations officer and he was chaperoning
a group of journalists on a flight over Hiroshima in 1945 a few weeks after it was
leveled by the first atomic bomb. ("All we knew about radiation back then," Tex
recalled, "was the men had to stuff a lot of tinfoil into their jock straps if they wanted
to preserve the ability to reproduce.") In reasonably good conscience given his job,
he urged the journalists touring four square miles of rubble at ground zero to refrain
from reporting the horror of, as he put it, "what we've done here." A year later, the
New Yorker graphically divulged the horrific dimensions of the devastation wreaked

by the bomb in an issue devoted entirely to John Hersey's grisly account. Tex waxed philosophic. "For me, it was the biggest damn story I never told—I covered it up and John Hersey uncovered it," he said. "That's the difference between a P.R. man and a reporter."

The con-man side of McCrary could have been acquired, or certainly honed, at the *Mirror*, where, like most Hearst papers at the time, literary license was liberally indulged. (One article famously featured vivid quotes from the survivor of a disaster on the front page—until the first edition of a rival newspaper identified the source of the supposed quotes as a deaf-mute. The suspect reporter, confronted by his editor, replied unfazed: "That's not what he told me.") Tex didn't necessarily believe that fiction was stranger than truth. Rather, he was amenable, if necessary, to redefining fiction *into* truth. "Covering the news bored him," Gabe Pressman said. "He wanted to make news." McCrary cast life as a heavyweight fight. "Ringside," he once said, "is not close enough."

Which was why, some ten months before the United States declared war against Germany and Japan in 1941, McCrary flew as a journalist with the Royal Canadian Air Force as it ferried American lend-lease bombers across the Atlantic to Britain. The mission (approved by Lord Beaverbrook, the British minister of aircraft production, as a personal favor to his friend Damon Runyon, the *Daily Mirror* columnist) was so dangerous that Runyon half-jokingly wrote McCrary's advance obituary, then transformed the eulogy into a triumphal column that was published when he landed safely in England. "Tex wanted to see what is going on over there with his own eyes," Runyon wrote. "He has insatiable curiosity about things, which is the true newspaper instinct." Though the American military would later assign him to a paper-shuffling public relations job, McCrary managed to dodge desk duty often enough to fly fifty missions and make sixteen parachute drops.

McCrary's gung-ho war reporting and military obligations during World War II interrupted the couple's romance well before Pearl Harbor. They finally found time to marry on June 15, 1945, just before Japan surrendered, in a civil ceremony in New York. By then Tex was nowhere as well known as Jinx, who, with two brothers in the military, feverishly buttressed morale as best she could. GIs embraced her as a voluptuous pinup and dazzling performer at 84 USO shows in Europe and the China-Burma-India war zone (plus hospital visits) and on the road again to Berlin in 1948 with Bob Hope and Irving Berlin during the airlift. "If there had been a vote to select the Body of the Year in 1945, it could have been Jinx Falkenburg," the television producer Norman Lear wrote in *Even This I Get to Experience* (2014). At one USO performance, he wrote, she appeared in tennis whites and heels and began lobbing autographed balls to the troops. "That was her entire act, but from the reaction of the troops at the sight of her in shorts and the escalating frenzy when she complained of the heat and whipped them off to reveal more skin in a bathing suit, Ms. Falkenburg had every right to feel she gave her all for the war effort."

After the war, Tex was enlisted as the editor of the *American Mercury*, the literary magazine founded in 1924 by H. L. Mencken and the critic George Jean Nathan. When the magazine spawned *Meet the Press*—on radio in 1945 and television two years later—Tex was already angling for his own pioneering leap into broadcasting.

Tex and Jinx didn't invent talk radio. Ed and Pegeen Fitzgerald had begun a regular interview format in 1938, and Dorothy (Kilgallen) and Dick (Richard Kollmar) launched their own version in 1945. But Tex had something altogether different in mind. Never shy nor short of passion, he was confident that with all his connections—and all the favors that countless political candidates, cultural icons, captains of industry, and wannabes he had befriended and defended owed him—he and Jinx could offer audiences a more sophisticated but still affecting conversation, a prelude to the next big thing they foresaw in mass media and in their professional evolution: television. He persuaded RCA's David Sarnoff to grant them a programming slot on WEAF, NBC's flagship New York radio station. On April 22, 1946, the modern celebrity talk show was born.

"They didn't know what to call it," Charles J. Kelly wrote in *Tex McCrary: Wars-Women-Politics, An Adventurous Life Across the American Century* (2009). "After a while Tex said, 'I'll just open with "Hi, Jinx." ' " That metaphor for playful or mischievous behavior became the theme of a show that would broadcast on radio and later television for thirteen years in one incarnation or another, pioneering a format that would be impersonated, perfected, parodied, but never quite duplicated. "We literally invented the talk show," Tex recalled unblushingly.

"While the Fitzgeralds bickered about Pegeen's weight on WJZ and the Kollmars preened amidst the birdseed on WOR," John Dunning wrote in *On the Air: The Encyclopedia of Old-Time Radio* (1998), "the McCrarys were interviewing Bernard Baruch, Margaret Truman, or Ethel Waters (who revealed on their air that, at her birth, her mother had been just 12 years old) . . . They got swimsuit actress Esther Williams to describe her first screen kiss, from Clark Gable, and Williams gave an uninhibited, hyperventilating account of how it had rendered her helpless and unable to act." Listeners to other programs never worried about spilling their morning coffee.

Fans of the McCrarys were never quite sure what to expect. "We didn't sidestep controversial issues," Tex recalled. "My newspaper experience had convinced me that the radio executives were all wrong when they said that people, particularly women, didn't want weighty stuff in the morning; I believed that minds were fresh and particularly open to the consideration of serious subjects in the morning."

Jerome Beatty Jr., a popular magazine writer, described the couple as "Mr. Brains and Mrs. Beauty," but that characterization gave Jinx short shrift. "She's the most intelligent uneducated person I know," Tex said. By today's standards, Tex (like Beatty) would be deprecated as a patronizing sexist, but at least he meant it as a compliment. She had dropped out of Hollywood High School at sixteen to pursue a career in modeling and acting, but on radio she persisted in quizzing guests until she understood them, which meant that listeners would, too. Bill Safire, a teenager at the time who would go on to become a speechwriter for President Nixon and a *Times* columnist, would pre-interview guests; he recalled how Tex coached his partner to pose questions and elicit anecdotes. (Given the wit of the guests, though, when some other shows offered only half as much, the hosts never knew what to expect. When Jinx asked the humorist Abe Burrows, "What was the low point of your life?" he paused a moment. "I never thought about that before," he replied, "but this must be it.")

Tex's mental acuity made up for his monotone. Jinx's quiver included a weapon that she fired successfully when all else had failed: "She studied the questions [Tex] told her to ask, but would add her own special one-word query that trumped all research," Safire recalled. "When the prickly Indian official V. K. Krishna Menon narrowly responded to a heavy question, Jinx would lean in, look closely into his eyes and whisper 'Really?' The cagiest diplomat would spill all."

As their megaphone got louder, Tex and Jinx were sustained by a supporting staff of young tyros who would not remain anonymous for long: Barbara Walters, Andy Rooney, Barry Farber, Hugh Downs, Ted Yates, Schuyler Chapin. The couple's friendship with John Hay Whitney, the Republican national finance chairman, eventually provided an intermittent residence for them and their two sons in a cottage on the venture capitalist's four-hundred-acre Greentree estate on Long Island's Gold Coast from 1947 to 1977, an enduring bond with the Republican Party, and a finder's fee when Whitney bought the *Herald Tribune* from their mutual friend Ogden Reid in 1958. (The McCrarys honored Whitney by confering his moniker, Jock, as the middle name of their younger son, Kevin. The storied paper would survive intact only until 1966, fulfilling Whitney's premonition when he

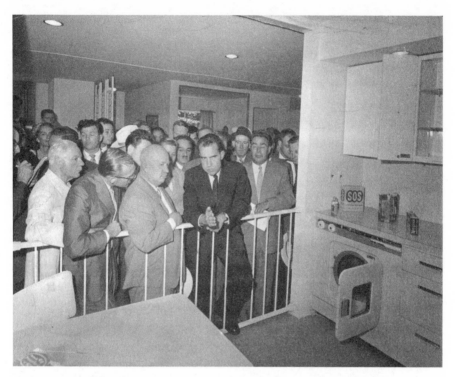

Tex's team staged this photo at an American exhibit at a fair in Moscow's Sokolniki Park. Vice President Richard M. Nixon, right, and the Soviet leader, Nikita S. Khruschev, engage in the "kitchen debate" on July 24, 1959. (Photo via the Associated Press)

toured the paper's headquarters as the new owner and compared the despair and decrepitude there to the atmosphere at the reporters' favorite watering hole, which was bustling with bonhomie. Whitney memorably declared, "I should have bought the bar.")

Whitney invited Jinx to head the Republican Party's women's division and helped lure Tex—it didn't take much convincing—into national politics. By mid-1951, Dwight D. Eisenhower, still in uniform as the commander of the North Atlantic Treaty Organization's armed forces, had persuaded the cognoscenti that while he could not reconcile himself to Truman's Fair Deal domestic platform as a Democratic presidential candidate in 1952, he just might be receptive to challenging Senator Robert Taft of Ohio for the Republican nomination.

Tex McCrary vowed to make that challenge viable in concert with other Republicans who favored Ike over Taft, the eldest son of former president William Howard

Taft and an anti–New Deal, anti-labor union conservative who was mounting his third bid for the G.O.P. nomination. Waiting until the new year, when the general would shed his uniform and could speak more freely as a civilian, McCrary staged a grandiose stunt in Madison Square Garden on February 8, 1952, aimed at galvanizing a single skeptic 3,600 miles away. By twenty-first-century digital standards, McCrary's caper would either have gone viral or backfired as the ultimate in flamboyantly orchestrated fake news. Only five hundred fight fans had loitered that night after Chico Vejar of Stamford, Connecticut, defeated Johnny De Fazio of Bayonne by a TKO in the ninth round, but by eleven thirty P.M. Tex had corralled fifteen thousand partisans committed to persuading their hero to throw his cap in the ring.

The showmanship was vintage McCrary. It kicked off with Miss New Hampshire, wearing only a bathing suit to introduce the delegation from the Granite State, where the first primary would be held, followed by Fred Waring's chorus, Ethel Merman, the Philadelphia Mummers, and the Brooklyn Dodgers Sym-Phony. Mary Martin, accompanied on the piano by Richard Rogers, sang "I'm in Love with a Wonderful Guy" from *South Pacific* by shortwave from London, and Irving Berlin delivered a revamped version of his "I Like Ike" from *Call Me Madam*.

Live and in person, McCrary's extravaganza was a crowd-pleaser, but pleasing the crowd at Madison Square Garden was beside the point. McCrary's carefully orchestrated spectacle of friendly persuasion targeted an audience of one. Eisenhower first heard it by shortwave radio in Paris. Two days later, he watched a three-hour kinescope version, personally delivered by the aviator Jacqueline Cochran in her own plane. "It was a moving experience to witness the obvious unanimity of such a huge crowd and to realize that everyone present was enthusiastically supporting me for the highest office of the land," Eisenhower later recalled. "As the film went on, Mamie and I were profoundly affected. The incident impressed me more than had all the arguments presented by the individuals who had been plaguing me with political questions for many months."

Ten days later, Eisenhower wrote McCrary: "While, as you know, I firmly believe that American interests demand that for the moment I remain outside the swirl of domestic political activity, it would be idle as well as false for me to attempt to deny that I am deeply touched by the obvious energy and conviction that you devoted to the Garden effort and by the extraordinary enthusiasm shown by the great crowd of Americans who gathered there. Even a clear personal knowledge of unworthiness of such confidence cannot overreach the pride that I feel." By merely asserting that he was a Republican, but without formally declaring his candidacy, on March 11 he narrowly defeated Taft in the New Hampshire Republican presidential primary through write-in votes. The Madison Square Garden rally, Bill Safire wrote, "did more than anything to bring him home from Europe to gain the 1952 nomination."

By 1956 McCrary had ended any pretense of impartiality. He launched a full-fledged public relations firm (at one point bipartisanly co-owned with Jerry Finkelstein, a New York fixer and Democratic power broker), which, by all accounts was a cover for the virtuoso impresario. "Shrewd, melancholy, aggressively well-connected," as Safire described McCrary, he quietly helped negotiate the racial integration of suburban Levittowns with his client the builder William Levitt and his friend Thurgood Marshall. In 1959 McCrary produced the United States Trade and Cultural Fair Exhibition in Moscow. He not only featured a "typical" American tract house in the fair (marketed by Tex's client Herbert Sadkin and dubbed the "splitnik," because it was divided especially for the display of American one upmanship by a walkway to provide a better view), but also maneuvered to immortalize Sadkin's model home on front-page photographs back home as the stage-setter for one of the most vivid episodes of the Cold War: the so-called kitchen debate between U.S. vice president Richard M. Nixon and Soviet premier Nikita Khrushchev. McCrary's dexterity in promoting the merits of capitalism over communism (and, not coincidentally, the homes built by Sadkin that American workers could afford) boosted Nixon's stock and contributed to his nomination as Eisenhower's prospective successor one year later.

McCrary had a knack "for making, manipulating and pyramiding friendships," the *New York Post* said. He was, his *Times* obituary proclaimed, "his own fable, a publicist's publicist." In his later years, Tex wasn't shy about emerging from the wings to take his share of the credit for inventing or promoting celebrities, candidacies, and events. He acknowledged that typically in public relations, "the catalyst doesn't always go along with the action; in fact, he mostly gets lost. He just makes it happen." McCrary was in a league of his own, however, "a catalyst on a hot tin roof," as he characterized himself. "McLuhan said the medium is the message," McCrary told a reporter in 1993. "I say the *messenger* is the medium."

Tex McCrary died in Manhattan on July 29, 2003, at the age of ninety-two. The couple had anchored sixteen weeks of coverage of the Billy Graham Crusade for Christianity in 1962, then had been separated since 1980 (but as Catholics, not divorced). Jinx became a spokeswoman for the American Gas Association and a vice president of Marian Bialac Cosmetics, a Whitney-owned company, played in celebrity and philanthropic tennis tournaments, and raised money for Republican candidates, but largely faded away from the public eye. She died barely one month after her husband, at eighty-four. Asked not long before his death what he would choose for his epitaph, McCrary didn't hesitate in harkening back to Arthur Brisbane's advice: be succinct. "To be continued," Tex replied.

28

Lillian Edelstein

Moses: "Let My People Stay!"

*R*ashomon was the epitome of consensus compared to the subjective and contradictory views of the 800 block of East 176th Street near Crotona Park in the
Bronx around 1940. The city government's official black-and-white property tax
photograph, on file in the Municipal Archives, depicts a Hopperesque vista, a spare
cityscape that might be credited to the Ashcan School, except that the pristine
cobblestone street is devoid even of potholes, much less of ash cans. The tranquil
thoroughfare is lined by six-story brick apartment houses, including one with
fancy striped awnings screening the windows (none of which appear to be broken)
from a lustrous summer sun. A solitary man, predictably a white man, wearing a
light-colored shirt and the blousy pants popular at the time, stands near his bicycle.
Both wheels are intact, the tires fully inflated.

Around the same time that the photograph was taken, the Federal Home Owners
Loan Corporation was dispatching surveyors to rate which neighborhoods around
the country were safe for public and private investors. Their color-coded "residential
security maps," which inspired the term "red-lining," rendered a far different perspective. On the survey drawn from the one-page report of an anonymous federal
mapmaker, the same arcadian community of Crotona Park pictured serenely in the
city's tax photo was bathed in rose-colored ink. That tint, alone, stigmatized it as
"hazardous."

The federal surveyor's judgment was by no means arbitrary. True enough, the neighborhood was very convenient to mass transportation, a major asset for any community. But, as in most of Greater Tremont, many of its buildings were already deemed démodé, and the population, nearly half of Russian or Polish descent, was undergoing profound change. "There is a steady infiltration of negro, Spanish and Puerto Rican into the area," the surveyor concluded, adding in bureaucratic shorthand, devoid of articles (of faith or otherwise): "Population is very unstable and relief load is heavy. Section is very congested with considerable small business scattered everywhere. One of the poorest areas in the Bronx." The report summed up Crotona Park's "trend of desirability" for the next ten to fifteen years in a damning, self-fulfilling one-word pronouncement: "Down."

Among the tenants on East 176th Street near Southern Boulevard in the 1940s was Lillian Edelstein. She was born on May 4, 1916, in the South Bronx to Jewish immigrants from Eastern Europe. Her father, Samuel Cohen, was a dress- and coat maker from Poland. His wife, Anna (Nemitz) Cohen, immigrated from Russia and also worked in the garment industry. Lillian, a graduate of Washington Irving High School, had studied patternmaking at Parsons School of Design and worked for the Simplicity Pattern Company in Manhattan. She lived on East 176th with her husband, Sam, who worked downtown, too, as a seventy-five-dollar-a-week ladies' hat finisher, originally for his father, who was also a milliner. They married in 1936 when Lillian was twenty. During the war, Sam tried to enlist but was rejected for medical reasons, so after putting in a full day at work, he would go home to the Bronx for a quick dinner and then take the subway to Brooklyn to labor in a munitions plant.

If federal bureaucrats defined East Tremont in one word—down—most of its residents could describe it just as succinctly and more devotedly, or, at least, forgivingly, as home. "We weren't rich, but we were a family," Lillian Edelstein would later recall. "East Tremont was a big family. There isn't a stronger bond than that." To mid-century regional planners, the neighborhood was decaying, headed down. It demanded visionary nostrums like wholesale slum clearance and vehicular escape routes to newly minted gated residential communities and even satellite cities in the suburbs. To many tenants and homeowners of the neighborhoods deemed to be deteriorating in an inescapable downward spiral, though, where they were living was still a step up from where they had lived before. It was typically better than any place else they could afford. Edelstein would venerate East Tremont as "an area where immigrants from European farms could get used to city life," as "a perfect location of our hardworking fathers who had good transportation to their jobs," where stay-at-home mothers "could get their weekly kosher food shopping done" and where "our parents and grandparents could set on benches playing chess while overlooking Southern Boulevard." Edelstein explained: "I became an activist against the Cross-Bronx Expressway after realizing how it would destroy the neighborhood so many people called their home."

With or without Robert Moses, though, their neighborhood was changing, to invoke the familiar euphemism. Greater Tremont began losing population in the 1940s, when the garment district in Manhattan's Midtown West began contracting and exporting jobs to nonunion shops out of town. Better-off Jews and Italians, who had migrated to the Bronx from the Lower East Side, were now graduating to Queens or the North Bronx or, better still, to the suburbs. But by the end of the decade, while a demographic upheaval—and with it, the devastation that transformed the borough into a shameful national symbol of urban blight—might have been inevitable, it did not seem to be looming apocalyptically. Lillian Edelstein had lived her entire life until then within a two-mile radius of her home on East 176th Street. "I was married from the building," she said. "I had my children from the building." She had no plans to move. Plans were being made to move her, however. The Edelsteins, like the vast majority of New Yorkers at the time, didn't own or need their own car (now, nearly half do). Lillian Edelstein never even bothered to apply for a driver's license ("she drove, but not very well," her sister said), which was about the only characteristic that she and Robert Moses had in common. Moses didn't drive either. Apparently, he knew how, but he didn't have to. Instead, he was chauffeured around the spiderweb of highways and parkways and expressways and bridges that he built as commissioner of planning, parks, and public works, chairman of the Triborough Bridge and Tunnel Authority and New York City's construction coordinator for a half century, beginning in 1924. All of these were appointed positions—Moses ran for office only once, for governor in 1934 as a Republican against Herbert H. Lehman, the incumbent. He was walloped.

But by the 1940s, the mightiest officials, elected and appointed, would capitulate to Moses: some because they became convinced that indeed he was a visionary; others because they secretly agreed with him but made him their foil, lacking the guts to confront their constituents; and still others because he was an implacable, capricious bully and had worn them down. If they were concerned about their own political survival, challenging him just wasn't worth the fight. And if elected officials, people with power that had, in fact, been vested in them by the voters, flinched at challenging Robert Moses, imagine the misgivings of average citizens who grew up believing you can't fight city hall, much less resist an unaccountable bureaucratic behemoth. "To really show political power," Robert A. Caro wrote in his magisterial biography of Moses, *The Power Broker* (1974), "you had to show the effect of power on the powerless."

The lopsided duel between Robert Moses and Lillian Edelstein would personify his effect on the powerless. "He looked right at us like we were little people," she said; "he made you feel you were little, and then he looked away." The Edelsteins lived at 867 East 176th Street, where they were raising their two daughters. They rented apartment 2F for fifty-six dollars a month (raised, recently, from thirty-six dollars). Lillian's sister and mother, a recent widow, lived in the same building, too, in 3G and 3F respectively. "We could still afford to live comfortably in a neighborhood full of Jewish families that shared our culture, language and experiences," Lillian said. "Moses deprived us all of this dream without any consideration for all the lives he held in his hands." What galled the powerless people of East Tremont most was Moses's single-mindedness, his refusal to discuss an alternative to his proposed route much less to seriously consider one. "It ruined our community, our families, friendships and the bonds we all shared; for which reason?" Edelstein asked. "The simple answer is that Robert Moses wanted his way." The Moses she invoked led her people away from the promised land, not toward it.

Suggesting an antidote to Manhattan's unforgiving street grid, Frederick Law Olmstead had proposed in the 1870s, as New York City began annexing what would become the borough and county of the Bronx, a greensward of parks and parkways traversing the rural topography. But by 1929, just two decades after mass production of the Model T began, the fledgling Regional Plan Association that William Wilgus had been mobilizing in favor of mass transit had turned to another priority: relieving the traffic congestion that was already inundating the Bronx by building more roads. Even more cars and trucks would be spilling off the George Washington Bridge after its opening in 1931, coming and going between New Jersey, New England, and Long Island. (It would become the world's most trafficked motor vehicle span.)

Propelled by Norman Bel Geddes, the industrial designer whose credo was "A straight line is the shortest distance between two points," Moses had turned away from the curvaceous and scenic parkways that he'd mapped earlier to harmonize with the region's natural terrain. In 1941 the New York City Planning Department fleshed out the 1929 traffic surveys as they considered how to go about building the proposed

"Cross-Bronx Expressway looking West from Boston Road," 1960. (Photo via the *New York Times* Photo Archives)

$17 million route bisecting the borough. "Topographical conditions, high land values and heavily built-up areas," the city's planners wrote, "make the construction of such a highway very difficult." Moses himself, elaborating on the proposal in a 1944 issue of *Bronxboro*, the Bronx Board of Trade magazine, admitted to being hampered by "difficult topography and cost of right-of-way." Statistics only begin to describe the magnitude of the challenge.

The western end of the highway would eventually be the Alexander Hamilton Bridge, spanning the Harlem River. The other, more than seven miles to the east, would ultimately connect to the Throgs Neck Expressway, which would lead to the eponymous bridge connecting Queens and the section of the Bronx known as Throggs Neck. (Moses deliberately removed one *g* from Throggs, a misnomer at the outset, supposedly to save money on signage.)

Only Moses would have had the audacity to blast a 225-foot-wide road through the billion-year-old Fordham gneiss that forms the bedrock of the Bronx and protrudes in ridges above the surface, in the process crossing 113 streets; 7 expressways or parkways; the Concourse line of the IND subway; the Pelham, Lenox–White Plains Road, Dyre Avenue, Third Avenue, and Jerome Avenue elevated lines; 2 branches of the New York Central Railroad and one of the New York, New Haven and Hartford; and innumerable pipes and utility lines. "Moses thinks he's God," skeptics said, "but he's only Moses."

But Moses was unfazed. He was a doer, the proverbial cook who breaks eggs to create an omelet. As he once told Detroit automakers, "There is no city traffic problem which cannot be largely solved, except at extraordinary peak hours, by simply giving adequate power and undeviating support to one official with guts."

By the 1940s the marathon court challenges by Anneke Jans's heirs against the Trinity Church holdings in Manhattan had just about ended. Those, arguably, were to some degree about greed. The tenants of East Tremont and Crotona Park, though, had no expectations of financial gain. They just wanted to keep what they had. And it began to seem as if time might be on their side. "It had gone on so long and you keep hearing and hearing and nothing happens," Edelstein told Caro years later, "and after a while it doesn't mean anything to you." When, by the late 1940s, nothing had happened, the tenants had come to feel it unlikely that even Moses could overcome the entropy that had stalled so many other public works projects and, in the style of his namesake, sunder the borough. (Moses would in fact emulate his namesake's biblical marvel even more literally when he relocated the Bronx River by five hundred feet.) "We continued to live our lives as if it was never going to happen," Edelstein said in the documentary *The World That Moses Built* (1988), part of the PBS American Experience series. "They were rumors, that was it. We thought we were going to live here forever."

But on Tuesday, December 4, 1952, without warning, Edelstein and some fifteen hundred other residents of fifty-four buildings were told that the highway had won: they had ninety days to vacate. Signed by Robert Moses under his auspices as city construction coordinator, the notices evoked those that Harlem's white tenants had received from Philip Payton earlier in the twentieth century. Edelstein and her neighbors were living in the path of what would, when it was completed, be the most expensive highway in the world, Moses informed the residents—as if that would make up for the loss of homes that, however humble, most of them cherished (and, in retrospect, idealized) as stable citadels in an anarchic city of nearly eight million. This Moses made no pretense of a promised land. He would follow the biblical script of uprooting the existing occupants, replacing them not by settlers staking their

perpetual claim to sacred ground, but by transients just passing through. (If the Isra-
elites had moved at the average speed of traffic on the Cross-Bronx Expressway, it
might not have taken them forty years to cross the desert, but they still would have
wasted a good three weeks.)

"It was like the floor opened up underneath your feet. There was no warning,"
Edelstein recalled. "We just got it in the mail. Everybody on the street got it
on the same day. A notice. We had 90 days to get out. I remember it was a nice day,
too, for that time of year. We all stood outside—'Did you get the letter? Did you
get the letter?' And 'What does it mean?' And then we all waited for our husbands
to come home. And my husband said, 'You can't do anything.'" How could a nobody,
even a coalition of nobodies—housewives, mostly—from the Bronx, without any
political connections and no money for lawyers, challenge the omnipotent Robert
Moses? "If this is what we have to do, this is what we have to do," Sam Edelstein
said. "And I said," his wife recalled, "'No way.'"

When Lillian Edelstein and the neighbors she helped band together in an East
Tremont Neighborhood Association delved into what had happened to those
uprooted during an earlier phase of construction, as the six-lane ribbon of concrete
snaked its way west from Bruckner Boulevard, their misgivings only grew. "My
mother was always a strong, very highly intelligent and independent person," her
daughter, Janet Weiner, said. "Her parents were strong role models, both coming to
the United States from Europe on their own." In the absence of sufficient subsidies
or alternative apartments, some long-term tenants had been transplanted to temporary quarters, while others were still stranded, subsisting like squatters in debris-
ridden buildings, sometimes devoid of basic services, that were being vandalized
and even demolished around them. "As soon as the top floor of a building was
empty, they'd start tearing off the roof and top stories, even," Edelstein said. While
people were being displaced, the wholesale demolition beckoned, or exposed, an
influx of fauna that endowed "changing neighborhood" with a whole new meaning:
"The rats were running like dogs and cats in the street."

"What we found was that families were not taken care of as Moses had promised," Edelstein said. "People were shown poor alternatives that were not even compa-
rable to the quality of their old homes but that still cost as much as twice that of
their old apartments. Those who couldn't afford these expenses had nowhere else to
go so they stayed in their apartments until the very end. They were forced to live in
such deplorable conditions and breathe the dirty, soot-filled air in close proximity
to the project site. Seeing these people was just unbearable. I did not want my family,

or any other people, to have to experience this suffering, so I knew someone had to speak up."

Moses refused to meet, much less listen. Local elected legislators expressed sympathy but little else. James J. Lyons, the resourceful borough president, was initially the most responsive. He listened, at least, although it's arguable whether the East Tremont women got a fair hearing. Lyons referred them to an engineer in his office, who for the first time offered a tantalizing glimmer of hope. The ingenious engineer suggested what seemed like a logical, face-saving, and relatively modest modification in Moses's map: to shift the expressway south two blocks, to the northern border of Crotona Park, for less than a mile. That detour would require the demolition of only six tenements, displacing nineteen families, instead of fifty-four multi-family apartment houses. "Surely, Construction Coordinator Moses could get Parks Commissioner Moses to give up a few blades of grass," Edelstein said snarkily. "And with these two important officials convinced, there could be no objection by City Planning Commissioner Moses."

Furious at being second-guessed, Moses wouldn't budge. Insisting that his route was inviolate, he threatened for the umpteenth time to resign as construction coordinator, take his marbles—in this case, federal and state highway funds—elsewhere, and apply them to other projects, leaving the Bronx with an embarrassing eyesore, a half-finished highway to nowhere. While Moses's obstinacy typically needed no further explanation, this time he attributed it, in part, to engineering and contractual challenges. The last-minute logistics would, in fact, not have been insignificant. Less justifiable were Moses's arrogant implacability and the appearance, at least (the accusation was never substantiated), of the cronyism he had often criticized in his political opponents: among the structures that would have been sacrificed by the shift in the expressway route was a bus depot that happened to belong to the Third Avenue Transit System—successor to the company Elizabeth Jennings had sued a century earlier—whose lawyer at the time was the fledgling political Mr. Fix-It, Roy M. Cohn.

Edelstein catalyzed the community with rallies, persuading local movie theaters to promote them on-screen. She taught herself to type and cranked out flyers and press releases. The conflict appeared headed for a showdown early in 1953 at a meeting of the all-powerful board of estimate, which consisted of the five borough presidents and the three citywide elected officials: the mayor, the comptroller, and the leader of the city's legislature. That March, with the board poised to consider what would ordinarily be a routine bureaucratic increment in the approval process, Moses issued an unequivocal warning in a letter to New York mayor Vincent R. Impellitteri: "The proposed kink in the Expressway," he wrote, "would represent a ridiculous and indefensible proposal from every angle and one which could not possibly be approved by the state and federal authorities in the light of the history of this undertaking and the steps already taken to carry it out, and that a new set of objecting owners and tenants would instantly appear in opposition."

On April 23, some two hundred Bronx housewives (their husbands were working) took chartered buses to city hall, where the board was meeting to vote on aptly named "damage maps" to get the condemnation process going. Borough president Lyons, furious because Moses had accused him of trying to mollify his constituents by only pretending to take their alternative route seriously, called the accusation a "damnable lie." He even dared to compare Moses to the Grand Poobah, the haughty, self-important Japanese minion in Gilbert and Sullivan's comic operetta *The Mikado*. But at the same public meeting, council president Rudolph Halley more or less concurred with Moses's claim that Lyons had already agreed to the original route earlier in the day, during the board's executive session, and had invited the house-wives just to let them vent. Unable to muster more than ten of the twelve votes needed for approval, the board punted and adjourned.

After weeks of indecision—or more likely because the decision had already been made—the board met again on May 15. This time, on second consideration, supporters of the expressway needed only a simple majority. The board concluded a vitriolic debate—the *Times* called it "acidulous"—by approving the expressway 10–6 as orig-inally mapped between Longfellow and Anthony Avenues, displacing some five thousand tenants and sixty shopkeepers. Only Halley and New York City comp-troller Lazarus Joseph voted no. Halley accused Moses of blackmail, with his threat to commandeer the funds appropriated for the expressway and transfer them to some other project. Lyons, who had by then capitulated to Moses, explaining lamely that municipal engineers had ultimately collectively agreed that the original route was in fact preferable, branded Halley a "demagogue."

Lillian Edelstein did not earnestly deliver her soliloquy, take a bow, and accept the board's praise for having taken a stand. Instead she fearlessly, and futilely, accused Lyons of double-crossing his Bronx constituents. At the final showdown, she was too distraught to demand that the mayor redeem his promise to vote no until all the residents were satisfactorily relocated.

By the end of 1953, with Halley and Joseph both gone (Halley lost the mayoral race; Joseph did not seek reelection as comptroller), Edelstein and her fellow tenants were clinging tenuously to one last hope: that Moses might still become reconciled to what he had called a "kink," which they insisted was only a wrinkle in the expressway's route. As he ran for mayor in the fall of 1953, Manhattan borough president Robert F. Wagner had already voted to start condemning the private property in the expressway's path under the city's power of eminent domain. But he promised repeatedly—once, only a few weeks before Election Day, in person to a thousand Bronxites assembled at P.S. 44 for one of Edelstein's rallies ("Every tenant who could walk was there," she said)—that he would vote against actual authorizing the city to take legal title to the properties until all of the 1,530 families living there had been properly relocated.

Deputy mayor Henry Epstein, who had embraced the tenants' alternative route, suddenly reversed himself—the result of browbeating, or blackmail, by Moses ("He was hit over the head with an ax," was all Moses admitted to Robert Caro). Even Wagner, the maestro of pondering, delegating, and mumbling, could hold out only so long. When push came to shove—the method by which Moses typically operated—Wagner, too, succumbed. "If you try to move this Expressway you'll never get another nickel from us," Moses recalled warning Wagner. "You will have to explain that it was all a mistake."

"On October 14, 1953, I had the rally, which was standing room only," Edelstein said. Every tenant who could walk was there. The public officials were there and they promised that no one would be dislocated. And everyone went away happy. That was October. Then came November, and after the election," she said. "That was it. We lost."

On December 3, 1954, almost two years to the day after the fifteen hundred households of East Tremont and Crotona Park were given ninety days to vacate their homes, Moses won the war of attrition. The board of estimate voted unanimously to take title to the 1.2-mile corridor that constituted Section 2 of America's first urban expressway. Moses's original ninety-day deadline, it turned out, had been an empty scare tactic. He could never by the spring of 1953 have been prepared to begin demolishing the obstacles that stood within the arterial's right-of-way.

"The prospect opened up by the thought of the Cross-Bronx Expressway and its tributaries is a pleasant one," a *Times* editorial effused in 1949. But the reality, Marshall Berman, the Marxist philosopher from City College, wrote, "turned potential long-range entropy into a sudden inexorable catastrophe." The six-lane, 225-foot-wide trench up to forty feet deep (which ironically, as Edelstein herself pointed out, could never have been broad enough to accommodate the thousands of vehicles that now snail along during the morning rush hour at an average speed of under thirteen miles per hour) would divide the Bronx physically and figuratively forever. "In the postwar era the geography and sociology of the Bronx was radically redefined by the construction of the Cross-Bronx Expressway," Robert A. M. Stern and his collaborators wrote in *New York 1960: Architecture and Urbanism between the Second World War and the Bicentennial* (1997). "It was a road *through* the Bronx, but not of it, offering motorists a means of traveling past—or, more precisely, cutting through—the borough on their way to New England and the rest of the United States." The route cleaved to no natural or historic course but was "the direct product of a willful engineering decision to link the George Washington Bridge with Long Island and New England by means of a straight line," the authors wrote, "as much bludgeoned as built." Stern vigorously challenged Moses's boast that the Cross-Bronx was "metropolitan architecture in the finest sense." Rather, he wrote, "it unalterably cut the borough in two, with the 'haves' to the north and the 'have-nots' cordoned off in the ancient tenements and industrial marginalis of the south."

By November 1955 the officially designated relocation company hired to evacuate the fifty-four apartment buildings in Section 2—a company in which three of Moses's aides were stockholders—crowed that 90 percent of the tenants had been relocated, a euphemism that could be more accurately defined as "driven from their apartments." Among them were the Edelsteins. Urban experts might question Moses's omnipotence; they might challenge the expressway's tectonic impact on the Bronx, or conclude that the social and economic upheaval blamed on this mammoth dry moat would have been unavoidable in any case. But they agreed nearly unanimously that the holdout tenants were given little help or recompense once they were forced to move. "The support provided for relocation," Ray Bromley wrote in "Not So Simple! Caro, Moses, and the Impact of the Cross-Bronx Expressway" (1998), "was hopelessly inadequate."

The 1.2 miles of Section 2 between the Bronx River on the east to just west of Webster Avenue, the stretch that routed Lillian Edelstein, her widowed mother, sister, and other neighbors, would finally open on April 27, 1960—more than seven years and four months after the East Tremont tenants had been given ninety days to leave. That was nearly as long as the time between President John F. Kennedy's 1961 pledge to Congress to place a man on the moon and the historic lunar landing—the 239,000-mile "one giant leap for mankind"—in 1969, seven years and ten months later. The full 8.3 miles that the expressway traversed across Manhattan and the Bronx would not be finished until 1963 and would take fifteen years longer to complete than the three-hundred-mile Erie Canal. Moses had vanquished the tenants and their toothless allies on the board of estimate. He had muzzled the entire chorus of naysayers. His completion of yet another in his litany of controversial public works inspired him to invoke another of his favorite, if affected, aphorisms, this one attributed to his friend, the economist Beardsley Ruml (who may be best remembered as the father of the withholding tax). "If the ends don't justify the means," Ruml liked to say, "what does?"

And yet . . . perhaps Moses sensed that this hard-fought victory was the beginning of his end. The graciousness that had surprised some adversaries suddenly gave way to a personal, and publicly displayed, vindictiveness. When the Cross-Bronx Expressway was finally dedicated, Robert Moses could no longer help but be a sore winner. He complained that he had been "thwarted, lampooned and libeled" by demagogues, and that his fellow public officials, more concerned about their reelection and (ironically) about "reprisals," were motivated primarily by self-preservation. "We have traversed in good company the spine of Manhattan," Moses gushed. "We have met rocks, rivers, and the resistance of modern Redskins. The whole Island of Manhattan cost only 24 dollars. Maybe in time this arterial expenditure, too, will be considered a bargain."

Originally the expressway was supposed to cost $17 million. By the time it was finished, with filigrees that evoked Moses's parkways, the official tab was at least $130 million (or more than $1 billion in today's dollars, nearly $130 million a mile). It became among the most congested freeways in America—the very worst by some measures—a mucilaginous flume of tens of thousands of gridlocked vehicles crawling at an average speed of thirteen miles per hour, belching noxious fumes, and fueling chronic road rage. "Ten minutes on this road," Marshall Berman wrote, "an ordeal for anyone, is especially dreadful for people who remember the Bronx as it used to be: who remember these neighborhoods as they once lived and thrived until this road itself cut their heart and made the Bronx a place to get out of." Motorists would traverse a borough that became a synonym for urban blight, a heartbreak highway overlooked by homey window shades and shutters that, on closer inspection, prove to be trompe l'oeil decals applied in the early 1980s to camouflage the shells of scores of abandoned apartment buildings.

Once the Edelsteins were finally forced to move, they relocated first to Sam's mother's apartment (she had moved in with a daughter) at 1700 Longfellow Avenue, just south of the Cross-Bronx Expressway near the corner of East 174th Street, about a quarter mile east of Crotona Park. Within a few years, the hat factory where Sam worked shifted its operations from Midtown to upstate New York. He couldn't make ends meet driving a taxi, so when he heard in 1959 about another hat factory opening in Framingham, Massachusetts, the couple moved there. Lillian worked at the Fabric Place, a decorating store in Framingham, until she was eighty. After Sam died in 1997, she moved to Northfield, New Jersey, near Atlantic City, where she served as a lunchroom aide in her great-granddaughter's school.

How long the Edelsteins would have remained in the Bronx if they and their neighbors had succeeded in blocking the Cross-Bronx is arguable. Their generation, and the one before, moved to the borough when newspaper classified columns were bursting with advertisements touting Crotona Park as the "most exclusive neighborhood," "exceptionally desirable," with "beautiful light rooms," and only "15 minutes from 42nd Street." The outward migration from the very same neighborhood began just as soon as the most successful transplants and the next generation could afford someplace better for themselves and their children. The stampede accelerated as high rents in mid-Manhattan and cheaper nonunion labor outside the city squeezed more and more firms, like Sam Edelstein's company, to flee the metropolitan area altogether (and, as in Philip Payton's Harlem, Black tenants began to move in).

With decades of hindsight, some critics of *The Power Broker* maintain that the book romanticized East Tremont and Crotona Park. They invoked Ed Koch's proverbial anecdote about the elderly woman who accosted him on the Brighton Beach boardwalk, pleading, "Make it like it was." Mayor Koch knew that it really never was as good as she remembered, only that she believed it was not as good now as it had been then, and that any further change was likely to make it even worse. To be sure, those Bronx neighborhoods were already in flux. Their residents were in the vanguard of white flight; many would migrate to self-contained communities like Co-op City. They were being replaced by poorer people, some of whom could not find jobs and could not afford to pay rent to landlords who found it more profitable to burn down their buildings and collect the insurance than to maintain them properly and pay their property taxes, which generated the revenue to provide the city services that the poor could not afford to replace with private alternatives.

What if Lillian Edelstein and her neighbors had defeated Robert Moses? Suppose the Cross-Bronx Expressway had never been built? "How many of us would still be in the Bronx today, caring for it and fighting for it as our own?" even Marshall Berman asked. "Some of us, no doubt, but I suspect not many, and in any case—it hurts to say it—not me. For the Bronx of my youth was possessed, inspired, by the great modern dream of mobility. To live well meant to move up socially, and this in turn meant to move out physically."

The memoirist Vivian Gornick remembered her own neighborhood, bounded on the south by East Tremont Avenue, mostly for "the bleakness of expectation, the stultified vision and resented courage." She recalled in the *New York Times Magazine* in 2001: "Our longing to get out of the Bronx was intense, and it induced, paradoxically, a solidarity that many were to carry well into other lives: the inevitable mixed legacy of the ghetto. For that's what the Bronx was for us: a working-class ghetto destined to be deserted by its young."

Marshall Berman never forgot his conversation with a futurologist at an academic reception. With Vietnam war protests and race riots raging among the next generation, the conversation quickly shifted from posterity to their shared past and to Berman's prediction that the recently completed Cross-Bronx Expressway would eradicate every remaining trace of their childhoods.

"'Fine, the sooner the better,'" Berman recalled the futurist saying. "'Didn't I understand that the destruction of the Bronx would fulfill the Bronx's own moral imperative?'

"'What moral imperative?' I asked.

"He laughed as he bellowed in my face: 'You want to know the morality of the Bronx? "Get out, schmuck, get out."'

"For once in my life, I was stunned into silence," Berman confessed. "It was the brutal truth: I had left the Bronx, just as he had, and just as we were all brought up to, and now the Bronx was collapsing not just because of Robert Moses, but because of all of us.

"It was true," Berman admitted, "but did he have to laugh?"

The Bronx would begin to come back; the abandoned buildings would be renovated so successfully during the Koch administration that the city would run out of tax-foreclosed apartments to rehabilitate. But Lillian Edelstein and her neighbors from East Tremont would not return. And it would take more than two generations for the Bronx to recover in population—only in 2020 flirting with its 1950 historic peak—as another influx of immigrants from other places discovered that, whatever its shortcomings, the borough was still better than where they were living before.

Lillian Edelstein's failed mutiny against Moses was not the first time that his grandiose projects had been resisted, of course. He obliged his influential benefactors by remapping the serpentine Northern State Parkway to spare their leafy estates on Long Island; he mollified the gentry in America's first suburb by transplanting the proposed

Brooklyn-Queens Expressway from their nineteenth-century neighborhood to an outer shelf (creating a stunning waterfront promenade overlooking the harbor atop a two-level highway); and he begrudgingly morphed his Brooklyn–Battery Bridge into a tunnel after preservationists howled that historic Castle Clinton would have to be demolished to accommodate the Manhattan approach to the span.

But the battle over the Cross-Bronx Expressway was different. "The tenants organized to fight the demolition of their homes and the adoption of an alternate route for the highway," the architectural historian Michael Caratzas wrote in 2002, "in what appears to be the first well-publicized, sophisticated effort by working-class people against expressway construction in the history of New York City, and possibly, the United States." Most of the press, except for the *New York Post* and the *World-Telegram*, paid little attention, since the fight took place in the Bronx, not in Manhattan, and was mounted not by puissant property owners and preservationists but by ordinary people. "I was just a housewife," Lillian Edelstein said.

Moses would lose his subsequent fights to replace a Central Park playground near West Sixty-Seventh Street with an eighty-car parking lot for Tavern on the Green. He would fail to ramrod a bus route through Washington Square Park as a prelude to another megaproject that would speed traffic between New Jersey and Brooklyn through the heart of Greenwich Village and the Lower East Side. Moses would lose those fights precisely because this time his opponents had learned from the defeat of Lillian Edelstein and her followers. This time they were typically wealthy and not working class, celebrities rather than nobodies, public-relations-savvy rather than starved for publicity, with a history of political organizing and a war chest of campaign contributions that provided the resources to hire a battery of lawyers and immediate access to power.

Lillian Edelstein's own fight failed, but it paved the way for the women with strollers whose protest blocked Moses's parking lot in Central Park and the "bunch of mothers" led by locals like Shirley Hayes and Mary Perot Nichols and joined by Jane Jacobs and Lewis Mumford and William H. Whyte and Eleanor Roosevelt, who stopped the downtown bus route and the highway through Lower Manhattan. (When Robert Caro interviewed Jacobs for *The Power Broker*, he recalled, "it turned out that we each had a question that we wanted to ask the other" about Robert Moses. "Jane wanted to ask me what it was like to meet him," Caro said. "I wanted to ask her, what it was like to beat him.") Jacobs's ascendancy as an apostle of natural surveillance to deter anti-social behavior (she called it "eyes on the street" and "the ballet of the sidewalk") and of mixed-income, low-rise apartment projects was triggered by the backlash to Moses's steamroller statecraft and to the lessons of Edelstein's lonely crusade.

In one sense, the clash between the tenants of East Tremont and the proponents of big government embodied the tension between two tenets of liberalism. On the one hand there was "a notion that ordinary citizens play a role in policy-making," Roberta Gold wrote in *When Tenants Claimed the City: The Struggle for Citizenship in New York City Housing* (2014). "It was a civics-class sort of belief—arguably a naive confusion of the electoral with the governing coalition—and it had likely been fostered by Franklin Roosevelt's savvy efforts to project personal concern with 'the forgotten man.'" At city hall, that textbook version collided with government bodies that were "liberal in the sense of supporting large-scale spending on infrastructure, not in the sense of a meaningful say for the ordinary citizen, or of openness to reasoned debate."

The groundwork for sparing swaths of Manhattan from *The Power Broker*'s radiating mosaic was laid in the Bronx. "I have no doubt that Edelstein was a source of inspiration for Jacobs," says the historian Stephen Petrus. "In many ways, Edelstein's work with the East Tremont Neighborhood Association was a blueprint for Jacobs and other activists in their successful endeavors to defeat the Moses plan to expand Fifth Avenue through Washington Square Park in the late 1950s, to save the West Village from demolition in 1961, and to kill the Lower Manhattan Expressway plan in the late 1960s."

Peter L. Laurence, the author of *Becoming Jane Jacobs* (2016), notes that while Jacobs mentioned the Cross-Bronx Expressway only once in her seminal *The Death and Life of Great American Cities* (1961), "the destructive effects of cars and 'expressways that eviscerate great cities' was a major theme—even before she fought LoMax in person. Another major theme of her book was community organizing, and cross-neighborhood organizing, and she definitely learned something about this from the Cross-Bronx Expressway battles."

The momentum that decentralized power in New York City, armed local community boards with jurisdiction, however limited, over planning and schools, and delegated the last word on public works to unelected judges responding to civil suits was provided by a backlash against the heavy hand of Robert Moses. By the early 1960s resistance to Moses's bulldozer diplomacy was merging into an equally intractable ideology, a reflexive not-in-my-backyard naysaying by New Yorkers discontented with the status quo, but so disillusioned by unredeemed promises that they worried that any change would be for the worse. A century earlier, even Parisians who acknowledged how much Baron Haussmann had accomplished were exasperated by his construction. "That's enough for the moment. There will be a 20th century. Let's leave something for them to do," the historian Léon Halévy wrote in the nineteenth.

The pace of traffic crawling on the Cross-Bronx begs the question whether an opponent of urban expressways, much less one only suggesting a minor detour, is a Luddite standing in the way of progress. In a 1961 episode of the TV series *Car 54, Where Are You?* (which was filmed in the Bronx), Officers Toody and Muldoon are assigned to evict the last holdout tenant in the path of the Cross-Bronx, played by the Yiddish stage actress Molly Picon. Chided for delaying progress, Picon scoffs: "Because some man in New York with Bermuda shorts and fancy socks wants to get to New Jersey ten minutes faster to play golf, I have to get out of my house? Tell him with the Bermuda shorts and the fancy socks, get up ten minutes earlier!" To which Toody replied: "She makes sense."

Perhaps the most definitive verdict on the expressway is recorded in the dozens of road signs that identify the route as I-95 (or, more esoterically, as Interstate Route Connector 511) or by its generic name only as the Cross-Bronx. In New York City's only borough denominated by a family's surname, nobody in the nearly sixty years since the Cross-Bronx was completed has seriously lobbied to anoint a namesake for the expressway. "No one wants the 'honor' of having this traffic nightmare named after him or her," the Automobile Club of New York said.

29

Preston Wilcox

The Pedigree of Black Power

In the 1960s, most of the chroniclers and combatants ensnarled in New York's seismic school wars overlooked an inconvenient parallel with the past. They all but disregarded the analogy between Archbishop John Hughes's campaign against the white Protestant establishment in the early nineteenth century on behalf of Catholic parochial education and the birth of Black empowerment embodied by Preston Wilcox in the twentieth.

Arguably, while Archbishop Hughes lost his battle in Albany for government funding of a separate Roman Catholic school system, he would win the larger war. Thanks largely to his lobbying, the city's public schools were ostensibly freed from the dominion of any one religion. Who won what—if anyone won anything—in the city's 1960s school wars was more ambiguous for two reasons: Wilcox, a gangly six-foot-three former professional basketball player, was just as comfortable calling the shots as an inconspicuous coach from the sidelines as he had been as a star player on the court; and, to the hand-wringing of white liberals, Wilcox had fundamentally rewritten not only the rules of the game but also the goals, or, at least, the strategy to achieve them.

In 1954, invoking the psychologist Kenneth Clark's conclusion that public school segregation contributed to "a sense of inferiority" on the part of Black children, the Supreme Court declared that providing them with a separate but equal education was unconstitutional. Barely a decade later, that seemed to be exactly what Wilcox wanted.

"The fallacy of Clark's argument," Wilcox wrote in 1969, "lies in his failure to cite the fact that Black students who want to become white suffer psychologically whether within segregated or integrated classrooms. Secondly, he made a basic assumption that 'white schools were right' even though the great majority of white students have been systematically educated not to respect Black students as people: as human beings in their own right. Finally, the Supreme Court decision itself was based on a faulty premise: it asserted that schools were 'separate and equal' at the time of the decision. The fact is that most schools were deliberately separate and deliberately unequal in terms of teacher turnover, overcrowding, number of textbooks, quality of the building, per capita expenditures, test scores, etc."

Wilcox defined the solution as separation rather than segregation, as genuine community control of local schools—the right of parents and civic and religious

Preston Wilcox, speaking as a professor at Columbia University, 1966. (Photo via the *New York Times* Photo Archives)

leaders to hire and fire teachers and principals and to shape curriculums—rather than some superficial bureaucratic decentralization. His strategy not only evoked Archbishop Hughes's parlous political platform but also echoed the agendas of two twentieth-century century educators, both white, who championed the special cultural needs of two other immigrant groups: Julia Richman, on behalf of Russian Jewish children on the Lower East Side; and Wilcox's exemplar, Leonard Covello, for Italian immigrants in East Harlem, as Professor Nicolous Mills of Sarah Lawrence College wrote in "Community Schools: Irish, Italians and Jews" (1974). But the intrusion of race, rather than ethnicity, produced a "curious turn of events," Professor Walter W. Stafford of New York University concluded: "White civic groups that had rejected blacks attending their schools, now protested blacks controlling schools in their own community." As a result, the version of community control applied experimentally and squeamishly by the city's board of education in the late 1960s functioned more like a gauzy bandage, barely even covering up a festering rupture, much less helping to cure it. Everybody concurred that the patient was sick. The medics disagreed not only on the remedy, but also on the diagnosis.

To Wilcox, a prolific and heterodoxical essayist, the brand name bandage itself represented the perfect metaphor for white America's hypocrisy. In 1920, on the eve of the Harlem Renaissance, Johnson & Johnson introduced the light beige Band-Aid. Its Caucasian hue was no coincidence (not unlike the original "flesh-colored" Crayola crayon color, which was tactfully relabeled "peach" on the eve of the civil rights revolution). While the nation's complexion became more diverse, the adhesive strip's pigmentation remained largely unchanged for a century, until 2020, a fact of American life that didn't go unnoticed by trenchant social critics. In 1970, a satirical book titled *White Is* included a scabrous caricature by Sandy Huffaker, a white political cartoonist, of a Black Panther militant, his eyes rolled upwards incredulously at the vanilla-colored adhesive bandage on his forehead. The caption bluntly read: "White is a flesh colored Band-Aid." The book was published by Preston Wilcox.

Wilcox was just the sort of unconventional provocateur for whom a monochromatic Band-Aid would represent both America's enduring racial insensitivity and the ineffectual remedies that had been applied to salve three centuries of discrimination. He was neither a balm-thrower nor a bomb-thrower, which may explain why, despite his sway, he never became a household name. Moreover, those New Yorkers who do remember him remain divided on his role in roiling a city that would be riven by race for decades as Black people staked a claim to political power commensurate with their expanding share of the population and struggled with white school bureau-crats who were uncaring at worst and ineffective at best. Wilcox galvanized a local movement to better educate Black New Yorkers that, though it indeed made a differ-ence, arguably impacted the city's politics and race relations as profoundly as it affected the public school system, and not always constructively.

Preston Rosenthal (a name he adopted from a friend) Wilcox, the great-grandson of slaves, was born in 1923 in Youngstown, Ohio, a Ku Klux Klan stronghold (that November, a mayor was elected with the Klan's endorsement for the first time) where only one in twenty residents was Black. He was the second of five children of southern transplants who came north in the Great Migration. His father, John, an illiterate Alabaman, was a laborer at the Youngstown Sheet and Tube plant in what was then the vast Steel Valley bordering Pennsylvania. His mother, Ida Mae Rous-seau, who hailed from Georgia, later worked as a housemaid.

Prophetically, Wilcox grew up on Harlem Street. Of the eleven families who lived there, seven were Black, but the color lines were blurred only so much. Youngstown's movie theaters were still segregated—Black people knew they belonged in the balcony—and so were public swimming pools. Wilcox remembered himself as a role model—among Black boys his age. A voracious reader, he acquired the nickname Sy because he always seemed to be toting a copy of *Silas Marner*, George Eliot's nineteenth-century novel justifying moral rectitude. "There was a neighbor in my block, Miss Haerian, who put her hand on my head one day when I was about seven years of age and said, 'you're gonna make a great contribution to your people,'" he recalled. "And at first I looked at it as a burden, man. Supposing I want to hang out, chase women, won't be of no good."

He remembered when he was in the second or third grade reciting the story of "Little Black Sambo" in class, "and the teacher loved the story so much from a stereo-typical standpoint. But I was telling the story from the standpoint that Sambo out thought the tiger, turned the tiger into butter." He told the *Amsterdam News*, "I remember the first Black teacher in my hometown and people admired her because she was very bright, but she didn't make a difference. I've always had this thing about making a difference."

Wilcox started to make a difference himself when he was only eight. That was the first time he walked a picket line, to support the Scottsboro Boys, accused of raping two white women aboard a train in Alabama in 1931. He later described himself as the first Black student elected as a class officer at Youngstown's Rand High School. "I made the honor roll and the football and the basketball teams," he recalled.

"But not one teacher encouraged me to go to college. As I think back on it, they were friendly enough toward me personally. Some even lent me money when I needed it. But they never thought of me as college material. I got a letter from one of those teachers, congratulating me on having been made a professor at the Columbia School of Social Work, but that woman doesn't know yet that I achieved it in spite of her. She's still unaware of what she failed to do."

Wilcox enrolled at the historically Black Morehouse College in Atlanta, hoping to become a doctor. As a freshman he was the leading scorer on the basketball team, playing center and averaging ten of the forty points scored by the varsity squad in a typical game. He remembered his stay there as "the major educational experience of my life," even though he only attended for a year before being drafted into the army. He served in the U.S. Army Air Forces from 1943 to 1946, part of his stint at a segregated base in Greensboro, North Carolina, where he played on a base basketball team. Black would-be pilots, many of them college graduates and Tuskegee Airmen further training or denied combat or command training, were instead assigned to KP duty, serving meals to German prisoners of war at the base, which was one of seven hundred camps for POWs in the United States. Wilcox defiantly counseled the airmen to feign illness rather than accept menial duties. They did, and white soldiers had to do the potato peeling.

He had never been to New York until he was twenty when he was dispatched to the city to retrieve a POW, but, having been born on Harlem Street, he imagined that he was predestined to belong there. "I had never seen that many Black people in one place in my life," he recalled in Herb Boyd's *The Harlem Reader: A Celebration of New York's Most Famous Neighborhood* (2003). "I knew after that one visit that I would return and spend the rest of my life here," he added. "So, when I got out of the army in 1946, I headed straight to Harlem and I've been here ever since."

After he was discharged, Wilcox first moved to Brooklyn, where his mother had relocated after his parents separated, and enrolled in City College. By the time he graduated with a bachelor of science degree in biology in 1949, he had already signed with the Brooklyn Gothams of the American Basketball League, becoming one of the first Black players in what would emerge as the National Basketball Association. He averaged 5.3 points per game in his sixty-six-game career, playing for the Gothams and the Saratoga Harlem Yankees. He was admitted to Howard University dental school and the New York Medical College at Flower-Fifth Avenue Hospital, but by then he was considering alternative careers. He married Katherine Knight, who he met at City College and would become a professor at Barnard. The couple would have two daughters (in 2021 Gwynne became the first Black woman member of the National Labor Relations Board) and a son. (Wilcox would later say that after attending Morehouse, it was a mistake for him to have enrolled in an integrated college; he also revealed that his wife's enduring commitment to racial integration cost him his marriage.)

Wilcox worked as a clerk for the Veterans Administration and an investigator for the city's Welfare Department, where he also became an organizer for the United Public Workers of America (which was ejected from the Congress of Industrial Organizations in 1950 because of its Communist connections). He managed a center for senior citizens in Brooklyn; organized tenants as director of the East Harlem Project, the community action arm of two settlement houses as the neighborhood evolved into a Puerto Rican "Island in the city"; drafted the strategic agenda for Massive Economic Neighborhood Development (MEND), East Harlem's antipoverty program; and earned a master's degree in 1957 from the Columbia University School of Social Work, where he also taught courses in community organization in the mid-1960s.

"The first thing I taught was how to keep me from manipulating them," Wilcox recalled telling his students. Like his role model, Malcolm X, the Black Muslim leader who was assassinated in 1965, Wilcox was an exponent of personal responsibility. He gravitated to the teachings of Black leaders like Marcus Garvey and W. E. B. Du Bois, he once said, because whites disregarded Black people as individuals and "if anything they wanted to advance you to become one of them." He also became a disciple of Michael Harrington, expanding on Harrington's definition of "the other America" to encompass the poor who "are not seen, and because of that they themselves cannot see" and whose "horizon has become more and more restricted; they see one another, and that means that they see little reason to hope."

By the mid-1960s, most hope was grounded in good intentions rather than material progress, and good intentions came at a cost to the beneficiaries as well as the givers. Schools were still largely separate and unequal even in New York, let alone the South. "The generous explanation," City College of New York professor Marta Gutman wrote in *Educating Harlem: A Century of Schooling and Resistance in a Black Community*, edited by Ansley T. Erickson and Ernest Morrell (2019), "is that demands from white parents for segregated neighborhood schools and from Black parents for integrated schools were irreconcilable in the face of extraordinary demographic change: 1.5 million white residents left the city between 1950 and 1965, and the number of school-age children increased with Black and Puerto Rican boys and girls making up 75 percent of students by 1960. Less generously, the board of education was, whether for reasons of racial ideology or inertia, comfortable operating a segregated school system." With no public school alternative that he deemed adequate available, in 1966 Wilcox became a founding member of the Manhattan Country School on the Upper West Side, which described itself as the city's first fully integrated private school—and one in which, he believed, the staff and curriculum were so progressive that Blacks could be taught self-respect while the entire student body could learn from one another.

In December 1963, on the basis of a report prepared by Wilcox, the NYC Commission on Human Rights concluded not only that the board of education had failed to sufficiently desegregate the city's schools, but also that its priority of improving schools in minority neighborhoods, rather than busing students across district lines, was incompatible with integration (if that had, in fact, been the board's goal to begin with). In February 1964 a grassroots coalition led by a Black Presbyterian minister, the Reverend Milton Galamison, agreed with the rights commission that the board, cognizant of the new Black and Hispanic majority in enrollment and the enduring white grip on political power, had all but given up on integration. To demonstrate their discontent, almost half of the system's students—nearly five hundred thousand— boycotted the schools for one day in what was billed at the time as the largest civil rights protest in American history. But while the goal of minority groups remained educational equality, a new strategy was emerging and Preston Wilcox would be its leading theoretician. "The concept of community control or 'power to the people' as it was termed in the 1960s had originated" with Preston Wilcox and Malcolm X, Murray Friedman wrote in *The Neoconservative Revolution* (2005). "They believed that since Blacks lived in a segregated world, they should take control of that world."

In the two years before that strategy would materialize on the streets of East Harlem, the civil rights movement could claim enormous legislative gains in Congress while progressives in New York City rekindled their own Camelot. In 1965 they toppled the Democratic old guard to elect a Republican-Liberal mayor, John V. Lindsay (a political upset that also incubated the Conservative Party in New York State and heralded a seismic rightward shift of the white working class). Lindsay cared about the schools *and* integration, but he inherited a board of education whose members had been appointed by the previous administration and were putatively independent of city hall. (Although, as Wilcox acidly observed, "in New York City we do not elect our school officials and indeed the educational system has for so long been perceived as being 'above' politics that its administrators are today alternately baffled and enraged to discover that they are squarely in the middle of it.")

On September 12, 1966, when the city's nearly 1.1 million students returned to classes from summer vacation, they were greeted by fifty-four thousand teachers armed with a new curriculum that, beginning in kindergarten, nobly taught that "all men are born free and equal in dignity and rights." The syllabus in upper grades was fleshed out with tropes elaborating "an understanding of our nation's heritage and its continuing progress toward liberty, equality and justice." Seventeen new schools that had been in the labyrinthine construction pipeline were completed to accept students that Monday morning. All of them opened on time except for one: the $40 million Intermediate School 201 on 127th Street at Madison Avenue in East Harlem, a windowless (so much for transparency, parents in the neighborhood carped) brick behemoth built on fourteen-foot-high concrete stilts abutting the Park Avenue tracks of the New York Central Railroad, which whisked oblivious white commuters to and from the segregated suburbs.

That I.S. 201 would be the city's first fully air-conditioned classroom building was insufficient to cool tensions that had been percolating since 1958, when the board of education announced plans for the five-hundred-seat school. It was gallantly intended to fulfill two creditable goals: relieving serious overcrowding in the Harlem neighborhood schools, and promoting integration by luring white students from Queens, the Bronx, and elsewhere in Manhattan with enriched programming, including music, art, and foreign languages. But from the beginning local parents warned the board against siting the school in the middle of Harlem instead of on the community's fringes, where it might become more of a magnet for skittish whites—a warning that in and of itself, Stokely Carmichael (Kwame Ture) and Columbia professor Charles V. Hamilton wrote in *Black Power: The Politics of Liberation* (1967), "clearly points up the colonial relationship of blacks and whites in the city; they knew the only way to get quality education was to have white pupils in the school."

By September 1966, not one non-Hispanic white family had applied to I.S. 201; the closest the board of education could come to declaring any sort of victory in achieving integration was that, according to the official roster, the expected enrollment was divided almost equally between Black and Puerto Rican students. Without consulting the community, the board named the school for Arthur Schomburg, who Harlemites initially mistook for a German Jew (he was, in fact, a Puerto Rican bank clerk, bibliophile, and literary figure in the Harlem Renaissance of African and German descent who had donated his collection to the New York Public Library).

To add insult to injury, the board appointed a white principal. Unwittingly recreating a New York version of "the best and the brightest," as David Halberstam would ironically describe the well-intentioned Washington phenoms who entrapped the White House into the war in Vietnam, the board had set the stage for a similar quagmire. Both efforts to pacify the local population failed because they refused to acknowledge the indigenous roots of the conflict or even the elemental players.

Preston Wilcox was not a teacher at I.S. 201. He was not the parent of a student enrolled there. He held no elective office. But he was not a newcomer to the dispute, nor an interloper who opportunistically leapt at the boycotts and other protests against the school as a pretext for political or personal aggrandizement. Instead, he was known and respected in the Harlem community and also came to be well regarded among educators who, instead of recoiling at inflammatory phrases wrested from his writings, were willing to actually read his agenda for community-centered schools that valued citizenship as well as scholarship. A confidante and close adviser to the ad hoc parent council of I.S. 201, Wilcox called the school as presented to parents merely a palliative contrived by aloof bureaucrats and academics that

Rhody McCoy, administrator of the Ocean Hill–Brownsville school district, raising a placard at a gathering of supporters outside his office during the 1968 teachers' strike. Beside him is the Rev. C. B. Marshall. Later, the group marched to Junior High School 271. (Photo by Patrick A. Burns via the *New York Times*)

embodied "the worst in community planning and public education" and "failed to handle the legitimate anger of the ghetto."

While I.S. 201 finally opened late that fall, after walkouts and other protests had fizzled, the community's lingering anger spilled over into still another boycott. This one was organized by civil rights leaders, including Stokely Carmichael, the chairman of the Student Nonviolent Coordinating Committee (SNCC), and Floyd B. McKissick, the director of the Congress of Racial Equality (CORE). But those early skirmishes at I.S. 201 allowed Preston Wilcox, by then already teaching at the Columbia School of Social Work, the opportunity to practice, or experiment with, what he had preached. As a result of the boycott, the white principal resigned, a Black administrator was hired, and Black history was incorporated into the curriculum. Black history was *made*, too. "The Black Power movement, as articulated by Charles V. Hamilton and Stokely Carmichael, took its first steps at the doorsteps of Harlem's Arthur A. Schomburg Intermediate School 201," Wilcox wrote in *Ebony* magazine in 1970. "The residents of that community decided once and for all that the educational problems of their children derived not from a *failure to integrate* but from the *success* of the New York City Board of Education in *failing to educate* their children."

Wilcox argued that if the public schools failed to provide marginalized students with the tools that had spelled upward mobility for previous generations of European immigrants, then they needed to be taught by superior Black and Hispanic teachers hired by caring administrators, principals like Leonard Covello, a transplant from southern Italy himself who had nurtured the children of Italian immigrants in East Harlem in the 1930s and Puerto Ricans in the 1940s. In theory, at least, Wilcox reasoned, community-controlled schools could unleash the "latent potential that an alien society has encouraged Black youth to hide under a bushel."

What was happening in East Harlem exposed the fundamental shift since *Brown v. Board of Education* in 1954. After decades of crusading for integrated schools, East Harlem parents had become ambivalent, at best, about the central board's commitment to integration, and even to their own. What divided Wilcox and his acolytes from white progressive idealists was not only the radicalism of their means, but also whether integration was an end in itself. "Making community versus individual uplift a priority in school reform had been an important value for New York's Black school activists since the beginning of their campaign in the 1950s," Karen Ferguson wrote in *Top Down: The Ford Foundation, Black Power, and the Reinvention of Racial Liberalism* (2013), "but after the I.S. 201 controversy it became their predominant goal." Challenging the verdict of James Coleman, a white Johns Hopkins sociologist, that a diverse socioeconomic classroom determined educational success, Wilcox declared in 1967: "I don't subscribe to the view that a Black kid must sit next to a white kid to learn."

The educational historian Diane Ravitch concluded that Wilcox had come to believe that integration "was explicitly based on the tenet that a predominantly Black and Puerto Rican school could never be a good school." If that struck white teachers, parents, and politicians as radical and separatist, Ravitch wrote, "Wilcox's position was strikingly similar to that of Bishop Hughes over a century earlier" when Hughes proselytized on behalf of Catholic schools. A shifting, amorphous boundary divided Black empowerment, which Wilcox had consistently embraced, from Black Power, to which his conversion would be completed by the white establishment's response to community control in East Harlem and later in Ocean Hill–Brownsville, Brooklyn. Wilcox, she said, was "an important figure in the decision to shift the demand for integration, which was never going to happen, to community control."

In 1968 Wilcox was still theorizing more generally when he said that the battle over the minds and aspirations of minority children—Black, Puerto Rican, Mexican American, and Appalachian white, as he defined them—had created a broader class confrontation between haves and have-nots. "They differ only in that the haves would say everybody can't make it—'somebody has to fail and/or be poor.' The have-nots would say that unless everybody makes it we will have no America." He characterized the community control movement as "an effort to develop at the local level, the ability to hold this nation accountable, and to employ dissent as an instrument to reshape the relationships between the have-nots and the haves."

By 1969, though, Wilcox wrote that "separation has become a concern for white Americans largely because it represents a shift within the Black community from a reliance on white paternalism to competition with whites for the right and responsibility for defining the Black condition." And by 1970, writing in *Ebony*, he cited the proliferation of Black student unions and Black studies programs on college and university campuses as direct evidence that "the movement which began at Harlem's I.S. 201 has become nationwide." The rising popularity of the Black Panther Party, he suggested, was forcing Black youth to confront a fundamental question that his generation had overlooked: "How can I become my brother's brother?" Instead, he said, "too many of us in the 1960s were asking how could we become the white man's brother—or brother-in-law."

Still, as Jerald E. Podair wrote in *The Strike That Changed New York: Blacks, Whites and the Ocean Hill–Brownsville* (2002): "Wilcox believed the events at 201 were about much more than the racial identity of its principal. He wished to show 'that a community can organize effectively around the process of educating its children.'"

"Education must enable Black students to comprehend their self-worth at a gut level as it operates," Wilcox wrote. "It must enable white students to de-honkify themselves at a gut level. It must convince both that their self-concepts are essentially intertwined; and that their destinies are deeply interrelated. Students who know who they are will demand that other students find out who *they* are. Respect will be based on mutuality. Deference will not be demanded because of differences in skin color, religious background or previous condition of servitude."

The board of education's faltering steps prompted Mayor Lindsay to recruit McGeorge Bundy, the newly minted president of the Ford Foundation, to find a more efficacious solution to the stalemate in East Harlem than he had in East Asia as Lyndon B. Johnson's national security adviser, a role in which he had advanced the Vietnam War before belatedly becoming a disillusioned exemplar of "the best and the brightest." In 1966, Bundy was challenged to draft a citywide plan, then in 1967 to come up with a replicable model for decentralized schools in East Harlem, on the Lower East Side, and in Ocean Hill–Brownsville, Brooklyn—three minority neighborhoods that would be dubbed demonstration districts, a term that unwittingly delivered a double entendre (as did community control).

Wilcox would publish some two hundred essays elaborating and embellishing his evolving versions of community control and Black power, but he never figured as a boots-on-the-ground combatant in the tectonic public clash over community control that roiled the city in 1968. He was, arguably, the movement's Marx to the front lines Lenins, avoiding the ranks of the lionized or loathed, like Milton Galamison and Rhody McCoy, who headed the Ocean Hill–Brownsville district; Sonny Carson, who was vilified because he recited a Black student's virulently anti-Semitic poem on a radio program; or Albert Shanker, the historically liberal leader of the United Federation of Teachers who transformed school decentralization into a chaotic showdown over union seniority and solidarity. (Woody Allen immortalized Shanker in the 1973 film *Sleeper*, in which the protagonist awakens after two centuries in suspended animation to learn that the United States has been destroyed because "a man named Albert Shanker got hold of a nuclear warhead.")

A series of vitriolic teachers' strikes touched off by the peremptory transfer of nineteen white teachers and principals out of the community-controlled Ocean Hill–Brownsville district by the district's Black superintendent and board finally ended on November 17, 1968, when Shanker, the board of education, and Lindsay—without the participation of leaders of the school district itself—announced an agreement. The union had won. The transferred teachers were reinstated; the local board was placed under state supervision. Wilcox—the theoretical godfather turned fleeting gladiator who, momentarily, could finally field-test his theses—scorned the settlement. The teachers flexed their muscles in Albany the following year when the legislature passed a largely cosmetic citywide school decentralization law. The 1969 New York Education Act granted nominal power to local districts, but fell far short of what Preston Wilcox had envisioned originally and what Rhody McCoy, Ocean Hill–Brownsville district administrator, had assumed to be his prerogative. Thirty district boards would be locally elected, but they were undeniably subordinate to board of education headquarters.

Wilcox might have largely lost the war in New York, but he remained in the vanguard of a national movement of educators who refused to let northern liberals get off the hook by sidelining segregation as an exclusively southern phenomenon or accepting integration or decentralization as a solution without community control—and accountability. "Many of us haven't overcome the damages of slavery in that we still turn our children over to be educated by someone else," Wilcox said. Decades of justifying rather than fixing failing social and economic policy had relegated the welfare state to the bottom of even the Democrats' political agenda.

Community control carried a risk, though. "The burden of proof rests not on the Establishment, but on the capacity of the ghetto to implement some of their own dreams—one that holds their children to be educable," Wilcox argued. Put more colloquially: "Education which fails to de-honkify whites and de-victimize Blacks is more of the same-o, same-o. The issue is not separation but who controls the nature and content of that separation." Encapsulating his credo of self-determination, Wilcox borrowed a graffitied slogan from a Harlem subway station and embossed it on his stationery: "No one can be free if someone else lets you be free."

Wilcox would go on to capitalize on his bitter experience with New York City's power brokers and bureaucracy by catalyzing a broader constituency among professionals across the country. He became the chairman of the National Association for Afro-American Education and founded Afram Associates, which was partially funded by the U.S. Department of Education and provided consulting services to community organizations and school districts. His career later evolved into a one-man band that, in an echo chamber, messianically beat the drum for Malcolm X.

Wilcox would be remembered by the establishment—Black and white—less for his philosophical arguments than for the protest movement those arguments fomented. He had been wide-eyed when he first arrived in Harlem, overwhelmed by the sheer numbers of Black people, their density and diversity. "Once upon a time here in Harlem," he recalled wistfully, "you had a basketball player, a parking lot attendant and a doctor all living in the same neighborhood, so their children came up together and they had an opportunity to learn from each other."

How Wilcox manifested his frustration may have changed as he grew older, but the fundamental conditions that provoked it—inequality in education, income, health, housing, and opportunity for economic mobility among Black people—varied only in degree. Harlem, however, was undergoing a remarkable demographic upheaval, as it had at the beginning of the century. In the late 1980s preservationists sought to freeze what was left of the old Harlem in legal amber by having the entire neighborhood declared an official city landmark. But while that chimerical "village" remained synonymous with Black America to out-of-towners and visitors from abroad, it had lost much of its cachet as a cultural capital to places like Detroit and Hollywood, and its reputation as an impregnable Black political bastion to Brooklyn and even beyond New York. By the second decade of the twenty-first century, the growing appeal of constituent neighborhoods like Hamilton Heights (Alexander Hamilton's house had been moved farther south, for the second time), the expansion of Columbia University into West Harlem, and creeping gentrification north of the once-unbreachable boundary of Ninety-Sixth Street conspired to reduce Black residents to a minority in greater Harlem. In 2017, for the first time since World War II, Harlemites were represented in Washington by a congressman who wasn't Black.

In the 1960s Wilcox was at the vanguard of a movement to create community development corporations, mobilizing low-income residents into an economic engine for self-determination. One of the earliest of these was the Harlem Commonwealth Council, established in 1967 by Wilcox and other Black community leaders. The council's prime target was a property on 125th Street, just down the block from the new State Office Building, a gift to Harlem from Governor Nelson A. Rockefeller that community activists saw as a symbol of the insensitive, top-down urban renewal driven by a commercial and distinctly middle-class ethos. Demanding low-income housing and the involvement of local stakeholders, radicals seized the 125th Street property in 1969, calling it Reclamation Site No. 1. The building they proposed on the disputed site would have been reserved for affordable housing, schools, and health care, but instead by 2002 a brand-name shopping mall had risen there, a brick-and-steel symbol of gentrification. It stands near the corner of Malcolm X Boulevard.

"By the late 1990s, the neighborhood represented the leading edge of the 'Second Renaissance' that touched many such neighborhoods," Brian D. Goldstein wrote in *The Roots of Urban Renaissance: Gentrification and the Struggle over Harlem* (2017). That change "came about in large part through the work of Harlemites like Wilcox who had struggled to reimagine and rebuild the neighborhood they called home." But, Goldstein concluded, the self-reliance envisaged by radical movements for community control revealed "a fundamental contradiction in their work: amid continued promises of self-help, these organizations came to depend instead on funds that flowed readily from the federal government." By refusing to revise his original vision, Goldstein wrote, "Wilcox could seem quite idealistic, even eccentric, in a neighborhood whose fate community leaders increasingly tied to the goal of economic integration."

Economic integration, which fulfilled one goal, accelerated gentrification, which inevitably rekindled a debate over community control. Would new jobs, even low-skilled dead-end positions, be offered to locals? Would Harlemites be priced out of existing rentals? Would they be granted preference for new or renovated affordable housing, or would giving them an advantage be stigmatized as another category of discrimination? The Black Power community organizations spawned in the late 1960s, Goldstein postulated, "depended on financial partnerships with the public sector even as they preached self-determination; remained subject to the whims of strong leaders even as they promised participatory democracy," and over time "came to idealize new objectives: the cultivation of a mixed-income population and integration into an economic 'mainstream.' In bringing that vision into physical form in the late 20th century, these organizations demonstrated their attainment of the long-sought power to shape Harlem's built environment. Yet their accomplishments also exemplified the distance they had traveled from the radical ideals that had once motivated their demands at locations like Reclamation Site No. 1."

Wilcox's Afram had devolved from a successful national consulting service on parental empowerment to an idiosyncratic neighborhood-based archive preserving the promise of what might have been if its hero, Malcolm X, had not been assassinated. The name on the door to his third-floor office at 271 West 125th Street— MALCOLM X LOVERS NETWORK—proclaimed Wilcox's preoccupation since the early 1990s.

No. 271 was built during the first decade of the twentieth century, the same year that the Bronx Zoo drew 250,000 visitors to behold an infamous exhibition in which an African bushman shared a cage with an orangutan. Wilcox moved into the building in the mid-1990s, when the Duane Reade drugstore chain made its Harlem debut by leasing the ground-floor space that had been vacant for four years since the failure of the Black-owned Freedom National Bank. Early in 2005, No. 271's owner, the United House of Prayer, announced a partnership with a private developer to transform the four-story building into commercial space and thirty apartments that would rent for as much as $5,300 a month for a two-bedroom. In one way, as Harlem revived through a mutated version of the strategy that he himself had originally advocated, Wilcox became a victim of his own success. The conversion of the building on 125th Street would take another twelve years to complete, but Wilcox was immediately evicted from the space his office had occupied for more than a decade. He died the following year.

30

Jack Maple

The Commonsense Cop

Jack Maple wasn't planning to go anywhere—not by train, anyway. So he must have been baffled the night in 1970 when his father asked Jack to meet him at midnight at the colonnaded General Post Office Building, across the street from Penn Station. Midnight was when George Maple, who worked at the post office, would be finishing his shift.

"My father knew I'd be a loser," Jack recalled years later. He had already defined himself by the role in which he was inevitably cast in Christmas pageants at his parish schools. "I never played Joseph," he said. "I was the beast in the manger" (hospitable, perhaps, but presumably stigmatized as a sinner nonetheless). George was afraid that Jack, still an immature teenager, would turn down an offer to join the Transit Authority police force, committing what amounted to the mortal sin of suicide.

Father and son crossed Eighth Avenue to Stanford White's original Pennsylvania Station, which, before it was demolished in the name of progress, had evoked comparisons to the Acropolis, the Vatican, the Bank of England, and the Brandenburg Gate. "One entered the city like a god," the art historian Vincent Scully said of the old station. "One scuttles in now like a rat." Even in its stunted labyrinthine reincarnation, the station remained the busiest transportation hub in the western hemisphere. Not so much at midnight, though. Midtown was still stirring, but rush hour's scrum of faceless figures had largely scattered by then, atomized into individuals who for a fleeting moment took on lives of their own.

The Maples descended the rickety escalators underground. They stepped onto the nearly empty platform. Precisely as George Maple planned, they got there just as the regular northbound train from Delaware arrived to unload its grim cargo from Dover Air Force Base: the latest consignment of coffins containing the remains of soldiers killed in Vietnam. John Edward Maple was just seventeen that night. He had come to Penn Station that night looking for answers. Instead, his father asked him a single question: "Do you want that to be you?" Like the Ghost of Christmas Future, George Maple showed his balky, unfocused son where his journey was fated to end. "My father said," Jack told the *New Yorker*, "'Kid, if you don't make something out of yourself, you're going to die in Vietnam.'"

The oldest son of seven children from a blue-collar Roman Catholic family—his father was a former Railway Express deliveryman, his mother, Isabel, a nurse's aide— Jack had been cajoled into punching all the right tickets to guarantee job security for life. He had undergone every test for a uniformed career that New York City government offered. "My father had me take all the civil service exams—police, transit, post office, Fire Department, all of them—when I was sixteen," Jack Maple remembered. When he received an acceptance from the Police Department, he'd

"Jack Maple, architect of New York City's Compstat program, in 1996." (Photo by John Sotomayor via the *New York Times*)

grabbed it, even going so far as to drop out of the elite Brooklyn Technical High School, where he was studying aeronautical engineering, in his senior year. One day before Maple was due to begin police force training, though, Mayor Lindsay imposed a hiring freeze. Overnight, Maple had been transformed from a promising police trainee to another anonymous blue-collar teenager, cannon fodder for an ill-conceived war nine thousand miles away. Already deleted from his public school roster, he'd also lost the temporary job he had been holding with the United Parcel Service as well as the promise of future employment with New York's Finest. And now, with the war in Vietnam escalating, he'd forfeited the draft deferment he qualified for as a student or as a police trainee.

Two months later, Jack was offered another trainee job, this time, though, with what even he considered to be a bush league uniformed service, the Transit Police. George Maple feared that his son would reject the offer and still pin his hopes on a second overture from the NYPD. The New York City Police Department fields the biggest uniformed, plainclothes, and undercover force in the country, some thirty-two thousand at the time, or the size of Sweden's army. Not for nothing had it earned the reputation as New York's Finest, a reputation that it struggled periodically to redeem against the recurring rot of racism, corruption, and goldbricking. But getting a second offer from the NYPD was going to be a long shot, at best.

There was only one respectable escape route available to the flummoxed teenage dropout from Richmond Hill, Queens. Three days after his eighteenth birthday in 1970, Jack Maple became a Transit Police trainee.

If the epiphany at Penn Station had been metaphorically intended to get Jack Maple on the right track—or any track, for that matter—the Transit Police position should have been a panacea. But Maple's first few years on the force were not very promising. He was married with a mortgage by the time he was twenty, but he didn't become a full-fledged officer until he was twenty-one. Once, he was conked on the head with a four-foot-long iron pipe wielded by a perp who he or a partner shot dead (both officers fired, but they weren't told which bullets proved fatal). About a year later, he was working undercover, about to arrest a pot dealer, when the guy grabbed his gun and fired two shots that whizzed close enough to burn his cheek.

But Maple's worst moment as a beat cop, he remembered, was on a winter night in 1975, when he was patrolling the IND underground platforms at Central Park West and Seventy-Second Street. Languorous late-night diners and partygoers were stumbling about. Prep cooks were shambling off the B and C trains before dawn to unlock the steel gates safeguarding greasy spoons. "I was bored to death, freezing my ass off on the eight-to-four-A.M. shift," he told David Remnick of the *New Yorker*. He found a door on the platform that led to a closet. Inside was a radiator and a box to sit on. "You'd think it was the pier at Key West," he recalled. "Then, suddenly, two guys—two transvestites in full gear—open the door slightly and start pissing on me. Maybe they thought I was the urinal, I don't know. So there I am, sitting on a box in the dark and transvestites are pissing on me, and I'm thinking, This is it. This takes the prize—my low point as a cop."

That was the same year that the White House perpetrated a similar, if figurative, frontal assault on the city, which was immortalized in the *Daily News* headline FORD TO CITY: DROP DEAD. But as bad as things seemed then, the city was still years away from being driven to its economic and emotional nadir by the primal forces unleashed during that 1975 fiscal crisis: layoffs of teachers and police officers; crowded classrooms because newly begun school buildings never got beyond half-finished steel skeletons; the imposition of tuition at City University; and a hike in subway fares to mollify bankers who had been complicit in decades of municipal profligacy but wanted proof that city officials finally profess fiscal responsibility and that taxpayers were sharing the pain.

For over a decade, as municipal debt was incurred to pay for operating expenses, hidden costs were rolled over from one year to the next, maintenance was deferred, and interest and principal from borrowing ballooned, virtually everyone had turned a blind eye. No generally accepted accounting principles, as they were euphemistically called, could justify the fiscal jujitsu officials practiced to both gratify the financiers and fulfill a progressive agenda while the federal government was abandoning urban America in favor of suburbia.

The threat of bankruptcy, layoffs from once-sacrosanct civil service jobs like the police force, and the Ford administration's initial rebuff left most New Yorkers agreeing with Maple that 1975 was their annus horribilis. In 1976 the nation's bicentennial celebration and the first Democratic National Convention held in New York since 1924 provided a temporary respite, but they were brief circuses without the bread. The state of the city would get even worse. "New York City was a horror show," Maple said. In 1977, bombs linked to Puerto Rican nationalists exploded in Manhattan office buildings and department stores. A Consolidated Edison blackout triggered looting that resulted in more than three thousand arrests. After a raucous primary campaign, hapless former comptroller Abe Beame became the first elected one-term mayor in more than half a century when he was defeated by Ed Koch. And a psychopathic serial killer dubbed Son of Sam, armed with a .44-caliber revolver, held New Yorkers hostage as no crime figure had done since the 1950s, when a disgruntled former Con Ed worker, George Metesky, periodically vented his rage as the folkloric Mad Bomber.

While Transit Authority cops had been exempted from the hiring freeze in 1970, Maple fully understood that transit officers were denigrated as the B-team, the "cave cops," branded with the same modifiers—*sub, under, below*—that applied to the trains. "In New York City, there were separate police forces for the streets, the subways and public housing, but only one had manpower equal to the fifth-largest army in the world and a reputation equal to the New York Yankees," Maple wrote in *The Crime Fighter* (1999). "I was with one of the other two. In the eyes of the world, Transit was junior varsity. Transit was Naugahyde."

Even so, until 1975 the Transit Police force was largely immune from personnel reductions; annual ridership was still nearly a billion passengers, and regardless of per capita crime statistics, New Yorkers felt more vulnerable trapped in a steel subway car ten feet wide or less and dead end station platforms. By 1980, though, layoffs and attrition had shrunk the force by nearly one fourth, from 3,600 to 2,800. Terrified mass transit riders felt that they were left to the mercy of random assaults by feral youth, their supremacy vividly illustrated by the kaleidoscopic graffiti with which they defaced subway cars.

Off-duty cops protesting layoffs stoked the anxiety by distributing a survival guide titled *Fear City*. "The pamphlet read like one more piece of the dystopia porn then filling American cinemas; these were the years of *Taxi Driver, The French Connection, Marathon Man, Escape from New York, Death Wish* and *The Warriors*, to name a few," the novelist and historian Kevin Baker recalled in the *Guardian* in 2015. "Jaded New Yorkers quickly turned the cover of *Fear City* into a tee-shirt, sold back to tourists in souvenir shops alongside other classics such as the 'Welcome to New York' shirt—with its image of a .45 handgun and the charming injunction, 'Now Hands Up, Motherfucker!'" Between 1965 and 1975 the number of recorded murders in the city had more than doubled, from 681 to 1,690.

Sometimes one face—of a crime victim or a criminal—eclipsed the escalating numbers, even as they reached new benchmarks. In 1978 the public's collective revulsion at rising crime was personified by a baby-faced killer, William James Bosket Jr., a fifteen-year-old boy born in Harlem to descendants of former slaves from South Carolina. He had been raped by his grandfather. His father had been convicted of double murder shortly after his son was conceived. Before being released from prison, charged with another crime, and committing suicide, Willie Sr. earned a college degree in computer science and psychology and became what was billed as the first prisoner elected to Phi Beta Kappa. Willie Jr. was also judged to be a genius but would spend all but eighteen months from the day he turned nine incarcerated. He slashed his mother's abusive boyfriend. She petitioned to declare him "a person in need of supervision." He suffered a head injury when he was hit by a car. All that happened before he turned eleven.

"Unable to provide for their families, the Bosket men sought respect outside their wretched homes—and outside the law," Peter Davis wrote in reviewing Fox Butterfield's *All God's Children: The Bosket Family and the American Tradition of Violence* (1995). Bosket himself later argued that society had reaped a whirlwind for which it only had itself to blame. "I laugh at this system," he said, "because there ain't a damn thing that it can do to me except to deal with the monster it has created."

Because he was only fifteen when he killed two men and wounded a third on the subway, Bosket was sentenced to just five years at a juvenile facility upstate. Prodded by public outrage at the short sentence, generated in part by *Daily News* headlines and editorials, Governor Hugh L. Carey convened a special session of the legislature, which mandated that defendants as young as thirteen charged with murder, as well as fourteen- and fifteen-year-olds accused of seventeen other felonies, be tried in adult courts, where more lenient juvenile sentencing would not apply. Arrested again and convicted of assaulting prison guards, Willie Bosket himself would not be eligible for release until 2062. But the profusion of handguns and the epidemic of crack in the 1980s propelled the crime rate higher and higher.

The creeping anarchy prompted New York senator Daniel Patrick Moynihan, writing in the *American Scholar* in 1999, to deplore a generation of social policy in which "we have been redefining deviancy so as to exempt much conduct previously stigmatized." One measure of just how far out of hand things had gotten was how exuberantly most New Yorkers embraced a mere baby step toward restoring the social contract. Seizing on a visceral, if pedestrian, pet peeve, the Koch administration began demonstrably enforcing the recently enacted pooper-scooper law, which required owners to clean up after their canines. People who had flouted the less onerous regulations for decades suddenly complied, as if grasping to prove their own civic virtue while the rest of the city was, well, going to the dogs. Vigilantism involving more serious violations was overlooked, though. In 1984 Bernhard Goetz, a scrawny electrical engineer, shot and wounded four teenagers who he said were menacing him on the subway. A Manhattan jury acquitted him of attempted murder.

The highly visible homeless population prompted editorial writers to dub New York a New Calcutta. Meanwhile, the city was building more jail cells than apartments—surely more jail cells than *affordable* apartments—and it would need every one of them. In the mid-1980s, police commissioner Benjamin J. Ward, returning from a visit to Los Angeles, issued a prophetic warning: "I've seen something out there called 'ice,' and when it hits New York it's going to undo everything we've done." Ward was right. Ice, or crack cocaine, helped drive crime rates to record highs.

By 1990 New York City's murder toll had reached a record 2,245—a modest tenth place in murders per capita among the twenty-five largest cities, but still nearly equal to one St. Valentine's Day Massacre every day. David Dinkins, the city's first Black mayor, inherited deficits that dashed dreams for his progressive agenda and provided a moving picture of New York with the grist for bizarre juxtapositions. A rosy television interview with parks commissioner Betsy Gotbaum at, fittingly, the Alice in Wonderland sculpture in Central Park ended abruptly when the body of a homeless man who had been stabbed to death bobbed to the surface of the nearby sailboat pond. The brief respite that the Koch administration's aggressive management had dangled before cynical New Yorkers gave way to the familiar trope that the city was ungovernable. "Not everyone who runs a city is elected," proclaimed the trailer for the movie *King of New York*—but this time, the unelected king of New York was not Robert Moses. In the movie, he was a drug kingpin.

"We had surrendered the city," Maple acknowledged, "and the citizens of New York were running up the white flags. Everywhere you went you saw cars with little cardboard signs hanging from the rearview mirrors that said 'No Radio in Car.' The next thing would be people putting signs in their windows saying 'No TV in House.' When they had to go out to the store, they'd hang placards around their necks saying 'No Wallet in Pocket.'" Armed with a knack for statistical analysis that may have been jump-started at Brooklyn Tech, Maple was less consumed by sociology and sociopathology than by criminology. Others could hypothesize about the root causes of crime; he was more concerned about identifying how many crimes were committed that day by whom, where, and when and figuring out how to prevent as many from being carried out the next day.

Nor did Maple's bravado augur great stability in his personal life. Maybe he was motivated by the self-confidence each promotion provided. He once mused that at birth he had been condemned to a civil service bassinet only by some mistake of fate and was determined to rectify the blunder. He did that at twenty-eight, when he became the department's youngest detective, and again in 1988 when, as the department's youngest lieutenant, he was upgraded after scoring first on the Transit Police exam to commander of its central robbery task force.

Maple so deftly managed a decoy squad who—armed with boom boxes and smoking joints stuffed with Lipton tea leaves—made themselves bait for chain snatchers, wolf packs, and other crooks in the mid-1980s that he was inspired to reinvent himself from the fat kid always cast as the beast in the manger, from the desultory dropout from blue-collar Queens, to role-play in real life as a dandified Hercule Poirot, a Roaring Twenties gangster or early nineteenth-century High Constable Jacob Hays wannabe without the gold-tipped walking stick. "The adventure had started purposively enough," he wrote, "with a five-week coffee-and-sardine diet that saved me ten inches on the waistline of three new designer suits I had purchased with the express intent of helping the crooks and the assistant district attorneys keep from lumping me in their category for 'just another shithead cop.'" He donned a signature Knox homburg hat, bow tie, and vintage two-toned spectator shoes. After work, he lived like there was no tomorrow, mortgaging his house to borrow twenty-eight thousand dollars—more than his annual salary at the time—from the Money Store, the mortgage lender ballyhooed by former Yankee Phil Rizzuto's ubiquitous low-budget TV commercials, hobnobbing at the Plaza Hotel's Oak Bar and Palm Court, mingling with the famous, infamous, and celebrity wannabes at Elaine's on the Upper East Side (staying sober, for the most part, he said, because "it would be hard to be an alcoholic at $4.50 a glass of Chablis"). His neighbors thought he was working undercover. "When the money ran out, so did the babes," Maple recalled. And so did his wife; he was now married to the Money Store. "But at least I had memories," he said later. As David Remnick wrote in the *New Yorker* in February 1997, "Maple's dandyism, his self-invention, was a defiant parody of New York class distinctions, an inside joke on how bleak and degrading the job could be."

The money did run out, but the act endured in full regalia, and the reputation grew. Maple was fearless, physically unafraid of the random mugger. He was just as unflinching in his confrontations with the hierarchical top-brass mossbacks, the recalcitrant bureaucrats, and his apathetic, burned-out colleagues, ploddingly awaiting their half-pay pensions after twenty years on the job. "Forty percent of the force hide behind their desks," Maple figured. "Another 40 percent perform competently but without passion and without having much impact. Ten percent hate the job so much that they try to destroy everything positive that somebody else might try to accomplish. The final 10 percent treat the job like a vocation; and those 10 percent do 90 percent of the work."

Maple's job, like that of Constable Jacob Hays, was to protect and inspire that ambitious 10 percent, to make sure the bastards—fearful department bureaucrats and fearless lawbreakers alike—didn't get them down. "Treat every case," he exhorted the cops he commanded, "as if your mother was the victim." Maple may not have looked threatening physically himself, relatively short and fat at five foot eight and 220 pounds. But Maple was no sap. He claimed to have developed a steel backbone, impervious to impudence or pretension, from having worked as a men's room attendant at the 21 Club before he became a cop. "After that, I wasn't intimidated," he said. "I realized that even the powerful people pull down their zippers to piss."

His willful conscientiousness as a one-man police force did not endear him to his bosses, particularly when he made so many arrests while off-duty and billed for his hours worked that the budget-strapped department placed a cap on overtime. Maple was making so many arrests outside the subway system on overtime, to and from the job when he was living in Howard Beach, Queens, that his bosses punished him with a post in the Bronx to make his round-trip between home and work as long as possible. They neglected to choreograph his route, though. To get to the Bronx, Maple had to switch trains in Midtown. During that brief interval waiting in and around the uptown platform of the sprawling, crime-ridden Times Square Station, he collared so many fare-beaters, pickpockets, muggers, and other miscreants that he never made it to his daily assignment in the Bronx.

The corporate ethos dictated by a calcified, risk-averse, paramilitary pecking order like a police department can be summed up as "Stay in your lane." Implicitly, the less discretion you exercise—in fact, the less you do at all—the less likely you are to screw up or be blamed when something goes awry. As a cop, Maple deduced that blindly performing by rote on the beat or in a radio car, following regulations, never questioning convention or exercising discretion or initiative, was the surest way to avoid being second-guessed. But rule-book policing also meant merely responding to crime after it occurred, not preventing it. To proactively slow the staggering proliferation of felonies demanded something different, a visionary strategy in a brass-bound bureaucracy, a willingness to fail on the part of a guy who was all but working for the Money Store anyway, and already so disdained by top commanders that he had little to lose.

So he went home and made maps. Hundreds of them. Maps of violent crimes, solved and unsolved. By station. By subway line. By time of day and day of the week.

Fifty-five feet of them affixed to his walls, maps that he called "Charts of the Future." They revealed patterns that might prove to be predictive. As Michael Daly wrote in *New York's Finest* (2021), the charts evoked a map that appeared in the *Brooklyn Eagle* in 1945. That map had fifty-one dots, each representing a violent crime that had occurred within the past month. One dot connoted the fatal knifing of a fifty-four-year-old deaf-mute who happened to have been Jack Maple's grandmother. By mapping constellations of lawlessness, Maple also charted his own career path. He became a star.

With subway crime breaking records and fresh from the war on graffiti, in April 1990 Robert Kiley of the Metropolitan Transportation Authority and David Gunn of the Transit Authority recruited William J. Bratton, chief of the Massachusetts District Commission force in Boston, to run the Transit Police in New York. Maple staked out Bratton's coffeepot, so the legend goes, to deliver to him a ten-page protocol for reducing crime. Within months Maple had been promoted to Bratton's special assistant, commanding a hundred-cop squadron of crime fighters. And none too soon. With subway robberies having risen 87 percent over three years, in September 1990 a twenty-two-year-old Mormon tourist from Utah named Brian

"'Great White Subway Fleet' painted for graffiti, 1983." (Photo by Carl T. Gossett Jr. via the *New York Times*)

Watkins was stabbed to death on a Midtown subway platform. Watkins and his parents had been on their way to dinner at a Moroccan restaurant in Greenwich Village when a rampaging gang slashed his father with a box cutter, and Watkins tried to protect his mother.

To vulnerable New Yorkers, Watkins became a symbol of random victimhood and the futility of resisting it. The headlines reporting his death, like those bemoaning Willie Bosket's murder spree a decade before, were too big for any incumbent elected official to ignore. DAVE, DO SOMETHING, the *New York Post* screamed. Weeks later, Mayor David Dinkins and city council president Peter Vallone finally did just that: they raised taxes and, through new hiring and by replacing officers performing administrative tasks with civilians, expanded the police force by six thousand, to a record thirty-eight thousand cops (or about as many as Chicago, Los Angeles, Philadelphia, Detroit, Washington, and Houston—combined). Recorded crime declined in other cities, too, but nowhere as dramatically as in New York. Most analysts attributed a substantial share of the decline to the hiring spree and to Maple's deployment strategy, which was grounded in anticipating and preventing illegal (or deviant) behavior.

"Two years after Maple hung his maps, subway crime had fallen 27 percent," Peter L. Bellenson and Patrick A. McGuire wrote in *Tapping into* The Wire: *The Real Urban Crisis* (2012). Under Bratton and Maple, misdemeanor arrests soared by 80 percent. In 1990 transit riders were victims of 17,497 recorded felonies—murders, robberies, rapes, assaults, and thefts. Two years later, the number had dropped to 12,199. By the end of 1993, the last year of Dinkins's term, overall crime in the city under police commissioner Raymond W. Kelly was already beginning to decline, too, from its 1990 peak. But for Dinkins, who never received sufficient credit, it turned out to be too little, too late. New Yorkers felt tormented enough by crime to turn to a law-and-order Republican that November for the first time. Former federal prosecutor Rudolph W. Giuliani would preside for two terms through 2001. He recruited Bratton from Boston, where he had returned in 1992 as its police chief, to be New York City's thirty-eighth police commissioner. By then Bratton and Maple were inseparable. Maple found himself not only employed by the police force he had pined for as a teenager nearly a generation earlier, but also a boss in police headquarters. By the time Bratton and Maple circled back to New York, Phyllis P. McDonald of Johns Hopkins University wrote, their "crime reduction strategy had become explicit. With Maple to articulate the management system while bringing the N.Y.P.D. in line with the plans—no easy task—crime began to plummet in the city."

"Within a span of two or three months, I was graduating from glorified Transit lieutenant to the N.Y.P.D.'s deputy commissioner for crime control strategies," Maple recalled in the memoir he wrote with Chris Mitchell. "The promotion—a product of Bratton's daring—was the equivalent of an ensign in the Coast Guard waking up as a three-star admiral in the Navy, and I felt a little like when I was a kid sneaking into the box seats at Shea Stadium. At any moment, a meaty hand was liable to land on my shoulder, and I would be swiftly escorted to the nearest exit. Only this time, I was in the dugout filling up the manager's ear with strategies."

Maple remembered telling John Miller, the intrepid television reporter whom Bratton recruited as deputy commissioner for public information, how the response of police brass to his own appointment reminded him of Jack Nicholson's Cheshire Cat grin in *Batman* as he proclaims his comeback. "You know," he said, "I met some of these chiefs at the Christmas tree lighting at Rockefeller Center, and I heard a few of their chuckles when Bratton told them I was going to be his crime guy. But inside, I'm smiling like Nicholson, and I'm thinking, 'Wait till they get a load of me.'" Bratton recalled: "Maple was gruff, like a kid pushing the big guys to see how far he can go." And with the support of Bratton and, for a time, of the mayor—until Bratton made the cover of *Time* magazine and Giuliani turned green-eyed—Maple went further than he or his father could have ever imagined.

Already on the job longer than many colleagues who had put in their twenty years and taken their half-pay pensions, Maple knew what was broken; he remembered, literally, where the bodies were buried and who had interred them; he challenged every orthodoxy. "I was 41 in 1993 when I finally got a seat at the table," he said. "I had been a cop since about the time I was first allowed to walk into a bar unaccompanied by an adult, but in the very profession that had consumed most of my life, I had until that year been very much on the outside, my cheeks red from the cold and my nose pressed up against the window."

Validated only by a high school equivalency diploma, Maple might have been the only cop in America who could invoke not only the Roman general Fabius Maximus and his enfeebled guerilla defense against Hannibal's rampaging army in 217 B.C. to exemplify the compromised mindset of American policing, but also the military tactician Vegetius's warnings against lowering recruitment standards. Maple's Charts of the Future eventually evolved into the four-pronged digital program CompStat. That no one can remember whether it was an abbreviation for computer statistics or comparative statistics makes the legend that it was visualized on a napkin by Maple over drinks at Elaine's with Bratton and John Miller all the more believable. (In addition to Maple and Miller, Bratton's core command included department chief John F. Timoney; chief of patrol Louis R. Anemone; chief of personnel Mike Julian; management consultant John Linder; and Mike Farrell, who became deputy commissioner for policy and planning.)

Inspired by the diligent efficiency of the restaurant's namesake, the program embodied accurate, timely intelligence; rapid deployment; effective tactics; and relentless follow-up. In retrospect, the concept was commonsensical: crime statistics would be collected, computerized, mapped, and shared promptly. "Wouldn't it be something if you punched in the name and found out that Jack Maple has never been arrested, he has never been convicted of a crime, but he has been a witness to 11 narcotics murders?" Maple said. "Wouldn't you want to know that?" If you did know that, you'd have good reason to question whether his presence was coincidental.

When precinct commanders told Maple they couldn't make it to weekly Comp-Stat grillings at nine A.M., he scheduled them for seven. At these sessions on the eighth floor of One Police Plaza, borough and precinct commanders were held accountable. "Maple would wield a laser pointer like an accusing finger," and they would squirm, Thomas A. Reppetto wrote in *American Police: The Blue Parade, 1942–2012* (2012). "Maple would occasionally flash a Pinocchio image on the screen, using his laser beam to make the nose grow as some commander struggled through his confused explanation."

Maple unflinchingly challenged other department norms, sometimes as an intellectual exercise to train minds to consider alternatives, but more often to question whether "the way it's always been done" was still the right way, or for that matter whether it had ever been right in the first place. Why, for example, were certain specialized squads on duty weekdays eight A.M. to six P.M., when their ostensible targets, the criminals, typically worked nights and weekends? When Maple asked for guesstimates as to what percentage of crime was attributable to the use or sale of illegal drugs, the reckoning ranged from 30 to 70 percent. Why then, he asked, did the narcotics unit account for only 5 percent of the police force? Instead of letting outstanding warrants for fugitives who failed to appear in court pile up unserved for months, his posse pursued them because his charts predicted that miscreants already wanted for one crime were more likely to commit another.

Commanding officers were grilled on crime rates in their jurisdiction. All crimes, including so-called quality-of-life offenses like loitering and public intoxication, would be addressed—not necessarily by an arrest, but through discretionary application of the "broken windows" theory advanced by George L. Kelling and James Q. Wilson in the *Atlantic* in March 1982—that maintaining public order also helps prevent crime. Maple was not a convert to the "broken windows" bromide. He revamped the theory conceived by two academics into a down and dirtier variant.

"It's not about broken windows, it's about breaking balls," Maple said. "But applied to any larger demographic, 'zero tolerance' is bad policy and a bad strategy" over time. His strategy predated the early 2000s tactic that became known as stop-and-frisk, in which during a single year the police reported stopping people on seven hundred thousand occasions to question and possibly followed up by frisking them if they further aroused suspicion. The tactic targeted Black and Hispanic neighborhoods, where most of the crime occurred. But it became counterproductive when it was employed excessively. Maple argued that his maps were more egalitarian. "Maps don't know the difference between a poor person and a rich person," he told *Government Technology Magazine* in 2010. "The dots are the same size regardless. A robbery is a robbery. Those ten dots tell you where to put your cops. The dots don't say, 'This affected Donald Trump; it's a press case.'"

"We realized that if we phoned the warrant desk every time we issued a summons," Maple concluded, "ball-breaking could be used to catch robbers, rapists and drug dealers so that they'd be displaced to where they belonged: the pokey." Cops needed to focus where the maps show concentrations of crime and to be more selective about who they arrest.

Criminologists, sociologists, demographers, and experts on law enforcement and the judicial and penal systems have all weighed in on why the number of recorded felonies has plummeted generally since the last decade of the twentieth century. More nonprofit organizations, neighborhood groups, and self-taxing business improvement districts began to take a preventative approach. More resources were devoted to private security, from guards and video surveillance to digital devices like Nest and LoJack. The evidence suggests that the criminal justice system—the police, in particular—learned something from Fabius Maximus, too, thanks to Jack Maple. Still, while crime dropped elsewhere around the country in the late 1990s, the decrease was more pronounced in New York. From 1993 to 1995, violent and property crime nationally declined by 3 percent; in New York it plunged by nearly 26 percent. With only 3 percent of the nation's population, New York accounted for one third of the 430,000 fewer crimes recorded nationwide. During the tenure of Bratton's team in New York, the number of murders plunged by 50 percent and overall crime fell by nearly 40 percent. Between 1993 and 1998, the number of murders dropped from 1,946 to below 1,000 for the first time since the 1960s. During that five-year period, the percentage decline was three times greater than the national average; overall, crime claimed 280,000 fewer victims than it had in any of the previous five years. "Jack has saved more lives than anybody in New York City, any doctor, anybody," said Richard Emery, a civil rights lawyer and rare defender of the police. "Just count."

Because Maple was a cop's cop, he understood that policing alone was insufficient to prevent crime, that the nightstick was needed only when the carrot didn't work. "Good policing doesn't feed people who are hungry," he said. "It doesn't care for people who are sick. It doesn't give a kid born in the Seven-Five Precinct as much a chance of meeting his or her potential as a kid born in the Silk Stocking District's Seventeenth."

Like Maple, Jacob Hays filled an office in the early nineteenth century that was sui generis and played a character that he invented. The short and stocky Hays would also stylishly patrol the city, in his case sporting a black suit, a stovepipe hat, and a white kerchief around his neck. Until recently, a pen-and-ink drawing of Jacob Hays hung at One Police Plaza as a reminder of the department's heritage. It was the only representation the department had of the high constable, until Benjamin Singleton was hired as a data scientist, a numbers cruncher whose job existed thanks to Jack Maple's obsession with statistics and his conviction that accurately charting crime patterns of the present could assure the safety of New Yorkers in the future. By 2019, when Singleton was twenty-eight, he had worked his way up to director of analytics for the NYPD Detective Bureau. In addition to his digital expertise, Singleton was able to make another contribution to the police department: a rare, faded photograph of Jacob Hays, which he just happened to have because he is the constable's great-great-great-great-grandson.

Besides his uncanny knack for identifying miscreants on sight, Hays kept a list of offenders in one notebook and another, which doubled as a prison ledger, of six thousand inmates, arranged by name, age, crime, and sentence. "Hays was the top cop because he knew the most, and hoarded information on crooks and their patterns in ledgers and in his head," said Patrick Bringley, who wrote his Hunter College thesis on the constable in 2014. "Nowadays you need a computer guy like Singleton for that and we call it data." Jack Maple picked up where Jacob Hays had left off. "Like him," Singleton said, referring to his forebear, "we try to filter out information in a systematic way to better understand the people who are driving crime patterns. We have a fancy database, but we still rely on the same techniques."

Maple and Bratton resigned from the NYPD in 1996, fed up with Giuliani's fit of pique when they—instead of the mayor—were credited with crime-prevention. Both went on to successful official and consulting roles in other cities. Maple was immortalized in no less than two television series: *The District*, in episodes he cowrote and produced and in which he is portrayed by Craig T. Nelson; and *The Deuce* on HBO, where he is played by Domenick Lombardozzi. He came up with other prescriptions to reduce crime, but he ran out of time to apply them. He died of colon cancer when he was forty-nine in 2001, a month before the 9/11 terrorist attack.

Maple's funeral was held at St. Patrick's Cathedral, an impressive ceremony for a kid from Richmond Hill, Queens, who never got to play Joseph in the Christmas pageants. Giuliani called him "the cop who cleaned up New York." Legend has it that Maple was determined, in a final gesture, to remind New Yorkers of the difference that one man—however hapless he may have seemed at the beginning—can eventually make. He left instructions for his funeral procession, which would naturally drive down Fifth Avenue from St. Patrick's, to creep crosstown along Forty-Second Street, regardless of how long it disrupted traffic. "For once," Maple supposedly said, "they would wait for the fat cop."

31

Carmelia Goffe

They Built This City

By the early 1940s, before the influx of people of color began changing Browns-ville's complexion, a foreboding had descended on the neighborhood. Just a few decades earlier, Brownsville had been idealized as an oasis for Jewish immi-grants escaping the bursting, squalid tenements of the Lower East Side. Even before kids turned ten, Alfred Kazin wrote in *A Walker in the City* (1951), those who had hopes of surviving "learned that Brownsville is a nursery of tough guys, and walk with a springy caution, like boxers approaching the center of the ring."

The Jewish exodus to Brownsville had begun slowly in the 1880s. There was no Moses to lead it, but in the forefront were clothing contractors like Elias Kaplan, who were seeking a sanctuary from the growing muscle of organized garment industry labor in Manhattan, which culminated in the shirtwaist strike of 1909. As the *Brooklyn Eagle* palatably put it, "the sweat-shop laws hampered his business." So Kaplan built a new clothing factory in Brownsville, complete with an on-site syna-gogue and nearby housing for his nonunion workers. By the end of the nineteenth century, after the El rumbled into Brownsville, the neighborhood had begun to flourish as a magnet for Manhattanites. As the twentieth century unfolded toward its midpoint, though, for first- and second-generation working-class Jews, as Kazin wrote, Brownsville—like the South Bronx—became "a place that measured all success by our skill in getting away from it."

Black people who began trickling into the neighborhood for the most part arrived with lower expectations. They were looking for a marginally better environment, not the promised land that Philip Payton had painted Harlem as at the turn of the century. Those modest prospects would be scuttled, too, within a few decades. "Even the Negroes who have moved into the earliest slums deserted by the Jews along Rockaway Avenue have been infected with the damp sadness of the place," Kazin wrote. By 1950 the block-by-block advance of Black buyers and tenants, often abetted by unscrupulous real estate brokers sowing panic among white homeowners increasingly desperate to sell.

In 1940 only about 5 percent of Brownsville residents were Black. By 1970, only 3 percent were non-Hispanic whites. The demographic shift was about more than race and ethnicity, though. The newcomers were poorer and more likely to be unemployed and living in households headed by single mothers. Once a mecca for middle-class aspirants, Brownsville had become a neighborhood largely without hope.

Brownsville's deterioration was mirrored in other East Brooklyn neighborhoods. Apartment buildings, no longer profitable to landlords, were neglected and left to scavengers. Meanwhile, the Kennedy and Johnson administrations' antipoverty

"Nehemiah Houses, East New York, Brooklyn, 1997." (Photo by Angel Franco via the *New York Times*)

programs were being defunded, losers in a growing guns-or-butter competition between defense and social services. The war in Vietnam was winning the battle over the war against poverty, a victory easier to justify when many domestic programs looked like failures anyway. Though some of those programs had never been given a fair chance, a few did succeed—Medicare, in particular—in holding the poverty rate lower than it would otherwise have been. The loss of local tax revenue in the mid-1970s, combined with the municipal overspending that had propped up the poor, produced a perfect storm of hypocrisy: after decades of complicity, New York's big banks suddenly got religion, refusing to loan the debt-ridden city government enough money to avoid default or bankruptcy.

The city's mid-1970s fiscal crisis became a pivotal test of whether New York's power brokers—ranked annually through the decade in Democratic Party reformer Edward Costikyan's *New York* magazine "Ten Most Powerful Men in New York" list—could still be assembled in one conference room and, for better or worse, *do something*. With a good deal of prodding and cat-herding by Governor Carey, it turned out that they could—back then. They banded together to impose tough love—laying off thousands of city workers, raising transit fares, imposing tuition at City University. The fiscal flagellation inflicted immediate pain and lasting repercussions, especially for the poor, but also persuaded federal officials and the financial community that the city had learned the lessons of profligacy and eventually steered it toward a surprisingly speedy economic recovery under Mayor Koch.

Since then, though, institutional and personal power has been diluted and diffused. In part this was due to a backlash against the concentrated clout wielded by unelected officials like Robert Moses. Globalization also played a role, reducing both the financial stake held by corporations and their customers, employees, suppliers, and stockholders in New York and their executives' emotional commitment to a city that their predecessors had considered home. Ultimately the fiscal crisis left a deep but incomplete impression when it came to allocating the blame for its cause, assessing the consequences of its draconian solutions, and deciding how much credit various players deserved for conjuring those solutions. Felix Rohatyn, the investment banker who was instrumental in navigating New York through its destructive deflection of default, recalled a personal example. Fifteen years later, he said, he and his wife had just left a restaurant on the Upper East Side one night when a young man snatched her Hermès leather purse and sprinted off. The thief escaped. A waiter who dashed out of the restaurant to join the unsuccessful chase said afterward that the brazen mugging just off Park Avenue had stunned him much less than its target. "God," the shaken young waiter said to Rohatyn, "how can they do this to you? You saved New York City."

But Rohatyn and the rest of the Ten Most Powerful effortlessly identified by Costikyan never could have saved the city by themselves. It was also rescued by unheralded heroes, men and women whose roles were largely overlooked or, at best, survive as a footnote. They were often immigrants, or the children of immigrants. They never landed on anyone's Most Powerful list. But the selflessness and passion of these private citizens who navigated the government bureaucracy and galvanized their communities produced a concrete legacy of its own. Their gusto has repeatedly propelled New York's resilient recovery from enemy occupation, fires, floods, civil unrest, political witch hunts, hurricanes, terrorist attacks, pandemics, and other crises that caused some early settlements like Jamestown to sink into the mud and modern Rust Belt cities to hemorrhage population while New York's set record highs into the twenty-first century.

Carmelia Walcott Goffe was one of those unsung paragons. She was born in January 1948 in Brownsville, not long after Alfred Kazin returned to the neighborhood to reflect on being raised in a borough nearing the final days of the era that inspired the author and historic preservationist Elliot Willensky's 1986 book *When Brooklyn Was the World: 1920–1957*. If Brownsville was not the refuge from the Lower East Side that Jews had fled to a generation or two before, it still boasted vestiges of upward mobility. Goffe's sister, Janis Borden, remembered the sanctuary provided by the Brownsville branch of the Brooklyn Public Library, an Andrew Carnegie gift that opened in 1908 with more than seven thousand books donated by the Hebrew Educational Society. "We were in there all the time," Borden said.

Just one year before Goffe was born, Branch Rickey, a teetotaling, Bible-quoting Republican from Ohio, had integrated major-league baseball—a quantum leap toward assimilation by a single private executive in Brooklyn even before the president of the United States desegregated the armed forces. Civil and voting rights laws and Supreme Court decisions would dismantle the legal framework of discrimination that had defied the Constitution since Reconstruction. But eliminating indelible racial bias would take more than legislation, and even more than Rickey's valorous spunk. On the very day Goffe was born, Democrats in the legislature were pressuring Governor Dewey to curb rents that were making scarce housing unaffordable. Residential segregation, to say nothing of prejudice, would endure for generations, not just in spite of the government's well-intentioned intervention but often because of it.

Brownsville, where Carmelia Goffe grew up, was one example. In America, low-income public housing began in 1935 in Manhattan's East Village, in a complex of eight four-and five-story red-brick buildings on Avenue A between Second and Third Streets. In dedicating the complex, aptly named First Houses, Eleanor Roosevelt explicitly described it as an experiment that would rise or fall depending on how well its scrupulously screened tenants maintained their homes. The prototypical apartments were supposed to be a temporary stopgap for the working poor. By the end of the twentieth century, though, more people were occupying New York City Housing Authority apartments than lived in either New Orleans or Cleveland. The selection criteria, such as they were by then, would have appalled the First Lady. In more than half the families, neither parent was employed. Fewer than half of new tenants placed in public housing projects were working families. Three in ten occupants were behind on their rent.

"Eastern Brooklyn, Nehemiah Plan. Carmelia Goffe in one of the homes already built, 1985." (Photo by Dith Pran via the *New York Times*)

At the beginning of the twenty-first century, when other Brooklyn neighbor-hoods began changing again, this time, arguably, for the better, Goffe's Brownsville seemed doomed—immune, or at least uncongenial, to gentrification because of decisions made by municipal slum clearance and public housing officials decades before. Within ten years of Alfred Kazin's brief homecoming, even he wouldn't have recognized his old neighborhood. Many of the three- and four-story multi-family homes had been bulldozed to accommodate what proved to be a cancerous core of high-rise public housing projects. They were not built there arbitrarily. They were sited, as Mayor Fiorello H. La Guardia said, in "areas where there is not the slightest possibility of rehabilitation through private enterprise" and where, given their politics and the complexion of the original tenants, progressive Jews in what had once been a socialist stronghold presumably would be less likely to vociferously object.

Thanks to Robert Moses's slum clearance mandate and the Housing Authority's complicity, Brownsville still has the highest concentration of public housing of any community in the country. Some one in three Brownsville residents live in public housing, perpetuating the neighborhood's residential segregation and isolation. "One of the unsustainable ideas behind 'projects' is the very notion that they are projects," Jane Jacobs wrote in *The Death and Life of Great American Cities* (1961), "abstracted out of the ordinary city and set apart."

The eldest of four sisters, Carmelia Goffe was raised in the mammoth Van Dyke public housing project on Mother Gaston Boulevard in Brownsville. Originally a dense complex of over 1,600 apartments in twenty-two buildings, up to fourteen stories high, Van Dyke Houses was constructed beginning in the early 1950s. What was so striking about the impersonal towers, which further isolated tenants in elevators, stairwells, and long corridors, was that they had been designed originally with people in mind. They were built so high specifically to provide as much open space between them as possible. But subsequent studies found that the crime rate in Van Dyke Houses was 65 percent higher than in the adjacent low-rise Brownsville Houses, and a large part of the disparity was attributed to its architecture. (As Oscar Newman wrote in *Defensible Space* [1972], "the removal of large numbers of units from visual contact with open space prevented proper public surveillance"—the kind of eyes on the street that Jane Jacobs romanticized.)

Brownsville was first settled in the mid-seventeenth century by Jan Thomasse Van Dyck, who arrived from Amsterdam with his wife and seven children and who later became a magistrate in Brooklyn's New Utrecht. Originally open farmland, it remained undeveloped well into the nineteenth century. The neighborhood's legacy for wanton violence may have begun when Van Dyck supposedly grabbed a young girl by the throat and assaulted a Samaritan who tried to intervene. By 1961 the arrest rate at Van Dyke was 14.1 per 1,000, the highest of any public housing project in the city.

"For many Brownsville residents, the Van Dyke Houses became the emblem for all the neighborhood's problems," Wendell Pritchett wrote in *Brownsville, Brooklyn: Blacks, Jews, and the Changing Face of the Ghetto* (2002). By 1963, when the housing project was still less than a decade old, only 25 of its 1,603 apartments were occupied by white families. "All of them," Pritchett wrote, "were trying to get out." As the project aged, so did its tenants. Instead of living in Van Dyke Houses as a temporary expedient, they would occupy their apartments there, on average, for nineteen years.

Goffe's expectations, if not her ambitions, had never exceeded her grasp. In her 1965 yearbook at Thomas Jefferson High School, she wrote that she hoped to attend Borough of Manhattan Community College and become a secretary. After high school, she worked as a bank teller, then followed in the footsteps of her parents, who, like Jack Maple and so many other New Yorkers seeking mobility and job security, made their way into the middle class by enlisting in government civil service. Her father, Alphonse, the son of an immigrant from Barbados, was a subway motorman. Her mother, Josephine, who had moved to New York from Illinois as a teenager, was a school crossing guard who enrolled in the first class of "meter maids," the much-maligned corps of revenuers recruited to replenish the city's depleted coffers by issuing tickets for illegal parking.

Goffe and Maple both witnessed the effects of the Great Society's failure on safety and service underground at first hand. Both were still in their twenties, working in the city's subway system. As a uniformed conductor, Goffe was still visible and vulnerable, but at least she was afforded the relative safety of the tiny compartment at each end of the car in the middle of the train. From there, she controlled the doors and made announcements, often rendered indecipherable by static or by the ear-piercing squawks of an obsolete sound system. She worked her way up to tower operator, a more cloistered cocoon and a promotion in the civil service hierarchy. What is incongruously known as a tower in the subway system is customarily a cramped, dingy underground bunker responsible for a modest sector of the 665 miles of trackage. Tower operators oversee signals and train traffic defined by snaking lights on a console. This windowless and poorly ventilated subterranean perch did Goffe's chronic asthma no good at all. After work, Goffe would return home to a Brownsville that, like Bushwick and East New York, was bearing the brunt of the city's fiscal crisis.

By the mid-1970s, for the first time since the Depression, the once-reliable sinecure of New York City civil service work was being attacked by number crunchers, and jobs for life were in jeopardy. Still, Carmelia Goffe and the public housing tenants she and her family epitomized were employed. They knew that moving up meant moving out of the projects, but most had nowhere else to go in a city where today a family of four making as much as seventy thousand dollars can be classified as low income. As a single mother with three sons, Goffe eventually found a heatless walkup near Van Dyke Houses on Dumont Avenue, not a vast improvement over the Lower East Side tenement that Annie Moore moved into when she first came to America.

Goffe would not give up on her neighborhood, though. Nor on her faith: she regularly attended services at the Pilgrim Baptist Church on Rockaway Avenue and later at the Brooklyn Tabernacle downtown. In 1973 she had married Arnold Goffe, but even after he abandoned the family, she never considered formally divorcing him.

In the late 1970s, an encounter with an after-school program run by the Roman Catholic Diocese of Brooklyn led Goffe to join other neighbors in launching East New York Christian Fellowships. Under the Reverend John Heinemeier, a Lutheran minister, Christian Fellowships became a founding member of a civic coalition called East Brooklyn Congregations in 1980. Unifying disparate groups behind a catalytic cause, Goffe and her neighbors hoped to recruit a leader charismatic enough to be taken seriously by the city's political establishment and persuade officials to *do something*. They were desperate. "We'd tried just about everything else—Model Cities, poverty programs, causes for this, causes for that," one civic leader said. "None of it worked. So we didn't have much to lose." Individually, they had failed to reverse or even slow Brownsville's decay. Grasping at straws, the coalition of faith-based groups enlisted the Industrial Areas Foundation, a network of religious and community organizations founded by Saul Alinsky in Chicago in 1940 that purposefully and painstakingly seeded itself in heartsick but not entirely hopeless urban neighborhoods.

Alinsky had learned the value of personal relationships from two pros whose alliances were, by necessity, transactional. As a criminology student, he mingled with Al Capone's gang, which enjoyed a well-deserved reputation for its power of persuasion. He was also a biographer (and largely an admirer) of mineworkers union leader John L. Lewis, whom Alinsky wrote, "does not flinch before authority." Alinsky was a radical, but also pragmatic; an idealist, but also a cynic, at least as far as his expectations of the bureaucracy's ability to deliver on the goals that an organized community had determined for itself. When public officials, expecting to be deferred to, begrudgingly agreed to meet with East Brooklyn Congregations and similar groups corralled by Alinsky's acolytes, they were galled to learn, as the journalist Jim Sleeper wrote in *City Limits* magazine at the time, "that the organization members were instructing their elected representatives, not the other way around." Alinsky was disinclined ever to give government and its abettors the benefit of the doubt. "You've got to goad the establishment into a ridiculous or rash action that convinces the underdog that you are for him," he advised, adding confidently, from experience: "I can always depend on the establishment to do the wrong thing at the right time."

The Industrial Areas Foundation was built primarily on church congregations. It was led locally by visionaries like the Reverends John Powis and Johnny Ray Youngblood, and Bishop E. L. White, the part-time pastor of a tiny church, St. James Holiness, in Brownsville. It was nurtured by Lucille Clark, a local mother of four; Ken Thorbourne, whose parents were Episcopal church leaders and founding members of East Brooklyn Congregations; and unheralded IAF acolytes like Stephen Roberson. But while the IAF shunned celebrity politics and publicity for its lead organizers, Alinsky's radical pragmatism would never have been promulgated without the skills, commitment, and unvarnished advice of Edward Chambers, the founder's successor in Chicago, and Mike Gecan, the organization's New York supervisor and later national senior adviser.

Chambers was a six-foot-five, 250-pound lapsed seminarian who defined himself as an organizer, rather than a movement person, whose individual marches and protests typically produce only temporary gains. "That's why a lot of movement people aren't good organizers," he said. "It takes a special cold, rational kind of anger." Mike Gecan, a history of literature major at Yale, had been angry since he was ten years old. In 1958, ninety-two of his fellow students and three nuns were killed in a fire that swept through Our Lady of the Angels school in Chicago because, he said, the same institution that supported and enriched life "exposed its most faithful followers to firetrap conditions." The anger and the visions it conjured up never vanished.

"I recall the sights and sounds of that first of December nearly every day of my life," he wrote in *Going Public* (2002), and how they reverberated wherever he went. "A siren, a news story, a charred building in Brooklyn, schoolchildren waiting on line or racing around an asphalt playground, inanities from the mouth of a public official trying to avoid responsibility—it doesn't take much to jog my memory." In the mid-1960s he relived that day in slow motion in the aftermath of urban riots, "when parish after parish experienced a near-total turnover in a matter of months, when hundreds of thousands of hardworking ethnic Catholics were driven from their homes and hundreds of thousands of hardworking Blacks and Hispanics were steered in, I saw the same kind of deadly disregard," he wrote. "This time, it was politicians benefiting from the profiteering of real estate hustlers. This time it was arsonists working for panic peddlers and landlords. This time, it was stunned and frightened pastors and rabbis drawing and redrawing the lines of their shrinking congregations until they had no people left to serve."

Ed Chambers was persuaded to visit Brooklyn from the IAF's Chicago head-quarters. He found the fledgling organizers gung-ho, but unschooled in the fundamentals of community organization. In his first meeting with East Brooklyn Congregations in a church basement, Gecan recalled, Chambers "told them precisely what they did not want to hear." Forget causes and personal charisma for now, Chambers counseled. Even as their neighborhood was sliding into an abyss, they needed to take the time to broaden their base, find allies, impose yearly dues to instill a tangible stake in the outcome, and train leaders to build a durable power base from the ground up. Given the odds against Goffe and the others—a city still reeling from the fiscal crisis, the absence of any local political organization, the barren moonscapes of shattered glass and broken bricks that Brownsville embodied, the entropy of a bureaucracy snarled in red tape—even Ed Chambers, who had begun at rock bottom before, left the group's meeting deeply discouraged. "When you get yourselves organized and raise the money to get your organization started," he said, "call me back."

Chambers had plenty of grounds for pessimism. Brownsville by the early 1980s, Goffe recalled, "was the end of the road, the worst of the bad." Many of her neighbors had lost faith. After witnessing decades of decline, of raised expectations and broken promises, they were inured to false hopes. Devoid of alternatives, many Black residents were stuck in place, having forgotten earlier generations' belief that Browns-ville, as Alfred Kazin described it, was "a place that measured all success by our skill in getting away from it." There were many reasons. "Public housing is perhaps the biggest barrier," Kay S. Hymowitz wrote in *The New Brooklyn: What It Takes to Bring a City Back* (2017). The projects, which were supposed to be a springboard to private rentals or ownership, "turned into quicksand," where residents endured on average for more than two decades. Their children and grandchildren were given the right to inherit their leases indefinitely when they died, "and so it is," she wrote, "that an apartment at Van Dyke can remain a family home for generations."

In 1980, when Gecan first met Carmelia Goffe, "she was living in an unheated flat with her three young sons on one of the most dangerous streets in East Brooklyn. Tutored by the IAF, she and fellow leaders were writing the grants that would provide some of the initial funding for the fledgling organization." Gecan instilled the iron credo that Alinsky had preached: "Never do for others what they can do for themselves." The Reverend Johnny Ray Youngblood, Alinsky's spiritual reincarnation in the impoverished communities of Brooklyn, would elaborate with his own corollary and cadence. "Don't do *for* us. Do *with* us. Don't believe what others say about us. *Ask* us. The Bible says to serve the poor, but it doesn't say to exempt the poor. The poor should still tithe. The poor should still be taking part in all the work of the church." Carmelia Goffe took that gospel to heart. "We realized that our power lied within ourselves," Dennis Deslippe quoted her as saying in the *Journal of Urban History* in 2019, "so from the ashes we started to rise."

In Brownsville, patches of ash still smoldered, the last gasp of the crepuscular hulks of burned-out buildings that flanked barren stretches of pulverized brick and broken glass. "In the spring of 1978, East Brooklyn was the South Bronx minus the presidential motorcades," Mike Gecan wrote, alluding to the obligatory campaign photo op for candidates hoping to affirm their bona fides for empathy. "I don't believe Mr. Chambers thought it could be done," Goffe herself said. "For that matter, I don't think *we* thought it could be done. But a fire had been lit under us that made us come together—Blacks, Hispanics, whites, Catholics, Protestants, and others. It was unprecedented. We held house meetings, one-on-ones, and we raised $150,000 in dues. We called Ed Chambers back and told him we were ready to start East Brooklyn Congregations."

Chambers and Gecan were surprised and impressed. "They did all this work themselves," Gecan said, "without a paid staff person, in one of the nation's poorest communities, at the very worst of times, while buildings continued to burn and bullets continued to fly. In September of 1980, after an eighteen-month period of base building, East Brooklyn Congregations 'began.' It was a quiet beginning. There was no grand press conference, no ribbon cutting, no march, no promise of spectacular success, no celebrity gushing praise and no political figures mugging for the cameras. A small team of local leaders met quietly with a newly hired lead organizer, me."

For Gecan, the first quandary was getting the vital players—Lutheran, Baptist, Roman Catholic, and Pentecostal ministers; the Brooklyn Democratic machine; insurgent party reformers; elected officials; and entrenched self-appointed civic leaders who were growing envious of the new organization's power base and at the same time feeling vulnerable to its potential to dislodge them—into the same room, much less to agree. His second challenge was to galvanize those diverse groups into a concerted and sustained campaign to empower the community and foster its revival—and to never forget one of Alinsky's signature axioms: "No permanent enemies, no permanent allies, only permanent interests."

Not surprisingly, Mayor Koch was among the first officeholders to put that credo to the test. He stormed out of a public meeting of the IAF's Queens Citizens Organization after its leaders insisted on setting the ground rules and refused to let him read his full opening statement. Koch could occasionally forgive, but never forget. He was so apoplectic that years later, when he invited Gecan to a private dinner at Gracie Mansion, the mayor's official residence, to bury the hatchet, Koch could no longer contain himself and compared his treatment by the Queens group to being in the dock at a Moscow show trial or a target at a Nuremberg rally of Nazis. This time it was Gecan who stalked out, and despite a two-page letter of apology from the mayor, he rejected an invitation to resume their dinner at a later date. Points of personal privilege or grandstanding aside, Gecan and Koch administration housing officials would eventually partner constructively to create thousands of affordable homes and apartments as a matter of mutual interest. "Intelligent action, even public confrontation, is at bottom an attempt to engage and relate," Gecan wrote, adding, "Most activists fail to appreciate this. Bureaucrats seek to stifle it."

To the eager East Brooklyn congregationalists, Gecan counseled perseverance—and patience: begin with modest goals, fulfill them, and then keep raising the bar. The group's initial agenda was humble, but highly visible: to replace three thousand metal street signs that had been pilfered and sold for scrap, rendering the burned-out neighborhood not only faceless but also nameless—as Gecan put it, "To put the area, quite literally, back on the map." The group also began flexing its political muscle, pressuring local elected officials to get the city to raze derelict housing. Fulfilling that agenda was a mixed blessing: the result was acres of rubble-strewn lots. Visionary EBC leaders evaluating the success of their demolition program were suddenly confronted with block upon block of vacant land given up by landlords for nonpayment of taxes and now owned by the city. Instead of despairing over this inhospitable dust bowl, they stumbled upon what would become their most ambitious priority. They transformed an eyesore and potential adversity into an opportunity, putting wholesale development of affordable housing on their agenda.

Their goal was not just to increase the number of "units," as bureaucrats bloodlessly described a household's habitat. Nor did they intend to replicate the massive complexes known generically as "the projects," where low-income tenants often felt warehoused in anonymous high-rises that, given their low rents and rising maintenance costs as they aged, were plagued by inoperable boilers and elevators and leaky roofs. Instead, they envisioned something entirely different, a less dense (and therefore less efficient) exploitation of scarce land, but serving a population more akin to the tenants whom New York City's original public housing program had first recruited in the mid-1930s: the working poor.

For years, a cantankerous *Daily News* newspaper columnist-turned-developer and municipal gadfly, I. D. Robbins, had been sermonizing about how to combine cheap land and mass production—the way Tex McCrary's client, William Levitt, did in a suburban Long Island potato field after World War II—to germinate swaths of modest, affordable city housing. Instead of hard-to-police and hard-to-maintain high-rises, the single-family homes conceived by Robbins would not merely provide housing but create a neighborhood of families with a stake in home ownership. "This is what the people want," Robbins said. "They come around here and they weep for these houses." Recalling a particularly inspiring sermon by the Reverend Johnny Ray Youngblood, Gecan christened the project Nehemiah, for the Old Testament prophet sent by the king of Persia to Jerusalem in 420 B.C. to help rebuild the walls of the holy city after the Babylonian captivity. "You know full well the tragedy of our city," Nehemiah told the local officials. "It lies in ruins and its gates are burned. Let us rebuild the wall of Jerusalem and rid ourselves of this disgrace!"

In June 1982, Alexander Von Hoffman wrote in *House by House, Block by Block* (2004), a delegation led by Francis J. Mugavero, the Roman Catholic bishop of Brooklyn, appealed to Mayor Koch to get Nehemiah off the ground. Joined by Gecan, Chambers, Robbins, and Youngblood at city hall, Mugavero wanted to convince Koch to donate vacant city land, defer property taxes, and grant each buyer a ten-thousand-dollar loan. "We've got $12 million, and we're ready to build," Mugavero boasted, borrowing the figure from his own supernal Book of Numbers (Gecan confessed that privately, so far, the group had managed to cobble together considerably less). Mayor Koch was impressed, but given the lingering impact of the mid-1970s fiscal crisis, he replied apologetically that the city had no money to offer. Mugavero replied: "Then steal it and I'll give you absolution." Koch agreed to find the funds, one way or another.

Alinsky's radical pragmatism transformed a ragtag group of do-good dreamers into a groundbreaking citizens' army. Their formula worked this way: the city would donate sixteen square blocks, or about twenty-five acres (most of which had been abandoned by its previous owners) for $1, abate property taxes (none were being paid anyway), and subsidize some of the construction costs. Member churches of East Brooklyn Congregations would also contribute. Residents, who would have to join a homeowner's association, received low- or no-interest state and federal loans (including a $20,000 subsidy, half in the form of a no-interest loan, payable when the property was sold). Buyers would put down $5,000 and make monthly mortgage payments of $300 for a 1,000-square-foot $30,000 two-bedroom house or $350 for a 1,200-square-foot $35,000 three-bedroom house for families that earned between $20,000 and $40,000. Assembled from prefabricated components built at the Brooklyn Navy Yard industrial park, the houses had tiled bathrooms, full basements, and off-street parking.

To many, the Nehemiah project's offer of affordable home ownership was just another sucker's bet, simply too good to be true. In October 1982, though, some five thousand jubilant Brownsville residents from forty congregations gathered to break ground for the first six-square-block phase of the project. They triumphally raised their hands above their heads as Mugavero blessed the barren lots and abandoned walkups where single-family row houses would rise. Mayor Koch led the countdown from ten to the first bulldozer bite for the excavation of four model homes. The crowd chanted "EBC!" after each number.

For years, Goffe had invested her time and sweat in Brownsville. She had urged her neighbors to do the same. Despite the skepticism of some of them, she put her money where her mouth was. "I said I wanted something more for my children than I had for myself," she said. "It was not easy to come home and wonder, can you make it upstairs to your apartment door safely or whether after school the kids were able to get home and get past drug addicts who were hanging out in the lobbies of our apartment building." She never lost faith, especially after reading an article in the *Daily News* about a builder's plan to build affordable housing. "I said this is the American dream, my dream," she said. "I wanted that. I said, maybe someday this could happen to me."

Goffe reserved a three-bedroom, one-bathroom house at 502 Powell Street near Riverdale Avenue, practically around the corner from the Van Dyke Houses apartment where she was brought up. In 1984, after making a down payment of five thousand dollars, she bought the newly completed house for forty-nine thousand dollars. "I couldn't afford to go to Queens or anything else," Goffe remembered. "I told myself that this a new phase in my life. As a single mom, I can finally give my children a safe and decent place to call home." Brownsville transubstantiated; Carmelia Goffe remained immutable. She would live her entire sixty-eight years within a few blocks' radius of where she was born. "We grew up here," her sister Janis said. "We felt safe here."

Not everyone did, though. "Most people in the neighborhood said, 'No, those are little stick houses over there. They're not gonna last and be successful,'" Goffe recalled. But by September 1985, after the first 140 families had settled in (their median income was twenty-six thousand dollars, and about one in three were transplants from public or subsidized housing), the waiting list of applicants for the next round of Nehemiah homes had grown to 3,000. Goffe would become head of the Brownsville Nehemiah Homeowners Association, representing the residents of 1,100 homes. (Another 1,050 homes would be built in East New York, 700 in New Lots and hundreds more later in Spring Creek, a new community created on forty-five acres of landfill between East New York and Jamaica Bay.) "An organization with a core budget of $300,000-a-year, a staff of four and a modest headquarters in a local apartment complex halted two decades of burning, deterioration and abandonment by building a critical mass of owner-occupied town houses and generating a chain reaction of other neighborhood improvements," Gecan wrote. Johnny Ray Youngblood said it succinctly: "We never wasted a moment whining. We kept focused on one thing: winning."

Nehemiah was no panacea. It didn't pretend to come close to replacing the housing that had been lost during the previous several decades. Nor, in a city where land can be recycled but for the most part not extended, were the single-family homes the most productive use of space (although the suburban enclave on Charlotte Street in the South Bronx—which became that iconic photo op for the presidential motorcades that Gecan mentioned as a barren wasteland transformed into a tiny urban oasis—had only six houses per acre, compared to the twenty-four Nehemiah brick row houses per acre). The South Bronx ranch houses were idiosyncratic anomalies constructed for ninety-two homeowners and countless gawkers, a permanent Potemkin village that eventually, helped herald the borough's revival. The Nehemiah project was proof of concept, a replicable solution that spawned other ambitious efforts like Community Solutions, begun by Rosanne Haggerty, who had already founded a successful supportive housing program called Common Ground. In the quarter century since 1982, Gecan said, more than 253,000 homes and apartments were rehabilitated, reconstructed, or built from scratch on formerly vacant city land. Youngblood and Gecan invoked a woman in a Nehemiah home in Brooklyn who casually strolled nightly through the streets of a neighborhood that not long before was the city's murder capital. "The sounds of her footsteps on the sidewalks," they wrote, "are as much the sounds of a better city and a healthier society as the opening bell of the New York Stock Exchange or the beeping of horns in Herald Square."

Without exaggerating, there was a religious fervor to the Nehemiah project, a biblical faith that gave Goffe and her neighbors the effrontery to pursue it and the fortitude to carry it out. Their prayers and perseverance were answered as if God were speaking to Nehemiah: "You return to me and obey my commands, then even if your exiled people are at the farthest horizon, I will gather them from there and bring them to the place I have chosen as a dwelling for my Name."

"They rekindled a spirit of the possible in a place that had grown dark with cynicism and despair," Gecan said of Goffe and her neighbors. "It's all been rebuilt, and not for the artists, God bless 'em, or the students or tourists or stockbrokers. It's all been built for the corrections officers and the health workers and the city workers, almost all Hispanic and Black buyers and renters." In Brownsville, what happened may have been more a reversal than a resurrection, but it helped make Brooklyn's adjacent neighborhoods safer and more habitable so that the artists, students, and stockbrokers and their families might discover more economical, safe, and convenient places to live in Bushwick, Williamsburg, Bedford-Stuyvesant, and other communities that were still considered no-man's-land for anyone who could afford to live anywhere else.

Grass roots don't begin to reach far enough down to describe the depth to which so-called faith-based organizations grounded their commitment to regenerate New York neighborhoods that otherwise might well have been neglected and forgotten by the government bureaucracy. Ed Chambers's formula for community organizing required resolve to nurture the roots and persistence to let them grow. "Movement is an emotional thing of marches, but organization is different," he told the *Times* in 1966. "When the marching was over in Selma, Negroes were still getting beaten on the head and nothing was really different. We're aiming for something much bigger. It means nothing unless you gain the power to deal with the problem yourself."

Goffe's name won't be found in other modern histories of New York, those accounts of the elected officials, union leaders, financial wizards, and civic cheerleaders who helped revive the city in the 1970s. But the "Drop Dead" sentence gleefully imposed by some Ford administration officials could not have been reversed as prodigiously without the religious fervor galvanized by grassroots groups like East Brooklyn Congregations and their anonymous members. New York University historian Jonathan Soffer described Nehemiah as "a model for community response in a neoliberal era" in his book on Ed Koch's New York.

Power in a limited space like New York, whether it was defined by the quixotic descendants of Anneke Jans Bogardus or the precision of John Randel Jr. or the stubborn persistence of Andrew H. Green or the gutsy neighbors of Carmelia Goffe, has been typically about territory. Goffe and her neighbors gained power and wielded it to great effect because their stake was never in doubt. It was not about a lofty but abstract feel-good principle. It was about place, property, shelter, security—more concrete than almost anything else in as mutable and unpredictable a city as New York. Goffe did the Bogardus heirs one better. Her family still has the home she purchased in 1984 for $49,000 with public and private support, and now, some forty years later, it's worth well over $500,000 (about twice the profit, when they sell, that she would have made leaving the same amount of money in a bank). "It's not an issue of propping people up in a crime-infested area and saying, 'You're on your own,'" Goffe said. "You have to have a culture in which people get a sense of ownership. That's what makes the difference, and that's what develops leadership."

In high school, Goffe aspired to be a secretary. But during thirty-six years of service to her neighbors, she would, like Barack Obama, in a way, rise from her beginnings as a community organizer to a position of leadership—to a presidency, too, no less, if only the presidency of her Nehemiah homeowner's association. Three years before she died, her path and Obama's would cross. As a member of the Brooklyn Tabernacle Choir she was invited to sing "The Battle Hymn of the Republic," the antislavery anthem written by New York poet Julia Ward Howe, at Obama's second inauguration on a high balcony outside the Capitol. Goffe and the other anonymous leaders of East Brooklyn Congregations never became household names. She would never be nominated to anyone's Ten Most Powerful list. But, as Mike Gecan said, "they saved East Brooklyn and helped save New York City as surely as any mayor or governor or banker did."

EPILOGUE

I f Thomas Carlyle was correct that "the history of the world is but the biography
of great men," he nonetheless left it to others quantify greatness and its legacy.
Do we measure it by the number of awards and medals those individuals collected
over their lifetimes, the prominence they achieved, or the streets and neighborhoods in which their names were memorialized for accomplishments long ago
forgotten? "Which was the greatest innovator?" Carlyle asked. "Which was the most
important personage in man's history, he who first led armies over the Alps and
gained the victories of Cannae and Thrasymene; or the homeless boor who first
hammered out for himself an iron spade?" Carlyle's point, the historian Margaret
MacMillan wrote, was that since society is the collective product of how countless
human beings lived and worked, history therefore "is the essence of innumerable
Biographies."

My goal in writing *The New Yorkers* has been to help readers envision history in
more engaging ways, to provoke them into challenging preconceived notions of the
past, to remind them that—to paraphrase Faulkner and Orwell jointly—not only
is the past not dead, it isn't even past, and whoever controls it can also determine
our collective future.

History is a story without end, not a static, unchanging set of facts to be accepted
at face value. It is a continuum, an opportunity to place current events in context,
to measure the terrorist attack on September 11, 2001, against the draft riots in 1863,
the Great Fire of 1776 and the following seven years of oppressive British occupation, and the Great Fire of 1835; to compare the Covid-19 pandemic with the suffering
and death toll inflicted in 1918 by the Spanish flu; to weigh how "the other half" lived
in the late nineteenth century as chronicled by Jacob Riis against the "two cities"
decried by progressive politicians at the beginning of the twenty-first; to correlate

the mid-nineteenth-century gangs of New York with the feral youth who rampaged unfettered in the 1970s; to place ourselves in the position of decision-makers of the past and to contemplate what, given the circumstances and the alternatives they faced, we would have done. As history ineluctably progresses, perspective demands that we take another look at its earlier chapters to see if and how they fit together, where they converged, and whether they still make sense in light of what has happened since—and of what didn't happen in between. If we can better understand the past, with all its accomplishments, promises, and imperfections, we can stake out common ground to forge a more providential future. Which way you explore history is like the difference in how we measure hours and minutes. A digital clock will tell you exactly what time it is. Looking at an analog clock, the kind with hands, will also remind you what time it isn't.

That's one reason why this is "*a* biography" of the city, not "*The* Biography." "A" places the defining article of faith in you, the reader. My choices of whom to include in this book were not arbitrary or capricious. But they were subjective. They were not meant to go unchallenged—anything but. "*The* Biography" might have required 923,380,602 chapters, if you accept that figure as the number of people who ever lived in New York.

From the very first years of New York's founding, naysayers predicted its doom. Some of their dire forecasts could have come true. Jolted by the murder of John Colman, Henry Hudson might have sailed for home without ever venturing north to identify the vital river route to the American interior. New Amsterdam might have been relegated to a provincial backwater if the West India Company hadn't told Peter Stuyvesant to grit his teeth and turn a deaf ear to the religious practices of the Quakers and other "vagabonds." The city might never have recovered from seven years of British occupation and, perhaps, have been overtaken by Philadelphia, Baltimore, or Boston, had John Jay not held his appointment as secretary of foreign affairs hostage to transplanting the nation's capital from Trenton to New York. It might not have become a world capital if Andrew Green had given up on consolidation. Would Franklin Roosevelt have become president if Charlie Murphy had scuttled the foundational New Deal's dry run in New York? Would Jane Jacobs have preserved Greenwich Village if she hadn't learned from Lillian Edelstein's trials and errors in the Bronx?

A few of those climactic outcomes may have been coincidental. But time and again, the city was poised to capitalize on its good fortune. Emboldened by each success, it demonstrated extraordinary resilience. It bounced back from the deepest depressions. It also ascended, often because of the faith placed in its future by people—people who kept coming and still do, and who today, after four hundred years of European, African, Asian, Caribbean, and South American immigration, have propelled New York's population to a record high. Some will achieve well-deserved fame. Most will labor in obscurity, remaining nameless and faceless, though their legacies to posterity may later prove to have been no less remarkable. The city began with natural geographic advantages, but it was people who seized those opportunities, people who already lived in New York and people who were destined to become New Yorkers, people who were willing to be lucky, and even to make history.

ACKNOWLEDGMENTS

The novelist Ben Cheever once observed that the litany of acknowledgments in virtually every nonfiction book suggest a fundamental conceit: that thanks to the inspiration, prodding, and prompting by the roster of selfless sources and despite their recommendation to write about some other subject, the author has nonetheless accomplished something. Given that caveat, *The New Yorkers* would not have been possible without the contributions of the subjects themselves and the historians, scholars, curators, archivists, librarians, authors, and genealogists who generously nominated the candidates (far more than thirty-one) to include, and who helped flesh out their biographies.

Thanks especially to, among others: Brian Andersson, Kevin Baker, Thomas Bender, William Brower Bogardus, Fergus Bordewich, Douglas Brinkley, Edwin Burrows, Robert A. Caro, Kenneth Cobb, Daniel Czitrom, Michael Daly, Jim Dwyer, Grace Friary, Elisabeth Paling Funk, Michael Gecan, Charles Gehring, Timothy Gilfoyle, James Golway, Robb K. Haberman, Andrew Hacker, Amy Hill Hearth, Harold Holzer, William Helmreich, Peter Hess, Clifton Hood, Kathleen Hulser, Amy Hill Hearth, Pooja Jhunjhunwala, Lisa Keller, Gerard Koeppel, William Kornblum, Jonathan Kuhn, Ken Jackson, Devan Lander, John Manbeck, John McClintock, Kevin McCrary, Donald Miller, John Miller, Timothy Miller, Susan R. Miller, Michael Miscione, Anthony Opelka, Nick Pileggi, Barry Popik, Diane Ravitch, Graham Robb, Russell Shorto, Megan Smolenyak, Jonathan Soffer, Walter Stahr, Jon-Christian Suggs, Mike Wallace, Will Wander, Robert Weible, Janet Weiner, Robert Whalen, and Justin White.

Thanks also to the institutions they and others represent: Tony Marx and the New York Public Library; Louise Mirrer and the New-York Historical Society; Whitney Donhauser and Sarah Henry and the Museum of the City of New York; Commissioner Pauline Toole and the New York City Department of Records and Information Services (the Municipal Archives); the New York State Archives, the New Netherland Project; Ken Bowling, Charlene Bickford, and William diGiacomantonio of the First Federal Congress Project of George Washington University; the National Parks of New York Harbor Conservancy; the Columbia University

Libraries; the Leon Levy Center for Biography at the Graduate Center of the City University of New York; the Cornell University Libraries and Trinity Church.

This project would not have been possible without the indulgence of my benefactors at the *New York Times*, first and foremost the Sulzberger family, who have steered this venerable yet nimble multimedia conglomerate while remaining faithful to its original mission as the nation's leading defender of the First Amendment. Thanks, too, to Bill McDonald and my colleagues on the Obituary Desk, my latest incarnation in a fifty-year career, where I am still writing about people, the most interesting subject of all, and about their lives in the form of on-deadline mini-biographies.

The unsung heroes of all my writing are the patient and generous researchers at the *Times*—Alain Delaquérière, Sheelagh McNeill, Susan Beachy, and Kitty Bennett, led by Jack Begg—who patiently plumb fathomless sources seeking answers to my esoteric and inscrutable queries. And special thanks, as always, to Jeff Roth, as the savior of the *Times*'s "morgue" and our resident polymath for his generosity in taking the time to share the unimaginable breadth of his expert knowledge.

Thanks to my indefatigable and enduringly gracious agent, Andrew Blauner, for his doggedness. The editors at Bloomsbury have supported the concept of a biography of New York from the beginning. Special thanks to Nancy Miller, Hattie LeFavour, Barbara Darko, Patti Ratchford, and Emily Fishman. Fred Chase's practiced eye sharpened the manuscript.

Shelby White deserves special mention for her generosity and her wisdom. Paul Neuthaler and Karen Salerno, too—they know how they helped. And Morty Matz, an unsung hero of New York.

None of what I do would be possible without the encouragement of my wife, Marie Salerno. She is a no-fail sounding board who never minces words and a rock-solid source of support. Thanks always to my two accomplished, funny, and sweet sons, Michael and Will; to my always empathetic daughter-in-law, Sophie, and to my granddaughters, Dylan and Isabella, the best little girls and source of joy in the world.

INDEX

The letter *f* following a page locator denotes a figure.

A NOTE ON THE AUTHOR

SAM ROBERTS, a fifty-year veteran of New York journalism, is an obituaries reporter and formerly the Urban Affairs correspondent at the *New York Times*. He has hosted *The New York Times Close Up* on TV, and the podcasts *Only in New York*, anthologized in a book of the same name, and *The Caucus*. He is the author of *A History of New York in 27 Buildings*, *A History of New York in 101 Objects*, *Grand Central: How a Train Station Transformed America*, and *The Brother: The Untold Story of the Rosenberg Case*, among others. He has written for the *New York Times Magazine*, the *New Republic*, *New York*, *Vanity Fair*, *Foreign Affairs*, the *Huffington Post*, and *Air Mail*. A history adviser to Federal Hall, he lives in New York with his wife.